Continuity, Innovation, and Connoisseurship

Old Master Paintings at the Palmer Museum of Art

Proceedings of an international symposium
held at the Palmer Museum of Art
on March 31 through April 2, 1995.

Organized in conjunction with the exhibition
*Continuity, Innovation, and Connoisseurship:
Old Master Paintings, Drawings, and Prints
from Pennsylvania Collections,*
on view at the Palmer Museum
from February 28 through April 30, 1995.

Mary Jane Harris, Editor

Cover: Master Jacomo, *Denial of St. Peter* (detail), c. 1630s.
          Palmer Museum of Art, The Pennsylvania State University.

ISBN 0-911209-56-5

U. Ed. ARC 03-258
Library of Congress Control Number: 2003100414

Designed by Catherine H. Zangrilli
Printed by Commercial Printing, State College, PA
Distributed by Penn State Press

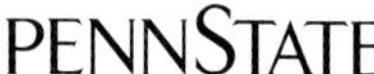

College of Arts and Architecture

Dedicated to the memory of

Morton B. Harris

Table of Contents

Foreword

Jan Keene Muhlert, *director*

In her introduction, Mary Jane Harris graciously acknowledges the role of those who helped to make all phases of *Continuity, Innovation, and Connoisseurship: Old Master Paintings at the Palmer Museum of Art* an unqualified success. She has, however, omitted one very key individual. It was Mary Jane herself who prevailed first and foremost. Her personal and long-standing relationship with each of the seven invited scholars was critical to the success of the symposium, and the accompanying exhibition could not have been organized without her intimate knowledge of Pennsylvania collections. Furthermore, her indefatigable editing skills, not to mention her contagious enthusiasm, have likewise been indispensable in moving the papers from presentation to publication.

I wish to also acknowledge Patrick McGrady who, despite his many other museum obligations, shared with Mary Jane the tasks of editing, checking, and double checking, and finally seeing this publication through its layout and printing—true labors of love for them both.

It is our sincere hope that *Continuity, Innovation, and Connoisseurship* will serve as a model for how the Palmer Museum's collections might be utilized by students, faculty, and other scholars in furthering our mission to provide opportunities for research, teaching, and appreciation.

Finally, in recognition of all that Mary Jane Harris has done to help bring this project to fruition, we at the Palmer Museum of Art join the authors of the papers herewith presented in dedicating this volume to Mary Jane's late husband, Morton B. Harris.

Introduction and Acknowledgements

Mary Jane Harris, *guest curator and editor*

The Palmer Museum of Art at The Pennsylvania State University acquired several European Old Master paintings under its distinguished first director, William Hull (1971-1983). By the mid-1990s, the museum had added three other works of particular interest. Those purchased in Mr. Hull's tenure were from the seventeenth century: the *Mystic Marriage of St. Catherine*, attributed to Pier Francesco Mola; the *Denial of St. Peter*, attributed to Trophime Bigot; and the *Holy Family with St. John the Baptist and St. Anne*, identified independently by the Italian scholars Mina Gregori and Federico Zeri as the work of the Florentine, Giovanni Francesco Vanni. Two Florentine sixteenth-century paintings by Maso da San Friano and Michele Tosini, called Michele di Ridolfo, were subsequently funded through the generosity of the Friends of the Palmer Museum of Art. My late husband, Morton, and I contributed the sixth, a baroque work by the Venetian artist, Pietro Vecchia.

During memorable years of studying and collecting Old Master paintings, Morton and I had the good fortune to meet many scholars in America and Europe, and we became acquainted with specialists on these six artists. It occurred to me how exciting it would be to invite them to research the Palmer pictures, come to Penn State and report their findings, and eventually publish their papers under the auspices of the museum. Thus, a symposium was born. (During the ensuing and challenging process, two of the attributions were revised and numerous related works were brought to light for the first time.)

Kahren Arbitman, director of the Palmer Museum in 1993, responded to my proposals with enthusiasm. We went to work directly and set a date for a symposium, the spring of 1995. The six scholars were invited, together with Mina Gregori, who was asked to preside as our keynote speaker. Few of them were aware at the time of the prominence and enormity of Penn State, or of its physical beauty set in the heart of Pennsylvania's mountains. They did not know that our museum had just doubled in size, redesigned by the noted American architect, Charles W. Moore in association with Arbonies King Vlock. But they were curious, even intrigued, and all accepted our invitation. The symposium took wing.

Symposiums generally develop out of exhibitions. Could we work in reverse and organize an exhibition to complement our symposium? Yes, said Kahren, if we could find the material and the resources. We decided to confine our search to Pennsylvania collections and set out for the Carnegie Museum of Art in Pittsburgh and the Philadelphia Museum of Art. We canvassed smaller institutions and even located a few private collectors. Everyone was receptive and pleased to cooperate. An exhibition began to take shape. To round out the selection, Morton and I added several works from our collection. Our late beloved friend, Robert L. Manning, contributed from his.

A symposium and an exhibition require an outlay of funds that would have posed a problem for the museum had it not been for the generosity of three institutions—the Samuel H. Kress Foundation, the Robert Lehman Foundation, Inc., and the Pennsylvania Council on the Arts— and two friends, Hester Diamond and the late Piero Corsini. We are infinitely grateful for their support.

Michael Heidelberg, a paintings conservator in New York, lent his skills, coming to Penn State before the exhibition to demonstrate conservation techniques to students and staff. Charles Schreiber, president and framing specialist at the House of H. Heydenryk, Jr., Inc., New York, generously restored the frame on our Vanni.

With the funding, the speakers, and the exhibition loans in place, invitations were sent out for a three-day weekend beginning March 31. The number of out-of-town acceptances was surprisingly gratifying. Among them was one from Ed Goldberg in Florence, Italy, and it was at the Palmer Museum symposium that he laid out his bold vision for what has become the Medici Archive Project.

The weekend turned out to be lively and enlightening, warmed by a spirit of camaraderie. To this day, guests and speakers declare that it was one of the most enjoyable symposiums in their experience. On Sunday, April 2, Kahren delivered her closing address with inimitable wit and charm. (See page 147).

Morton's health was fragile and declined rapidly that spring. He was gone before the end of the year. Each of the speakers asked that their paper be dedicated to his memory.

I wish to express my profound gratitude to each person who contributed to the success of the Palmer Museum's symposium and exhibition. First and foremost, congratulations to the distinguished speakers whose insights and scholarship have expanded an appreciation for the importance of our Old Master paintings: Bernard Aikema, Francesca Baldassari, Philippe Costamagna, Mina Gregori, Heidi J. Hornik, Erich Schleier, and Leonard J. Slatkes. Heartfelt thanks go to the outstanding staff at the Palmer Museum who gave of their time and expertise without reservation: Ronald Hand, Ok-Hi Lee, the late Mary F. Linda, Patrick McGrady, Betsy Warner, Barbara Weaver, Glenn Willumson, and especially to Kahren Arbitman, for her unique talents and her leadership and friendship. I am indebted to other scholars and friends who gave counsel and information: Robert Behrman, Richard A. Berman, David Alan Brown, Marian Burleigh-Motley, Miles Chappell, Frank Dabell, Michael Flack, Lynn Gamwell, Edward L. Goldberg, William Griswold, Hellmut Hager, Ann Sutherland Harris, Anna LoBianco, Catherine Monbeig Goguel, Susan Clare Scott, and Catherine Whistler.

The Palmer Museum staff and I are deeply indebted to the lenders, as well as particular individuals at the lending institutions who were on staff during the exhibition's organization, for their cooperation and collegiality:

> Allentown Art Museum, Peter Blume, director
> An anonymous collector
> Carnegie Museum of Art, Pittsburgh, Phillip M. Johnston, director;
>   Louise Lippincott and Linda P. Batis, curators
> Center Gallery, Bucknell University, Lewisburg,
>   Cynthia Peltier, acting director
> LaSalle University Art Museum, Philadelphia,
>   Brother Daniel Burke, director; Caroline Wistar, curator
> Philadelphia Museum of Art, Anne d'Harnoncourt, director;
>   John W. Ittmann, Ann B. Percy, Joseph J. Rishel, and
>   Innis Howe Shoemaker, curators; Carl B. Strehlke, adjunct curator
> Saint Vincent Archabbey, Latrobe, Brother Nathan M. Cochran, O.S.B.
> Trout Gallery, Dickinson College, Carlisle, Peter M. Lukehart, director

Publishing the symposium papers would not have been possible without three elements. The first is a belief in their importance, which Kahren passed on to her esteemed successor, our current director, Jan Keene Muhlert. Under Jan's stewardship, Patrick McGrady, recently named Charles V. Hallman Curator, saw the job through. No expression of thanks is adequate acknowledgement of Patrick's intelligence, dedication, and patience. He worked closely with me from symposium to exhibition to publication.

The second element concerns the exacting demands of preparation time needed to produce this volume. It was a painstaking process for which I was most fortunate to have at my side Professor Susan Clare Scott, editor of Penn State's highly regarded *Papers in Art History.* She shared generously with me and the Palmer Museum the benefits of her long experience. Critical editorial skills were contributed by R. Aaron Rottner, Scott Schweigert, Richard A. Berman, Suzanne Wayne, Amy Milgrub Marshall, Betsy Warner, and Barbara Weaver. Cathy Zangrilli designed this publication with distinction and style, and made the task seem effortless. Countless thanks to each of these contributors for their invaluable assistance.

The third and critical element is the funding. We are grateful indeed that the Robert Lehman and Samuel H. Kress Foundations came through with additional grants, and that an anonymous donor made a generous gift. A special contribution, applied toward the cost of photographic reproduction, was given by The Vero Group, Mark Fehrs Haukohl, president, in Morton's memory.

Keynote Address

Mina Gregori

The themes "continuity" and "innovation" give us an opportunity to examine the dynamics of art in Italy from the fifteenth to the seventeenth century. Italian artistic heritage has been supported throughout the centuries by the coexistence of "continuity" and "innovation" perceived in the changes and varying interpretations that unceasingly nourished its creativity.

Two Florentine artists examined in this symposium demonstrate these themes. Giovanni Battista Vanni reflects "innovation" in his response to the profound changes that occurred in the latter part of the sixteenth century after the death of Vasari and the reform of Florentine painting. Michele Tosini in his early career represents "continuity," which can be interpreted as conservatism. Tosini trained within a deeply rooted tradition preserved in the workshop founded by Domenico Ghirlandaio, who gained fame replacing episodes in the *Life of the Virgin,* which had been frescoed by Andrea Orcagna in the choir of Santa Maria Novella. Utilizing some of the original iconography, Ghirlandaio paid homage to the tradition of Trecento fresco.

Tosini, in his *Madonna and Child with St. John* (Hornik, Fig. 1) at the Palmer Museum, repeats the central composition of a large altarpiece in the church of SS. Jacopo and Lorenzo, which he executed in collaboration with Ridolfo Ghirlandaio, Domenico's son, who inherited his father's workshop (Hornik, Fig. 3). This altarpiece was commissioned by Leonardo di Giovanni Buonafé, the Bishop of Cortona, who ordered works from Ridolfo for over a quarter of a century, from 1500 to 1528, during his directorship of the Florentine hospital, Santa Maria Nuova. The bishop's inclinations were conservative; he favored late Quattrocento style and imagery.

The structural conception of the altarpiece for SS. Jacopo and Lorenzo and the Palmer panel is rooted in the art of Fra Bartolommeo. In the Palmer work, the presence of the young John the Baptist expresses the persistent religious sentiment of the early years of the Cinquecento which, inspired by the art of Leonardo, favored pictorial allusion to the Passion. The *cangiantismo* (iridescence) of the drapery colors at the Virgin's shoulder and upper arm, although a more "up-to-date" stylistic element, has no structural significance. Bishop Buonafé exerted considerable influence over his favorite workshop whose style remained conservative, although many other commissions in Florence were being awarded to more innovative Mannerist painters. Buonafé's preferences, however, may be understood by the destination of paintings like the Palmer Tosini, which were ordered for convents and confraternities in outlying areas.

Ultimately, Tosini became one of Vasari's collaborators in the Palazzo Vecchio. In the independent works painted shortly before his death in 1577, he brings the Classicism of the very early years of the century together with the first anti-Mannerist reactions that were responding to the dictates of the Council of Trent. Tosini was one of the proponents of *pittura sacra* that represented a distinct genre of painting with its own rules.

As noted by David Franklin, the compositional repetition in the altarpieces commissioned by Bishop Buonafé from Ridolfo Ghirlandaio and his workshop fulfilled a need to foster a unity of function and taste over a broad geographic area.[1] Indeed, repetition of images in *pittura sacra*, which has been considered a mere commercial expediency, is closely linked to functional, devotional needs and to the veneration of the "icon." In the Seicento, this repetition of imagery is seen in the work of artists such as Carlo Dolci and Sassoferrato.

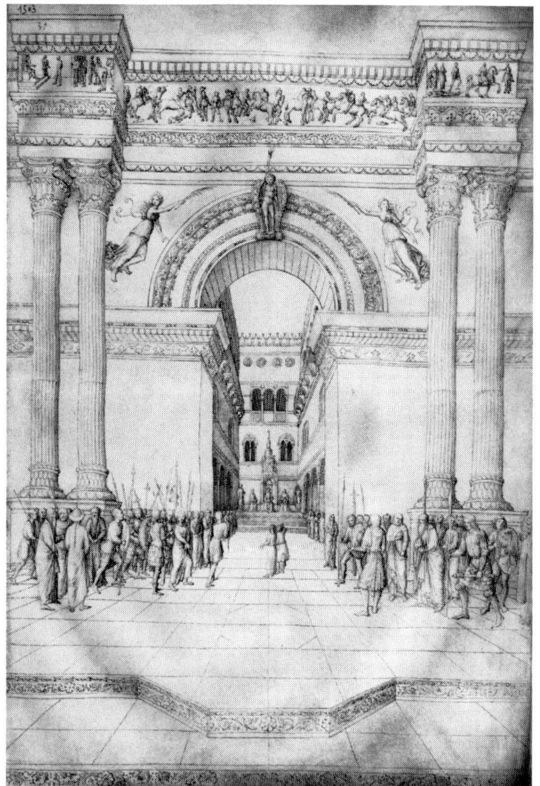

Fig. 1

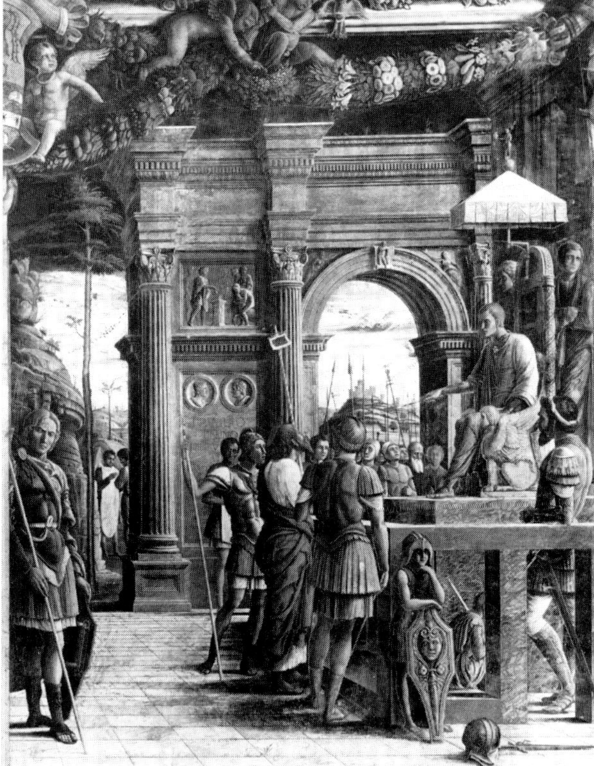

Fig. 2

A significant aspect of "continuity" in Italian art began at the end of the thirteenth century, when Italian artists first garnered the legacy of the Antique. After the Quattrocento, when it was most keenly felt in Italy, this legacy was to flourish throughout Europe. Although Greek and Roman civilization is accepted as the foundation of Western civilization, not enough attention has been given to the notion that everything that was innovative or anticipated innovation was based on an impulse to seek the approval of the Ancients. Charles Sterling reminds us of the axiom that nothing happened in the arts "sans la bénédiction des anciens."[2] The axiom holds true at the end of the sixteenth century with the origins of naturalism (imitation of nature), where images without an evident subject, as in the works of the young Annibale Carracci and Caravaggio, resemble literary examples that can be found in Pliny. Continuity and innovation are deeply engaged in an ongoing dialogue with the Ancients.

These observations lead to others. The Quattrocento was a century enamored with the artistic and theoretical imitation of the Antique. The Florentine artists were the first to make liberal use of architectural elements and motifs derived from antiquity. We find a similar practice in the Veneto, brought largely by Donatello and his prominent use of motifs *all'antica*. The drawings of Jacopo Bellini (Fig. 1) and the two lower registers of the Paduan frescoes of Mantegna in the Ovetari Chapel (Fig. 2) depict monuments that appear to be real architecture but are largely inventions *all'antica* inspired by antique examples. We need to be aware of their complexity and the imagination of their creators. In Mantegna's *St. Sebastian* at the Louvre and in one of his frescoes in the Camera Picta at the Ducal Palace, Mantua (Fig. 3), representations of imagined cities with remains of antique monuments convey a sophisticated sense of history. In the Seicento, imagery of the antique monuments is prominent in the rigorously classical compositions of Domenichino, especially his frescoes in San Gregorio Magno (Fig. 4) and San Luigi dei Francesi. Antique imagery was carefully studied and utilized extensively by Nicolas Poussin and 150 years later by Jean Louis David. This vision is part of an artistic continuity of thought that is not a matter of style but of sustained admiration for antiquity.

Another important facet of the *stile all'antica* and its persistence from the Quattrocento through various forms in the Seicento and the Settecento, concerns the rendering of action, figural movement, and pathos. What will here be designated as the *stile concitato*, to borrow a term applied to music by Claudio Monteverdi, expresses the inner agitation of the soul and the dynamic tension of the body. To search for its sources, we turn again to Donatello—to his Florentine Cantoria (Fig. 9), the Paduan reliefs, and the two pulpits in San Lorenzo in Florence (Fig. 5).

The *stile concitato,* which Aby Warberg termed the *antik-Pathetischen Stil* or *antikisierenden Idealstil,* derived from a Dionysian vision of the Antique as opposed to Apollonian. Warberg examined it in a lecture of 1914,[3] pointing to the second half of the Quattrocento in Florence where Antonio Pollaiuolo developed precepts of Donatello (Fig. 6) and Domenico Ghirlandaio adopted the formulas of the Roman triumphal arch. In northern Italy, this vision extended to Mantegna and art of Ferrara with the art works of Francesco del Cossa, mentioned by Warburg, and Ercole de' Roberti, not previously noted (Fig. 7). It should be pointed out that the basic concept of this mode was already implicit in the humanistic principles of Leon Battista Alberti, who stated in his treatise, *Della Pittura,* that the aim of the painter is to represent history with the "movimenti d'animo" and the "movimenti del corpo."[4] In the late Quattrocento, the characteristics of the style can be recognized by studying the dynamic tension in Dionysian subjects and battle scenes on ancient sarcophagi and triumphal arches and by awareness of the emphasis on expressiveness and pathos rather than beauty.[5]

We digress here to indicate another mode in Quattrocento art, designated the *stile prospettico*. It was based on the science of perspective discovered early in the century and was less concerned with the imitation of antiquity or dynamism. Outlined by Roberto Longhi in a famous essay of 1914 (a landmark year for art history),[6] the *stile prospettico* was developed by Piero della Francesca throughout the Adriatic region and northern Italy, and by Giovanni Bellini (Fig. 8) and Antonello da Messina in Venice. It bears mentioning that the relationship in this mode between space and figures was profoundly different from that of Mantegna.

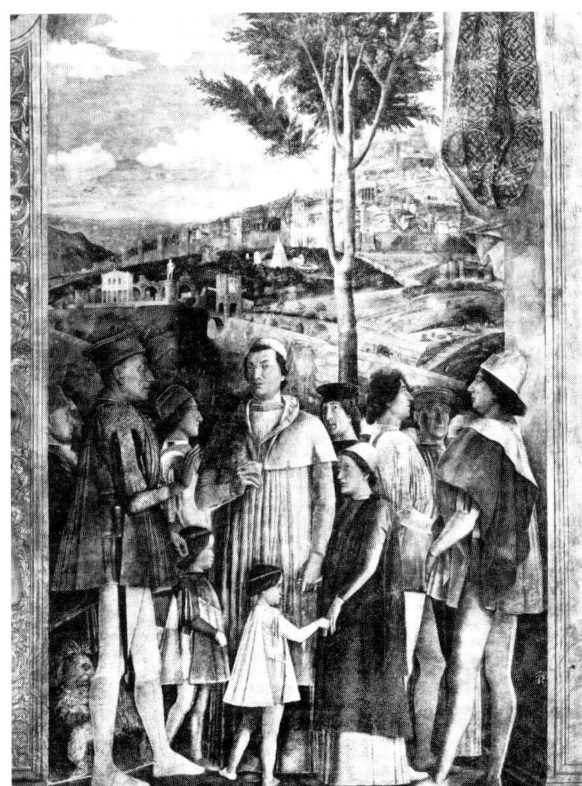

Fig. 3

The distinction between two modes inspired by the Antique, the *stile concitato* or *antik-Pathetischen Stil* and its counterpart, the calm *stile neo-attico,* was already evident in the Florentine Quattrocento in the differing visions of Donatello and Luca della Robbia (Figs. 9 and 10). These differences are also discernable in the contrast between the dynamic style of the late Quattrocento, investigated by Warburg, and the protoclassicism of Perugino from which the art of Raphael was born. In the Stanza della Segnatura at the Vatican, Raphael perfected a spiritual and meditative style appropriate to the fresco's religious and philosophical program. For the *Expulsion of Heliodoros,* however, in the Stanza di Eliodoro, 1511–14, Raphael adopted the *stile concitato* that later found its grandest expression in the *Battle of Constantine.* Executed by Giulio Romano on Raphael's designs in the Stanza di Costantino, 1521–24 (Fig. 11), this fresco contains a violence of action

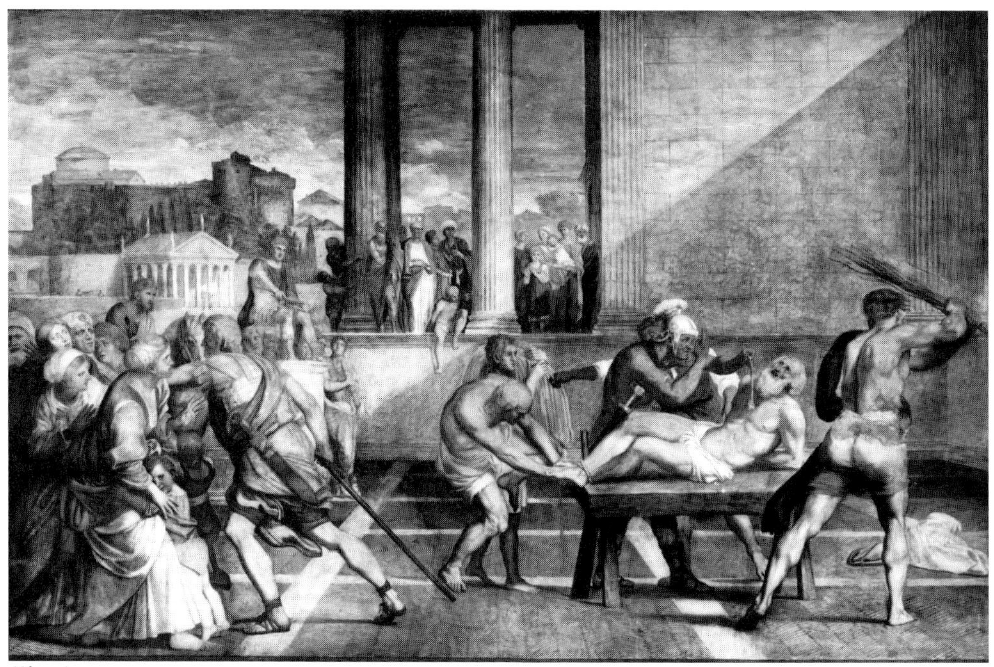

Fig. 4

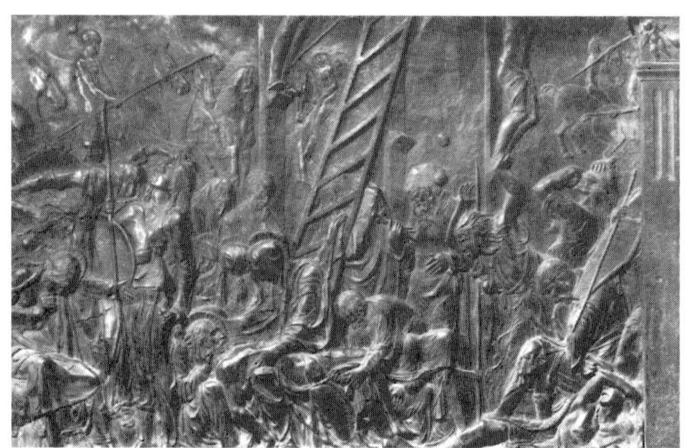

Fig. 5

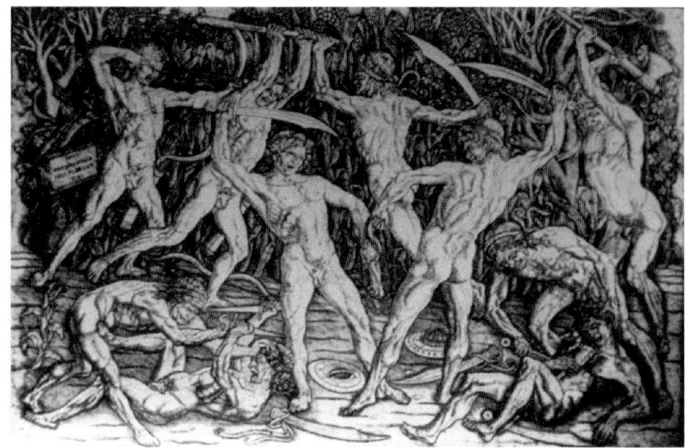

Fig. 6

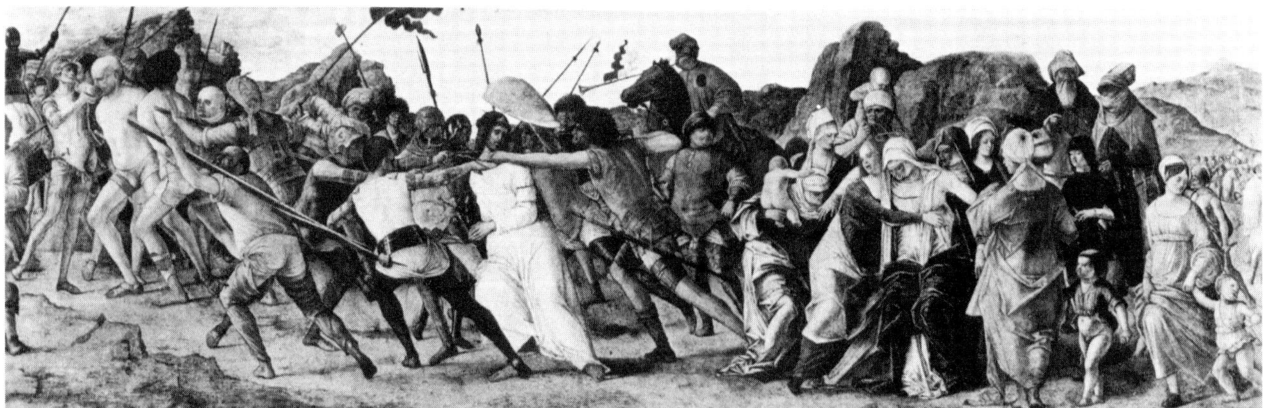

Fig. 7

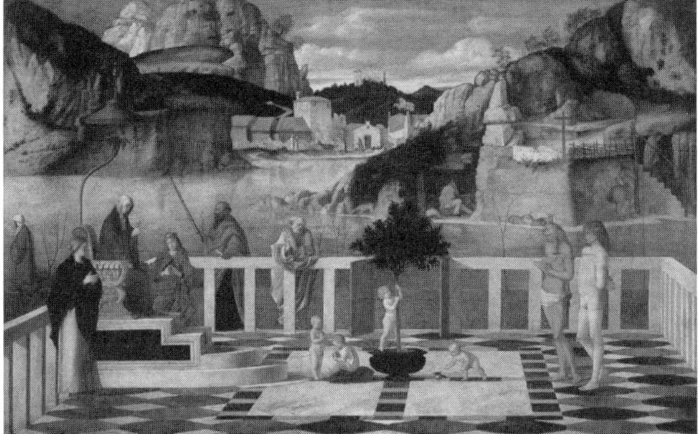

Fig. 8

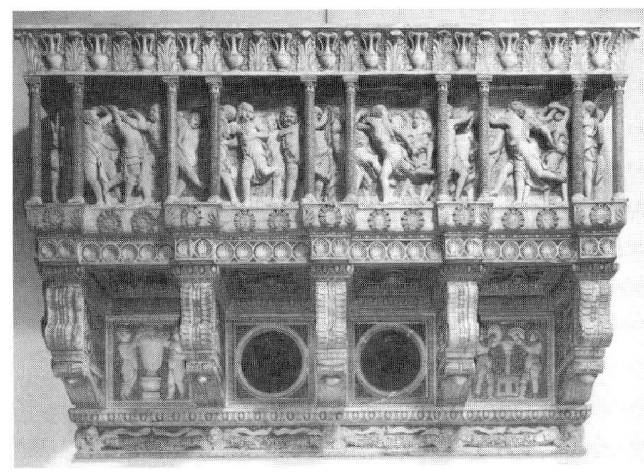

Fig. 9

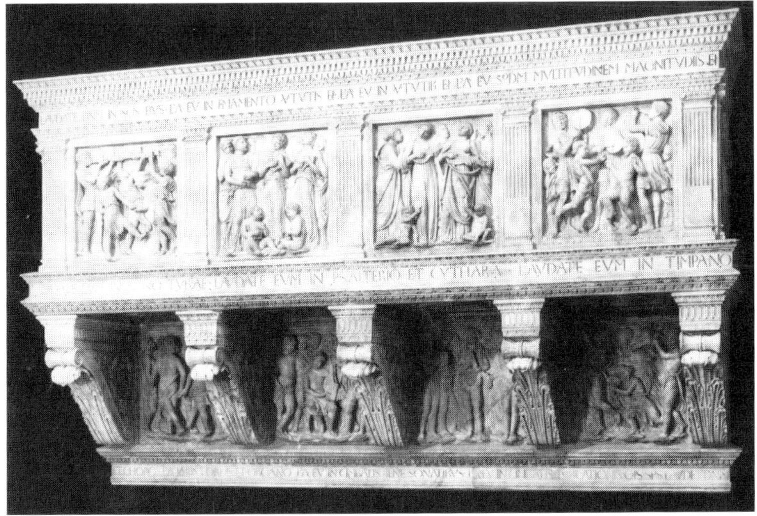

Fig. 10

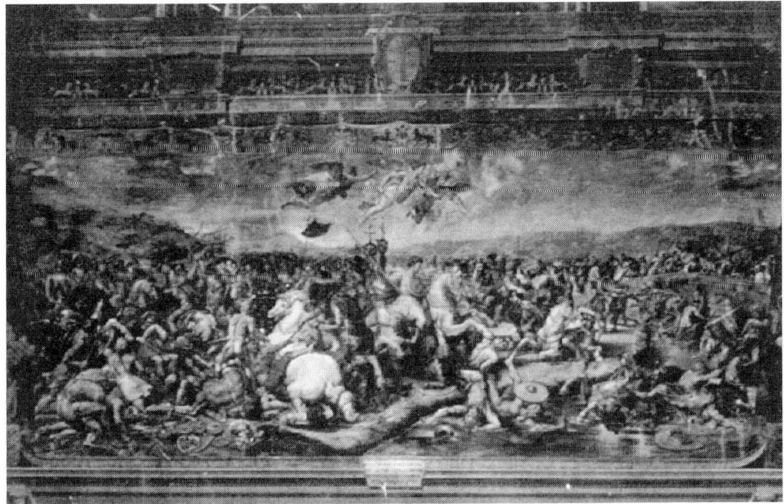

Fig. 11

Fig. 4 Domenichino, *Flagellation of St. Andrew,* 1609. Rome, San Gregorio Magno, St. Andrew Chapel. Photo: Alinari.

Fig. 5 Donatello, *Deposition,* 1460–65. Florence, San Lorenzo, south pulpit.

Fig. 6 Antonio del Pollaiuolo, *Battle of the Nudes,* 1471.

Fig. 7 Ercole de' Roberti, *Road to Calvary* (predella for altar in San Giovanni al Monte), 1483–86. Dresden, Gemäldegalerie.

Fig. 8 Giovanni Bellini, *Sacred Allegory,* c. 1488. Florence, Uffizi.

Fig. 9 Donatello, *Cantoria,* 1433–39. Florence, Museo dell'Opera del Duomo.

Fig. 10 Luca della Robbia, *Cantoria,* 1431–38. Florence, dell'Opera del Duomo.

Fig. 11 Giulio Romano, after design by Raphael, *Battle of Constantine,* 1521–24. Rome, Vatican Palace.

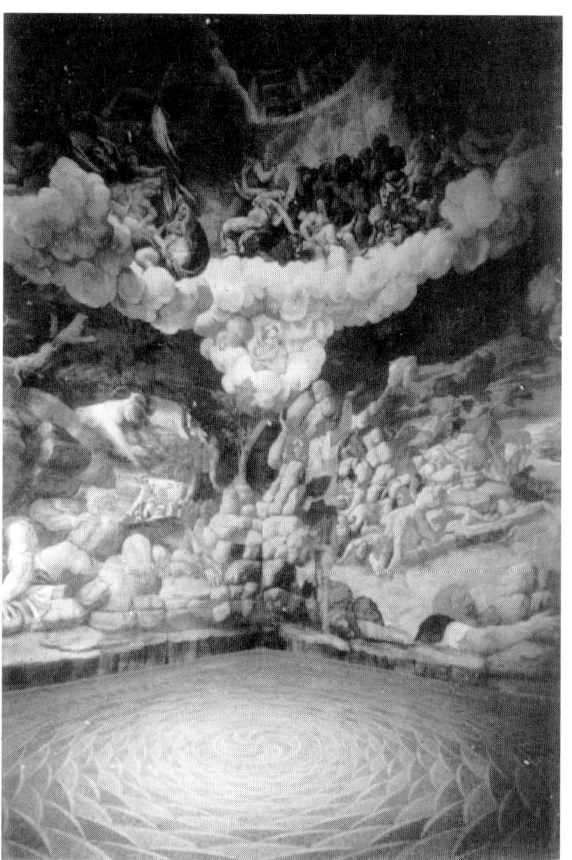

Fig. 12

and expression that had been explored earlier by Leonardo in the *Battle of Anghiari*. The *Battle of Constantine* was to become the touchstone for all subsequent battle painting and its vigorous development throughout the Seicento.

Giulio Romano, the favored and most prominent pupil of Raphael, brought the *stile concitato* or *antik-Pathetischen Stil* to Mantua, one of the great centers of humanistic culture in northern Italy. It is epitomized in Giulio's fresco, *The Fall of the Giants*, in the Palazzo del Te (Fig. 12) and the frescoes of the Sala di Troia in the Ducal Palace (executed for the most part by Fermo Ghisoni da Caravaggio). These are extremely important precedents for Seicento ceiling painting. Until the third decade of the Seicento, the city of Mantua preserved not only the frescoes of Mantegna and Giulio Romano, but also Mantegna's *Triumphs of Caesar* (Fig. 13), considered the most precious of the Gonzaga treasures, as well as the great collections of Isabella d'Este. These incomparable riches made Mantua a center of antiquarian culture and humanism.

Diverse elements from northern Italy gave birth to late Cinquecento artistic reforms and to the Baroque movement of the grand decorators. In understanding the genesis of Baroque painting, three components are intrinsic: Venetian colorism, Lombard naturalism, and, from the profane and mystic realms of Correggio's art, the *affetti*. *Quadratura* was born in northern Italy. For Bernini and the great decorators beginning with Pietro da Cortona, the *stile concitato* rooted in humanism was fundamental. Precedents were established not only by the late Raphael and the flourishing of the humanistic, antiquarian culture of Mantegna and Giulio Romano, but later by Ludovico Carracci and Peter Paul Rubens.

Indeed, we should understand Ludovico Carracci and Rubens as the initiators of the Baroque style. Ludovico was important for Giovanni Lanfranco; Rubens for Bernini and Pietro da Cortona. Rubens and his Mantua years are better known (though further research is needed), but Ludovico, whose anticipation of the Baroque style was discussed by Sydney Freedberg,[7] has been far less considered. It should be remembered that Malvasia himself chronicled Ludovico's visit to Mantua.[8] Ludovico derived figural movement and other elements from Mantegna's *Triumphs of Caesar* (Fig. 13) in his gigantic *Funeral of the Virgin*, painted for the Piacenza Cathedral, now in the Pinacoteca of Parma (Fig. 14). He drew inspiration as well from the *stile concitato* and the "terribili" (Malvasia) works of Giulio Romano. His direction was already manifest in paintings before 1590, such as the *Conversion of St. Paul* in the Pinacoteca of Bologna (Fig. 15) and the *Assumption of the Virgin* in Raleigh (Fig. 16), which became, in turn, powerful models for Lanfranco.

One of the factors that caused a decisive break between Ludovico and his cousin, Annibale, was Ludovico's continual striving for urgency of action. The *gigantismo* of Mantuan origin spread throughout Lombardy with Camillo Procaccini and other Lombard painters. Annibale, however, sought to attain ideal beauty through the *stile neo-attico* of Raphael's Stanza della Segnatura. Comparing the art of the Carracci cousins, we see that their differences are based on two distinct ways of approaching the principles and models of the Antique, a dichotomy that was to echo later in the debates at the *Accademia di San Luca*, Rome, between Pietro da Cortona and Andrea Sacchi. Consider, on one hand, Cortona's dynamic compositions crowded with foreshortened figures, and on the other, Sacchi's serene compositions with a limited number of figures placed in a controlled and rational space. As different as they are, Cortona's dynamism and Sacchi's classicism derived equally from the Antique.

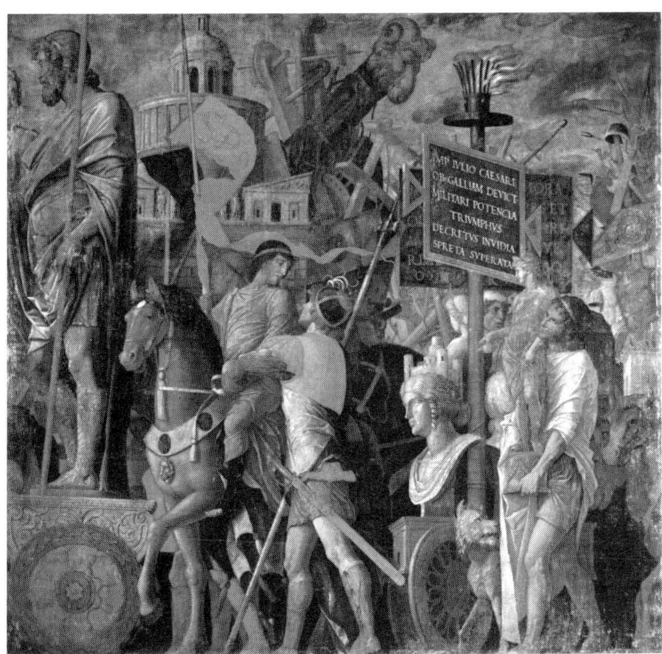

Fig. 13

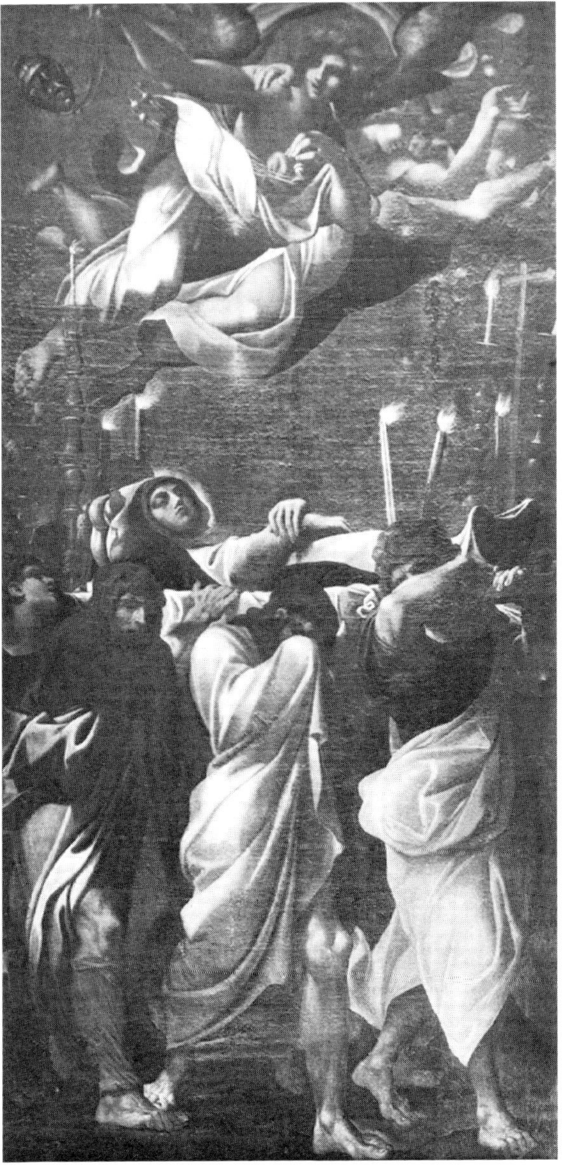

Fig. 14

Fig. 12 Giulio Romano, *The Fall of the Giants*, 1526–35. Mantua, Palazzo del Te.

Fig. 13 Andrea Mantegna, *Triumphs of Caesar*, canvas II, 1485–95. Hampton Court.

Fig. 14 Ludovico Carracci, *Funeral of the Virgin*, 1606–09. Parma, Galleria Nazionale.

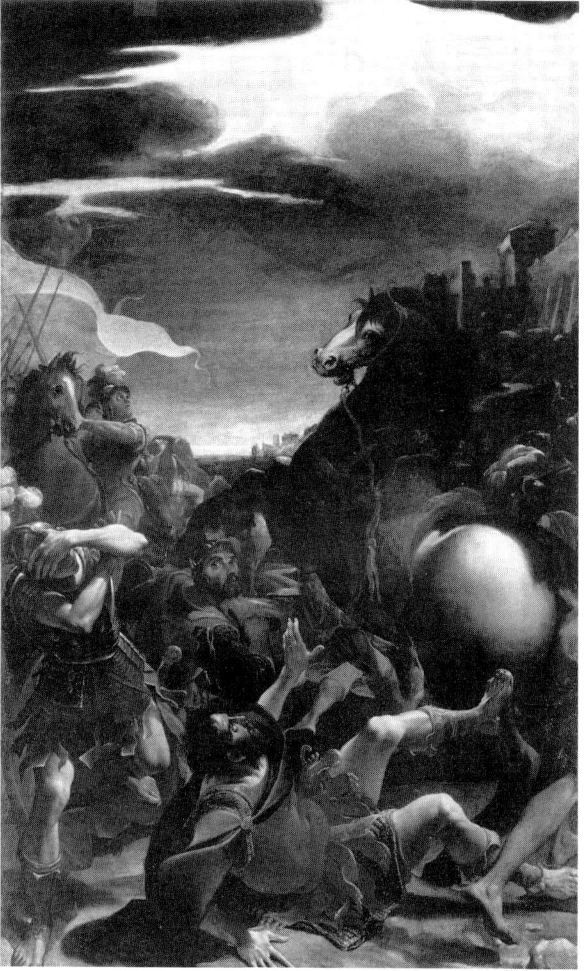

Fig. 15

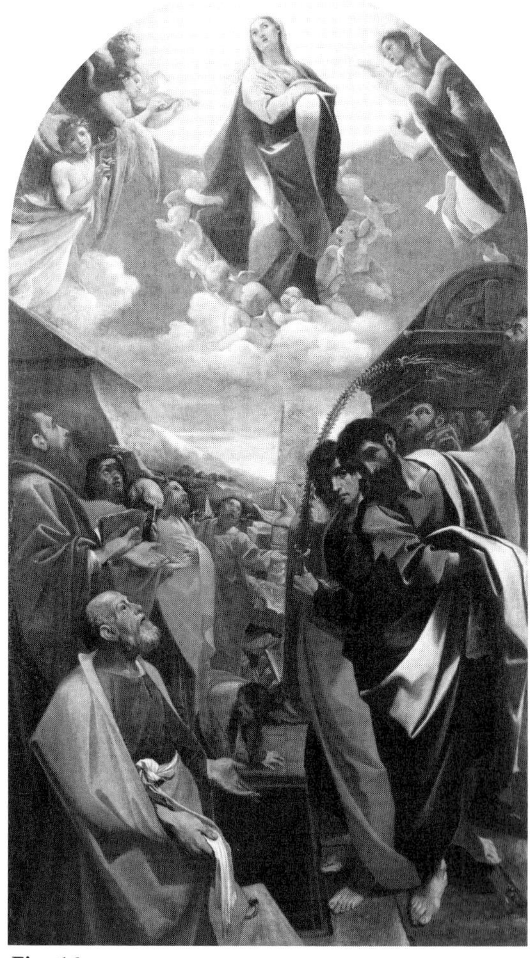

Fig. 16

Caravaggio was well aware of these contrasting approaches to painting. In the Cerasi Chapel in Santa Maria del Popolo, his first *Conversion of St. Paul*, now in the Odescalchi collection (Fig. 17), may have been prompted by the dynamic urgency of Ludovico's example of the subject (Fig. 15). His second version, however, for a chapel in which Annibale's *Assumption* was already installed on the central altar, reveals Caravaggio's replacement of the *stile concitato* by a composition more in harmony with the classicism of Annibale (Fig. 18). There are other examples of Caravaggio's duality, such as the contrast between his crowded *Seven Acts of Mercy* in Naples and the solemn calm of the *Beheading of St. John the Baptist* in Malta.[9]

The interplay between the *stile concitato* and the meditative *stile neo-attico*, between the realms of Dionysus and Apollo, provides a useful framework to assess the art of many centuries. In the study of Italian art, we can profit by these concepts, as they offer unexpected and fruitful insights.

Fig. 15 Ludovico Carracci, *Conversion of St. Paul,* 1587–89. Bologna, Pinacoteca Nazionale.

Fig. 16 Ludovico Carracci, *Assumption of the Virgin,* 1585–88. Raleigh, North Carolina Museum of Art.

Fig. 17 Caravaggio, *Conversion of St. Paul,* 1600–01. Rome, Odescalchi collection.

Fig. 18 Caravaggio, *Conversion of St. Paul,* 1600–01. Rome, Santa Maria del Popolo, Cerasi Chapel. Photo: Alinari.

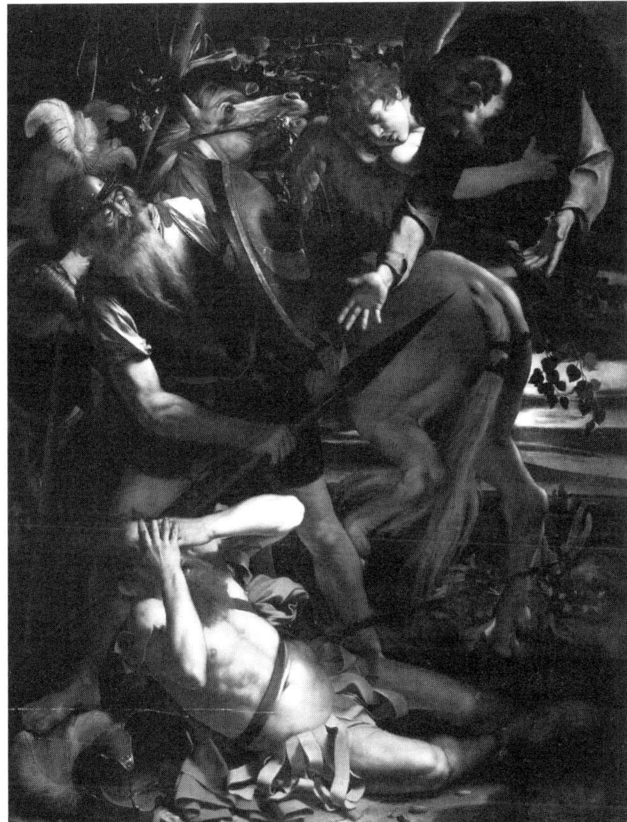

Fig. 17

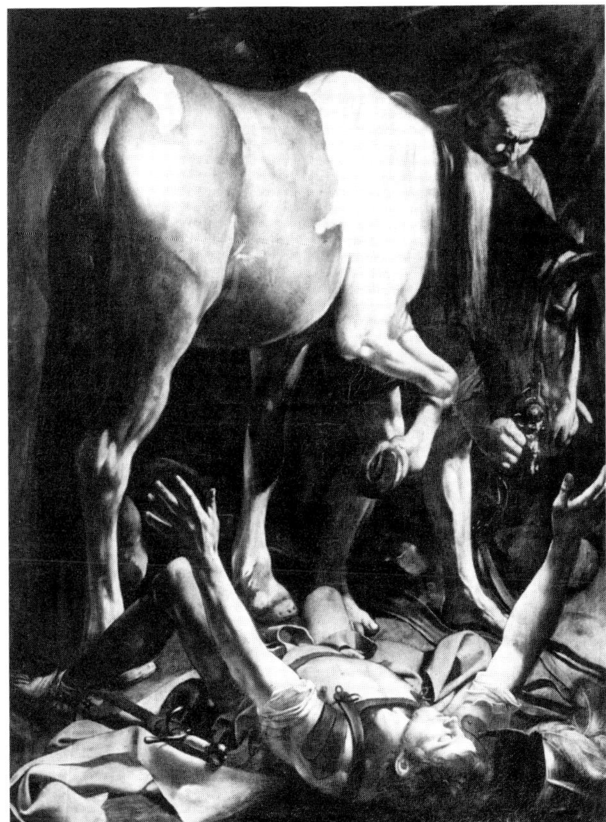

Fig. 18

Endnotes

1 D. Franklin, "Ridolfo Ghirlandaio's altarpieces for Leonardo Buonafé and the Hospital of S. Maria Nuova in Florence," *Burlington Mag.* CXXXV, 1078, 1993, p. 15.

2 C. Sterling, *La Nature Morte de l'Antiquité à nos jours*, Paris, 1959, p. 38.

3 A. Warburg, "Die Eintritt des antikisierenden Idealstil in die Malerei des Frührenaissance," *Gesammelte Schriften*, Leipzig and Berlin, 1932 (presented at a conference, April 20, 1914, Kunsthistorisches Institut, Florence); reprinted in A. Warburg, *La rinascita del paganesimo antico: Contributi alla storia della cultura*, Florence, 1966, pp. 285–307.

4 L. B. Alberti, *Della pittura*, ed. L. Mallé, Florence, 1950, pp. 87, 93, 94.

5 My article "Rubens, Bernini, e lo stile concitato" appeared in *Paragone*, 24–25, 1999, pp. 3–22. The initial ideas were formulated in this keynote address at the Palmer Museum, March 31, 1995.

6 R. Longhi, "Piero dei Franceschi e lo sviluppo della pittura veneziana," *L'Arte* XVII, 1914, pp. 198–221, 141–256; reprinted in R. Longhi, *Scritti giovanili, 1912–1922*, Florence, 1961 (Opere complete, vol. I), pt. 1, pp. 61–106.

7 S. J. Freedberg, "Ludovico Carracci" in *Circa 1600: A Revolution of Style in Italian Painting*, Cambridge, Massachusetts, and London, 1983, pp. 83, 97–100; reprinted as "An artist between two centuries," in A. Emiliani, *Ludovico Carracci*, exh. cat., Milan, 1993, pp. lxxi, lxxvii–lxxix. (Not included in American edition of the catalogue.)

8 G.C. Malvasia, *Felsina pittrice. Vite dei pittori bolognesi*, Bologna, 1678, ed. Bologna, 1841, p. 264.

9 M. Gregori, "Decollazione del Battista" in *Caravaggio da Malta a Firenze*, Milan, 1996, pp. 28–30; and "Decollazione del Battista" in *Caravaggio al Carmine*, Milan, 1999, pp. 33–36.

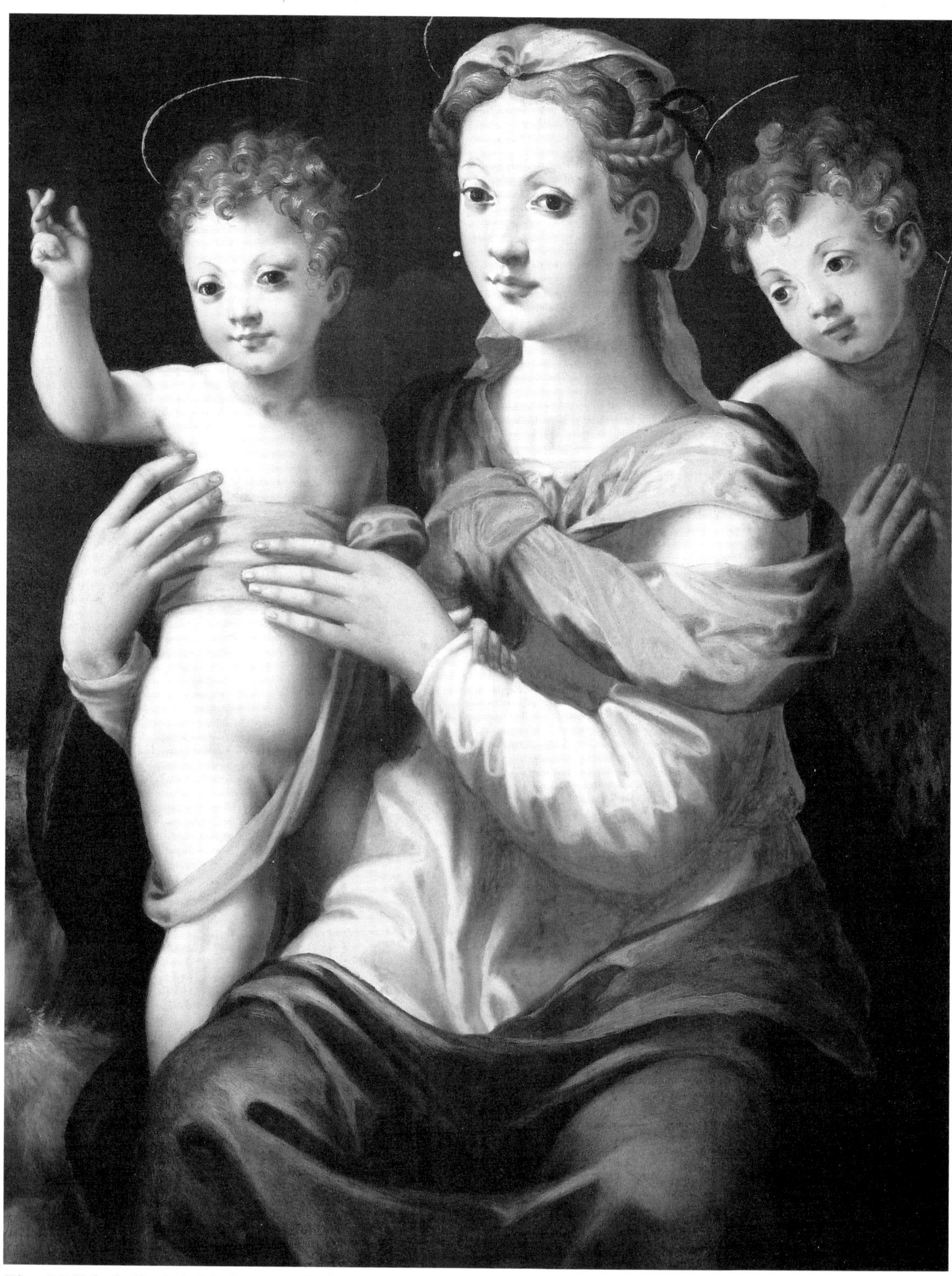

Fig. 1 Michele Tosini, *Madonna and Child with St. John the Baptist*, c. 1545-50. Palmer Museum of Art, The Pennsylvania State University. (See color plate 1.)

Michele Tosini: The Artist, the Oeuvre and the Testament

Heidi J. Hornik

The themes of the symposium: continuity, innovation, and connoisseurship,[1] can be identified with three phases of the work of Michele di Jacopo Tosini, who was born on May 8, 1503, and died October 26, 1577, in the city of Florence. [2]

The first phase encompasses the artistic training of Michele Tosini in the conservative workshop of Domenico Ghirlandaio and his son Ridolfo, where Tosini absorbed an artistic tradition that had been successful for generations. Michele ultimately established himself as the *capo* of the Ghirlandaio workshop, directing a skillful team of artists. Later, he became engaged in the major Florentine commissions of the 1560s because of his ability to produce the works and nurture the artists who carried on this tradition.

The second phase defines the mature style of Tosini, in which he broke with the conservative tradition and began a period of innovation and experimentation. The Palmer Museum's *Madonna and Child with St. John the Baptist* is pivotal between the first and second phases of his career (Fig. 1).[3] Although never as daring as Agnolo Bronzino, Francesco Salviati, or Giorgio Vasari, Tosini incorporated aspects of their work into the Ghirlandaio tradition, and was pivotal in the dissemination of their style in a broad range of private commissions and public projects.

The third phase of Tosini's oeuvre comprises his late half-length portraits and his secular and mythological subjects. The problems of attribution associated with these late works require connoisseurship and further study.

The recently discovered Testament of Tosini has been important for my study, as it discloses new information concerning his family and patrons.[4] Michele di Jacopo Tosini, "a wise man and being of sound mind, perception, reason and body, not willing to die intestate, but making declaration concerning his own goods dictated his Testament without writing in vulgar speech," was recorded by Notaio Giovanni di Matteo da Falgano on March 20, 1575. The document, written two years before the artist's death, contributes much to our understanding of Michele Tosini as a man and an artist.

ARTISTIC TRAINING— CONTINUITY

Tosini's artistic life began with his training under Lorenzo di Credi (1459–1537) and then possibly with Antonio del Ceraiolo (d. 1525?). Lorenzo di Credi was the head of a conservative and enduring workshop that produced works of consistent if unexceptional quality. His artists were thoroughly schooled in traditional techniques and not encouraged to experiment. Ceraiolo too received his early training with Lorenzo and became an assistant and friend to Ridolfo del Ghirlandaio (1483–1561).[5] It may have been Ceraiolo who introduced Ridolfo and Michele Tosini.

Tosini entered the workshop of Ridolfo Ghirlandaio around 1516. Ridolfo was the son of Domenico (1449–94), but from the age of 11, after the death of his father, he was educated by an uncle, Davide (1452–1525).[6] Tosini's training between 1516 and 1545 was honed under the watchful guidance of Ridolfo, but Tosini gradually asserted his individuality. Tosini looked upon his master as a father, and Ridolfo loved him like a son. He became known as Michele di Ridolfo, and modern scholarship has tended to underestimate his role.[7] In establishing his style and chronology, it is necessary to consider his development alongside and beyond his teacher.

As author of *Le Vite de'più eccellenti pittori, scultori ed architettori*, Vasari is one of the prime contemporary sources for Michele's biography. He valued Tosini as a friend, the head of a thriving workshop, and a fellow founding member of the *Accademia del Disegno*, which suggests a significant role for the artist in late sixteenth-century Florence. Vasari states that together Michele and Ridolfo controlled one of the most successful workshops in Florence, with commissions so numerous it was impossible to complete them all.[8] The conservative High Renaissance style continued to be in demand for many decades and there were other shops in Florence even more conservative than that of Ridolfo.[9]

In the 1568 edition of *Le Vite*, Vasari lists four collaborative works by Michele and Ridolfo.[10] The *Marriage of St. Catherine* of circa 1520, today in a convent outside Florence, is one of the works produced by the workshop, and it typifies the balanced compositions of the High Renaissance (Fig. 2).[11] Michele was 17 in 1520 when Carlo Gamba wrote, "Ridolfo is associated with a young man, who is still inexperienced in the science of art but already self-assured."[12]

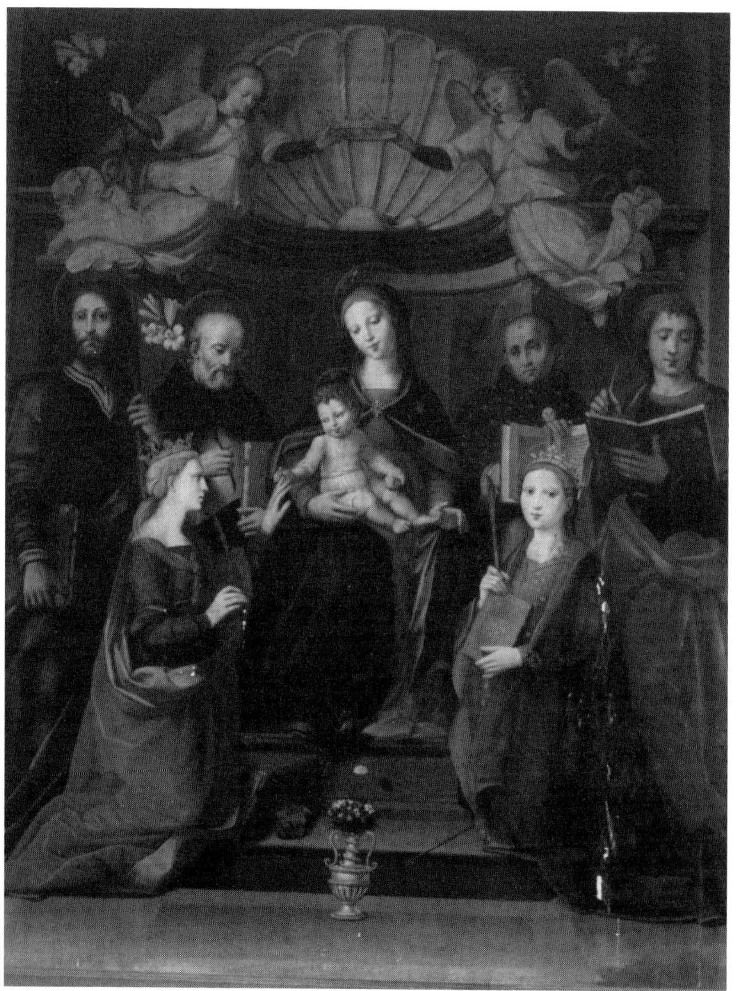

Fig. 2

As Michele matured, Ridolfo gradually allowed him to exert more influence. Another collaborative work cited by Vasari, an altarpiece for the monastic church of SS. Jacopo and Lorenzo on Via Ghibellina, Florence, reveals Michele as a distinctive talent (Fig. 3). This *Madonna and Child with Saints James, Lawrence, Francis, and Clare, and Bishop Buonafé*, illustrates his emergence from the Ghirlandaio style. The Palmer Museum painting is based on its central composition.[13] Recently discovered documents in the Florentine Archivio di Stato clarify the patronage and provide a time frame in which to date the altarpiece and the Palmer painting.[14] Vasari stated that the altarpiece was ordered by the Florentine, Leonardo di Giovanni Buonafé (c. 1450–1545).[15] David Franklin, who has studied the altarpieces commissioned by Buonafé during his tenure (1500–28) as director of the hospital in Florence, Santa Maria Nuova,[16] points out that the work was ordered by Buonafé after he was elected Bishop of Cortona in 1529.[17] The saints represented have specific significance for the church. St. James and St. Lawrence are its patron saints; St. Francis is invoked during its opening prayer; St. Clare is referred to in the documents as the mother of the affiliated monastery.

The dating of the altarpiece has heretofore been problematic because it was unclear whether it was painted before or after the death of Buonafé in 1545. Recent documents establish that it was completed before 1551, when the Church of SS.

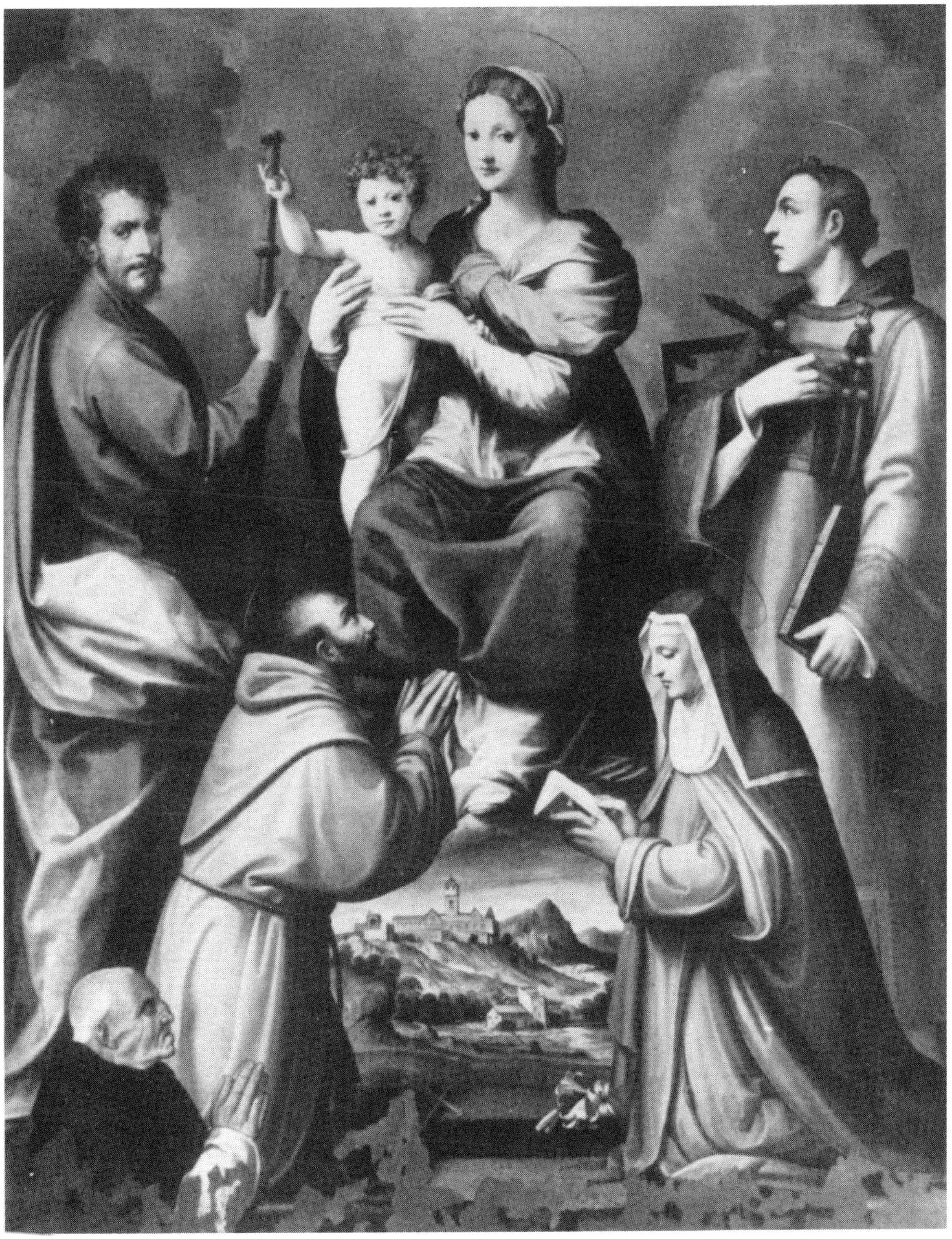

Fig. 3

Jacopo and Lorenzo was dedicated to the bishop's memory.[18] I believe the altarpiece was begun about 1540. The bishop is shown in profile at the lower left, the usual position of patrons in altarpieces by Ridolfo Ghirlandaio. The central Madonna and Child were painted, as stated above, by Michele Tosini. The *changeant* (iridescent) colors on the mantle of the Virgin, as well as the lightening and brightening of the palette in the two central figures are different from the pure colors used by Ridolfo for the saints and donor. Michele achieved texture by thicker application of paint and glazes, which increased the reflection of light. Ridolfo continued to depend on the late Quattrocento use of local color.

In the late 1540s, Tosini completed his years of training in the Ghirlandaio workshop. His paintings reflect a dilemma between meeting his obligations to continue in the traditional Renaissance style and a desire to incorporate the modern techniques of the *Maniera* artists, Bronzino, Salviati, and Vasari. Michele's use of *changeant* colors, already employed for decades by these artists, is evident on the Virgin's mantle in the Palmer *Madonna and Child with St. John the Baptist*, and I would place it between 1545 and 1550, after the S. Jacopo altarpiece was well underway.

The Palmer painting presents other *Maniera* elements that were to become characteristic of the second phase of Michele's career, such as bringing the figures forward in the picture plane and positioning them directly before the viewer. Compared with the altarpiece, one notes the sweeter expression and firmer modeling of the Child. His head turns slightly to the right as he looks outwards. *Pentimenti* are evident between the first and second fingers of the Madonna's left hand, reflecting the pains the artist took to render the pressure of her fingers against the flesh of the Child. Her headdress and hairstyle are elaborate, and her mantle of *changeant* mauve and blue-green reflects a bold *Maniera* palette. St. John the Baptist, the patron saint of Florence, is now included. His delicate features and slightly unaligned eyes are characteristic of the artist.[19] Looking adoringly toward the Madonna and Child, St. John is positioned behind her left shoulder and slightly separated from the pair. Tosini's faces and palette differ from Ridolfo's, but his poses retain a traditional format that recalls Andrea del Sarto.

A second *Madonna and Child with St. John the Baptist*, formerly in the Museo Bandini, Fiesole, and known to me from a photograph (Fig. 4), is almost identical to the Palmer composition, but until I can study the picture I will reserve judgment on its quality and attribution.[20] The Fiesole and Palmer painting were probably commissioned by private patrons, suggesting that the S. Jacopo altarpiece must have been known and well regarded.

Tosini's personal life underwent many changes between 1520 and 1545. According to his Testament, he married a woman named Felice and had four children. Baccio, their first child, was born circa 1530–35. Following tradition, Baccio took the profession of his father and entered the Company of St. Luke in 1555. After his father's death, he inherited the Ghirlandaio workshop. Dionora, the first daughter, was born in 1540 and joined the convent of S. Vincenzo, Prato, in 1553. A second son, took the name Fra Santi upon his ordination into the monastery of San Domenico in Fiesole. Michele's youngest child, Lisabetta, joined the convent of S. Jacopo in Ripoli, a suburb of Florence.[21] Michele was occupied with obligations of family during this period but he continued to advance his professional career within the security of the Ghirlandaio workshop. In the 1530s, his prestige and accomplishments grew, and he was elected a member of the Company of St. Luke on April 14, 1538.[22]

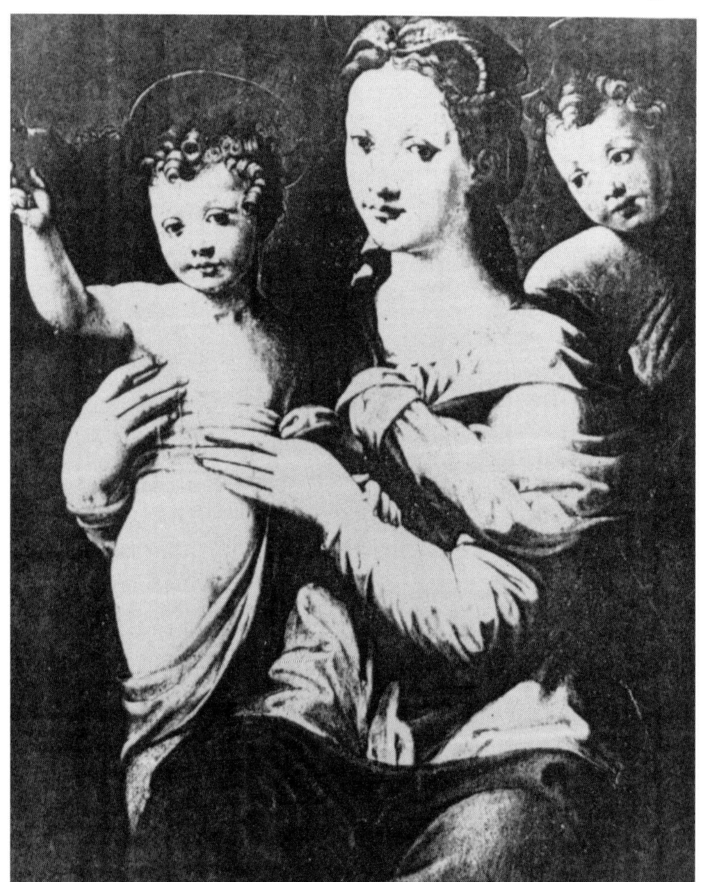

Fig. 4

ECCLESIASTICAL, PRIVATE, AND CIVIC PATRONAGE — A PERIOD OF INNOVATION

SAN VINCENZO, PRATO

The second phase of Michele's oeuvre was a period of innovation and experimentation. During the 1550s he developed a style fully independent of Ridolfo, which is reflected in an altarpiece for the chapel of the convent of S. Vincenzo, Prato, executed between 1559 and 1561. In 1553, his daughter Dionora, as mentioned, entered S. Vincenzo, a convent with ties to the Tosini and

Ghirlandaio family church, S. Maria Novella in Florence. Both convent and church were Dominican, and many of the nuns were Florentine. Dionora served for seventeen years under the direction of the venerable Catherine de'Ricci, who was eventually elevated to sainthood. Dionora's presence in the convent helped her father secure several commissions, the largest and most important being the Chapel of the Madonna of Loreto.

Michele was commissioned to fresco the ceiling of the chapel (unfortunately lost when it was repainted in 1743) and to execute the altar panel.[23] The panel remains, but the upper area is lost, also painted over in the eighteenth century (Fig. 5) with a Madonna and Child surrounded by *putti* in clouds. Fortunately, the six flanking saints are original and reveal Tosini's interest in Bronzino, Salviati, and Vasari. The colors are bright and vivid pinks, blues, and greens, typical of the *Maniera* palette that Michele adopted by the 1550s. It is worth noting that Francesco Salviati worked in the Sala d'Udienza at the Palazzo Vecchio between 1543 and 1548.[24] Eight years later Tosini painted in the adjacent room, which must have sharpened his interest in *Maniera* color.

The poses of the six saints are expressive, even theatrical. The elegant profile, long neck, small mouth, and deep-set eyes of St. Catherine became part of Tosini's vocabulary, as in his half-length *St. Mary Magdalene* in the Museum of Fine Arts, Houston, which falls into what I have designated as his third phase (Fig. 9).[25] The face of St. Catherine recalls those of Vasari in the Palazzo Vecchio decorations circa 1557 where he worked with Tosini,[26] as well as Vasari's *Judith and Holofernes* (Fig. 10) circa 1554 in the St. Louis Museum.

The background of the San Vincenzo altar is a cityscape, a frequent element in Tosini's work. It depicts a triumphal arch, a cylindrical fortress, a long basilica, and other buildings.

THE STROZZI VILLA

In the second phase of Tosini's career, his patronage expanded. He received a commission to decorate the chapel of the Villa Caserotta outside Florence for the Strozzi family (Figs. 6–8). Vasari mentions it in the 1568 edition of his *Vite*, stating that Matteo Strozzi (d. 1541) ordered several paintings as well as sculpture.[27] Bottari, in his 1759 edition of *Le Vite*, was the first to attribute the chapel fresco cycle to Tosini.[28] Milanesi maintains the attribution in 1878 and states that the villa was owned, as today, by the Ganucci-Cancellieri family.[29] These early references mention neither a precise date nor a location.[30]

Villa Caserotta is situated twenty miles from Florence near San Casciano in the small town of Paolini in the Pesa River valley.[31] The Strozzi family purchased the property in the first quarter of the sixteenth century[32] and retained ownership until Diacinto Ganucci bought it in 1741. The villa as it appeared during the Strozzi possession can be seen in the background of Tosini's painting behind the figure of St. John (Fig. 6).[33] This branch of the Strozzi, like their more famous relatives, Palla and Filippo, were active patrons of the arts in Florence and their outlying villas. Alessandro (1501–70), a banker and the son of Matteo mentioned by Vasari, was already living in the villa when he commissioned the work from Tosini.

The Chapel of the Madonna of Loreto is approximately eleven feet wide, fifteen feet long, and twelve feet high and has a barrel vaulted ceiling. Tosini's frescoes are intact and in excellent condition. They have undergone little restoration except for overpainting of some Latin inscriptions. The central altarpiece has been temporarily removed for restoration and replaced by a twentieth-century work. The wall frescoes depict the Four Evangelists and scenes from the life of Christ. A date of 1561 is faintly visible in Roman numerals on the gospel book of St. John the Evangelist (Fig. 6). The open book of St. Mark refers to the baptism of Christ, a subject in the chapel, whose iconographical program represents the life of Christ from the Annunciation to the Crucifixion. The *Adoration of the Magi* (Fig. 7), the largest of the scenes, the *Marriage at Cana*

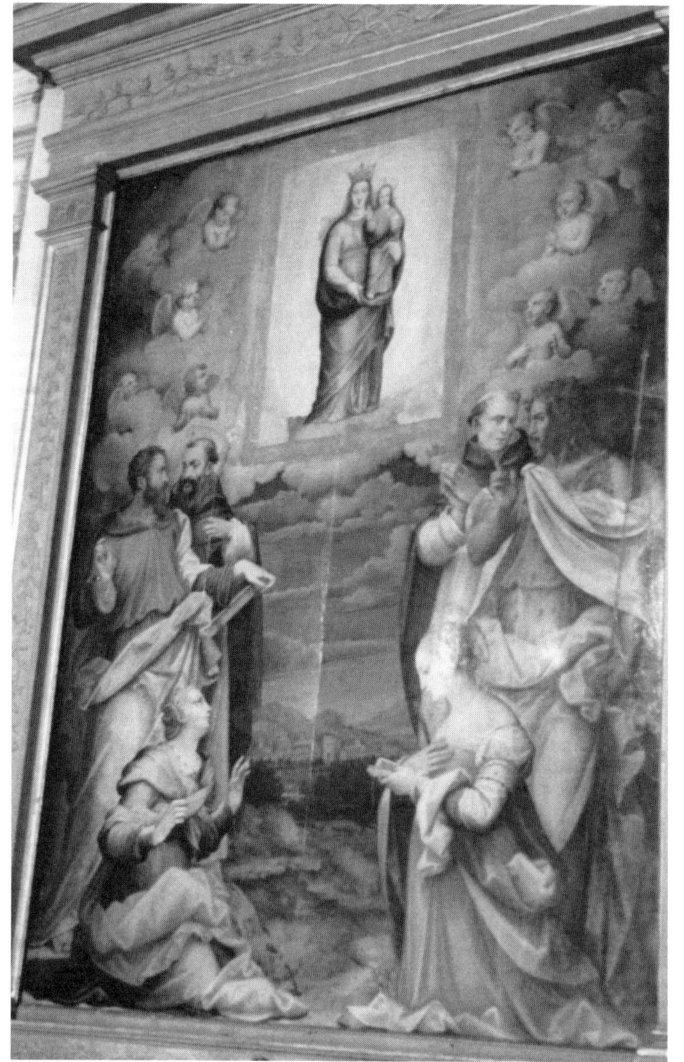
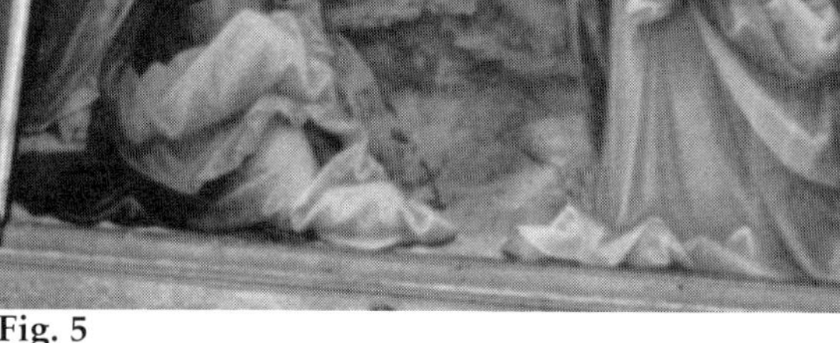

Fig. 5

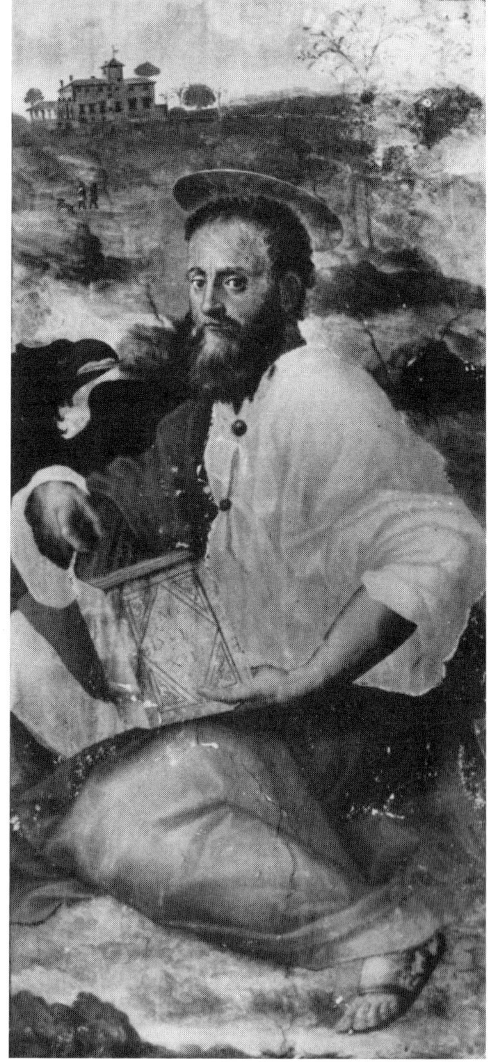

Fig. 6

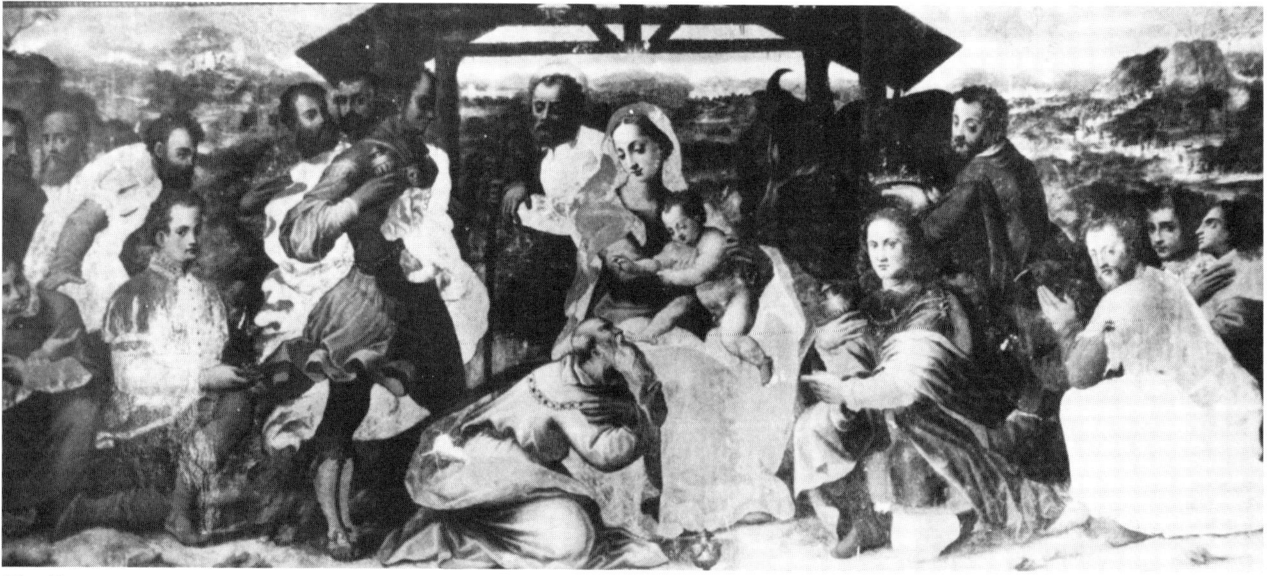

Fig. 7

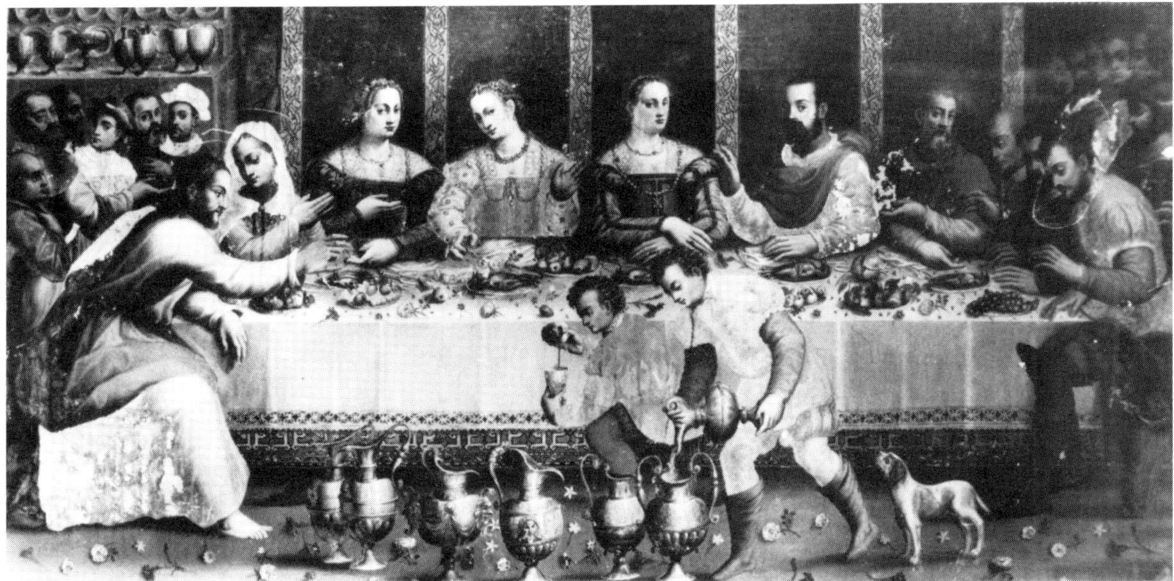

Fig. 8

(Fig. 8), and the *Baptism of Christ* comprise the three events celebrated on Epiphany.[34] This chapel was decorated at a critical point in the life of Michele Tosini. Ridolfo Ghirlandaio was dying, and Michele was assuming responsibility for the workshop. Although he seems to have painted the larger portion, other hands may be detected. As Vasari attests, Michele was known for his ability to attract and to train talented artists.

CIVIC PROJECTS FOR FLORENCE

In addition to commissions for ecclesiastical and private patrons during the second phase of his career, Tosini was engaged in major civic projects for Florence. He had an advantage over other artists in that he was a personal friend of Giorgio Vasari (1511–74). Their first documented collaboration was the Sala di Cosimo I in the Palazzo Vecchio, August 1557.[35] Tosini was 54 years old and Vasari 46. Later Vasari called upon Tosini and five other artists to assist him in additional remodeling and decoration of the Palazzo Vecchio for Cosimo I, who had taken up residence there in 1549. Besides the Sala di Cosimo, Michele participated in the decoration of the Sala di Giovanni dalle Bande Nere and the Sala dei Cinquecento.

Vasari remodeled the Sala dei Cinquecento or Sala Grande in the style of the Doge's Palace in Venice. The ceiling contains thirty-nine small compartments each painted with a city significant for the growth of Florence. Unity of the project being the prime consideration, it is difficult to discern individual hands. According to a document published by Edmund Pillsbury, Tosini worked on the project in 1564.[36] Although his proficiency in landscape was acknowledged, Pillsbury does not say which landscapes might be by him. Paola Barocchi has proposed his authorship for three of the compartments, identified as the *quartiere* of S. Giovanni and S. Maria Novella, the allegory of Prato, and an allegory of Certaldo.[37] These works suggest that Tosini never lost touch with established tradition even after his commissions reflected a more innovative style.

FOUNDING OF THE ACCADEMIA DEL DISEGNO

In 1563, Vasari called upon Tosini to assist him in founding the *Accademia del Disegno*.[38] His name appears in numerous documents and correspondence between Grand Duke Cosimo de'Medici, Don Vincenzo Borghini, and Vasari regarding the formation of the Academy and

Fig. 5 Michele Tosini, *Madonna and Child with Saints,* 1559–61. Prato, S. Vincenzo. Photo: author with permission.

Fig. 6 Michele Tosini, *St. John the Evangelist,* 1561. Paolini, Villa Ganucci-Cancellieri, Strozzi Chapel. Photo: author with permission.

Fig. 7 Michele Tosini, *Adoration of the Magi,* 1561. Paolini, Villa Ganucci-Cancellieri, Strozzi Chapel. Photo: author with permission.

Fig. 8 Michele Tosini, *Marriage at Cana,* 1561. Paolini, Villa Ganucci-Cancellieri, Strozzi Chapel. Photo: author with permission.

its projects.[39] As a founding father, Michele participated in the formulation of the forty-seven articles comprising the Code of Rules.[40] One of the first and most important projects of the new body was the planning and execution of a grandiose funeral celebration for Michelangelo in 1564 under Tosini's direction, for which his workshop painted a large part of the catafalque.[41]

The workshop also assumed an important role in the ephemeral decorations for the marriage celebration of Francesco I and Giovanna of Austria.[42] Preparations, begun in June 1565, included elaborate *apparati* (temporary structures) erected throughout Florence that would be admired by the wedding procession as it wound through the streets of the city. Contemporary documents indicate a hierarchy of artists in Florence at that time. Tosini was in the first rank, together with Carlo Portelli, Alessandro Allori, Battista Naldini, Santi di Tito, and Giovanni Maria Butteri. Borghini records that seventeen artists were engaged to assist Vasari in the marriage decorations, eleven for Bronzino, and seven for Michele di Ridolfo.[43] Several of Michele's students were among artists of second and third rank. Borghini describes Michele as "*di buon giudizio e valente*" (of good judgment and worthy) and as having excellent relations with young artists.[44] He comments that anything Michele and his pupils created would be "pleasing and well received."[45] Michele, by then the sole head of a highly productive workshop, was a respected artist of wealth and prestige.

THE MATURE WORKS — ISSUES OF CONNOISSEURSHIP

The mature works of the third phase of Tosini's career require an exercise of connoisseurship in its most straightforward definition. It is a term coined by the art historian Bernard Berenson (1865–1959) indicating the ability to identify by the work of art alone, the artist, its period, its relationship to other works, and its aesthetic merits or lack of them. With regard to Tosini, for the most part modern scholars have had to rely on attributions based on connoisseurship. Scholarship for Tosini ranges from lists with little stylistic analysis and no documen-

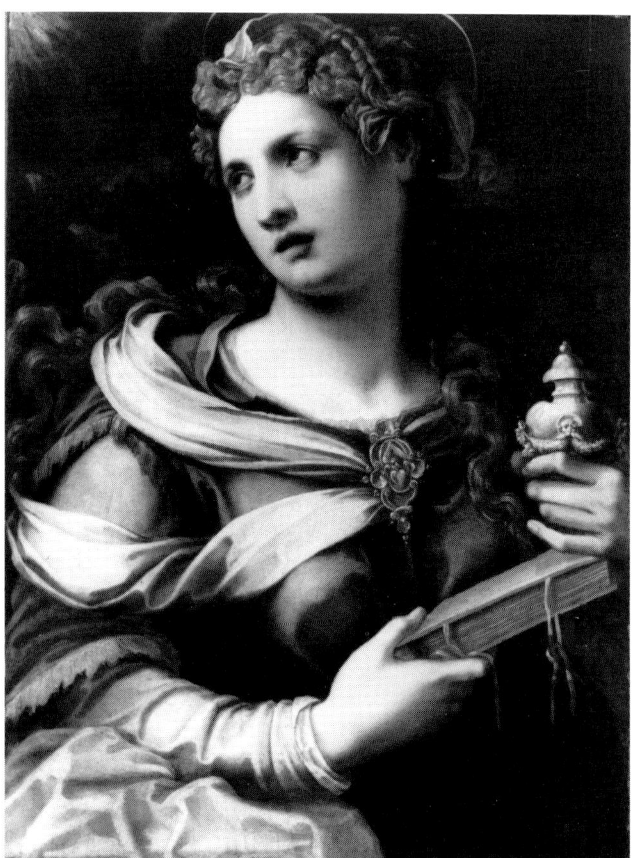

Fig. 9

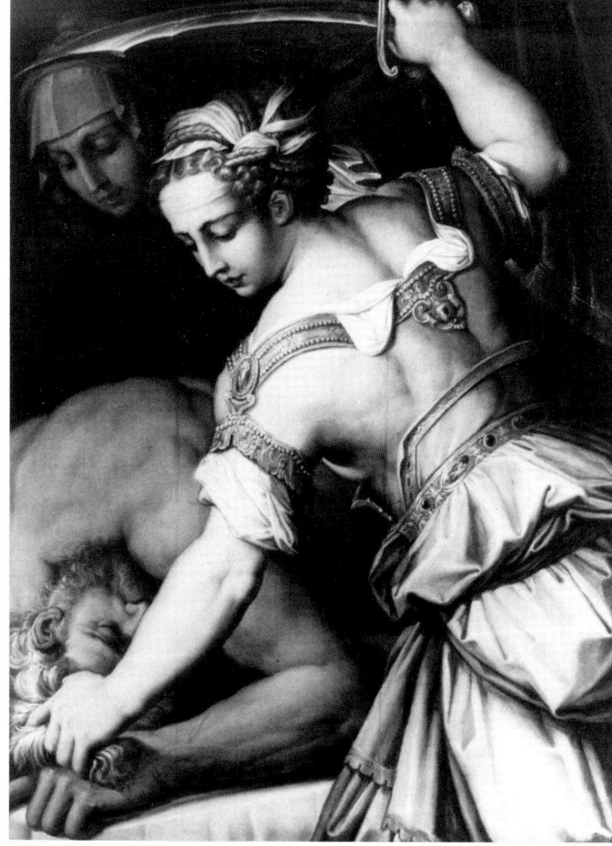

Fig. 10

tary reference—such as those made by Gamba, Venturi, and Freedberg—to catalogue entries proposing the attribution without supportive explanation.[46] Lists can be useful, however, in assembling a body of work agreed upon by several scholars.

Although it is not possible here to discuss every Tosini work that has generally been agreed upon, it is possible to substantiate many attributions by comparison with a small group of eight securely documented paintings. My study has focused on tracing the development of Tosini's style by checking the most reliably attributed pictures against this benchmark group of the eight examples.[47]

After 1561, Tosini's paintings have virtually no documentation and are difficult to pin down. In the recent twenty years, a large number of new attributions has been put forth by auction houses to Tosini or his workshop.[48] In my best judgment, seventy-four paintings can be correctly assigned to Michele Tosini and twenty-six to his workshop. Several of the most convincing examples are female half-length figures that demonstrate Tosini's assimilation of the Vasarian *Maniera*. A prototypical example is Tosini's *St. Mary Magdalene*, Houston, circa 1570 (Fig. 9), which may be compaired with Vasari's *Judith and Holofernes*, in St. Louis, circa 1554 (Fig. 10). In the 1550s and 1560s, Tosini exhibited a predilection for Vasari's rich costumes and hair ornaments, and by the 1570s we find him using elaborate light-catching jewels. Tosini has also mastered Vasari's graceful profiles and long sensuous necks, as in his *St. Barbara* in the Accademia, Florence, dated circa 1575 (Fig. 11).[49] In this late phase, Michele tends to demonstrate attention to facial expression and strong *contrapposto*.

Portraiture is a challenging area of connoisseurship in sixteenth-century Florentine painting.[50] At times, the individual style of the artist makes it difficult to identify the sitter. On the other hand, hairstyle, costume, and to some extent pose, are determined by the sitter and fashion rather than the artist. I call attention to two examples: *Portrait of a Gentleman* in the North Carolina Museum of Art, Raleigh (Fig. 12), and *Portrait of Cosimo I, Francesco I, and Another Man*, from a private collection in Florence (Fig. 13).[51] The attributions to both pictures have hovered between Salviati, Vasari, and Tosini. William Suida, in 1956, was the first to assign the Raleigh portrait to Tosini. The sitter holds a note bearing the date 1575, indicating that he is in his 31st year. Karla Langedijk attributed the group portrait to Tosini in 1981. Both attributions are correct in my view. I place the group portrait among Tosini's late works, circa 1573, close to Cosimo's death in 1574, and to the Raleigh painting.[52]

CONCLUSION: THE GHIRLANDAIO WORKSHOP

Tracing the continuation of Tosini's late production and the fate of his workshop is speculative. His son, Baccio, inherited the shop after his father's death in 1577, but virtually nothing further is known about the son or the workshop itself, and no works of art have been attributed to him.

The Brina brothers, Francesco (1540–86) and Giovanni (d. 1599), were documented as fairly late members of Tosini's workshop, and several paintings dating to the 1570s have been attributed to them.[53] A few of Tosini's students were employed by Vasari in the Studiolo, such as Andrea del Minga, but were no longer producing the type of works associated with the last years of the workshop.

Michele Tosini's rather late assimilation of the *Maneria* style of Vasari, Salviati, and Michelangelo took place at a time when a younger generation of artists, including some who had originally been trained in this style, was turning back to the work of Andrea del Sarto, the young Pontormo, and to a lesser degree, Fra Bartolommeo.[54] One such artist was Tommaso Manzuoli known as Maso da San Friano (1532–71). Maso's *Adoration of the Shepherds*, purchased by the Friends of the Palmer Museum of Art in 1986, represents the newer tendency, which was evolving in Florence in the mid-1560s. The Palmer Tosini (Fig. 1) and the Maso da San Friano (Costamagna, Fig. 1),[55] reflect two different directions taken by Florentine artists in the middle of the sixteenth century.

Fig. 9 Michele Tosini, *St. Mary Magdalene*, c. 1570. Houston, The Museum of Fine Arts, Samuel H. Kress Collection. Photo: Museum of Fine Arts.

Fig. 10 Giorgio Vasari, *Judith and Holofernes*, c. 1554. St. Louis Museum of Art. Photo: St. Louis Museum of Art.

Fig. 11 Michele Tosini, *St. Barbara,* c. 1575. Florence, Museo del Accademia. Photo: Soprintendenza per i Beni Artistici e Storici, Florence.

Fig. 12 Michele Tosini, *Portrait of a Gentleman,* 1575. Raleigh, North Carolina Museum of Art, gift of Mr. and Mrs. Arthur Erlanger. Photo: North Carolina Museum of Art.

Fig. 13 Michele Tosini, *Portrait of Cosimo I, Francesco I, and Another Man,* c. 1573. Florence, private collection. Photo: Florence, Kunsthistorisches Institut (Fototeca).

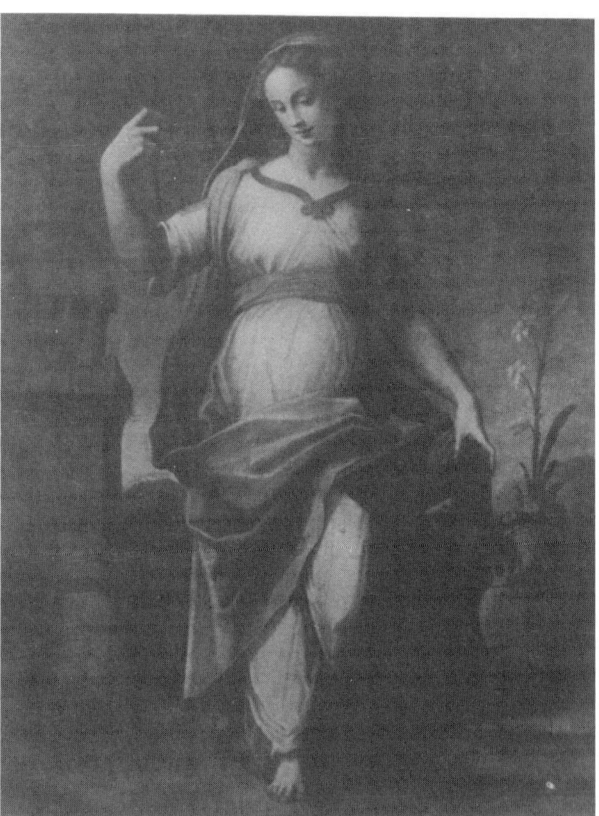

Fig. 11

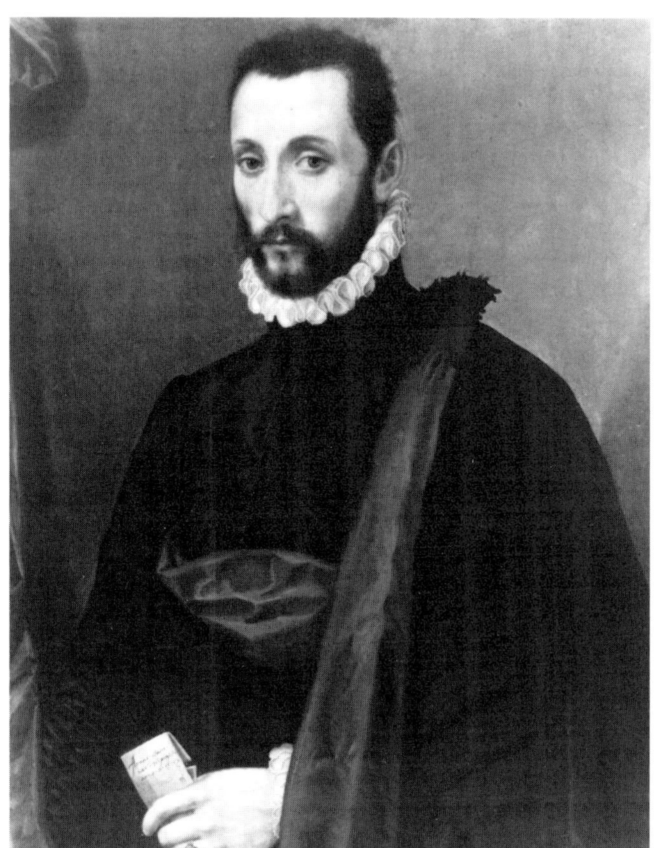

Fig. 12

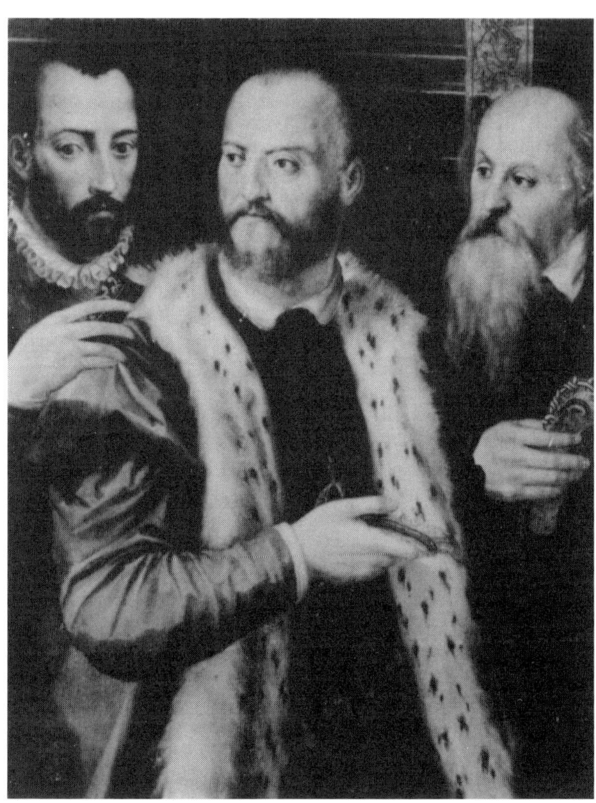

Fig. 13

Endnotes

1 In 1986, Mary Jane Harris initiated an exhibition of Renaissance works from the Piero Corsini Gallery, New York, for the Museum of Art, The Pennsylvania State University, now the Palmer Museum of Art (see Wollesen-Wisch, note 3 below). The exhibition was shown in Springfield, Massachusetts, the College of William and Mary, Williamsburg, Virginia, and Marquette University, Milwaukee, Wisconsin. This painting was part of the exhibition. I am greatly appreciative of the support that I have received from Ms. Harris over the years and thank her for the opportunity to have participated in the symposium and contribute to this volume.

My research on Michele Tosini was funded by Baylor University Summer Sabbaticals in 1993 and 2002, a University Research Grant, 1993, and an Allbritton Grant for Faculty Scholarship from the Department of Art, 2002. The Pennsylvania State University Dissertation Research Fellowship and the Francis E. Hyslop Memorial Fellowship for Dissertation Research Travel supported my research in Florence in 1988–1989.

2 Sources for the biography of Michele Tosini are: G. Vasari, *Le Vite de'più eccellenti pittori, scultori ed architettori scritte da Giorgio Vasari pittore Aretino*, 1881, pp. 533–48 (includes Vasari's life of Ridolfo Ghirlandaio), in *Le Opere di Giorgio Vasari*, ed. G. Milanesi, Florence, 1878–85, (hereafter cited as Vasari, *Opere*, 1881); C. Gamba, "Ridolfo e Michele di Ridolfo del Ghirlandaio," *Dedalo* 9, 1928–29, p. 463–90 (hereafter cited as Gamba, "Ghirlandaio"); H. J. Hornik, "Michele di Ridolfo del Ghirlandaio (1503–1577) and the Reception of Mannerism in Florence," Ph.D. diss., The Pennsylvania State University, 1990 (the first monographic study of Tosini, hereafter cited as Hornik, diss.); H. J. Hornik, "The Testament of Michele Tosini," *Paragone* 543–45, 1995, pp. 156–67 (hereafter cited as Hornik, "Testament").

For Tosini's date of death see Hornik, "Testament," pp. 156–67. Vasari, *Vite*, 1881, vol. VI, p. 547, note 3, records the date as October 28, 1577. Gamba, "Ghirlandaio," states that the death date is October 3, 1577. *Le Opere di Giorgio Vasari: Le Vite de'più eccellenti pittori, scultori ed architettori scritte da Giorgio Vasari pittore Aretino*, ed. P. della Pergola, Milano, 9 vols., 1966, vol. VI, p. 386, note 5 records the correct date. The birth date for Tosini is not recorded in any primary source of which I am aware. The date of May 8 is given by Milanesi (in Vasari, *Opere*, 1881, vol. VI, p. 543, note 3). D. Colnaghi, in *A Dictionary of Florentine Painters*, London, 1928, p. 263, also uses this date without citing a primary source.

3 Michele Tosini, *Madonna and Child with St. John the Baptist*. Oil on panel, 35 3/4 x 28 3/4 in. (90.8 x 73 cm.). Palmer Museum of Art, The Pennsylvania State University, University Park, inv. no. 90.4. Purchased by the Friends of the Palmer Museum of Art with supplementary funds provided by the Office of the President. See B. Wollesen-Wisch, *Italian Renaissance Art: Selections from the Piero Corsini Gallery*, University Park, Pennsylvania, 1986, pp. 40–41, for a catalogue entry written shortly before the painting's acquisition. The panel appears to be cut slightly on the left and bottom edges.

4 For a complete discussion of the relationships see Hornik, "Testament."

5 Vasari, *Opere*, 1881, *op. cit.*, vol. IV, p. 462.

6 Ridolfo was known among his contemporaries as one of the best draftsman in Florence and was much beloved, particularly by Raphael. For a discussion of Ridolfo del Ghirlandaio, see Vasari, *Opere*, 1881, *op. cit.*, vol. VI, pp. 533–48.

See three recent works by D. Franklin, *Painting in Renaissance Florence, 1500–1560*, New Haven, 2001, pp. 117–25; "Ridolfo Ghirlandaio and the Retrospective Tradition in Florentine Painting," *Italian Renaissance Masters*, Milwaukee, 2001, pp. 17–23; "Towards a new chronology for Ridolfo Ghirlandaio and Michele Tosini," *Burlington Magazine* 140, 1998, pp. 445–55. For more extensive chronology, see S. Freedberg, *Painting of the High Renaissance in Rome and Florence*, Cambridge, Massachusetts, 1961, vol. I, pp. 589–90, and, more recently, Hornik (as in note 1), pp. 25–56.

7 Vasari, *Opere*, 1881, *op. cit.*, vol. VI, p. 534.

8 Vasari, *Opere*, 1881, *op. cit.*, vol. VI, p. 547.

9 On the other hand, the workshop of Ridolfo turned out some of the more progressive artists of the 1520s and 1530s in central Italy, who were Michele's contemporaries. Vasari mentions Giuliano Bugiardini (1475–1525), Baccio Ghetti (d. Jan. 1535/6), Toto del Nunziata (1475–1525), Domenico Puligo (1492–1527), Giovanni Sogliani (1492–1544), Perino del Vaga (1500–1547), Mirabello Cavalori (c. 1520–1572), and Carlo Portelli da Loro (before 1510–1574). For further discussion on the relationships between these artists and Ridolfo, see Hornik, diss., pp. 30–35.

10 Vasari, *Opere*, 1881, *op. cit.*, vol. VI, p. 543–45.

11 The altar panel was a collaborative work by Ridolfo and Michele for the nuns of the convent of Ripoli (Vasari, *Opere*, 1881, vol. VI, p. 544). Milanesi (Vasari, *Opere*, 1881, vol. VI, p. 544, note 4) could not locate the painting. Its current location is the Villa La Quiete, which functions as a convent and children's day-care center. The painting has recently undergone cleaning and is now being restored. The photograph was taken after the cleaning. J. Crowe and G. Cavalcaselle, *A New History of Painting in Italy*, New York, 1914, vol. VI, p. 151, cite the painting as a joint work for S. Jacopo de Ripoli. A. Venturi, *Storia dell'arte italiana*, vol. IX, *La Pittura del Cinquecento*, Milan, 1925–34, pt. 1, p. 512, and Gamba, "Ghirlandaio," p. 546, also cite the work as by Ridolfo and Michele. It was attributed to Michele Tosini alone by B. Berenson, *Italian Pictures of the Renaissance, Florentine School*, London and New York, 1963, p. 150.

12 Gamba, "Ghirlandaio," p. 463–490.

13 For information specifically related to the S. Jacopo altarpiece see the following references: Vasari, *Vite*, 1881, vol. VI, p. 544; F. Bocchi, *Le bellezze della città di Firenze*, ed. G. Cinelli, 1581 (repr., Florence, 1677), p. 347; G. Richa, *Notizie istoriche delle chiese fiorentine divise ne'suoi Quartieri*, Florence, 1755, vol. II, p. 217; E. Pieraccini, *Guida della R. Galleria Antica e Moderna*, Florence and Rome, 1893, p. 90; J. Crowe and G. Cavalcaselle, *A New History of Painting in Italy*, New York, 1914, vol. VI, p. 151; H. Voss, *Die Malerei der Spätrenaissance in Rom und Florenz*, Berlin, 1920, p. 194; Colnaghi, 1928, p. 53; Gamba, "Ghirlandaio," p. 546–48; Venturi, *Storia dell'arte italiana*, vol. IX-5, Milan, 1932, p. 273, note 1; O. Giglioli, *Catalogo delle cose d'arte e di antichità d'Italia. Fiesole*, Rome, 1933, p. 221; U. Procacci, *La Galleria dell'Accademia di Firenze*, Rome, 1936, p. 51; W. Paatz, *Die Kirchen von Florenz*, Frankfurt am Main, 1955, vol. II, pp. 431 and 433, note 22; B. Berenson, *Italian Pictures of the Renaissance, Florentine School*, London and New York, 1963, vol. I, p. 149; G. Leoncini, *Illustrazione sulla Cattedrale di Volterra*, Siena, 1978, p. 32; C. d'Afflitto, M. Mannini and C. Pizzorusso, *Il paesaggio nella pitura tra cinque e seicento a Firenze*, Poggibonsi, 1980, p. 100; S. Padovani and S. Meloni Trkulja, *Guida al Museo di San Salvi. Il Cenacolo di Andrea del Sarto a San Salvi*, Florence, 1982, pp. 26–27; Wollesen-Wisch, *Italian Renaissance Art: Selections from the Piero Corsini Gallery*, University Park, Pennsylvania, 1986, pp. 40–41.

14 Florence, Archivio di Stato, Corporazioni religiose soppresse dal governo francese, Conventi soppressi, 97 N. 40, carte 1, 8, 9, 11.

15 Vasari, *Opere*, 1881, *op. cit.*, vol. VI, p. 544. Leonardo Buonafé was a Carthusian monk. He was elected Bishop of Cortona in 1529 and died in 1545. Buonafé was the prior and protector of the abbey known as the Certosa di Galuzzo, outside of Florence, and the church of SS. Jacopo and Lorenzo. The monastery records of the sixteenth century state that the "monasterio e monache" of S. Jacopo were located on Via Ghibellina, 33, Florence.

16 D. Franklin, "Ridolfo Ghirlandaio's altar-pieces for Leonardo Buonafé and the Hospital of S. Maria Nuova in Florence," *Burlington Magazine* 135, 1993, pp. 4–16.

17 *Ibid.* See also Hornik, diss., pp. 42–45, 202–4 for a discussion of the dating of this altar panel.

18 Florence, Archivio di Stato. See note 14. D. Franklin, *op. cit.*, 1998, p. 455, has found archival documentation that confirms a completion date of 1544.

19 See Hornik, diss., pp. 241, 243–44, 246.

20 The panel is 2.8 cm. shorter in length than the Palmer panel and may have been cut. It has been traditionally attributed to Francesco Brina, one of the leading pupils and imitators of Michele Tosini, because of an inscription noted by O. Giglioli, *Catalogo delle cose d'arte e di antichità d'Italia. Fiesole*, Rome, 1933, p. 221. The painting is inscribed on the reverse: "Di mano di Francesco del Brina—ritrovata nel 1763 da Santi Pacini." Giglioli records that the painting was in the convent of Annalena, then stored in the Regia Gallery, Florence, and finally placed in the Museo Bandini, Fiesole. The Museo Bandini is currently undergoing restoration and the painting cannot be viewed at this writing. Giglioli considers it to be a copy by Brina from the altarpiece in SS. Jacopo and Lorenzo. Gamba, *op. cit.*, pp. 548–49, gives the same citation referring to the S. Jacopo altarpiece as by Ghirlandaio alone. S. Freedberg, *Painting in Italy 1500–1600*, New York, 1971, p. 620, notes that Brina often imitated Tosini's Madonna and Child subjects.

21 For all of the preceding, see Hornik, "Testament," pp. 157, 161–62, notes 10–13.

22 Florence, Archivio di Stato, Accademia del Disegno, N. 4, c. 8r. Registro intitolato = entrata e uscita della compagnia di S. Luca segnato a 1 Gennaio 1535–18 Maggio 1556. (D. Colnaghi, *A Dictionary of Florentine Painters*, London, 1928, p. 263, gives an incorrect date of April 1537.)

23 Information in Tosini's Testament led me to the convent of San Vincenzo. The construction and decora-

tion of this chapel are carefully documented from conception to completion. Prato, Archivio del Monastero di San Vincenzo, ms. 22, c. 11 v., in Di Agresti and Guglielmo, vol. V, *op. cit.*, pp. 11–12. S. Bardazzi and E. Castellani, *Il Monastero di S. Vincenzo in Prato*, Prato, 1982, p. 19. R. Villani, "Contributo a Michele di Rodolfo del Ghirlandaio," *Antichità viva* 21, 1982, pp. 19–22.

24 I. Cheney, "Francesco Salviati," Ph. D. diss., New York University, 1963, pp. 161ff.

25 See C. Wilson, *Italian Paintings XIV–XVI Centuries in the Museum of Fine Arts, Houston*, Houston, 1996, pp. 266–71, for an entry on this securely identified Tosini. Wilson's detailed study of the *St. Mary Magdalen* and discussion of the infrared reflectograms of the painting are invaluable.

26 Vasari, *Opere*, 1881, *op. cit.*, vol. VI, p. 547, states that his first collaboration with Michele was the decoration in the Palazzo Vecchio. See also note 40.

27 Vasari, *Opere*, 1881, *op. cit.*, vol. VI, p. 59; vol. VII, p. 595.

28 *Ibid.*, 1881, vol. VI, p. 548, note 2. "Il Bottari, alla fine della Vita di Ridolfo e di Michele, cita le pitture di quest'ultimo fatte nella cappella della villa di Caserotta presso San Casciano, villa della quale è fatta menzione a pag. 59 e ivi nota 1." G. Carocci, *Il comune di San Casciano in Val di Pesa*, Florence, 1892, pp. 70–71, and F. Lumachi, *Guida di San Casciano*, Milan, 1952, p. 17, also cite Tosini as the artist of the fresco cycle.

29 For a complete study of this rediscovered chapel, see the article by H. Hornik, "The Strozzi Chapel by Michele Tosini: A Visual Interpretation of Redemptive Epiphany," *Artibus et Historiae* 46, Autumn, 2002.

30 S. Meloni Trkulja, *Firenze e la Toscana dei Medici nell'Europa del Cinquecento*, vol. III: *Il primato del disegno*, Florence, 1980, p. 146, states that the frescoes and altar panel in the chapel of the Villa Caserotta, formerly owned by the Strozzi, are by Michele di Ridolfo. She is the first to record the correct date for the fresco cycle, 1561.

31 Paolini is five miles east of the larger town of San Casciano, which is often used to locate it, and five miles west of Mercatale. See Hornik, diss., pp. 121–25, for a discussion of the ownership of the villa.

32 M. Bullard, *Filippo Strozzi and the Medici. Favor and finance in sixteenth-century Florence and Rome*, Cambridge, 1980, p. 46.

33 Vasari, *Opere*, 1881, *op. cit.*, vol. VI, p. 548, note 2.

34 For a discussion of the Epiphany as "The Feast of First Appearances," see M. Lavin, *Piero della Francesca's 'Baptism of Christ'*, New Haven, 1981, p. 123; and T. Martone, book review of same, *Art Bulletin* 70, 1988, p. 523–28.

35 The document records payment for Michele's work in the Sala di Cosimo I, Palazzo Vecchio. See Florence, Archivio di Stato, Fabbriche Medicee, N. 7, c. 28v, cited in E. Allegri and A. Cecchi, *Palazzo Vecchio e i Medici, guida storica*, Florence, 1980, p. 153. The date and the archival reference should be corrected. The document states, "22 agosto 1557. micele di ridolfo p[er] essere ito fuori ordine di G[i]org[i]o a fare dissegni di vari siti e lu[o]ghi. 5 piccioli fiorini 22.20." See also note 26. For a discussion of the iconographic program and accompanying diagrams of the Sala di Cosimo I, see Allegri and Cecchi, *op. cit.*, pp. 143–53.

36 See Firenze, Archivio di Stato, Fabbriche Medicee, N.4, c. 45v, quoted in E. Pillsbury, "The Sala Grande Drawings by Vasari and his Workshop: Some Documents and New Attributions," *Master Drawings* 14, 1976, pp. 127–46, pp. 145–46.

When Cosimo requested that the ceiling be finished for the marriage of his son, Francesco I, to Giovanna of Austria in March 1565, Vasari hired three additional artists: Prospero Fontana (1512–1597), September 4 to December 18, 1563; Michele di Ridolfo [Tosini], February 19 to March 11, 1564; and Santi di Tito (1536–1603), September 16 to October 14, 1564. See Firenze, Archivio di Stato, Fabbriche Medicee, N. 10, c. 35–37, 54–55v, and 73–76v, quoted in Pillsbury, *op. cit.*, p. 139. Tosini received the highest daily wage.

Assessment of Michele Tosini's participation in the decoration of the Palazzo Vecchio will appear in my forthcoming article, "Giorgio Vasari and Michele Tosini: A Classic Friendship."

37 P. Barocchi, et al., *Mostra di disegni dei Fondatori dell'Accademia delle Arti del Disegno*, Florence, 1963, p. 58.

38 Vasari, *Opere*, 1881, *op. cit.*, vol. VI, p. 656, brought the painters Bronzino and Tosini, the sculptors Ammanati and Rossi, and the architect Francesco da Sangallo together on a project in SS. Annunziata, a

donation of Fra Giovann'Agnolo Montorsoli, as a starting point to unite all artists, regardless of their guild affiliations. It was Vasari's goal to improve the social status of the artist.

39 Florence, Archivio di Stato, Academia del Disegno, N. 24, c. 15. Registro intitolato = Giornale di riccordi dell'universita e societa del disegno segnato e dal provveditore. 1563–1571. A document dated February 10, 1565 (1566) lists as *riformatori*: Francesco di Giuliano da Sangallo, Agnolo Bronzino, Giorgio Vasari, Pier Francesco di jacopo, Micele di jacopo di ridolfo. These men, as the document indicates, called themselves "reformers" and created the Accademia del Disegno to lift the artist above that of a mere craftsman to the status of a respected professional.

Borghini wrote to Vasari several times regarding the founding of the Academy. Borghini also recommended to Vasari in a letter on August 14, 1564, that Michele be appointed the principal artist to replicate Michelangelo's *Last Judgment* in the decorations for his funeral (see main text below). See K. Frey and K. Hermann, *Il Carteggio di Giorgio Vasari dal 1563 al 1565*, Arezzo, 1941, pp. 188–91.

40 Florence, Biblioteca Nazionale, Manoscritto II-I-399, "Capitoli dell'Accademia del Disegno" as quoted in N. Pevsner, *Academies of Art, Past and Present*, Cambridge, 1940, pp. 296–304; Florence, Archivio di Stato, Accademia del Disegno, N. 157, c. 9. Letter from Don Vincenzo Borghini to Duke Cosimo dated February 1, 1562 (1563). See K. Barzman, *The Florentine Academy and the Early Modern State: The Discipline of Disegno*, Cambridge, 2000.

41 R. Wittkower, *The Divine Michelangelo: The Florentine Academy's Homage on His Death in 1564*, London, 1964, p. 102.

42 For the workshop's participation (under the direction of Michele) in the marriage decorations see the following documents quoted in *L'apparato per le nozze di Francesco de'Medici e di Giovanna d'Austria nelle narrazioni del tempo e da lettere inedite di Vincenzo Borghini e di Giorgio Vasari*, ed. Piero Ginori Conti, Florence, 1936, Appendix II, Nota di cose da farsi [rimessa da Vincenzo Borghini a Giovanni Caccini]; Appendix II, 2. 45r, N. 5 Ponte Rovinato; Appendix V, Dal libretto di appunti delle cose fatte o da farsi per l'apparato, tenuto da Vincenzo Borghini, 3. (Elenco degli artisti colle opere loro assegnante); Appendix V, 4. c. 66v (Elenco di artist assegnati per aiuto al Vasari e al Bronzino; Appendix V, 4. c. 67v. (Nota di artisti di Firenze e di fuori.) See also Vasari, *Opere*, 1881, *op. cit.*, vol. VIII, pp. 617–22.

43 L'apparato per le nozze di Francesco de'Medici e di Giovanna d'Austria ..., *op. cit.*, Appendix V, p. 4. c. 67v. *Ibid.*, Appendix V, p. 4. c. 66v.

44 See G. Bottari, *Raccolta di lettere sulla pittura, scultura ed architettura*, Milan, 1822, vol. I, p. 195. Don Vincenzo Borghini wrote in a letter dated 5 April 1565 to Duke Cosimo I about the marriage of Francesco. "Michele di Ridolfo è di buon giudizio e valente, ed ha una buona mano di giovani, ed a costui si può sicuramente fidare quel che è piglierà. Seco sono (ed avanzadone cosi a lui, come agli altri serviranno a chi ne mancasse) Baccio di Michele suo figliolo, Andrea del Minga, Coccheri (?) detto di Michele, Giovanni del Brina, Giovanni Benci, Bartolomeo Gobbo, Salvi di ... ed altri."

45 *Ibid*. Seven students/workshop members are listed in the document previously cited. Four additional members, Francesco di Mariano del Cialdonaio, Rinaldo di ..., Iacopino di Meglio detto Pino, and Malfatta con Michele di Ridolfo, are quoted in *L'apparato per le nozze* (as in note 42), c. 66v, c. 67v. See S. Freedberg, *Painting in Italy 1500–1600*, New York, 1971, p. 620, for a discussion of Francesco del Brina (c. 1540–1586) as a student of Michele di Ridolfo.

46 Gamba, "Ghirlandaio," *op. cit.*, pp. 463–90; A. Venturi, *Storia dell'arte italiana*, vol. IX: I *La Pittura del Cinquecento*, Milan, 1925–34, pp. 490–512; S. Freedberg, 1961, *op. cit.*, pp. 239, 463, 616, 620, and 713, note 10.

47 The eight extant documented works are as follows: (1) Ridolfo and Michele, *Marriage of St. Catherine with Saints*, panel, 1520-25, Ripoli, Convent of S. Jacopo, today outside Florence, La Quiete Istituto delle Montalve; (2) Ridolfo and Michele, *Madonna and Child with Sts. Anne, Sebastian and Roch*, panel, 1530–35, Prato, S. Rocco, today Helsingor, Denmark, Carmelite Cloister; (3) Ridolfo and Michele, *Madonna and Child with St. Anne and other Saints*, panel, c. 1545, Florence, S. Spirito, Segni chapel; (4) Ridolfo and Michele, *Madonna and Child with Saints and Bishop Buonafé*, panel, 1540–44, Florence, S. Jacopo e Lorenzo, today, Florence, Museo di San Salvi; (5) Michele, *Madonna and Saints*, panel, 1559–61, Prato, Convent of San Vincenzo, Chapel of the Madonna di Loreto; (6) Michele, *Scenes from the Life of the Madonna della Quercia*, marble tabernacle, 1570, Viterbo, S. Maria della Quercia; (7) Michele, *Ten Thousand Martyrs*, c. 1570, Florence, S. Pancrazio, today Florence, Museo di San Salvi; (8) Michele, *Scenes of Epiphany and the Four Evangelists*, 1561, fresco cycle, Paolini, Ganucci Cancelleria Villa, Caserotta. See also, D. Franklin, 1998, note 39, for an "update" of Vasari's list of paintings, both extant and lost.

48 Late scholarship on Michele Tosini concerns paintings after-restoration. See A. Negra, "Venere e

Amore di Michele di Ridolfo del Ghirlandaio: Il mito di una Venere di Michelangelo fra copie, reliche e pudiche vestizioni," Rome, 2001. For three articles related to an attributed *Adoration of the Shepherds*, see Udine. Bollettino dlle civiche istituzioni culturali, Udine: Artis Grafiche Friulane, 3 n. 4, 1998, pp. 36–64.

49 For a discussion of the *St. Barbara*, see Hornik, diss., pp. 163, 240; Gamba, "Ghirlandaio," pp. 560–61; Procacci, *La Galleria dell'Accademia di Firenze*, Rome, 1936, p. 52; B. Berenson, *Italian Pictures of the Renaissance, Florentine School*, London and New York, 1963, vol. I, p. 149; and S. Meloni Trkulja, *Firenze e la Toscana dei Medici nell'Europa del Cinquecento*, vol. III*: Il primato del disegno*, Florence, 1980, p. 146.

50 For recent work on portraiture that includes attributions to Tosini, see three articles by P. Costamagna, "De l'idéal de beauté aux problèmes d'attribution. Vingt ans de recherche sur le portrait florentin au XVIe siècle," *Studiolo. Revue d'historire de l'art de l'Académie de France à Rome*, 1, 2002, pp. 192–220; "Il ritrattista," in *Francesco Salviati (1510–1563) o la Bella Maniera*, Catherine Monbeig Goguel, ed., Milan, 1998, pp. 47–52; "Mécènat et Politique Culturelle du Cardinal Giovanni Salviati," in *Francesco Salviati et la Bella Maniera. Actes des colloques de Rome et de Paris (1998)*, C. Monbeig Goguel, P. Costamagna and M. Hochmann, eds., Rome, 2001, p. 227.

51 For a discussion of *Portrait of a Gentleman*, see W. Valentiner, *Catalogue of Paintings: North Carolina Museum of Art*, Raleigh, 1956, pp. 79–80; G. Rosenthal and S. Merritt, "Bacchiacca and His Friends," *News Quarterly* 24.2, 1961, p. 64; G. Rosenthal, "Il Bacchiacca at Baltimore," *The Connoisseur* 149, 1962, pp. 58–63; K. Foster, "Probleme um Pontormos porträtmalerei (III); ein Beitrag zum Porträtwerk Michele Tosini," *Pantheon* 25, 1967, pp. 30, 32; E. Bowron, *The North Carolina Museum of Art: Introduction to the Collections*, Chapel Hill, 1983, p. 192; Hornik, diss., p. 261; K. Langedijk, *The Portraits of the Medici, 15th–18th Centuries*, Florence, 1981, p. 865.

52 For a discussion of *Portrait of Cosimo I, Francesco I and Another Man*, see Hornik, 1990, diss., p. 262.

53 Freedberg, 1961, *op. cit.*, p. 620, and Vasari, *Opere*, 1881, *op. cit.*, vol. III, pp. 238–39, note 1. Francesco del Brina worked in the Strozzi Chapel in 1561 with Michele and the Ghirlandaio workshop and he copied the *Adoration of the Magi* (Fig. 7) for the high altar of S. Maria sul Prato that is today in the Museo di S. Salvi, Florence. S. Padovani and S. Meloni Trkulja, *Guida al Museo di San Salvi. Il Cenacolo di Andrea del Sarto a San Salvi*, Florence, 1982, pp. 31–32, discuss the work as by Francesco del Brina but were not aware of its source in the Strozzi chapel fresco cycle.

54 Scholars have begun to study the direct influence of Michelangelo and his work on Mannerist artists. Michele di Ridolfo is included with Pontormo and Bronzino in this group. See F. Falletti and J. Nelson, *Venere e Amore: Michelangelo e La Nuova Bellezza Ideale = Venus and Love*, Florence, 2002, pp. 164–67.

55 See P. Costamagna's paper on Maso da San Friano included in this volume.

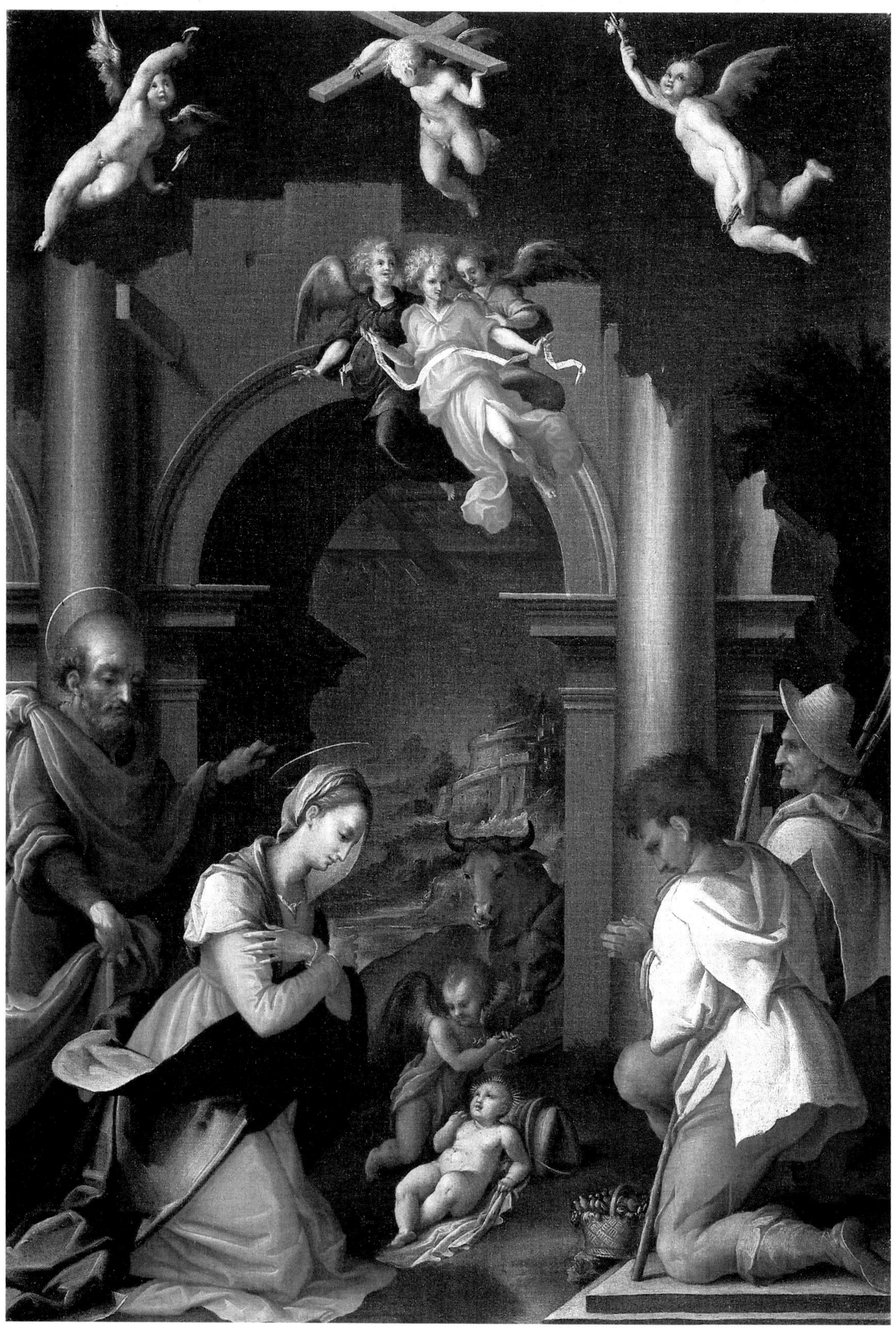

Fig. 1 Maso da San Friano, *Adoration of the Shepherds*, c. 1570. Palmer Museum of Art, The Pennsylvania State University. (See color plate 2.)

Continuity and Innovation: The Art of Maso da San Friano

Philippe Costamagna

Maso da San Friano's artistic personality fits perfectly with the theme "Continuity, Innovation, and Connoisseurship." Although our knowledge of his production is rather fragmentary and encumbered by problematical attributions, it is quite clear that his career developed along two distinct paths: on the one hand, large altarpieces painted in purest Florentine tradition combining motifs from his predecessors, and on the other, paintings of smaller format with small figures whose zenith is represented by Maso's two panels in the Studiolo of Francesco de' Medici in the Palazzo Vecchio. Vasari praised his early works,[1] but later Maso pursued a path that led him away from Vasari's emphatic rhetoric. Maso, the "pro-Vasarian," eventually became "anti-Vasarian," a change Maso's second biographer, Raffaello Borghini, seems to have approved.[2] An historical event is at the core of this transformation: the publication in 1564 of the decrees on the arts issued by the Council of Trent, which articulated the artistic style of the Counter Reformation.

Although admired by his two early biographers, Maso da San Friano, whose given name was Tommaso Manzuoli, was eventually forgotten. For a long time, a victim of haphazard attributions, his artistic personality remained hazy and undefined. At the beginning of the twentieth century, his name was still associated with countless Florentine paintings from the 1560s and 1570s that should be traced to the active workshops of Michele di Ridolfo, Michele Tosini himself, and Francesco del Brina. In the 1960s, references to Maso by Luciano Berti, Peter Cannon-Brookes, and Sydney Freedberg provided useful insights but failed to define the artist in a comprehensive manner.[3] Then, in the following decade, Catherine Monbeig Goguel's publication of the Louvre's considerable fund of Florentine drawings,[4] as well as Valentino Pace's monographic article,[5] marked the essential steps toward a long overdue evaluation of Maso's graphic and painterly production. We shall describe and illustrate Maso's work in relation to the previously defined view of his career in order to place the Palmer Museum's *Adoration of the Shepherds* (Fig. 1)[6] in context. In doing so, we will note Maso's form of "International Mannerism" and the shift in his style related to events of 1564 and 1565.

Maso da San Friano was born in November 1531, and died in the fall of 1571 at a relatively young age. He seems to have received training in two workshops. In 1568, Vasari identified him as a pupil of Pier Francesco di Jacopo Foschi, while in 1584, Borghini wrote that he had trained under Carlo Portelli.[7] A direct analysis of Maso's works allows us to confirm that he studied with both painters and probably spent a much longer period in Portelli's workshop. Studying with a conservative teacher such as Portelli insured that Maso would learn from paintings by artists of the previous generation. Art historians have noted the influences of Andrea del Sarto and Pontormo. John Shearman, in fact, identifies Maso as one of the principal representatives of the so-called "Sarto revival."[8] It is therefore not surprising to find copies by Maso after Sarto and Pontormo in the drawing collections of major museums (e.g., Fig. 2).[9] For example, a sheet in the Louvre (Fig. 3)[10] appears to be Maso's copy after one of the motifs on the famous carnival chariots that Pontormo decorated in 1513 (Fig. 4).[11] The drawing style with its short parallel strokes is typical of Maso, and his name has been suggested by Annamaria Petrioli Tofani on the drawing's mount.

After the decrees of the Council of Trent were implemented, the Accademia del Disegno established copying after Andrea del Sarto as part of its curriculum. Pontormo's works had been regularly copied before 1563. Maso, like his contemporaries, had copied Pontormo's *Madonna of the Book* (Fig. 5), the original of which is now lost.[12] Pontormo was later discredited, possibly because of his religious orientations, which did not conform with the new precepts of the

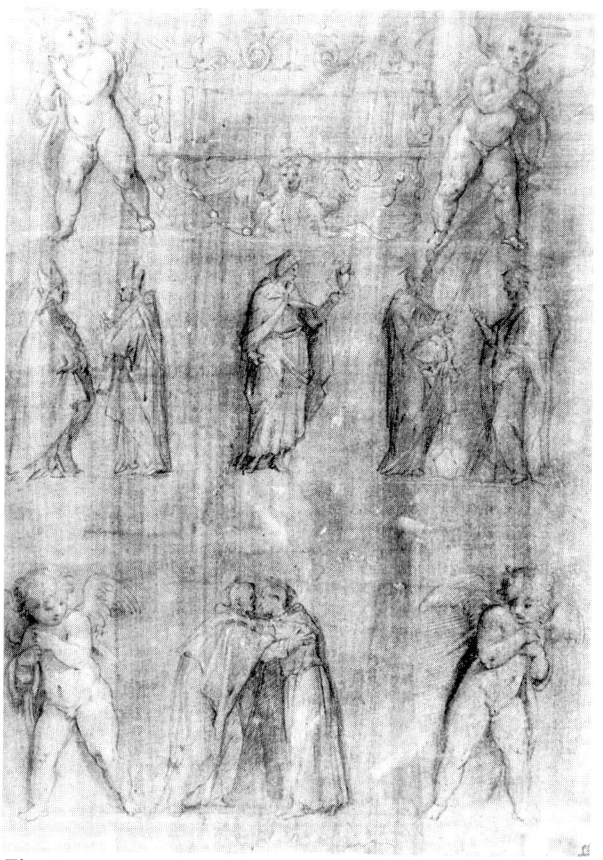

Fig. 2

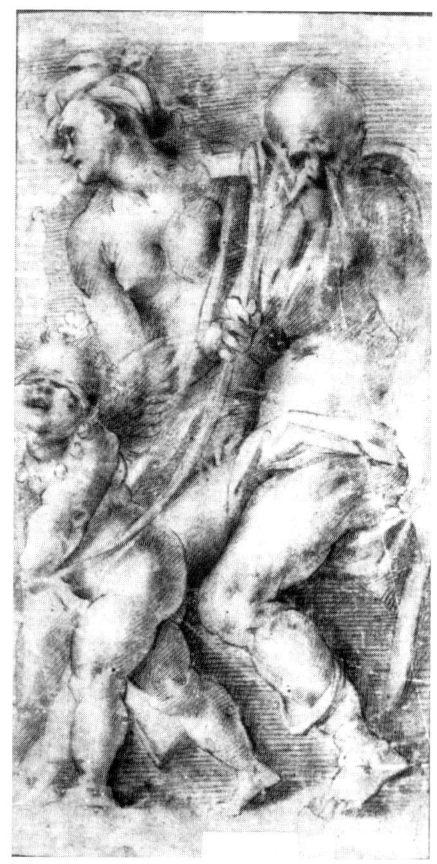

Fig. 3

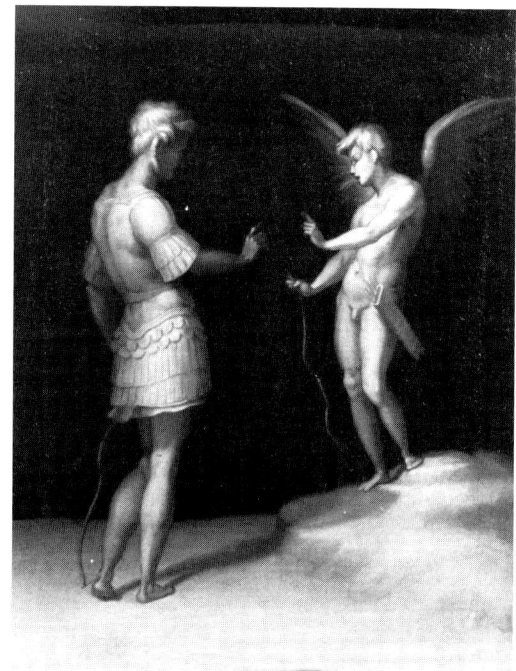

Fig. 4

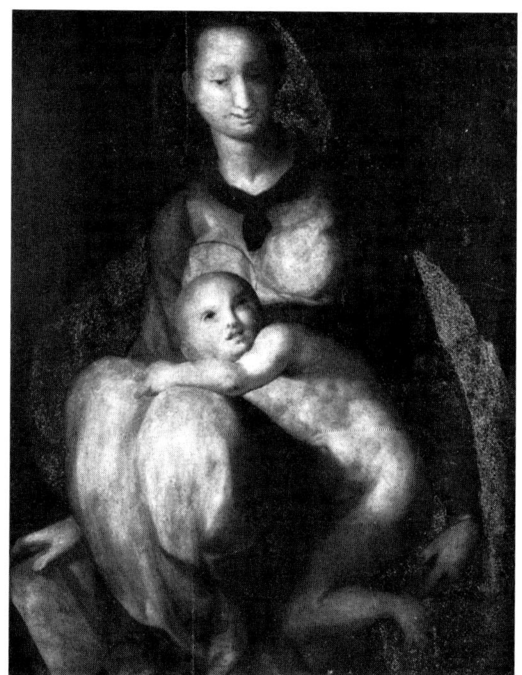

Fig. 5

Church. Younger artists, however, probably continued to follow in his steps, perhaps even espousing his religious principles, which may have been the case with Maso.

Of course, Maso copied not only artists of the previous generation, but also earlier masters. A drawing from Christ Church, Oxford, ascribed convincingly to Maso (Fig. 6), is a copy of the *Dudley Madonna*, a famous relief sculpture in the Victoria and Albert Museum, London, attributed variously to Desiderio da Settignano and Donatello.[13] This celebrated relief had been copied by Baccio Bandinelli and was a source of inspiration for Pontormo and other artists in his workshop, such as Bronzino and Jacone.[14] Copying the Old Masters was common practice in Florence; Michelangelo's drawings after Masaccio are well-known.[15] In a symposium of 1990, I discussed the integral role of copying in the training of all artists in Florence.[16] There is an aspect of this activity, however, which has not been stressed sufficiently: the special interest of Florentine painters in relief sculpture. The Philadelphia Museum of Art, for example, has a copy by Francesco Salviati after one of Lorenzo Ghiberti's bronze reliefs for the doors of the Baptistry in Florence.[17]

Maso copied works by artists of other schools; for example, his drawing in the Wallraf-Richartz Museum, Cologne (Fig. 7) is after Parmigianino's famous engraving, *The Entombment of Christ*. Although the style is very close to the engraving, Maso's authorship is verified by the inscribed monogram "TO" with which he signed his works.[18] Maso also copied Florentine works by the michelangelesque miniaturist, Giulio Clovio. A painting ascribed to Clovio, preserved at the Kunsthistorisches Museum, Vienna, reveals the miniaturist's characteristics.[19] Its partial copy by Maso was probably destined for the door of a tabernacle, and its refined style looks ahead to Maso's panels for the Studiolo of Francesco de' Medici (Fig. 8). Besides presenting attribution problems, which are particularly sensitive when dealing with copies, these examples help us to identify Maso's principal sources: the great Florentine masters, especially Michelangelo, the sculptor-painter who revolutionized the artistic world and inspired a younger generation of artists.

Fig. 6 Maso da San Friano, drawing after *Dudley Madonna*. Oxford, Christ Church, cat. no. 182. Photo: author.

Fig. 7 Maso da San Friano, *The Entombment of Christ*, drawing after Parmigianino engraving. Cologne, Wallraf-Richartz Museum. Photo: author.

Fig. 8 Maso da San Friano, *The Resurrection*, copy after Giulio Clovio (?). New York, Collection of Richard L. Feigen.

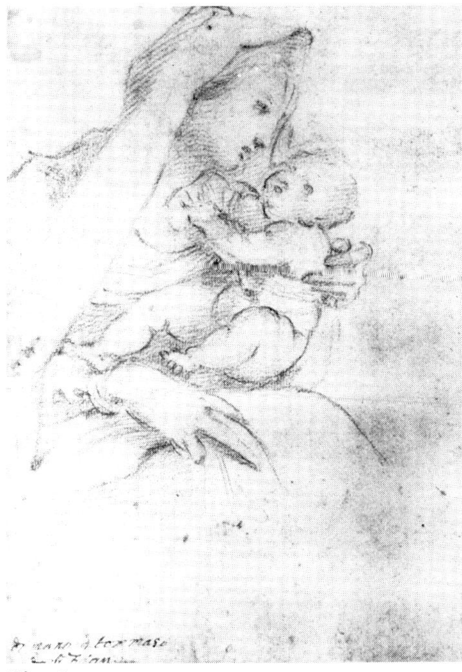

Fig. 6

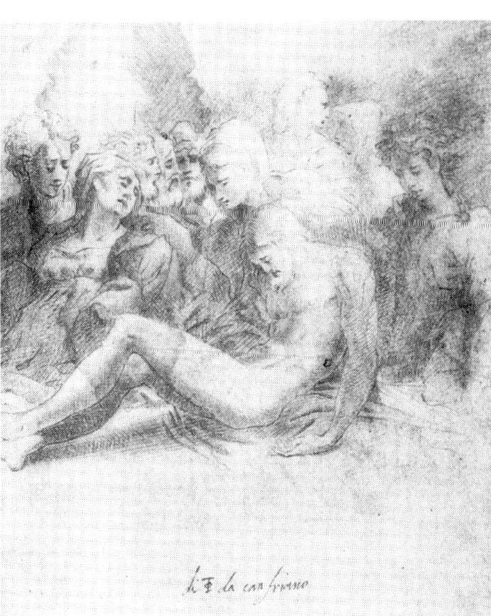

Fig. 7

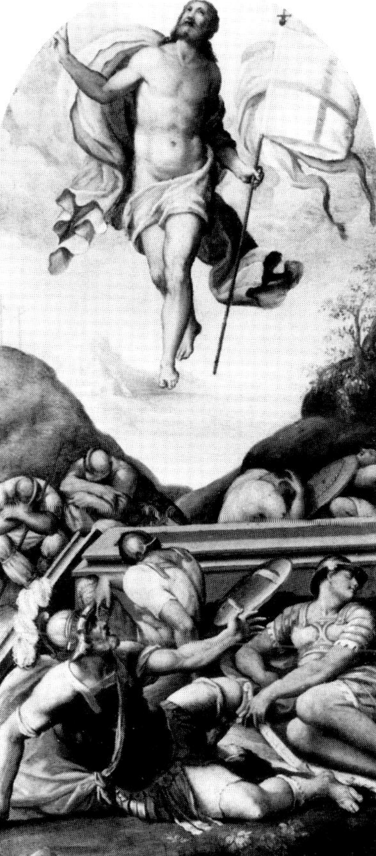

Fig. 8

Maso's first paintings can be dated between 1555 and 1560. The earliest known is the *Double Portrait* in the Galleria Nazionale di Capodimonte, Naples, signed with his monogram "TO" and dated 1556 (Fig. 9).[20] It is viewed as formal evidence that Maso had trained in the workshop of Pier Francesco Foschi, whose most celebrated painting is the *Portrait of a Woman in Pink* in the Thyssen-Bornemisza collection, Madrid. Almost all of Foschi's portraits share a typically Florentine format characterized by an extremely balanced design, exemplified in the works of Bronzino. Maso's portrait in Naples, on the other hand, more resembles the Mannerist portraits inspired by Rosso and Salviati, such as Carlo Portelli's *Portrait of a Young Man* in the Abbaye de Chaalis (Fig. 10). A comparison of the two reveals the extent to which Maso was indebted to his second teacher, from both stylistic and formal standpoints. Some scholars have tried to disclaim Maso's training with Portelli, but the evidence in his early works belies this view.

In the years following, Maso da San Friano appears to have been very active, and his workshop produced four noteworthy altarpieces. The *Virgin and Child Enthroned between St. Catherine of Alexandria, Mary Magdalene, St. Bernard, and St. Benedict*, dated 1560, is still in its original location, the church of the Convento della Trinità in Cortona (Fig. 11). Of all Maso's works, it is the closest to Foschi, especially to his altarpieces, not only in style but in its dependence on Sarto and Pontormo. On the other hand, the preliminary sketch for the *Virgin Enthroned…* (in the Uffizi) cannot fail to recall Salviati's draftsmanship (Fig. 12).[21] In fact, Maso's altarpiece appears to be a kind of summation of the principles set forth by the creators of the *Maniera*.

Maso's other major altarpieces from the same period reveal a more complex stylistic matrix. Rediscovered by the author is a *Pietà* for the Florentine church, Santa Maria dei Candeli, that had long been missing (Fig. 13).[22] It was acquired by the Gismondi Gallery, Paris, and attributed to Daniele da Volterra. A preliminary drawing is preserved in Chatsworth signed "Tommaso da San Friano" (Fig. 14),[23] which confirms the attribution of the altarpiece as a work of the young Maso. The drawing style, somewhat different from the artist's graphic production in the next decade, is again suggestive of Portelli.[24] The completed work was probably in place

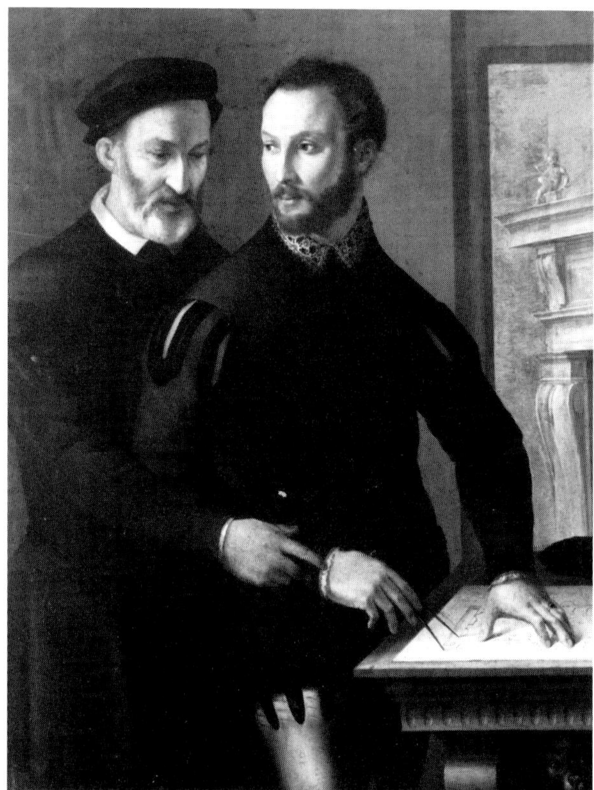

Fig. 9

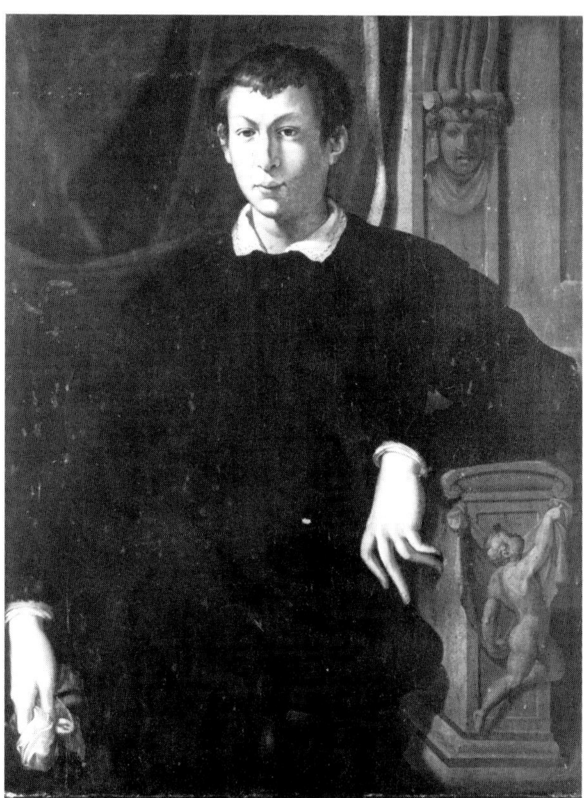

Fig. 10

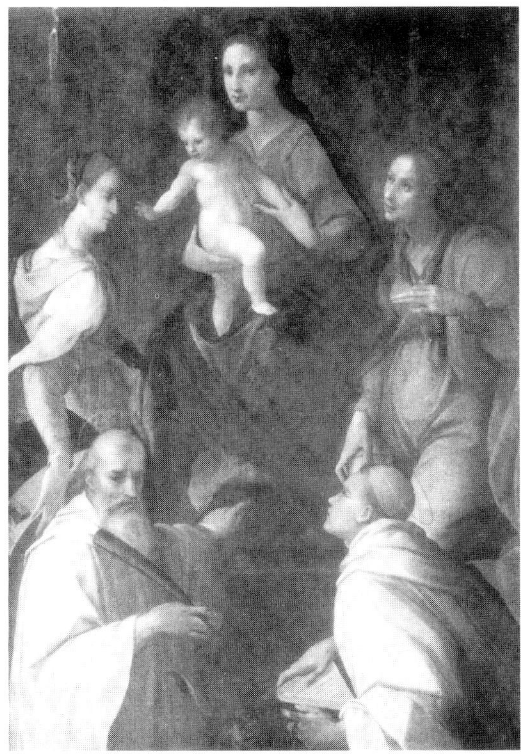

Fig. 11

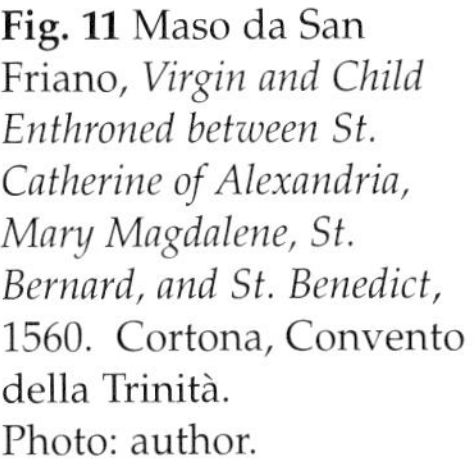

Fig. 12

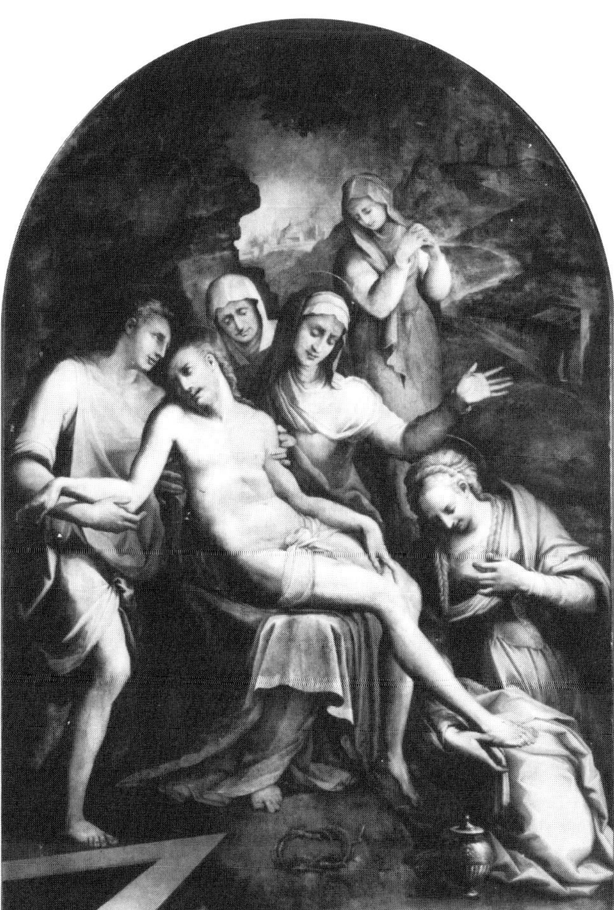

Fig. 13

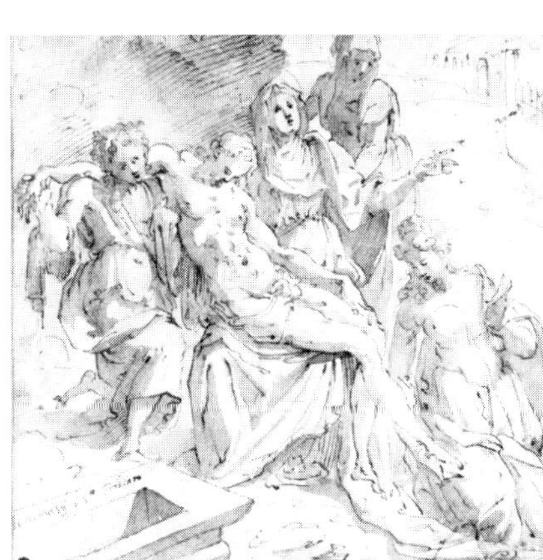

Fig. 14

Fig. 11 Maso da San Friano, *Virgin and Child Enthroned between St. Catherine of Alexandria, Mary Magdalene, St. Bernard, and St. Benedict*, 1560. Cortona, Convento della Trinità. Photo: author.

Fig. 12 Maso da San Friano, preliminary sketch for *Virgin and Child Enthroned* (Fig. 11), c. 1560. Florence, Uffizi. Photo: author.

Fig. 13 Maso da San Friano, *Pietà*, c. 1557. (Altarpiece for Santa Maria dei Candeli, Florence.) Paris, Gismondi Gallery. Photo: author.

Fig. 14 Maso da San Friano, *The Entombment*, before 1557, preliminary sketch for Santa Maria dei Candeli altarpiece. Chatsworth, Devonshire Collection. Reproduced by permission of the Duke of Devonshire and the Chatsworth Settlement Trustees. Photo: Photographic Survey, Courtauld Institute of Art.

on the high altar of the church at the time of its consecration in 1557. *The Pietà*, Maso's early undisputed masterpiece, embodies specific compositional ideas inherited from Michelangelo and developed in Florence during the mid-sixteenth century in the workshops of Ridolfo del Ghirlandaio and Pontormo/Bronzino. The central group with Christ and the Virgin is a reprise of two motifs of Buonarroti. The position of Christ's body, stretched out on the Virgin's knees, recalls his celebrated *Pietà* in St. Peter's, which had already inspired many other Florentine artists.[25] The Virgin's mourning gesture with wide-open arms had been conceived by Michelangelo in a drawing of a *Pietà* for Vittoria Colonna (Boston, Isabella Stewart Gardner Museum). The two motifs had been combined also by Portelli in another *Pietà* for the Compagnia della Misericordia at Loro Ciuffenna, the artist's birthplace (Fig. 15).

Michelangelo's appeal for Maso was sharpened by his lively interest in Giulio Clovio's Florentine production. The *Pietà* of Santa Maria dei Candeli is more specifically a reprise of a composition by the Croatian miniaturist, known to us in a drawing at The British Museum (Fig. 16).[26] The idea that a work by Clovio was the model for an important Florentine altarpiece is unusual enough to be worthy of notice. It may also enable us to understand the increasing miniaturization of Maso's late style. Indeed, even at the beginning of his career, Maso displayed skill with small figures, as in three predella panels for an altarpiece in Arezzo at Casa Vasari that represent *The Holy Women at the Sepulcher, The Resurrection of Christ*, and *Noli me Tangere* (Figs. 17a, b, c).[27]

One further conspicuous element in the Santa Maria dei Candeli *Pietà* is the prominence of landscape, a genre of painting that had previously been accorded little attention in Florence. Landscape was revived by such artists as Michele Tosini and Maso da San Friano, possibly under the influence of Salviati and of Northern artists who had been invited to Florence to execute tapestries in the newly-established Medici factory. Maso's execution of landscape here is light and swift. It is even more prominent in a painting circa 1560 in the Luzzetti collection, Florence, *The Samaritan at the Well* (Fig. 18).[28] The *Pietà* and the *Samaritan* exhibit a high degree of refinement, especially in the treatment of the female figures, which must have evoked Vasari's admiration.

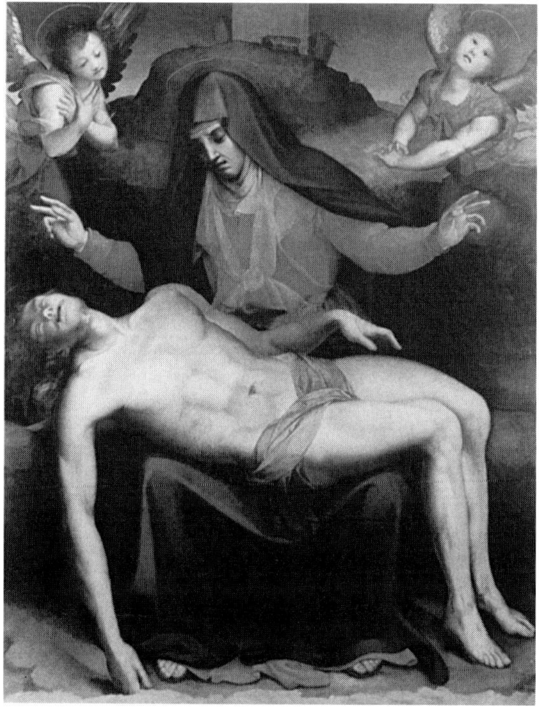

Fig. 15

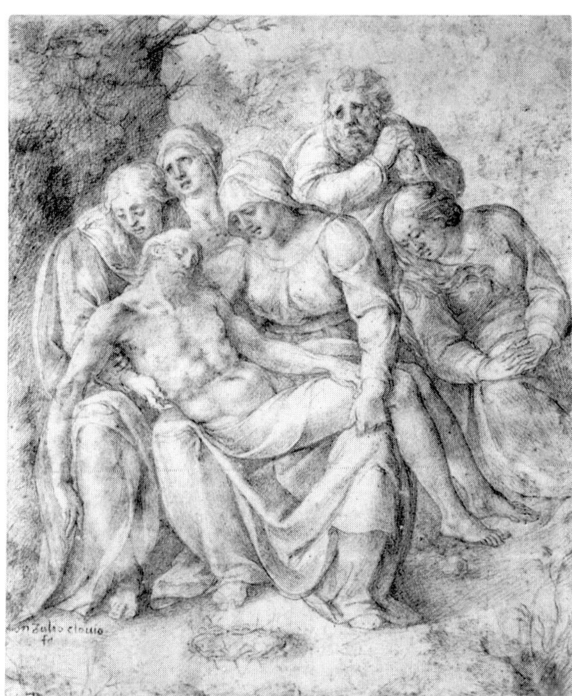

Fig. 16

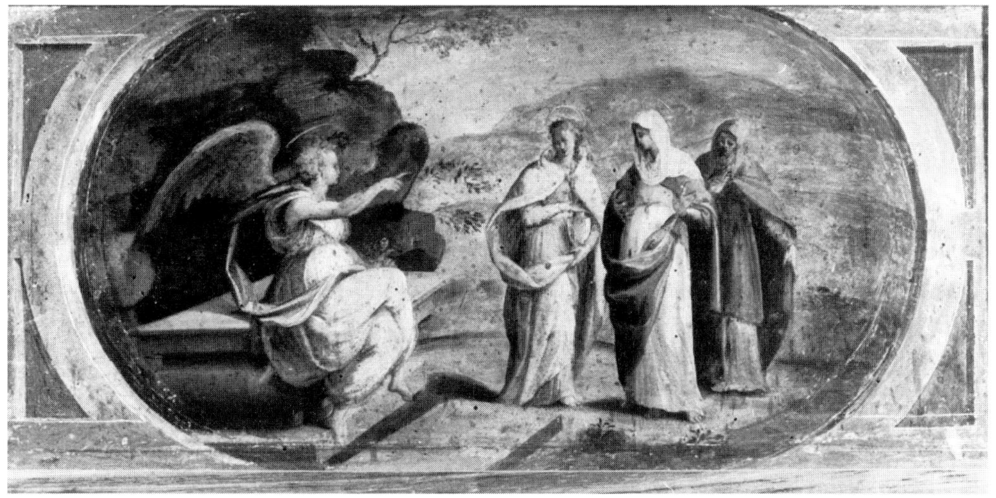

Fig. 17a

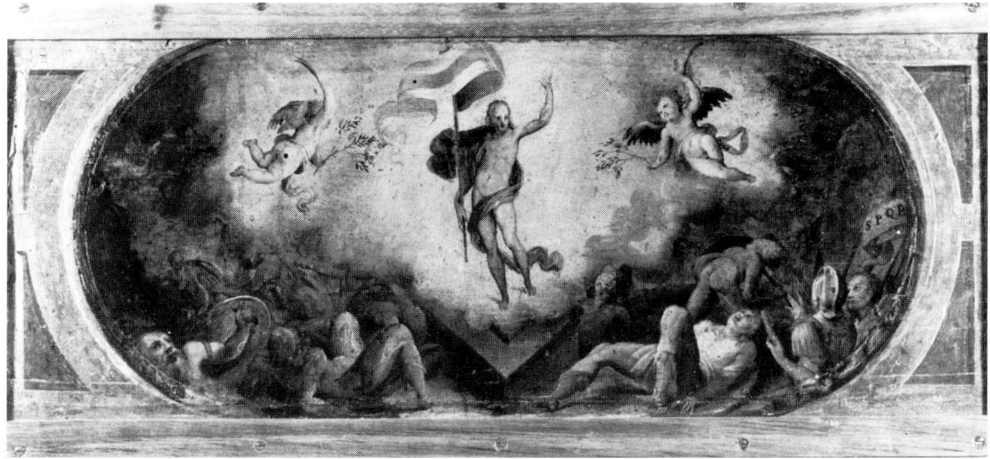

Fig. 17b

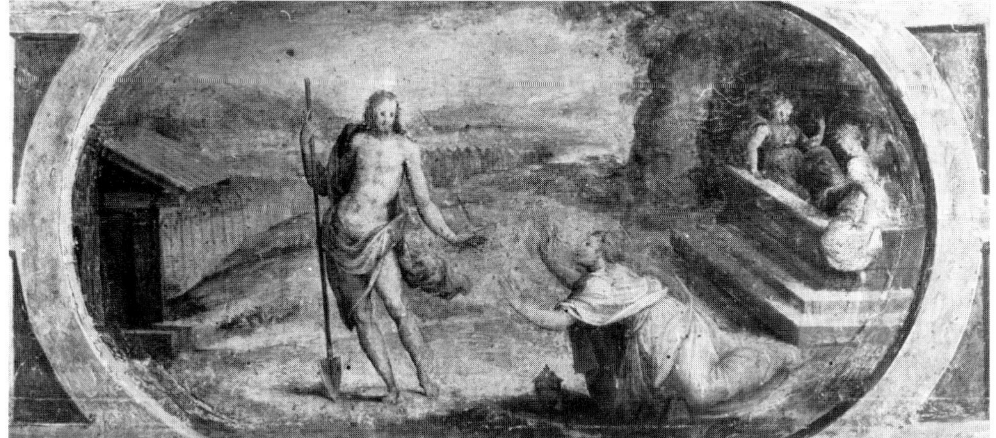

Fig. 17c

Fig. 15 Carlo Portelli, *Pietà*, 1561. Loro Ciuffenna, Compagnia della Misericordia. Photo: Gabinetto fotografico, Soprintendenza ai beni artistici e storici di Firenze.

Fig. 16 Giulio Clovio, *Pietà*, c. 1551–55. London, British Museum. Photo: © The British Museum.

Fig. 17a Maso da San Friano, *The Holy Women at the Sepulcher*, predella panel, c. 1557. Arezzo, Casa Vasari. Photo: Archivio fotografico, Soprintendenza ai Monumenti e Gallerie di Arezzo.

Fig. 17b Maso da San Friano, *The Resurrection of Christ*, predella panel, c. 1557. Arezzo, Casa Vasari. Photo: Archivio fotografico, Soprintendenza ai Monumenti e Gallerie di Arezzo.

Fig. 17c Maso da San Friano, *Noli me Tangere*, predella panel, c. 1557. Arezzo, Casa Vasari. Photo: Archivio fotografico, Soprintendenza ai Monumenti e Gallerie di Arezzo.

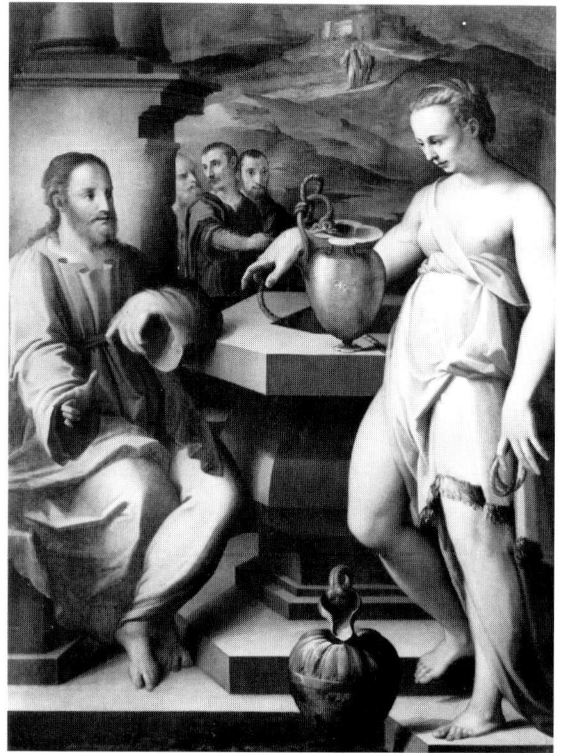

Fig. 18

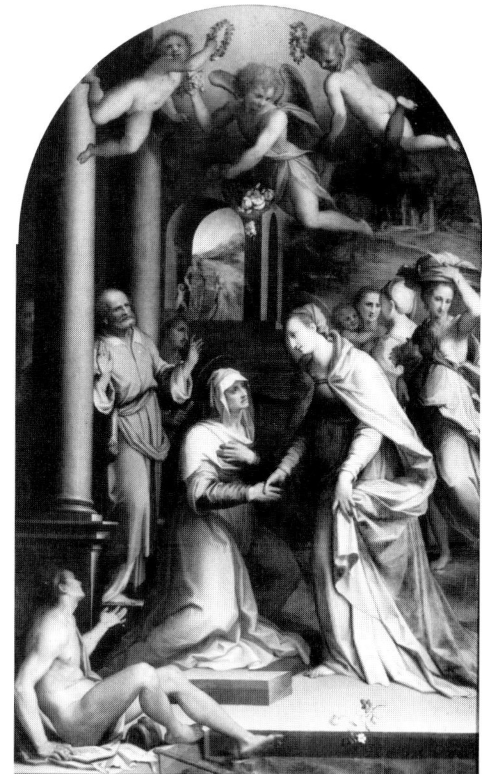

Fig. 19

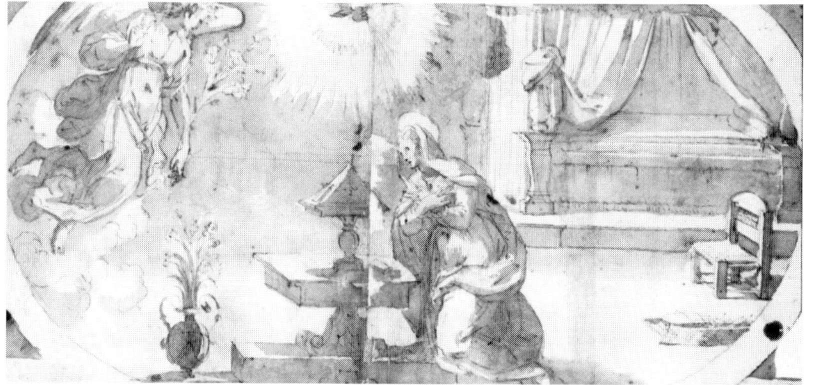

Fig. 20

Maso's next altarpiece, the *Visitation* (Fig. 19) dated 1560, now at the Fitzwilliam Museum, Cambridge, was originally executed for the church of San Pier Maggiore in Florence.[29] Here, Maso brilliantly combines elements from the earlier masters who inspired him, Sarto and Pontormo. One is reminded of Pontormo's *Visitation* in the atrium of SS. Annunziata, Florence. In particular, Vasari praised the monumentality of Maso's youthful *Visitation*, which he deemed worthy of a more experienced master.[30] In fact, at 29, Maso was already in full control of his skills, as attested by a study of the details. The central portion enables us to appreciate the artist's unparalleled chromatic range. His palette moving from saturated to subtle color follows in the steps of Bronzino and Vasari. The faces in the second plane show Maso's masterful control of modeling. The background reveals the deft handling of small figures evident in his predella panels. The Fitzwilliam *Visitation* must have once had its own predella. A drawing in the Louvre (Fig. 20), evidently for such a panel, is possibly a preliminary study for one of the sections.[31] Its subject, an *Annunciation*, would accord with the theme of the altarpiece. The central predella panel may have depicted an *Adoration of the Shepherds*, a subject which Maso did several times. It is the subject of the altarpiece from the same period that Maso painted for SS. Apostoli in Florence.

Painted a few years after the *Visitation*, the SS. Apostoli *Adoration of the Shepherds* (Fig. 21) is the quintessential example of Maso's "Sarto revival."[32] While the angels in the upper sector echo the angels of Bronzino at the top of the Besançon *Pietà*, those in the middle ground can be traced to Sarto models. A drawing by Maso at the Uffizi (Fig. 22), generally associated with the angel in the center, is based on the angel that Andrea del Sarto painted at the top of the *Birth of the Virgin* in the atrium of SS. Annunziata.[33] The Louvre owns the preliminary drawing for the group of three angels, which has been viewed as a copy (Fig. 23).[34] The differences, however, between the drawing and the finished work, as well as the swift execution of the former, appear to negate this assumption. It is possible to detect a development in the artist's graphic style, which induces us to date the altarpiece to 1565, slightly later than previously thought. For the central scene of the *Adoration of the Shepherds*, there exists a preliminary drawing by Maso in a private collection that echoes Sarto's classicism (Fig. 24).[35]

Although clearly related to the altarpiece in SS. Apostoli, the *Adoration of the Shepherds* in the Palmer Museum cannot be viewed as a *modello*. The drawing style is swift and sharp, not sketchy as one would expect. From 1565, Maso da San Friano was moving towards a *fare piccolo* mode that would culminate in the Studiolo panels. A study of the artist's drawings enables us to illustrate clearly this shift in style. A splendid sheet from the Louvre with six drawings by Maso comes from Vasari's drawing collection, *Libro dei Disegni* (Fig. 25).[36] Vasari is the author of the extravagant framework in pen and ink, which echoes Maso's style. Maso's minute execution is reminiscent of the production of the Northern artists active in Tuscany and connects Maso with

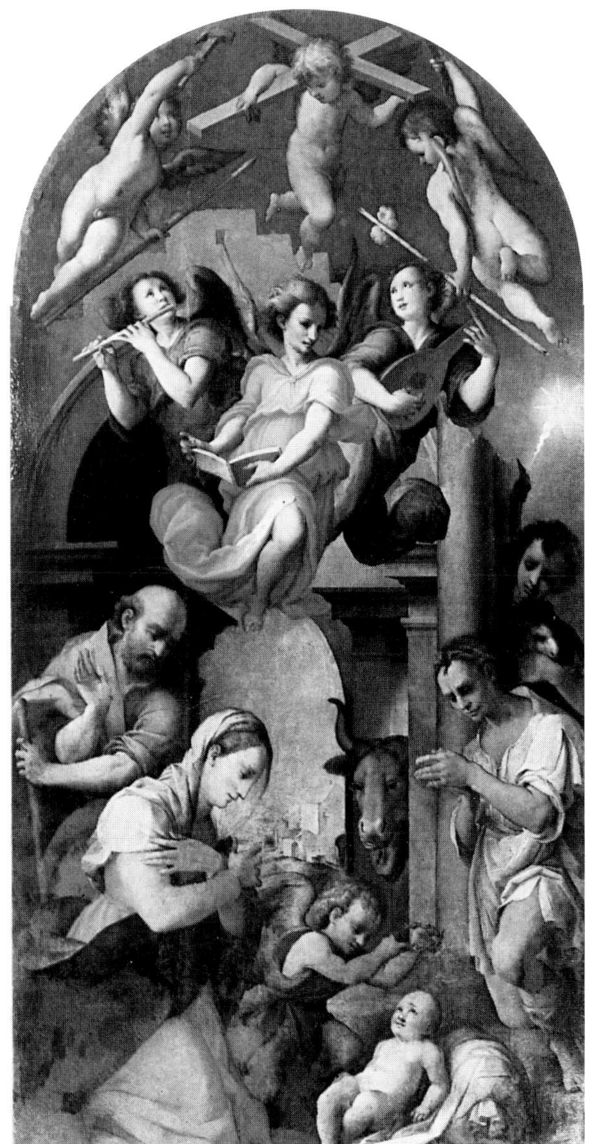

Fig. 21

his Florentine contemporary, Jacopo Zucchi. These two artists, Maso and Jacopo, with their Northern-looking small figure style, were the leading Florentine representatives of "International Mannerism." The small oval at the lower right is the only one on the Vasari sheet whose attribution is doubted.[37] The attribution of pen drawings to a painter is often problematic, since it is a technique preferred by sculptors and goldsmiths. However, it appears to be Maso's hand, and we do not see why we should reject an attribution that Vasari made while the artist was still alive. The same mode is present in a drawing in Rennes, Musée des Beaux-Arts, which Monbeig Goguel recently attributed to Maso (Fig. 26).[38] This grouping of Eastern figures derives from those found in engravings by Lucas van Leyden that circulated in Florence from the beginning of the century. It reinforces the observation that Maso was developing a lively interest in Northern artists.[39]

The shift in style can be especially noted in Maso's production for private clients. The *Holy Family* in the Ashmolean Museum, Oxford (Fig. 27), is an adaptation of Pontormo's *Madonna of the Book*,[40] though it is clearly reminiscent of the large altarpieces in Maso's early production. A drawing in the Uffizi is a project for a similar Holy Family, with a *sfumato* quality typical of the works of his second period (Fig. 28).[41] Maso here draws inspiration from paintings by his teacher, Carlo Portelli, such as the *Madonna and Child* at Princeton (Fig. 29), and the *Holy Family*

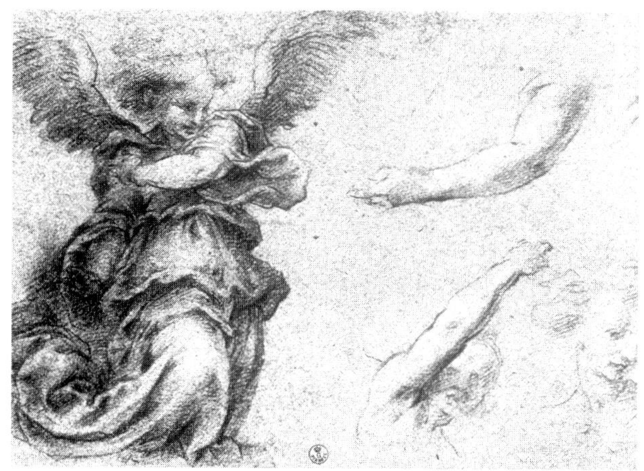

Fig. 22 Maso da San Friano, *Angel*, study (after Andrea del Sarto) for *Adoration of the Shepherds* in SS. Apostoli, Florence. Florence, Uffizi. Photo: author.

Fig. 22

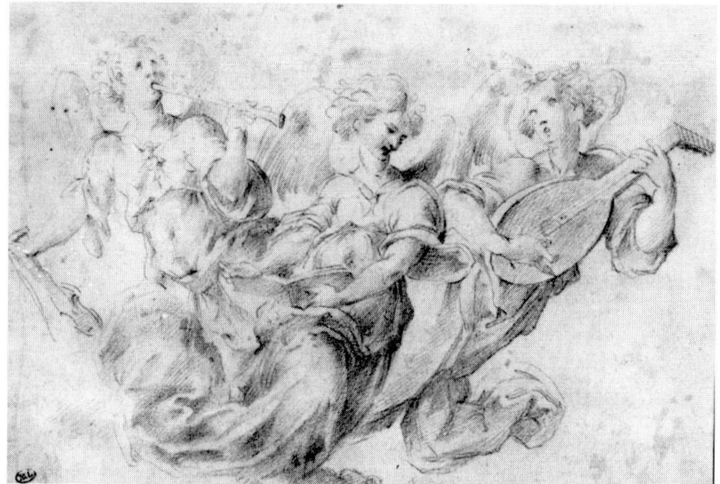

Fig. 23 Maso da San Friano, *Three Angels*, study for *Adoration of the Shepherds* in SS. Apostoli, c. 1565. Paris, Louvre. Photo: © Réunion des Musées Nationaux.

Fig. 23

Fig. 24 Maso da San Friano, *Adoration of the Shepherds*, study for *Adoration of the Shepherds* in SS. Apostoli, c. 1565. U.S., private collection. Photo: author.

Fig. 25 Maso da San Friano (drawings) and Giorgio Vasari, leaf from Vasari's *Libro dei Disegni*. Paris, Louvre. Photo: © Réunion des Musées Nationaux.

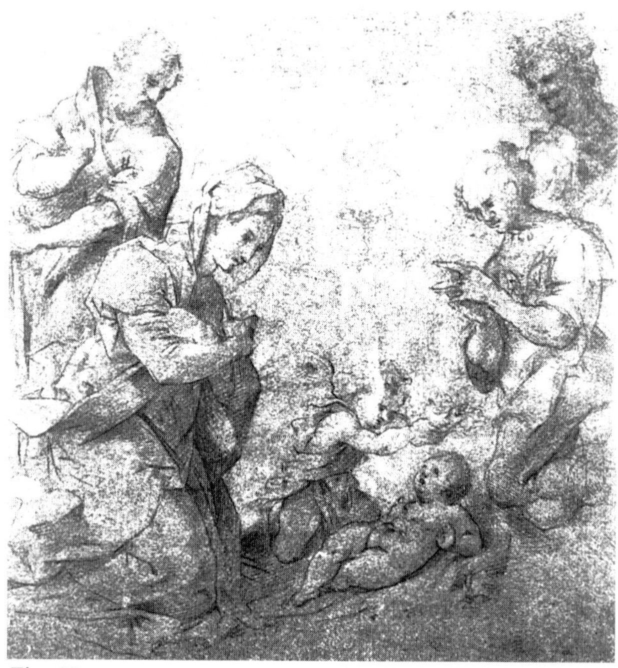

Fig. 24

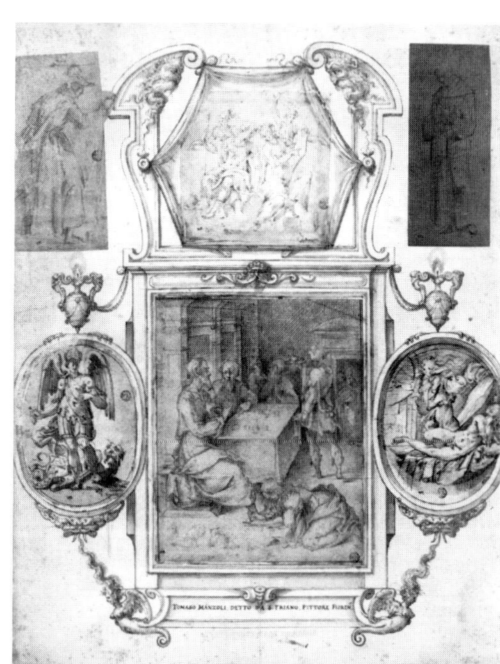

Fig. 25

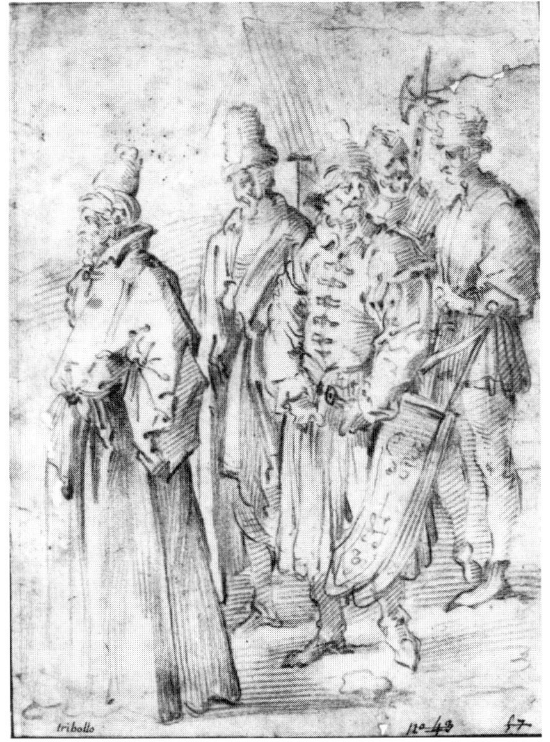

Fig. 26

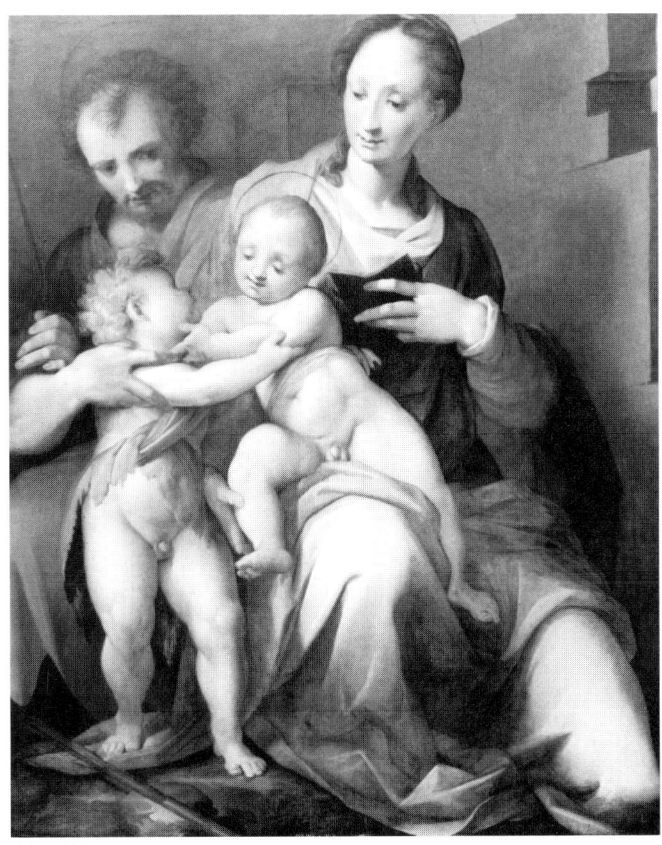

Fig. 27

Fig. 28

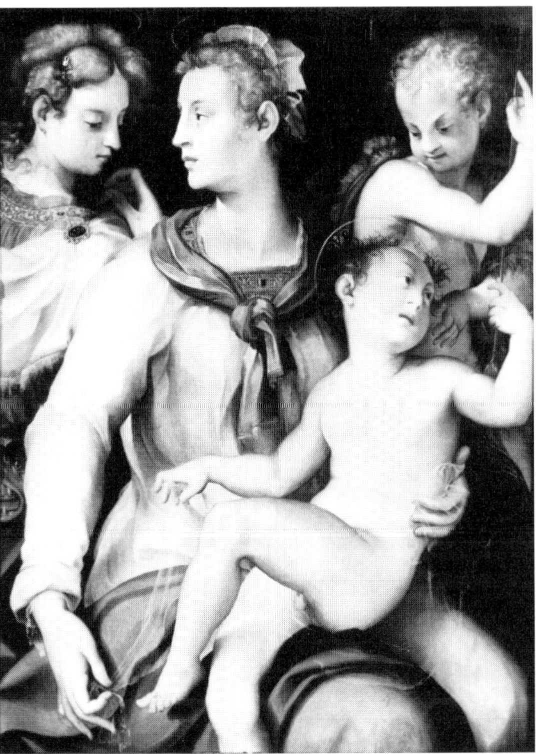

Fig. 29

Fig. 26 Maso da San Friano, *Group of Eastern Figures*. Rennes, Musée des Beaux-Arts. Photo: Musée des Beaux-Arts de Rennes.

Fig. 27 Maso da San Friano, *Holy Family and St. John,* c. 1560. Oxford, Ashmolean Museum. Photo: © Ashmolean Museum, Oxford.

Fig. 28 Maso da San Friano, *Holy Family,* 1560s. Florence, Uffizi. Photo: author.

Fig. 29 Carlo Portelli, *Madonna and Child with St. John and St. Margaret,* c. 1555–60. Princeton, The Art Museum. Photo: © 1984 Trustees of Princeton University.

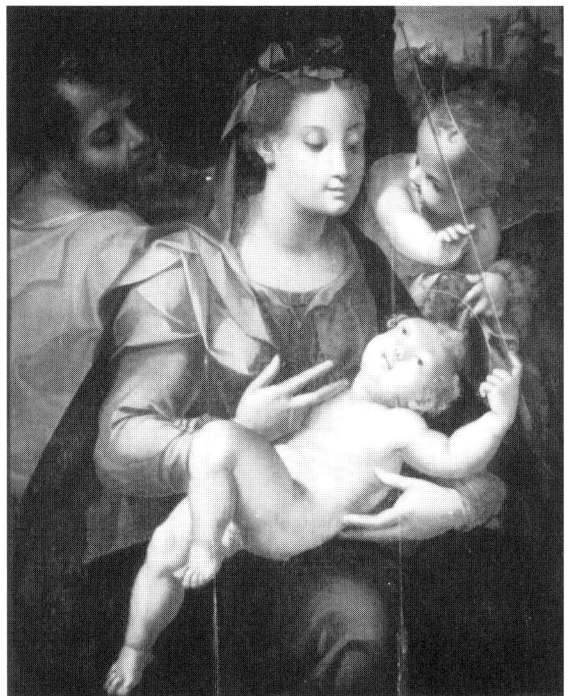

Fig. 30

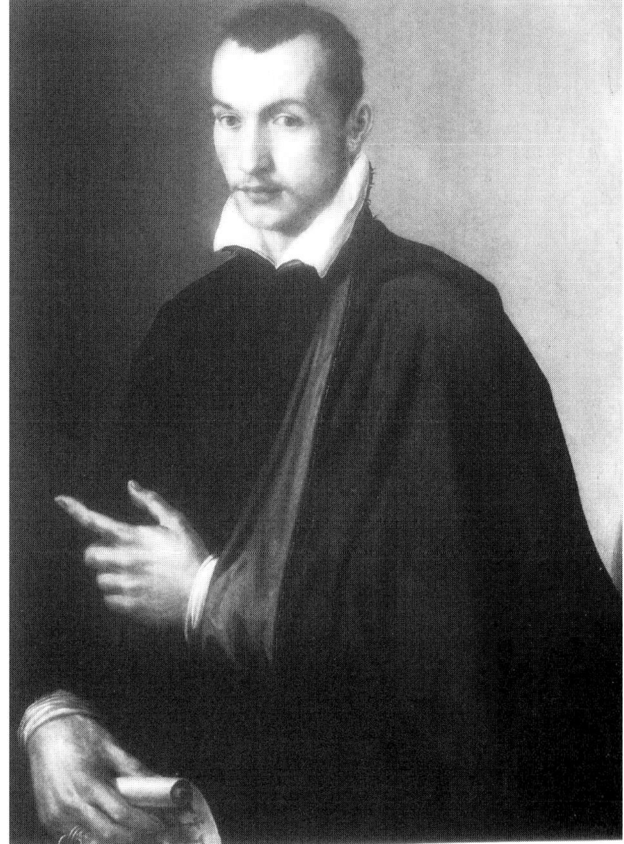

Fig. 31

Fig. 30 Carlo Portelli, *Holy Family with St. John,* c. 1560. Rouen, archepiscopal coll. Photo: Kollmann ©1989 Inventaire Général [Haute-Normandie, Rouen] SPADEM.

Fig. 31 Maso da San Friano, *Portrait of an Architect,* 1560s. Formerly London, Colnaghi's. Photo: author.

Fig. 32 Maso da San Friano, *Adoration of the Child,* 1565. (Project for the decoration of the central door of the Duomo, Florence.) Paris, Louvre. Photo: © Réunion des Musées Nationaux.

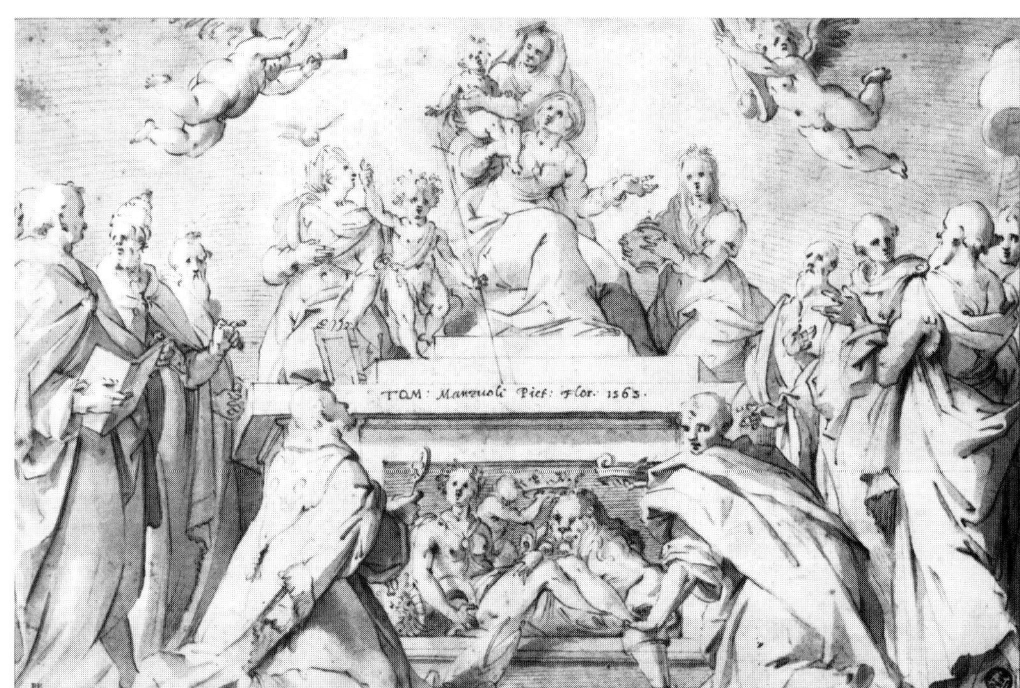

Fig. 32

in Rouen (Fig. 30). (The latter entered the collection without an attribution but is undoubtedly a work by Portelli.[42]) Maso eventually developed another type of Madonna and Child whose *sfumato* effect is a clear departure from the *Holy Family* at Oxford. His workshop produced a number of paintings of this subject from a single cartoon[43] (not unlike Tosini's workshop, which specialized in the production of Madonna and Child compositions that enjoyed wide dissemination, such as the example [Hornik, Fig. 1] in the Palmer Museum.) The *sfumato* effect can be observed in the domain of portraiture. The *Portrait of an Architect*, formerly with Colnaghi Gallery, displays similar characteristics, though the sitter is shown standing and already exhibits the features typical of Counter Reformation portraits (Fig. 31).[44]

In the years 1564–65, three historic events took place. As mentioned, in 1564, the Council of Trent published its edicts concerning the arts. The year 1564 also witnessed the solemn celebration of Michelangelo's funeral, and in 1565, the Florentine Medici prince, Francesco, married Giovanna of Austria. For both latter occasions, extravagant programs of ephemeral decorations were ordered, and most of the Florentine artists participated in their execution.[45] A Maso drawing in the Louvre, *Adoration of the Child* (Fig. 32), is a study for an ephemeral decoration of the central door of the Duomo that Maso realized for the princely nuptials.[46] Here he created an image that would not have been conceivable two years earlier. More inventive than traditional altarpieces, ephemeral decorations met the new requirements and desires of the Church.

In the years following the publication of the Tridentine decrees, the principal basilicas of Florence under Vasari's supervision were redecorated according to the new edicts.[47] Maso, however, was not among the leading participating artists; he was given only one altarpiece, an *Ascension of Christ*, for the church of the Carmine. For this project he made a large number of preparatory drawings, among them a highly finished sheet in the Uffizi (Fig. 33),[48] but he never completed the altarpiece. It was eventually completed by Naldini and subsequently lost in a fire.[49] Maso's preparatory drawings for the project were quite influential among his contemporaries, such as Stradano (Jan van der Straet). In the collection of Jak Katalan, New York, there is a drawing by Stradano which illustrates this point (Fig. 34).[50] From the time of the Carmine commission, Maso himself apparently produced no more large scale works. But he almost certainly continued to design large projects entrusting their execution to his workshop, as attest-

Fig. 33 Maso da San Friano, *Ascension*, after 1565. Study for altarpiece for the church of the Carmine, Florence. Florence, Uffizi. Photo: author.

Fig. 34 Jan van der Straet (Giovanni Stradano or Johannes Stradanus), *Ascension*, c. 1569. Preliminary drawing for *Ascension* in Asini Chapel, Sta. Croce, Florence. New York, collection of Jak Katalan. Photo: author.

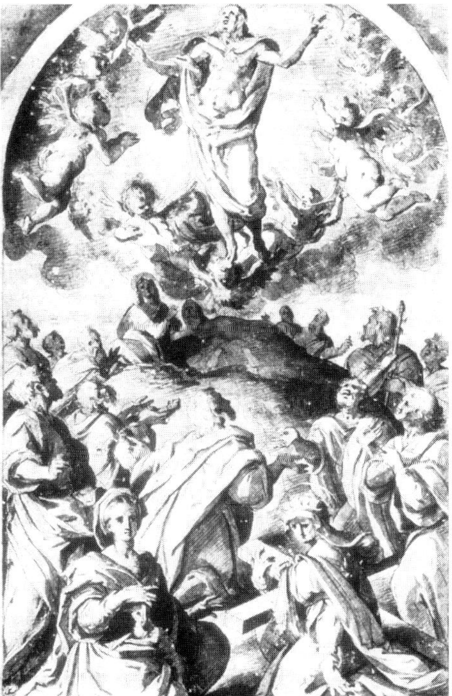

Fig. 33

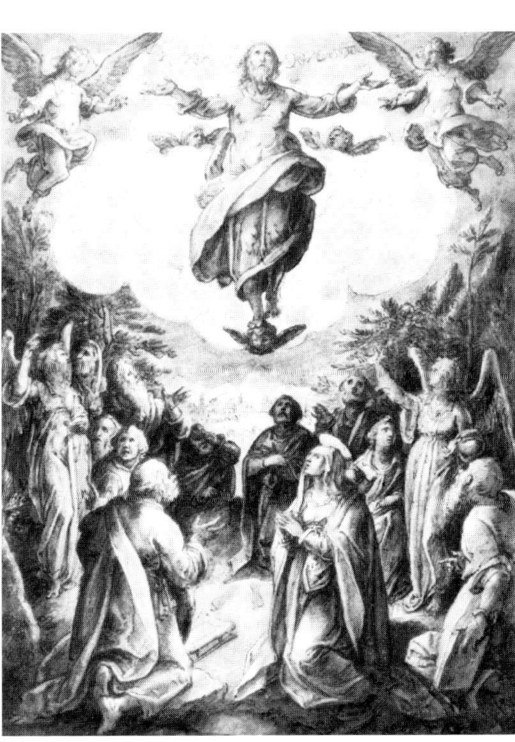

Fig. 34

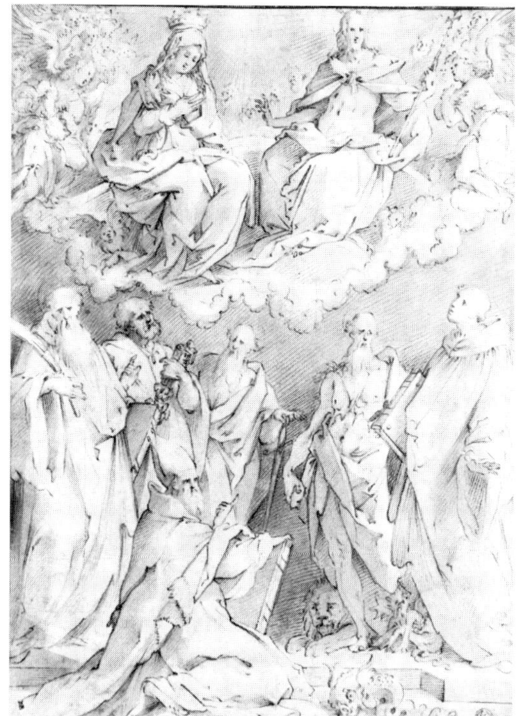

Fig. 35

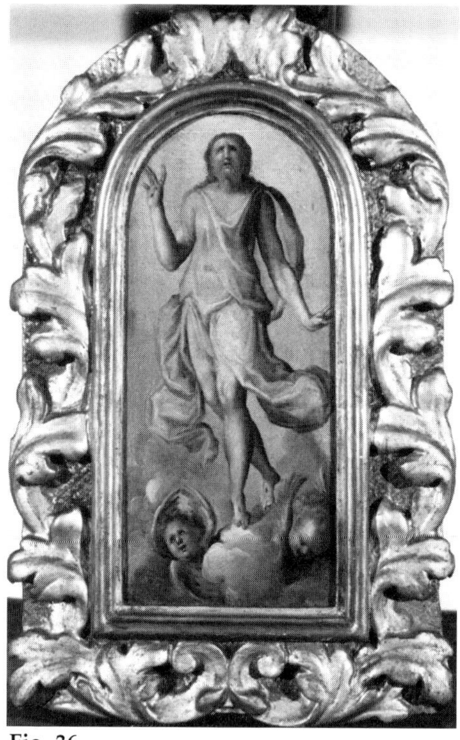

Fig. 36

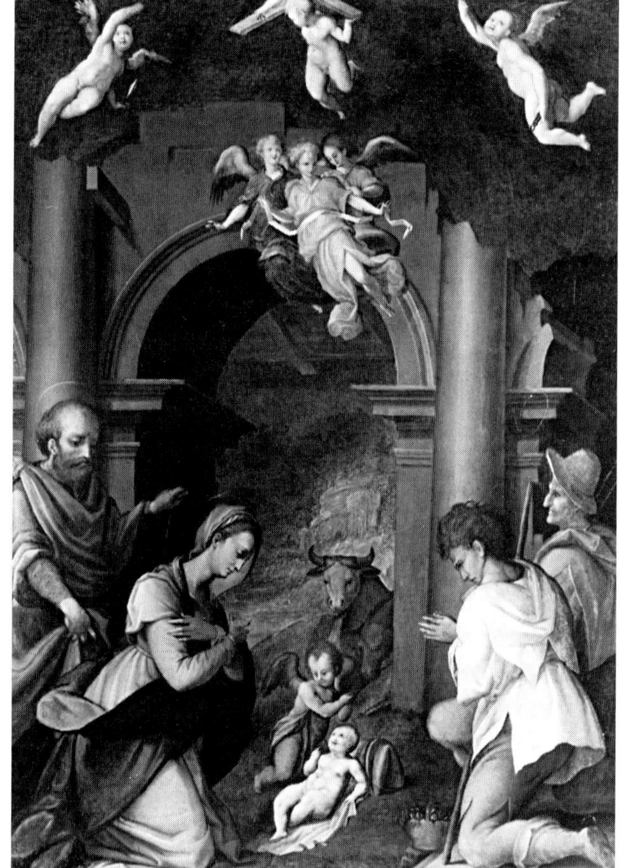

Fig. 37

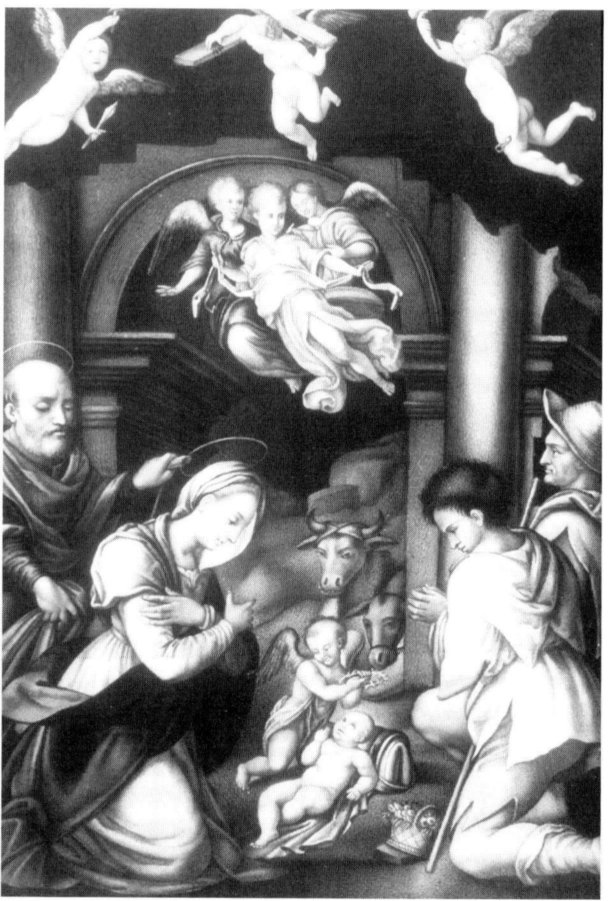

Fig. 38

ed by a sketch for an altarpiece in the Louvre (Fig. 35).[51] He made little effort to establish himself as an official artist, and in this respect he can be considered "anti-Vasarian." His new and
sought-after specialty was small paintings for private patrons.

A tabernacle door in the Musée de Chambéry (Fig. 36) is based on Maso's sketches for the
Ascension in the Carmine,[52] and in our judgment its high quality places it among the autograph
works of the artist. The same observation may be made for the *Adoration of the Shepherds* in the
Palmer Museum,[53] and an earlier version in a private collection, New York (Fig. 37), and a third
version, as yet unknown to us. The latter was engraved as part of the Sanford collection at
Corsham Court (Fig. 38), where it was attributed to Andrea del Sarto. (It later passed to Lord
Northwick's collection as a painting by Pontormo.[54])

We have suggested that these works are not *modelli*. They reflect Maso's new artistic direction,
away from the earlier large altarpieces and towards a *fare piccolo* or miniaturization. The difference is not only of scale but of increased refinement, calling to mind the other artists of the
Studiolo, rather than Andrea del Sarto. At the expense of a seeming contradiction, they also
recall an early work by Vasari, the *Adoration of the Shepherds* at Camaldoli. The resemblance
between the poses of the angels is striking, but more importantly, both pictures prefigure the
rarified aesthetic of the Studiolo, which was to incorporate Northern influences. The version in
private hands (Fig. 37) was executed in our view during the 1560s. Based on its success, Maso,
possibly while working in the Studiolo, painted the nocturnal and more refined version now at
the Palmer Museum of Art. We suggest a date of circa 1570.

An even closer resemblance to Vasari's altarpiece at Camaldoli is demonstrated in another
Adoration of the Shepherds attributed to Maso, a predella panel sold at auction in 1985 (Fig. 39).[55]
The quality is high and the attribution convincing, inviting comparison with the Palmer picture. Maso, it seems, re-used figures and poses in his drawings, and he varied their arrange-
ment. Since, as observed above, he is unlikely to have executed large altarpieces after 1565, the
Sotheby predella, which includes a *Baptism* and an *Annunciation*,[56] may have belonged either to
an altarpiece by his workshop or to one from a different workshop.[57] A preliminary study for
the *Annunciation* is preserved at the Istituto Nazionale per la Grafica, Rome (Fig. 40).[58] Maso's
graphic style here, minute and refined, achieves such perfection that the drawing can stand as
an independent work.[59]

Fig. 35 Maso da San
Friano, *Coronation of the
Virgin with Saints*, study
for an altarpiece,
c. 1565–70. Paris, Louvre.
Photo: © Réunion des
Musées Nationaux.

Fig. 36 Maso da San
Friano, *Ascension*, taber-
nacle door, c. 1570.
Musée de Chambéry.
Photo: Musée de
Chambéry.

Fig. 37 Maso da San
Friano, *Adoration of the
Shepherds*, c. 1565-70.
U.S., private collection.
Photo: Richard L. Feigen
& Co.

Fig. 38 Engraving after
Maso da San Friano,
Adoration of the Shepherds.
Illustration from
*Catalogue of Paintings
belonging to the Rev.
Sanford…*, London, 1838.
Photo: Artini, Florence.

Fig. 39 Maso da San
Friano, *Adoration of the
Shepherds*, predella panel,
c. 1570. Photo: Sotheby's.

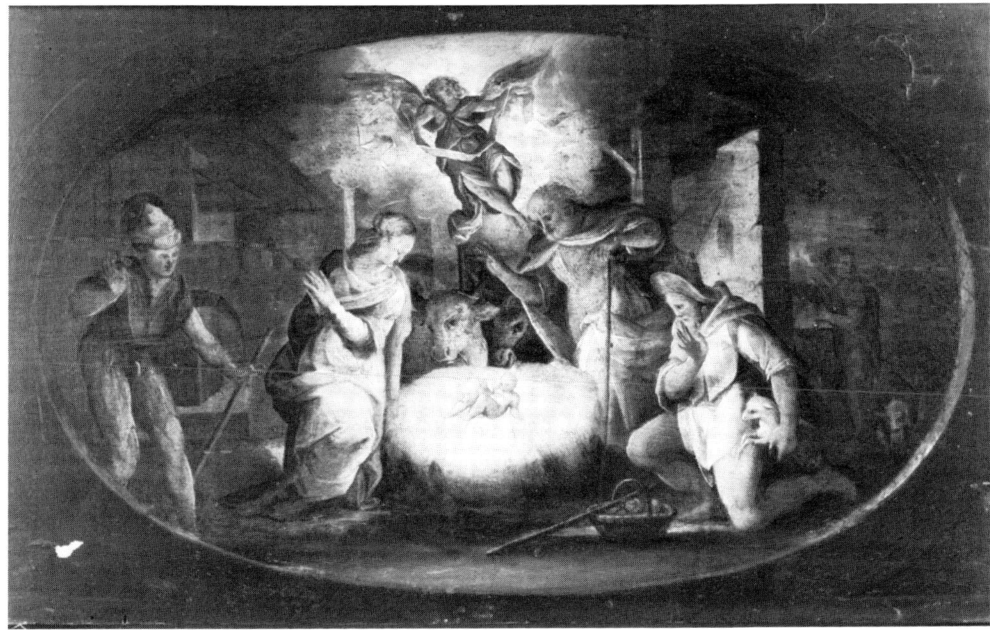

Fig. 39

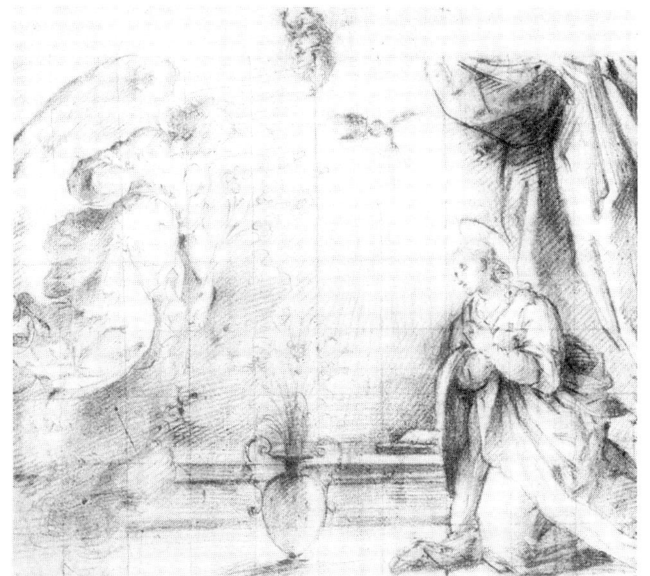

Fig. 40

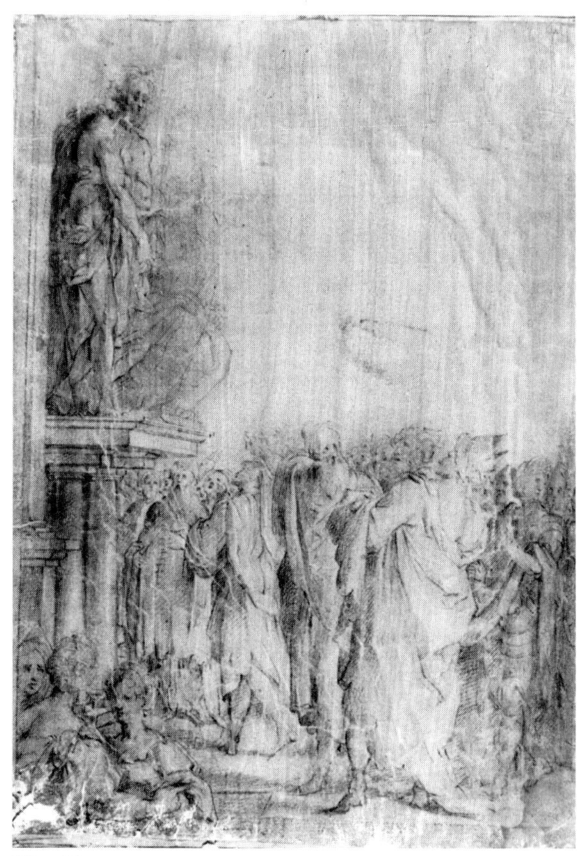

Fig. 41

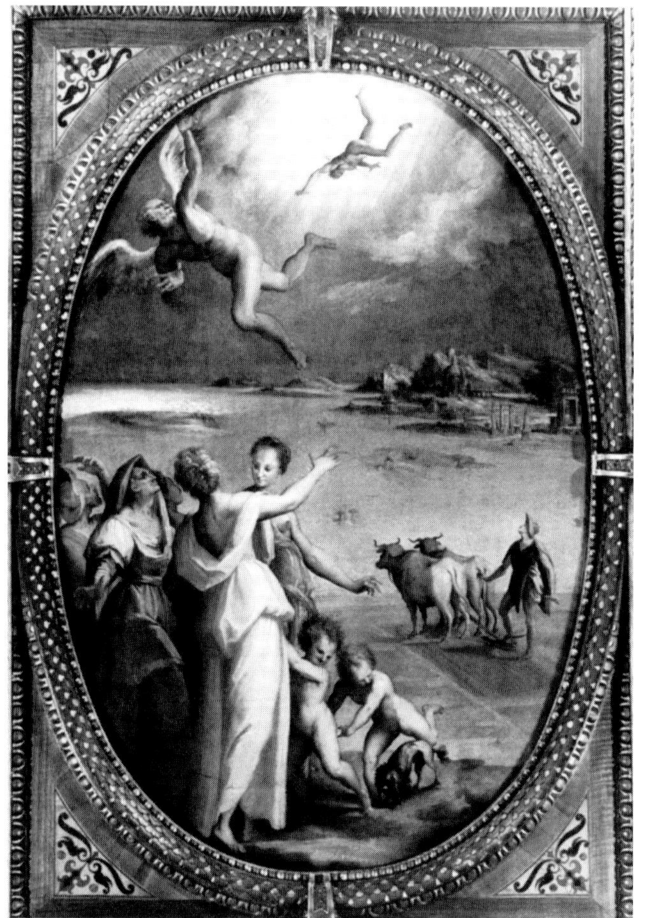

Fig. 43

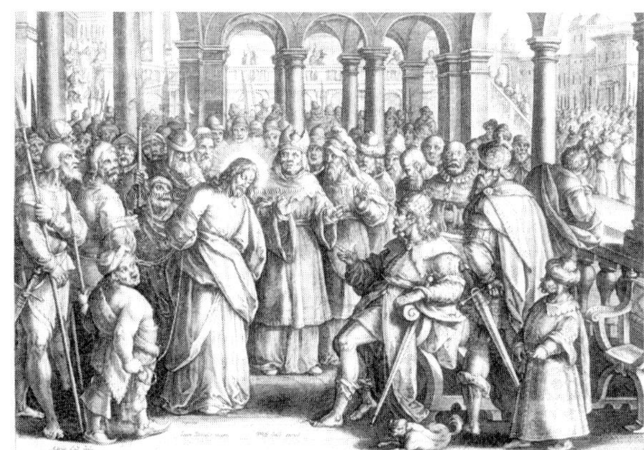

Fig. 42

Maso may have marketed his drawings. An *Ecce Homo*, a fairly large sheet at the Louvre, appears to be a finished work that could have hung in a private collection next to, perhaps, a miniature (Fig. 41).[60] It calls to mind Stradano's output of the period, such as his engraving, *Christ before King Herod*, which was in the Palmer Museum exhibition that accompanied the symposium (Fig. 42). The *Ecce Homo* may be considered one of Maso's last drawings, close in style to the Studiolo panels.

Francesco I, Grand-Duke of Tuscany, commissioned the construction of the Studiolo as a *Kunstkammer* for his personal treasures. Implementing a program conceived by Vincenzo Borghini, Vasari supervised a team of artists in the execution of panels covering the doors of the cupboards containing the Medici Grand-Duke's rarities.[61] Maso's talent for small figure works explains his presence in the Studiolo, and he produced two masterpieces: *The Fall of Icarus* (Fig. 43) and *The Diamond Mines* (Fig. 44). His panels are unmatched by Alessandro Allori or Santi di Tito, who reduce the size of traditional Florentine compositions. Maso's panels relate to Flemish paintings, the school of Fontainbleau, and especially paintings from the workshops of Prague; he had become an exponent of "International Mannerism," whose compelling quality is refinement. With these panels, Maso revealed his originality, proving to be more than equal to his celebrated contemporaries. It is lamentable that his early death prevented the full maturation of his gifts. Maso might have become one of the most prominent artists of the Cinquecento. A drawing in the Louvre, a preliminary for the figure in the lower left of *The Diamond Mines*, suggests the vigor of Michelangelo (Fig. 45).[62]

Maso's style was carried on by his workshop, especially by Jacopo da Empoli, his most important follower. Empoli's early altarpiece in Sassetta di Vernio (Fig. 46) had probably been ordered from Maso and recalls several of Maso's compositions. The Annunciation group derives from the drawing in Rome,[63] and Saint Michael is identical to a figure in a drawing owned by Vasari (Fig. 25). The Saint Francis is adapted from a figure for the Carmine altarpiece. Maso's style was taken up by a later generation and is discernible in Giovanni Balducci's *Christ in Glory* of 1586 (a gift to the Palmer Museum from Mary Jane Harris) where the figures of Christ and the musical angels recall those in the paintings by Maso that we have been considering (Fig. 47).[64]

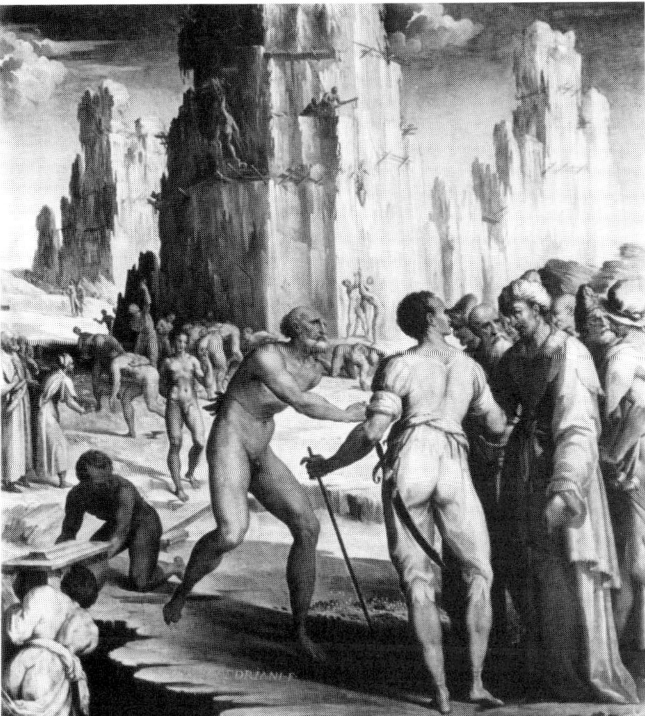

Fig. 44

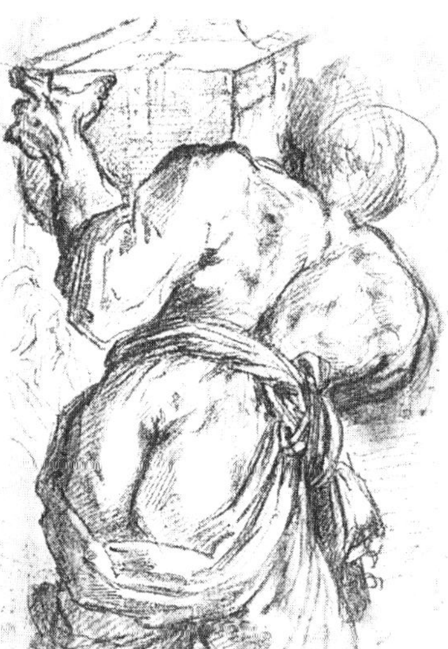

Fig. 45

Fig. 46 Jacopo da Empoli, *Annunciation with St. Michael, St. Francis, and Donors*. Pieve, Sassetta di Vernio. Photo: author.

Fig. 47 Giovanni Balducci, *Christ in Glory*, 1586. University Park, Palmer Museum of Art, The Pennsylvania State University, gift of Mary Jane Harris in memory of her husband, Morton B. Harris.

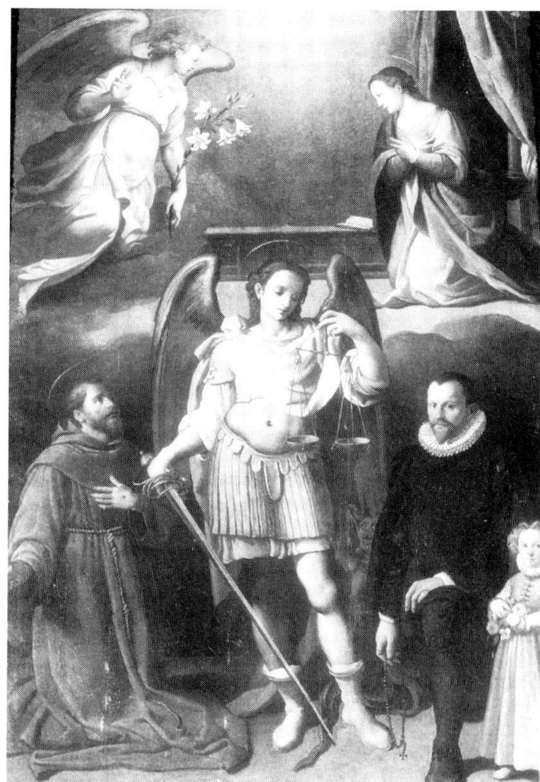

Fig. 46

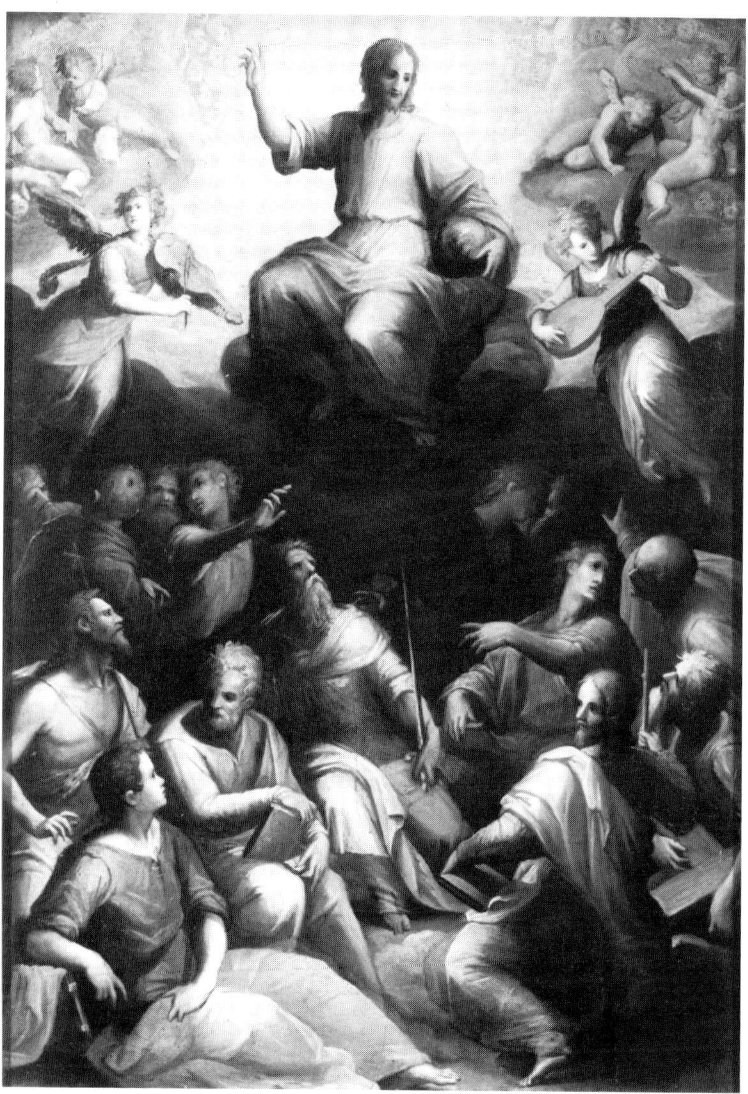

Fig. 47

Endnotes

1 G. Vasari, *Le Vite de'più eccellenti pittori, scultori et architettori*, Florence, 1568, ed. G. Milanesi, Florence, 1878–85, 9 vols., vol. VII, pp. 611–12.

2 R. Borghini, *Il Riposo*, Florence, 1584, pp. 539–40.

3 L. Berti, "Nota a Maso da San Friano," in *Scritti di Storia dell'arte in onore di Mario Salmi*, Rome, 1963, pp. 77–88; P. Cannon-Brookes, "Three Notes on Maso da San Friano," in *Burlington Mag.* CVII, 1965, pp. 192–97; P. Cannon-Brookes, "The Portraits of Maso da San Friano," in *Burlington Mag.* CVIII, 1966, pp. 560–68; P. Cannon-Brookes, "A Madonna and Child by Maso da San Friano," in *Apollo* XCII, 1970, pp. 346–49; S. Freedberg, *Painting in Italy*, 1500 to 1600, New York, 1971, pp. 465–67.

4 C. Monbeig Goguel, *Musée du Louvre, Cabinet des dessins, Inventaire général des dessins italiens: I, Maîtres toscans nés après 1500, morts avant 1600: Vasari et son temps*, Paris, 1972, pp. 59–68.

5 V. Pace, "Maso da San Friano," in *Bollettino d'Arte* LXI, nos. 1–2, 1976, pp. 74–84.

6 Inv. no. 87.2, oil on canvas, 28 15/16 x 20 5/16 inches (73.6 x 51.6 cm.). Acquired from the Piero Corsini Gallery, New York, in 1987 with funds from the Friends of the Palmer Museum of Art.

7 G. Vasari, *op. cit.*, note 1, vol. VII, p. 612; Borghini, *op. cit.*, note 2, p. 539.

8 J. Shearman, *Andrea del Sarto*, 2 vols., Oxford, 1965, p. 170.

9 As C. Monbeig Goguel has already remarked (*op. cit.*, note 4, p. 61, under no. 45), the drawing in the Ashmolean Museum, Oxford, inv. Parker 680, that Shearman (*op. cit.*, note 8, p. 60, Fig. 23b) cited as a copy of certain figures on the dado in the Monastery of the Scalzo, Florence, is in fact, an original by Maso.

10 Inv. no. 1025; see P. Costamagna, *Pontormo: Catalogue raisonné de l'oeuvre peint*, Paris and Milan, 1994, p. 104.

11 *Ibid.*, pp. 105–6. *Cupid and Apollo*, a grisaille painting (possibly a copy) of one of the carnival chariot designs by Pontormo, is preserved in the Samuel H. Kress Collection of the Center Gallery, Bucknell University, Lewisburg, Pennsylvania, K.1618 (Fig. 4). It was shown at the Palmer Museum of Art in the exhibition that accompanied the symposium.

12 Inv. 1890 (supp.), no. 9255; see *ibid.*, p. 287, no. A38. For the lost original, see *ibid.*, pp. 225–29, no. 73. A panel in the Uffizi, by Maso, records the middle part of the missing picture (Fig. 5).

13 Inv. no. 0180; concerning the relief in the Victoria and Albert Museum, see F. Caglioti, in *Il Giardino di San Marco: Maestri e compagni del giovane Michelangelo*, exh. cat., Florence, 1992, pp. 72–78.

14 See Costamagna, *op. cit.*, note 10, pp. 305–7.

15 Munich, Staatliche Graphische Sammlung, inv. no. 2191; Vienna, Albertina, inv. no. 116.

16 P. Costamagna, "L'étude d'après les maîtres et le rôle de la copie dans la formation des artistes à Florence au XVIe siècle," in *Disegno, actes du congrès, Rennes*, 9–10 October 1990, Rennes, 1991, pp. 51–62.

17 Inv. no. 1984-56-78; see C. Monbeig Goguel, in *Francesco Salviati ou la Bella Maniera*, exh. cat., Rome and Paris, 1998, p. 111, no. 17.

18 Regarding the drawing, see C. von Heusinger, *Herzog Anton Ulrich-Museum Braunschweig: Die Handzeichnungs-sammlung*, I, *Von der Gotik zum Manierismus*, Brunswick, 1992, no. 136. The engraving was frequently utilized by the Florentines and in particular by the artists of the Studiolo, see M. Privitera, "Invenzioni parmigianesche in disegni e dipinti di Girolamo Macchietti (1535–92)," in *Kunst des Cinquecento in der Toskana*, Munich, 1992, pp. 273, 276, note 24.

19 See P. Costamagna, "A propos du séjour florentin de Giulio Clovio," in *Kunst des Cinquecento in der Toskana*, Munich, 1992, p. 170. For a different attribution of the panel, see A. Wied, in *Vittoria Colonna: Dichterin und Muse Michelangelos*, exh. cat., Vienna, 1997, pp. 477–78, no. IV.58.

20 Inv. 1912, no. 385. L. Vertova, "Domenico di Baccio d'Agnolo: due ipotetici ritratti e un omaggio al maestro," *Artista* 3, 1991, pp. 68–77, proposes identifying the portraits as Giuliano Baglioni and his younger brother, Domenico, the two sons of Baccio d'Agnolo, architects like their father. G. Bertini, "Ottavio Franese e Francesco De Marchi: una proposta d'identificazione nel 'Doppio ritratto maschile di Maso da San Friano," *Aurea Parma*, LXXVIII, 1994, pp. 149–55, on the other hand suggests that the two portraits represent Duke Ottavio Farnese and his military architect, Francesco De Marchi.

21 Regarding the altarpiece and its preparatory drawing, Florence, Gabinetto dei Disegni et Stampi degli Uffizi, inv. no. 7276F, see Pace, *op. cit.*, note 5, pp. 76, 83, 86–87.

22 See P. Costamagna, *Maso da San Friano: La "Pietà" de l'église florentine de Santa Maria dei Candeli redécouverte*, Saint Laurent de Var, n.d. [1993]. Another important altarpiece by Maso, also dating from the 1550s, is the *Deposition with Two Saints* on the third altar to the right in San Agostino, Montepulciano, attributed to a follower of Pomarancio. This identification was made independently by Alessandro Bagnoli who will publish the work after its restoration. In the church of Santa Lucia, Montepulciano, there is a seventeenth-century copy.

23 Coll. of the Duke of Devonshire, no. 1084. See M. Jaffé, *The Devonshire Collection of Italian Drawings: Tuscan and Umbrian Schools*, 1994, pp. 78–79, no. 40.

24 Regarding the drawings of Carlo Portelli, see V. Pace, "Carlo Portelli," in *Bollettino d'Arte* LVIII, 5, 1973, pp. 27–33. For two recent additions to the graphic catalogue of the artist, see C. Monbeig Goguel, "Alphabet pour Roseline Bacou: Dessins italiens peu connus ou redécouverts (XVe–XVIIIe siècles)," in *Mélanges offerts à Roseline Bacou*, Rimini, 1996, p. 118; and C. Monbeig Goguel, *op. cit.*, note 17, p. 45, note 8.

25 Such as the central themes of the altarpieces by Pontormo in the Capponi Chapel, Santa Felicità, and by Bronzino for the chapel of Eleanora di Toledo, Palazzo Vecchio (now in the Musée d'Art et d'Archéologie, Besançon).

26 Inv. no. 1895-9-15-654; see Costamagna, *op. cit.*, note 19, pp. 170, 175.

27 On deposit with the Soprintendenza di Belle Arti, Florence, under joint inv. 1890, no. 5906; see Costamagna, *op. cit.*, note 22, pp. 13–17.

28 See A. Tartuferi, in *Collezione Gianfranco Luzzetti: Dipinti, sculture, disegni, XIV–XVIII secolo*, Florence, 1991, pp. 96–98; L. Vertova, "Il prestigio delle corti e il clan Traballesi," in *Kunst des Cinquecento in der Toskana*, Munich, 1992, pp. 283, 291, note 5; Costamagna, *op. cit.*, note 22, pp. 11–12.

29 Inv. no. 496; on loan, the main altar of Trinity Hall chapel. See Pace, *op. cit.*, note 5, pp. 76, 83.

30 Vasari, *op. cit.*, note 1, p. 612.

31 Inv. no. 1310. The drawing at the Louvre has been rightly seen as close to a sheet in the Gabinetto Disegni e Stampe at the Uffizi (*Birth of the Virgin*, inv. no. 7279F), and could also be considered preparatory for one of the missing predella panels. See A. M. Petrioli Tofani, in *Il primato del Disegno*, exh. cat., Florence, 1980, p. 142, no. 299.

32 Regarding the altarpiece described by Vasari, see M. Privitera, in *Magnificenza alla corte dei Medici: Arte a Firenze alla fine del Cinquecento*, exh. cat., Florence, 1997–98, p. 193, proposing a date of 1565.

33 Gabinetto Disegni e Stampe, inv. no. 6466F; see Shearman, *op. cit.*, note 8, pp. 212–13.

34 Inv. no. 9896; see C. Monbeig Goguel, *op. cit.*, note 4, p. 61, no. 47. V. Pace excludes the sheet from the corpus of the artist; see Pace, *op. cit.*, note 5, p. 90.

35 See L. Feinberg, *From Studio to Studiolo: Florentine Draftsmanship under the First Medici Grand Dukes*, exh. cat., Oberlin, 1991, pp. 122–23, no. 26.

36 Inv. no. 1306; see C. Monbeig Goguel, *op. cit.*, note 4, pp. 59–61, no. 45.

37 See P. Cannon-Brookes, "Book review of *Dessins italiens du musée du Louvre: Vasari et son temps*," in *Burlington Mag.* CXVII, 1975, p. 57.

38 Inv. no. 794.1.3201; see C. Monbeig Goguel in *Disegno: Les dessins italiens du Musée de Rennes*, exh. cat., Rennes, 1990, pp. 100–101, no. 44.

39 Maso's interest in Northern art is also evident in his portrait drawings, such as the *Portrait of a Man* in the Gabinetto Disegni e Stampe degli Uffizi, inv. no. 7285F, but also in the studies of facial expression recently attributed to him: the *Portrait of a Man in a Turban* at the Louvre, inv. no. 11963 (see C. Monbeig Goguel, "Vasari's Attitude toward Collecting," in *Vasari's Florence: Artists and Literati at the Medicean Court, Acts of the Congress, New Haven, Yale Univ.*, 16–18 April 1994, Cambridge, 1998, pp. 129, 277, note 67), as well as the *Head of an Old Man* at the Courtauld Institute, London, inv. no. 2162, shown in Sarrebruck (*Zeichnungen aus der Toskana: das Zeitalter Michelangelos*, exh. cat., Sarrebruck, 1997, not in the catalogue) under the name of Pontormo and attributed to Maso by J.-C. Baudequin in the review of the exhibition published in *Bulletin de l'Association des Historiens de l'Art italien*, 5, 1998, p. 45, ill. This interest of Maso was the direction taken by Pontormo in the years of the *Adoration of the Magi* at the Pitti Palace, Florence (see P. Costamagna in *L'Officina della Manieria*, exh. cat., Florence, 1996–97, pp. 292–93, no. 102).

40 Inv. no. 391. See also his autograph copy, contemporary with the Studiolo panels in the Hermitage, St. Petersburg (inv. no. 9868), to which the artist added an architectural background with small figures (see Pace, *op. cit.*, note 5, pp. 77, 78, 84). The *Head of a Woman* in the Casa Buonarroti, Florence (inv. 1896, no. 60) is a fragment of a similar Madonna, most probably by the hand of Maso, datable circa 1565–70 (see P. Costamagna, *op. cit.*, note 10, p. 289, no. A42).

41 Inv. no. 7100F. See Pace, *op. cit.*, note 5, p. 86.

42 The painting entered the Archbishop's palace in Rouen at the beginning of the twentieth century with a painting collection formed by Monseigneur Edmond Frédéric Fuzet. For the Fuzet collection see D. Lavalle, "La Vierge et l'Enfant avec saint Jean-Baptiste et saint Jacques: une peinture inédite de Francesco Brina conservée à l'archevêché de Rouen," in *Kunst des Cinquecento in der Toskana*, Munich, 1992, pp. 277–80. I wish to thank Jean-Christophe Baudequin, who informed me of the work's existence. For the Princeton painting, see P. Costamagna, "La formation de Carlo Portelli: précisions et adjonctions au catalogue," in *Annali* II, 1989, pp. 20, 24, note 24. Also by Portelli is a *Holy Family* sold at Christie's, London, Dec. 17, 1985, no. 97, as Maso.

43 Birmingham, City Museum and Art Gallery. Formerly New York, private coll. See Pace, *op. cit.*, note 5, pp. 82, 84.

44 See *Colnaghi a Firenze*, exh. cat., Florence, 1989, p. 54. Among the lesser known portraits by Maso, one should mention the *Portrait of a Nobleman of the Order of St. Michael* shown at Colnaghi's London as Salviati, in 1955, as well as the *Portrait of a Man* also with Colnaghi's in 1982, and the *Portrait of a Man Holding a Letter*, Raleigh, North Carolina Museum of Art, as Tosini. (See P. Costamagna, *op. cit.*, note 22, p. 17, note 25.)

45 See Z. Wazbinski, *L'Accademia del Disegno a Firenze nel Cinquecento: Idea e Istituzione*, Florence, 1987, pp. 155, 381–397.

46 Inv. no. 1307; see C. Monbeig Goguel, *op. cit.*, note 4, p. 61, no. 46. For the figures in the lower part,

Maso drew upon the great altarpieces of Andrea del Sarto, an orientation probably stressed in the newly formed Accademia del Disegno.

47 See the study of M. B. Hall, *Renovation and Counter-Reformation: Vasari and Duke Cosimo in Sta. Maria Novella and Sta. Croce 1565–1577*, Oxford, 1977.

48 Gabinetto Disegni e Stampe, inv. no. 602S. The drawings of the Uffizi, inv. nos. 7283F, 14419F, 14423F, 14424F, 14426F, 14428F, are also preparatory for the figures in the same altarpiece (see Cannon-Brookes, *op. cit.*, note 3, 1965, pp. 195–196). Pace (*op. cit.*, note 5, pp. 77, 84) published a bozzetto in a private Genoese collection.

49 See also the modello by Naldini in the Ashmolean Museum, Oxford, illustrated by Hall, *op. cit.*, note 47, pp. 69–70 and Fig. 61.

50 Black chalk, sold at auction, Phillips, London, 7 December 1994, no. 160. For the *Ascension* in the Asini chapel of Santa Croce, Florence, by Stradano, dated 1569, see Hall, *op. cit.*, note 47, pp. 64–65, 142–43, Fig. 43, as well as the monograph by A. Baroni Vannucci, *Jan Van Der Straet detto Giovanni Stradano flandrus pictor et inventor*, Milan and Rome, 1997, pp. 128, 224, 263, 429, who also published the engraving of Philippe Galle, dated 1580 (*Illustrated Bartsch* 56, no. 046) and its preparatory drawing, Frederikssund, J. F. Willumsen Museum, inv. no. G.S.631. For the Katalan drawing see also our review of Baroni Vannucci's mongraph in *Bulletin de l'Association des Historiens de l'Art italien*, 5, 1998, p. 46.

51 Inv. no. 10212; see C. Monbeig Goguel, *op. cit.*, note 4, pp. 61–65, no. 48. See also the most finished version in the Galleria Estense, Modena, inv. no. 985 (see A. Cecchi, in *Disegni della Galleria Estense di Modena*, exh. cat., Modena, 1989, pp. 132–33).

52 Inv. no. M907; see V. Damian, *Collections du musée de Chambéry, Peintures florentines*, Chambéry, 1990, p. 71, no. 26.

53 The version on canvas was with the Piero Corsini Gallery, New York, and sold to the Palmer Museum of Art in 1987. See B. Wollesen-Wisch, *Italian Renaissance Art: Selections from the Piero Corsini Gallery*, exh. cat., University Park, 1986, pp. 44–45, no. 16. A small drawing of a *Nativity* in the Louvre, inv. no. 9969, is contemporary with the Palmer canvas.

54 *Catalogue of Paintings belonging to the Rev. Sanford collected in Italy from 1815 to 1837*, London, 1838. *Northwick Park Collection: Important Pictures by Old Masters c. 1400–c. 1600*, Christie's, London, 28 May 1965, p. 20, no. 16.

55 *Natures mortes des XVII et XVIII siècles: Tableaux Anciens*, Monaco, Sotheby's, 22 June 1985, no. 113.

56 A panel representing the *Baptism of Christ*, probably the central panel of the same predella, was sold at Christie's, London, 14 March 1975, no. 37. A simplified workshop replica of the panel sold at Monaco appeared in Sotheby's, Florence, 3 December 1990, no. 1078. It was accompanied by an *Annunciation* that conforms to a drawing in Rome (see note 58).

57 Similar conclusions may be drawn concerning the predella panels on view in the Chapel of the Church Painters, SS. Annunziata, Florence; see Pace, *op. cit.*, note 5, p. 85.

58 Istituto Nazionale per la Grafica, inv. F.C. no. 127655; see S. Prosperi Valenti Rodinò, in *The Golden Age of Florentine Drawing: Two Centuries of Disegno from Leonardo to Volterrano*, exh. cat., Fort Worth, 1994, p. 60, no. 22.

59 The drawing in Rome is, however, preparatory for the third panel (whereabouts unknown) of the predella panels sold at Christie's, London, and Sotheby's, Monaco, as confirmed by its replica sold at Sotheby's, Florence (see note 56).

60 An autograph version of the drawing in the Louvre (inv. no. 11423; see C. Monbeig Goguel, *op. cit.*,

note 4, p. 65, no. 51) is in the Gabinetto Disegni e Stampe of the Uffizi, inv. no. 999S.

61 For the Studiolo, see especially M. Rhinehart, "A document for the Studiolo of Francesco I," in *Art the Ape of Nature: Studies in Honour of H.W. Janson*, New York, 1981, pp. 275–89, and S. Schaefer, "The Studiolo of Francesco I de' Medici: A Checklist of the Known Drawings," in *Master Drawings* XX, 2, 1982, pp. 125–31.

62 Inv. no. 10879; see C. Monbeig Goguel, *op. cit.*, note 4, p. 65, no. 49.

63 See A. Marabottini, *Jacopo di Chimenti da Empoli*, Rome, 1988, pp. 31–32, 176. For the *Adoration of the Shepherds*, Plymouth, City Museum and Art Gallery, considered by Marabottini (pp. 28, 175) as the first certain work of Jacopo da Empoli, the artist takes as his model not the altarpiece in SS. Apostoli but the composition in the Palmer Museum of Art.

64 Inv. no. 1996.32; see B. Wollesen-Wisch, *op. cit.*, note 53, pp. 60–61, no. 22.

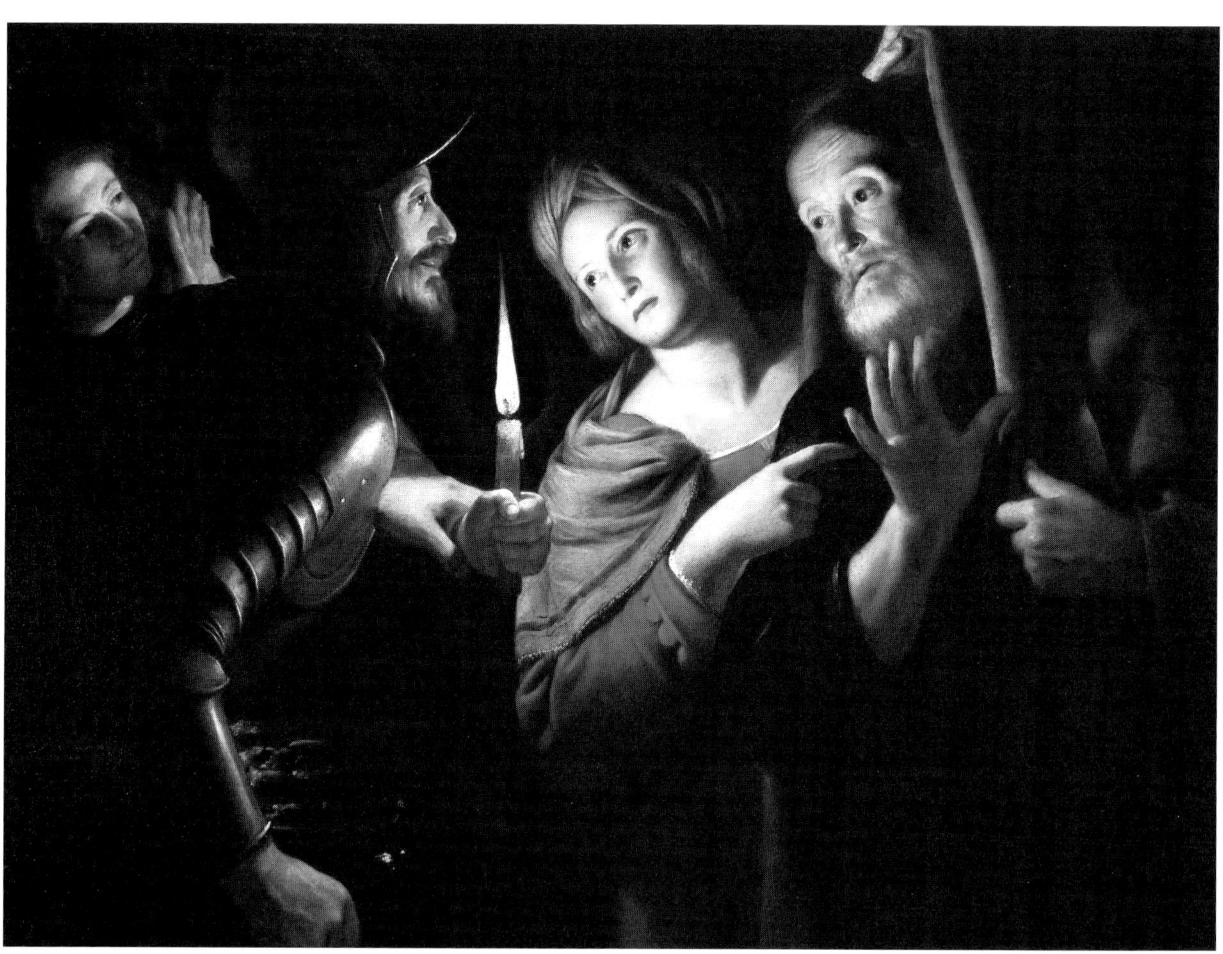

Fig. 6 Master Jacomo, *Denial of St. Peter,* c. 1630s. Palmer Museum of Art, The Pennsylvania State University. (See color plate 3.)

Master Jacomo, Trophime Bigot, and the Candlelight Master

Leonard J. Slatkes

No topic could be more appropriate for a symposium in which connoisseurship is one of the central themes than the problems surrounding a group of nocturnal pictures variously assigned to Gerrit van Honthorst,[1] Georges de La Tour,[2] Crijn Hendricksz. Volmarijn,[3] and even Matthias Stom, called Stomer,[4] before Benedict Nicolson described the *oeuvre*, first under the note name of the Candlelight Master,[5] and later as the work of the Provence painter, Trophime Bigot.[6] Even the short summary given here of the present state of the Candlelight Master/Bigot question quickly reveals the triumphs as well as the inadequacies of connoisseurship, and serves as a reminder that today connoisseurship in the service of art history is but one step in the increasingly complex process of establishing the identity and authenticity of works of art. Those who have followed the increasingly contentious debates surrounding the findings of the Rembrandt Research Project,[7] or have seen the exemplary Caravaggio exhibition organized by Mina Gregori,[8] will realize that today connoisseurship includes the mastery of a growing body of technical means from the interpretation of X-rays and infrared reflectography to the findings of dendrochronology and the thread count of canvas types. Unfortunately, none of these scientific techniques, which might solve some of the problems I will be discussing, has as yet been systematically applied to the works under discussion.

In his 1686 guide to the churches of Rome, Filippo Titi attributed the three pictures in the Passion Chapel of S. Maria in Aquiro to the Dutch artist Gerrit van Honthorst, known in Italy as Gherardo delle Notti.[9] Later, this attribution was accepted by Hoogewerff in his pioneering article on Honthorst's Italian period production,[10] and followed by Voss in his monumental study on the Roman baroque.[11] Judson also catalogued these paintings as the earliest Roman works by Honthorst, although by assigning different dates to each of the canvases—from c. 1612 for the *Flagellation* (Fig. 1), to late 1613 or early 1614 for the *Lamentation* (Fig. 2) and late 1615 or 1616 for the *Christ Crowned with Thorns* (Fig. 3)—he indicated that the stylistic differences discernable in these pictures were products of Honthorst's development during his early years in Italy.[12] In 1960, Nicolson assigned the entire chapel to a follower of Honthorst, whom he named the Candlelight Master. Like Judson, Nicolson noted differences in the canvases, although he credited them to the participation of an assistant.[13]

Even before Nicolson's publication, however, there had been a growing dissatisfaction with the attribution of the Passion Chapel to Honthorst. In 1954, for example, Roberto Longhi[14] opened a new phase of scholarship when he grouped the three S. Maria in Aquiro pictures with the Spada collection, Rome, *Capture of Christ*[15] (Fig. 4) and the *Allegory of Justice* (then identified as an *Allegory of Death* or a *Vanitas*) in the Ashmolean Museum, Oxford, and assigned them to an unknown follower of Honthorst. Today, the Spada canvas still remains central to our group. The lovely and subtle Oxford picture, however, was correctly dropped from Nicolson's lists in 1960 and has yet to find a convincing attribution.[16]

In 1955, Judson grouped some of the same works somewhat differently and assigned the Spada *Capture of Christ*, and several other candlelight pictures, to the Rotterdam painter Crijn Hendricksz. Volmarijn.[17] Volmarijn did indeed produce documented candlelight scenes, including his signed and dated (1631) *Supper at Emmaus* (Fig. 5), in the Rotterdam Historical Museum.[18] An examination of this rather wooden and unsophisticated composition quickly reveals that Volmarijn is not Nicolson's Candlelight Master. Indeed, none of the unsigned candlelight pictures Judson designated as Volmarijn still carries that attribution. For example, the Palmer Museum *Denial of St. Peter* (Fig. 6, p. 58)[19] and the Chantilly, Musée Condé, *Supper at Emmaus* (Fig. 7),[20] both assigned to Volmarijn by Judson, were later included in Nicolson's

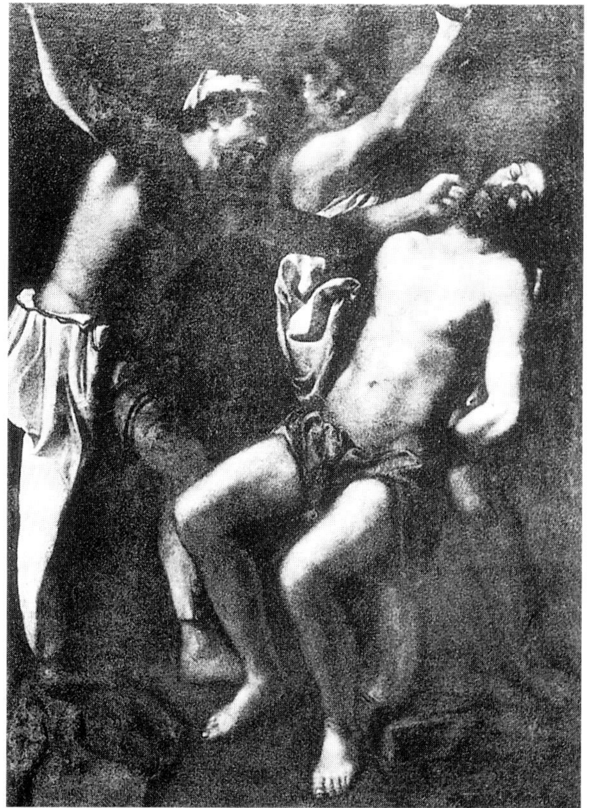

Fig. 1

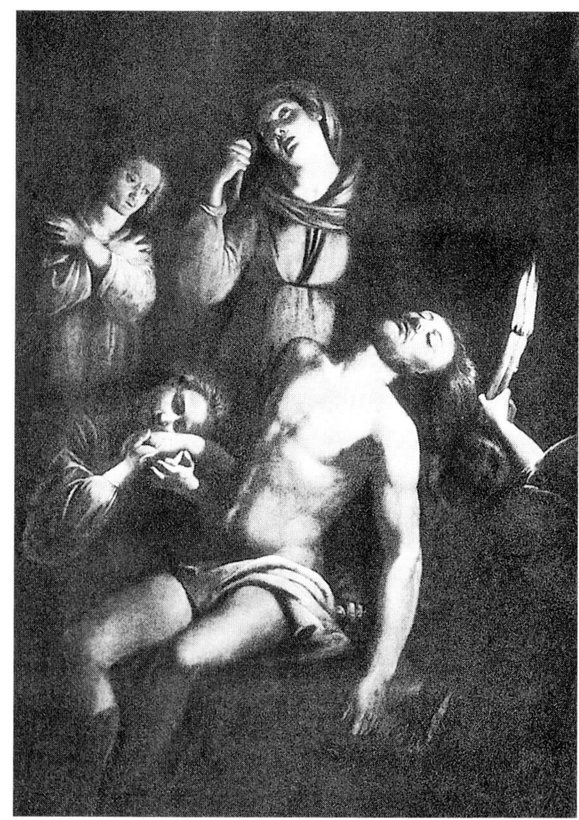

Fig. 2

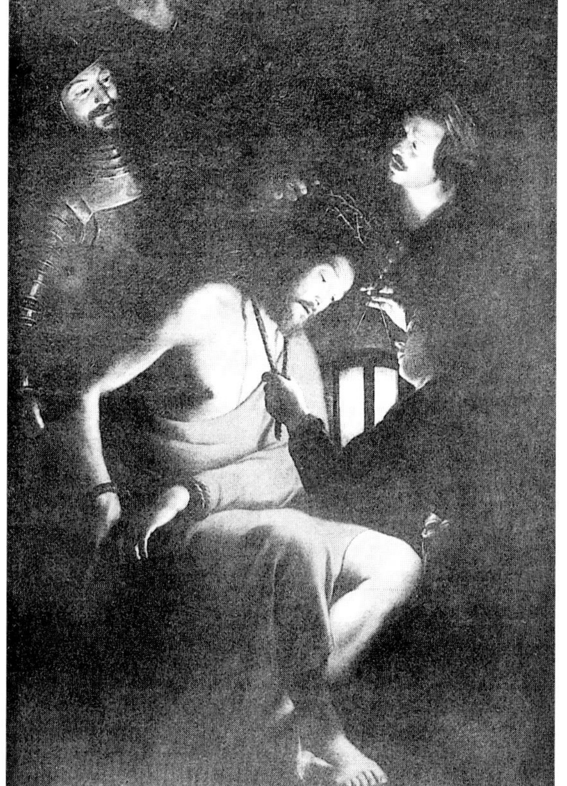

Fig. 3

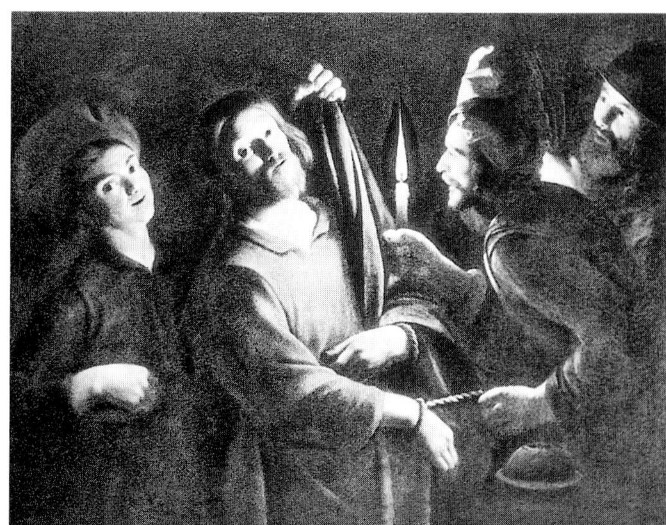

Fig. 4

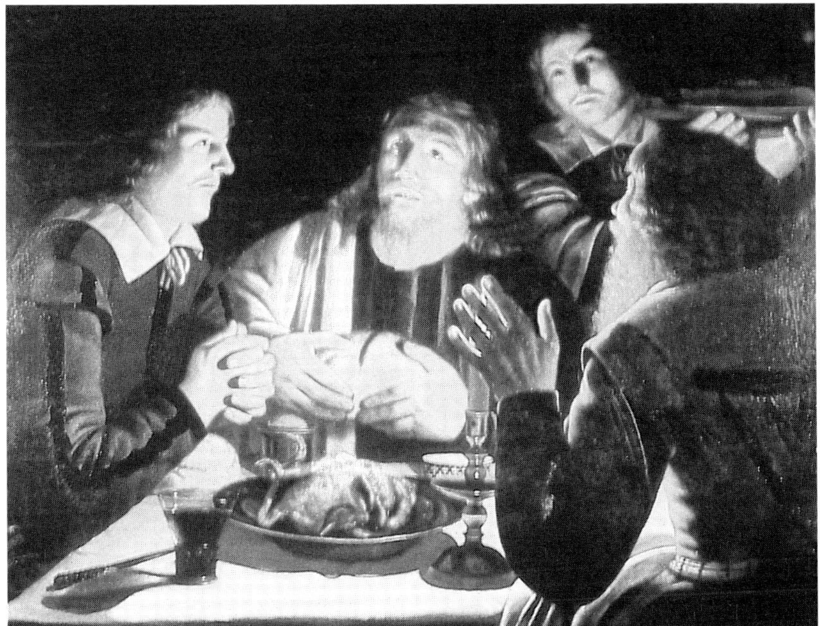

Fig. 5

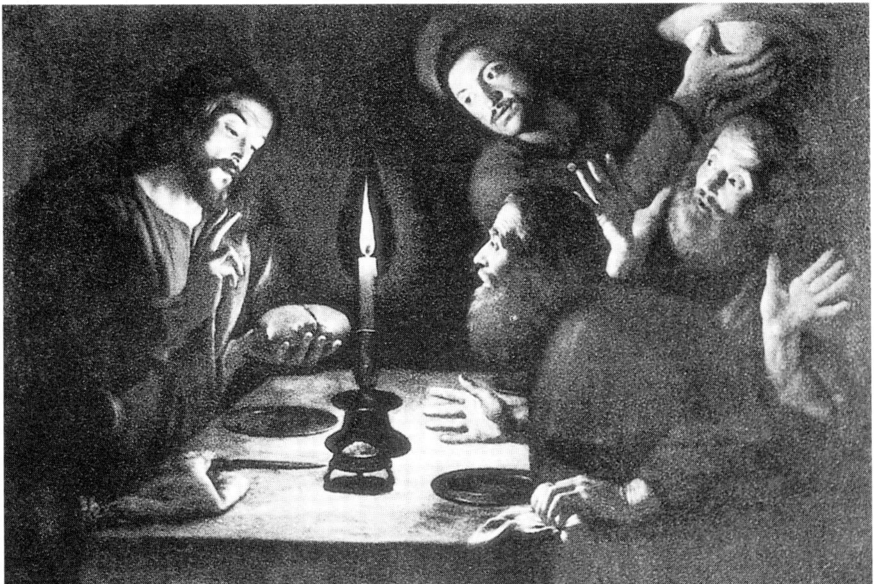

Fig. 7

Candlelight Master group. Oddly, it has often been overlooked that the subtitle of Nicolson's article, "A Follower of Honthorst in Rome," and the place it was published, the *Nederlands Kunsthistorisch Jaarboek*, indicates that he, like Judson and others, at first believed the artist to be Dutch. This accounts for the fact that Honthorst and Volmarijn were major points of stylistic reference for the nocturnal oeuvre that Nicolson brought together.

The situation changed a few years later when Nicolson published a completely revised and updated version of his 1960 article under the title: "The Rehabilitation of Trophime Bigot."[21] With the revelation that the Candlelight Master was French, a new group of players entered the art historical debate hoping to shed some French light on the formerly Dutch nocturnal master.

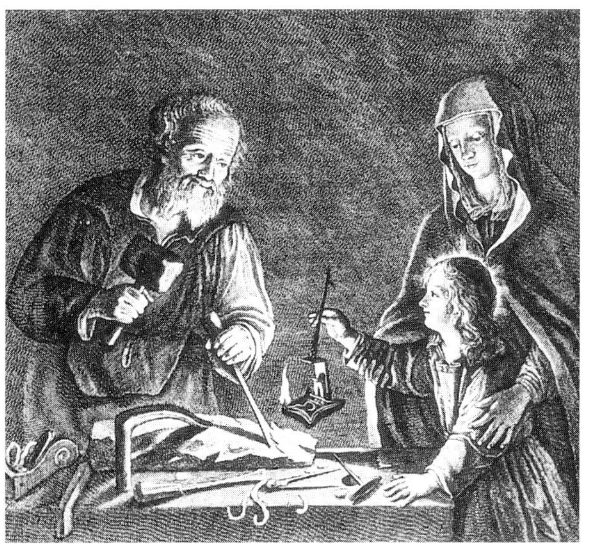

Fig. 8

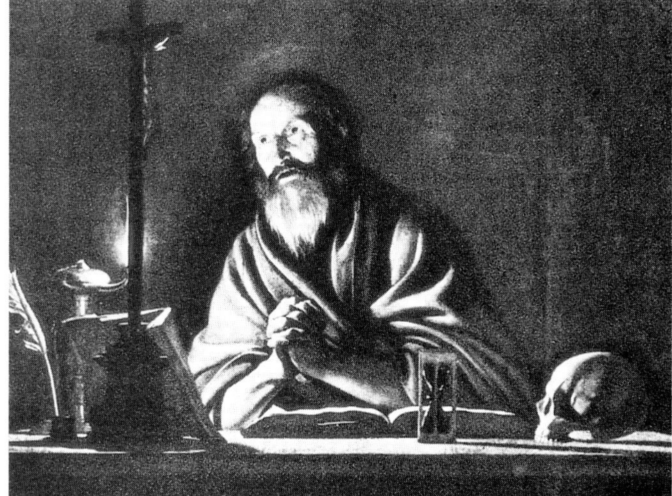

Fig. 9

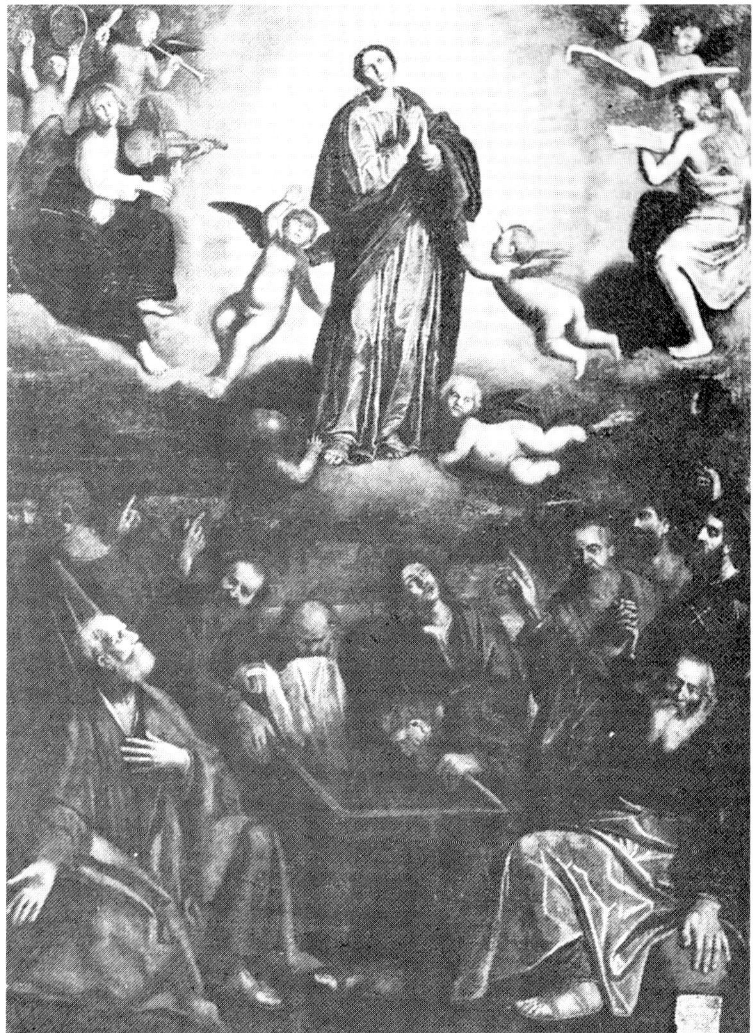

Fig. 11

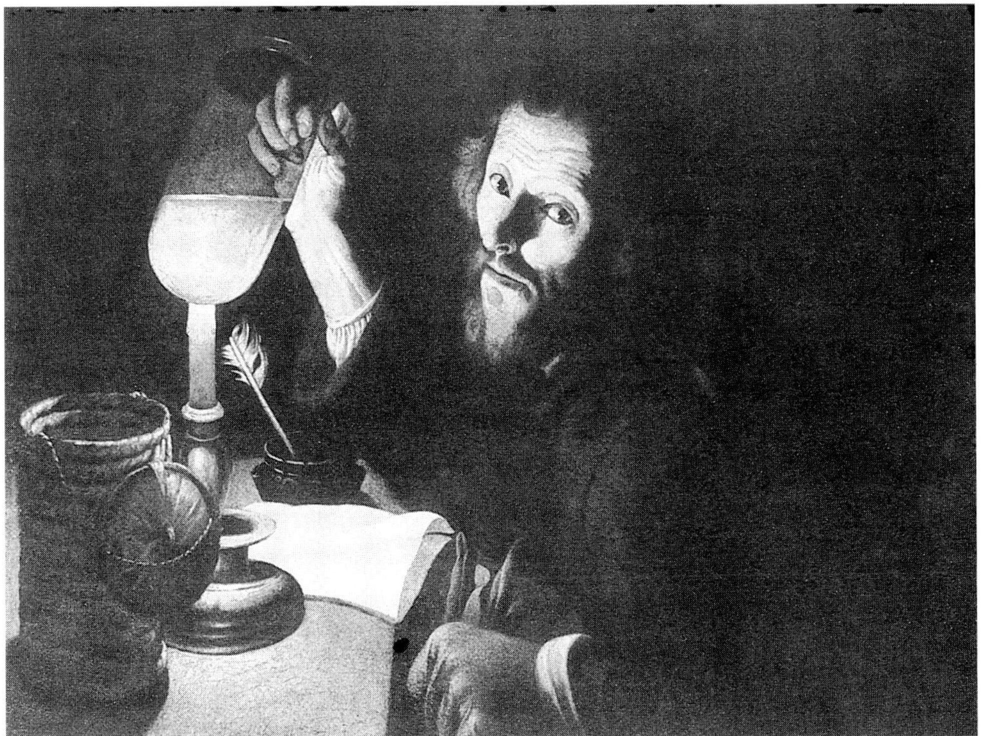

Fig. 10

Trophime Bigot, it should be noted, was hardly unknown to those scholars interested in French Caravaggism before 1960. In 1948, for example, Pariset, on the basis of Coelemans' 1708 engraving with its subscript telling us that it is after Bigot's *Christ in the Carpenter Shop* (Fig. 8),[22] noted a stylistic and thematic connection between the reproduced composition and Georges de La Tour's Louvre picture of the same subject.[23] Furthermore, Anthony Blunt called attention to the relationship between the *St. Jerome* (Fig. 9) in St. Leu-St. Gilles, Paris[24] (which he had earlier published as anonymous French), and the *Doctor Examining a Sample of Urine by Candlelight* (Fig. 10) in the Ashmolean Museum, Oxford,[25] and suggested both were by a French follower of de La Tour, although he ended up ultimately begging the question of nationality when he added "or possibly even a Dutchman."[26] However, the following year Blunt reaffirmed the relationship between the two pictures, especially their French origins, and suggested an attribution to Trophime Bigot.[27] At first, Nicolson followed Blunt and included the St. Leu-St. Gilles painting in his Candlelight Master lists. Later, however, he dropped the work from his posthumously published Bigot list;[28] correctly so, since the picture is by a Flemish hand close to Gerard Seghers.[29] The Ashmolean Museum *Doctor* still remains part of the central Candlelight Master group.

With a French name and a more or less agreed-upon oeuvre, French art history joined Nicolson and attacked the Bigot problem on several fronts. In 1978, Jaques Thuillier, troubled by the stylistic disparity between what was believed to be Bigot's Roman-period nocturnal scenes and the signed and dated Finson-like altarpieces in Provence—for example, Bigot's signed and 1639 dated, *Assumption of the Virgin* (Fig. 11), La Tour-d'Aygues, Parish Church[30]—suggested there were two Trophime Bigots, father and son.[31] Indeed, he created individual biographies and oeuvres and even divided the works into separate catalogue sections for "Trophime Bigot the Elder"[32] and "Trophime Bigot the Younger."[33] Thuillier's resourceful solution—too resourceful as it turned out—neatly disposed of the irreconcilable stylistic differences by assigning to "Bigot the Elder" the ungainly but documented Provence altarpieces, while "Bigot the Younger" was assigned Nicolson's Candlelight Master paintings. Thus, Thuillier's attempt to turn what had previously been a stylistic discrepancy into a generation gap seemed to eliminate the impasse.[34] Never mind that the dates remained irreconcilable, or that the awkward Provence altar pictures began to appear in 1635, after the "younger Bigot" left Rome, or that the "son's" work was earlier than the "father's," it was a solution. Thuillier's hapless creation did not survive long. Jean Boyer, in 1988, after searching the Provence archives, published his findings in an article titled "The one and only Trophime Bigot."[35] Although the demise of the "two Bigots" theory by Boyer's hand was unfortunate for Thuillier, it has been an unmitigated disaster for those scholars who wished to identify Bigot as the Candlelight Master. With no way of reconciling the candlelight pictures—which were assumed to be a product of the nearly twenty years Bigot spent in Italy—and the ungainly but signed Provence altar paintings, there remained no way to associate "the one and only Trophime Bigot" with the Candlelight Master. Nevertheless, some scholars, including Thuillier, have held on to this identification and continued to attribute these nocturnal works to Bigot.[36] Oddly, the death knell to Bigot as the Candlelight Master was sounded in the same exhibition catalogue that gave rise to the "two Bigots" theory. Olivier Michel, who searched the archives of S. Maria in Aquiro in hopes of finding some documentation concerning Bigot, found instead something more puzzling, a 1634 payment for the Passion Chapel in which the artist's name was given as *Mr Jacomo pittore*.[37] Unfortunately, no surname was given. What must be the same artist's name was modified in a 1653 document where the painter of the *Lamentation* (Fig. 2) was named as *Jaccobe*.[38] Significantly, the payment listed in 1634 was only thirty *scudi*; this, plus the fact that the 1653 account cited only the *Lamentation*, has been taken as an indication that the document does not deal with the entire chapel. Suddenly, interested scholars and connoisseurs alike, eyes sharpened by the lens of documentation, found it possible to discern two distinct hands in the chapel, where previously Nicolson had found only a master with some intervention by an assistant. Having suggested, in a 1962 note appended to my dissertation, that the Passion Chapel and Nicolson's oeuvre for the Candlelight Master was the product of at least two hands,[39] I was hardly surprised by these findings.

When viewed closely but dispassionately, the pictures in the Passion Chapel reveal that there is no reason to assume that the two nocturnal scenes, the *Lamentation* (Fig. 2) and the *Christ Crowned with Thorns* (Fig. 3), are by radically different hands. Certainly, there is no longer reason to assign any of the three paintings to Trophime Bigot, although this association is still maintained in the expanded edition of Nicolson's *International Caravaggism*.[40] There are, undeniably, significant differences in the states of preservation of the canvases. One, the *Flagellation* (Fig. 1), is in especially poor condition; nevertheless, condition aside, there are discernable differences between the execution of this canvas and the other two. Most notably, it is the only picture lacking the hallmark device of the Candlelight Master, artificial illumination. However, all three paintings are similar in the scale of the figures, anatomical structure, and physiognomic type, as well as being compositionally coordinated, suggesting that they were all designed together and in the same workshop. Thus, I would assign the damaged *Flagellation* to an assistant or associate of Master Jacomo.[41] Since there is no mention of Trophime Bigot in the archives of S. Maria in Aquiro, and there is no documentation linking his name with any work in Nicolson's Candlelight Master group, there is no need for his name to enter into discussions of the Passion Chapel or, for that matter, in relation to the Candlelight Master. When the best preserved of the Passion Chapel pictures, the *Christ Crowned with Thorns*, is compared with central works always assigned to the Candlelight Master, such as the Pesaro, Musei Civici, *Capture of Christ* (Fig. 12),[42] the Palmer Museum *Denial of St. Peter* (Fig. 6), or the Prato, Galleria Comunale, *Mocking of Christ* (Fig. 13),[43] they are clearly by the same hand. There is only one possible conclusion, Master Jacomo—not Trophime Bigot—is the Candlelight Master.

TROPHIME BIGOT

This does not mean that Trophime Bigot should be completely forgotten. There is abundant documentation concerning the activity of Bigot in Rome. Indeed, *Teofilo Bigotti* appears with certain regularity in the Roman parish records as well as those of the Roman Academy of St. Luke, where he seems to have achieved some prominence during the 1620s. Furthermore, in 1963, Boyer associated *Bigotti* with the Trophime Bigot cited on the subscript of the 1708 engraving as the painter of the *Christ in the Carpenter Shop*,[44] and the following year, independent of Nicolson, he came to the same—erroneous as it now turns out—conclusion: Trophime Bigot was the Candlelight Master.[45]

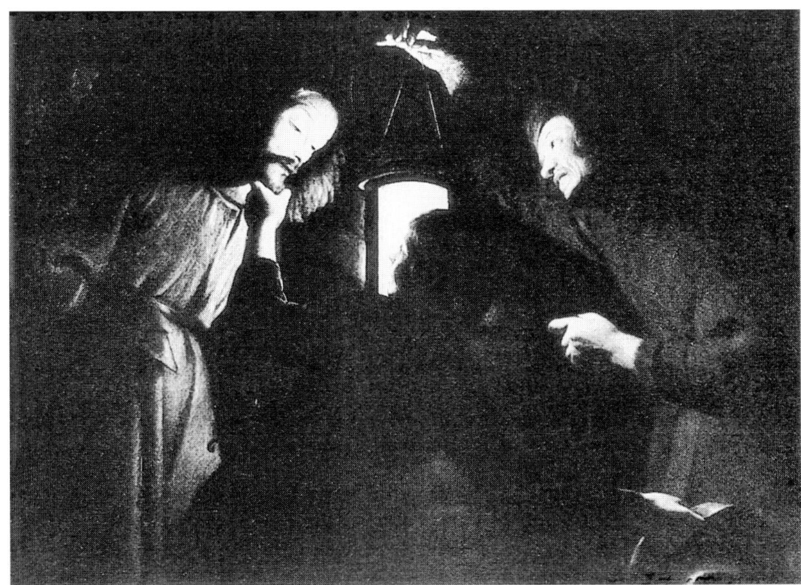

Fig. 12

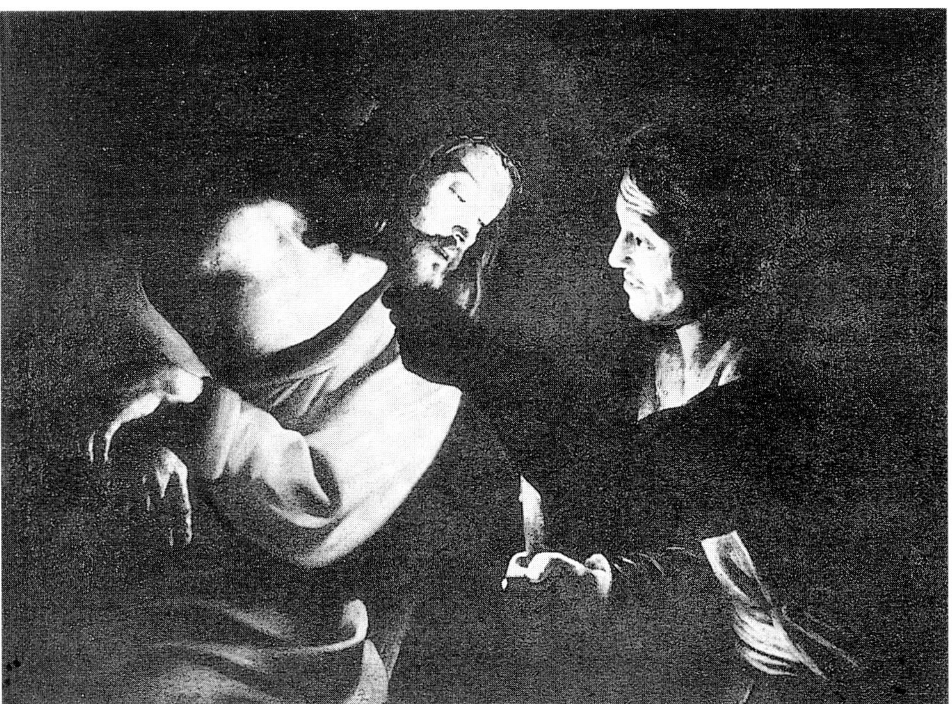

Fig. 13

Boyer also made another significant connection when he suggested that the mysterious *Trufemondi* mentioned by Joachim von Sandrart as a Provence painter of half-length nocturnal scenes was also Trophime Bigot.[46] Thus, the *Teofilo Trufamonti*, who appears as the author of two paintings in the 1638 inventory of the Giustiniani collection, must also be Bigot. Unfortunately, both pictures, a *Holy Family* and *Soldiers Gambling for Christ's Robe*,[47] are either lost or unrecognized.[48] This identification accords with Bousquet's 1960 discovery that in 1630 a certain *Trofamone*, described as a painter, was living with Claude Lorrain and another French artist on the Via Margutta, a street well-known for its hospitality toward foreign artists in Rome.[49] In 1634, still living with Claude, his name was listed as *Teofilo*. This locates Bigot within the artistic circle that Sandrart sometimes frequented in Rome. Despite these provocative connections and relationships, it has not been possible to associate any documented Roman period nocturnal scene with Bigot, although there have been valiant attempts. At the moment, the only certain Roman period Bigot, recently published by Tiberia, is the *Adoration of the Magi* (Fig. 14) in the sacristy of San Marco, Rome.[50] During a recent cleaning, this picture, painted in the style of the large altarpieces in Provence, revealed a signature, "Teofilo Trufam . . ."; unfortunately, only the first three digits of the date, "163(?)," are legible. Nevertheless, one cannot ignore the evidence of the Giustiniani inventory, or Sandrart's report that Bigot painted nocturnal scenes in Rome. Since Sandrart lived in the Palazzo Giustiniani, and must have known the two pictures, as well as Bigot himself, there is no reason to doubt his statement. However, the Giustiniani inventory does not indicate that these lost pictures by Bigot, described as supraports, were nocturnal scenes, although Sandrart's report suggests that they very well might have been. Boyer has published two candlelight works, a *St. Jerome* (Fig. 15),[51] and a *Denial of St. Peter*.[52] Unfortunately, neither work is signed and there is no documentation to confirm the attributions. Nevertheless, if nothing else, it does at least tentatively affirm Sandrart's statement and point to a tradition of nocturnal representation in Provence. However, neither work appears to be by the same hand responsible for any of the three key pictures in S. Maria in Aquiro.

That Trophime Bigot produced some nocturnal pictures is hardly news. Earlier, both Blunt and Pariset cited the subscript on the 1708 engraving of Bigot's now lost *Christ in the Carpenter Shop* (Fig. 8) in connection with Georges de La Tour. Although the 1744 catalogue of Boyer d'Aguilles collection, in Aix-en-Provence, in which the print later appeared, reports that the painting was acquired locally, nothing else about it is known.[53] There is no reason to assume that any of the several painted versions of the composition noted by Nicolson and Cuzin is based on the lost original rather than the print. Indeed, they are in the same sense as the engraving.[54]

Of somewhat greater interest for our understanding of Bigot's art is the fact that the theme, *Christ in the Carpenter Shop*, as well as the composition in the engraving can be related to two Roman period paintings by Honthorst, the earliest of which can be dated to 1617.[55] This is hardly surprising since Bigot was active in Rome during the 1620's, when Honthorst's influence was at its zenith. There is also a third composition of *Christ in the Carpenter Shop*, at Bob Jones University, attributed to Bigot by Judson,[56] but more reasonably assigned to Honthorst by Nicolson.[57] Also related to the print and its theme—although in mirror image—and thus also comparable to the Bob Jones University painting, is a canvas of the same subject in a French private collection (Fig. 16). Cuzin has published a close variant of this composition in Rome (Fig. 17).[58] This does not mean, of course, that these works were painted in Rome. Indeed, the 1744 catalogue of Boyer d'Aguilles collection tells us the picture was acquired locally. Thuillier has published still another variant of this provocative composition that he attributed—certainly incorrectly—to Stomer.[59] Despite the fact that he reproduced the picture on the same page as the Bigot engraving, Thuillier did not come to the obvious conclusion, or, indeed, to any con-clusion, since he makes no mention of the painting in his text. This is probably due to the fact that Thuillier still apparently believes that Bigot is the Candlelight Master.[60] Nevertheless, this interesting painting, with its subtle sense of color and light, is close to the 1708 print without being a direct copy. I can see no reason why it should not be by the same hand as the lost Bigot original reproduced by Coelemans. Indeed, Cuzin has, correctly in my estimation, attributed the Roman variant of this work to Bigot, and has added still another painting seemingly by the same hand, a *Denial of St. Peter* (Fig. 18), in a French private collection.[61] One must remain cau-tious, however, given the lack of supporting documentation.

What Cuzin has to say about Bigot's stylistic sources does raise some questions in my mind. He compares, for example, the soldier in Bigot's *Denial of St. Peter* with Honthorst's famous *Christ Before the High Priest*.[62] This circa 1617 painting, now in London, was originally in the Giustiniani collection and is one of the early monuments of northern Caravaggism in Rome. Understandably, Cuzin would like to link Bigot's style with Honthorst's Roman period mas-terpiece, thus placing him in the mainstream of northern Caravaggism in Italy. But there are far more cogent relationships one can make for the *Denial of St. Peter*, although they locate Bigot's candlelight production in a different artistic circle, and closer to such Flemish Caravaggesque artists as Adam de Coster, active in Antwerp, who specialized in nocturnal

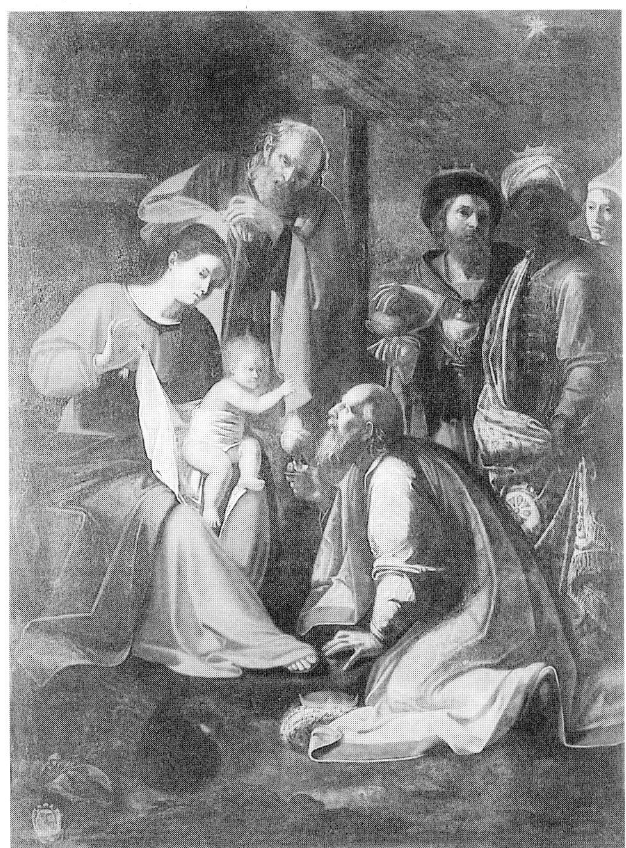

Fig. 14

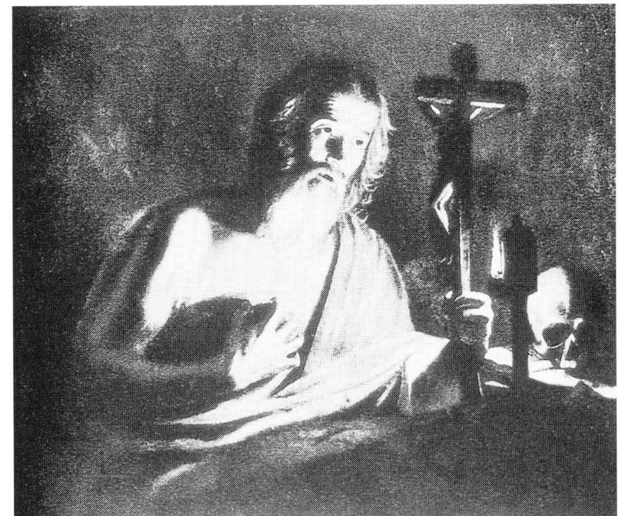

Fig. 15

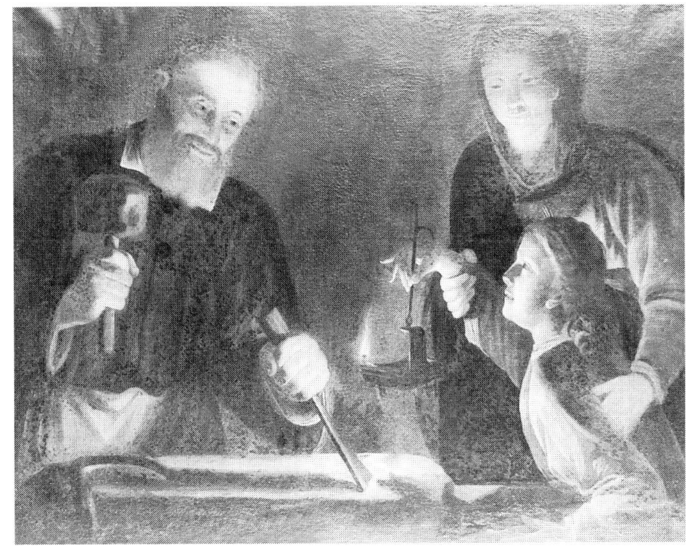

Fig. 17

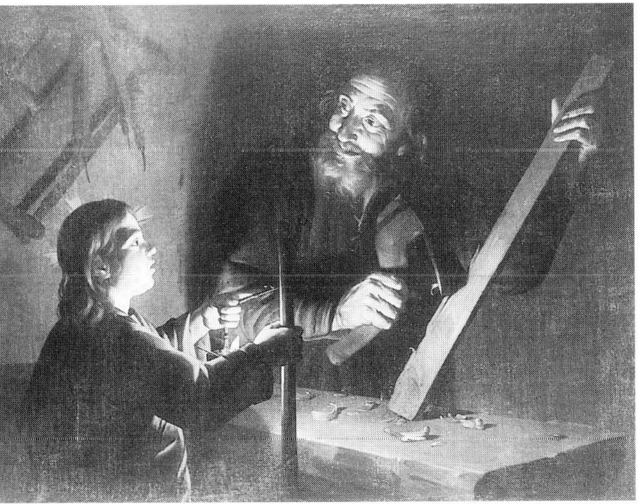

Fig. 16

depictions. For example, the lost profile on the left of the Bigot, in which Cuzin saw the influence of Honthorst, can be more directly compared with works like de Coster's *Scene of Mercenary Love* (Fig. 19), in an American private collection.[63] It is also worth noting that during the 1620s another Flemish Caravaggesque painter, Gerard Seghers, painted a number of nocturnal depictions of the *Denial of St. Peter,* for example, his important canvas in the North Carolina Museum of Art, Raleigh.[64]

As for Bigot, I would like to add another picture to his small oeuvre, the *Angels Lamenting the Dead Christ* (Fig. 20).[65] As the heads of the angels and the patterns of light are comparable to an unfortunately damaged *Supper at Emmaus* (Fig. 21) in the Carmelite Convent, Aix-en-Provence,[66] it was most likely executed in Provence, like the other nocturnal pictures assignable to him.

Granted, none of the nocturnal paintings now given to Bigot is especially close to the large, Finson-like altarpieces he executed after he left Rome in 1634, but this may be a product of the conservative tastes of his ecclesiastical patrons. The smaller easel pictures, however, apparently made for a more discerning clientele, provided him with an opportunity to produce the kind of nocturnal depiction that Sandrart had admired in Rome.

MASTER JACOMO

Given the confusion in the names found in the archives of S. Maria in Aquiro, it is likely that Master Jacomo was a foreigner in Rome, possibly French, or perhaps, like Renieri, Franco-Flemish. Some support for this can be found in a superior and better preserved version of the Teramo, Museo Civico,[67] *Cupid and Psyche* (Fig. 22) that appeared in a 1983 Christie's, New York sale. This work may be compared with one of Vouet's rare excursions into artificial illumination in his circa 1625 rendition of the same subject, in Lyon.[68] Significantly, there were several artists named Jacques who lived with Vouet in Rome,[69] and others are mentioned in the various Roman archives, for whom we have no certain works, any one of whom could be our Master Jacomo.[70]

It is also possible to add several new pictures to the oeuvre of the former Candlelight Master, Master Jacomo. The most interesting of these works is the *Boy with Dead Birds and Fish* (Fig. 23). This unusual painting, formerly on the English art market (1987), can be related, at least in general approach to the theme, to pictures like the Doria collection, Rome, *Boy Singeing a Bat* (Fig. 24).[71] Unfortunately, there is no technical evidence concerning the canvas of this latter picture and the other related Doria works, but it seems plausible to think that it has been reduced in size. Indeed, three of the four Doria pictures now assignable to Master Jacomo have unusually tight compositional formats; for example, the *Young Singer Crowned with Laurel* (Fig. 25).[72] Furthermore, there is no thematic or iconographic reason to link these pictures, aside from their nocturnal light. Certainly their themes have nothing in common. Only the *Girl Delousing Herself* (Fig. 26) has sufficient space around the figure.[73] Even the San Francisco *Singer* (Fig. 27), often related to the Doria paintings,[74] reveals more in the way of space and setting. Thus, it seems probable that the sizes of the Doria pictures have been adjusted to make a pseudo series. The more typically northern Caravaggesque *Boy with Dead Birds and Fish* (Fig. 23), with his exposed shoulder and arm, may be an early work by Master Jacomo, representing his first response to Caravaggio and especially to his many northern followers in Rome. Importantly, the surface of this new version reveals a sense of modeling closer to the *Cupid and Psyche* than any of the more broadly executed Doria pictures, also suggesting an earlier date.

It is also possible to assign to Master Jacomo another picture, a *Pipe Smoker* (Fig. 28), in the Ambrosiana, Milan.[75] In several elements, this picture can be related to the *Boy with Dead Birds and Fish*, including the off-the-shoulder blouse and the use of a foreground barrier. By including a prominently displayed sword in his picture, Master Jacomo links his theme with a typical Utrecht Caravaggesque type.[76] Indeed, Utrecht pipe smokers and such related themes as

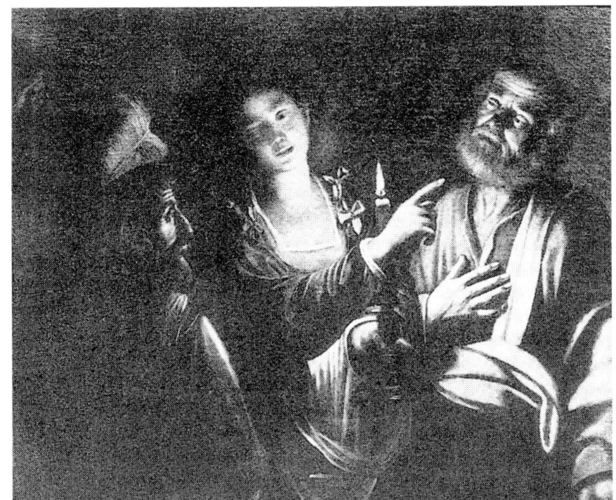

Fig. 18

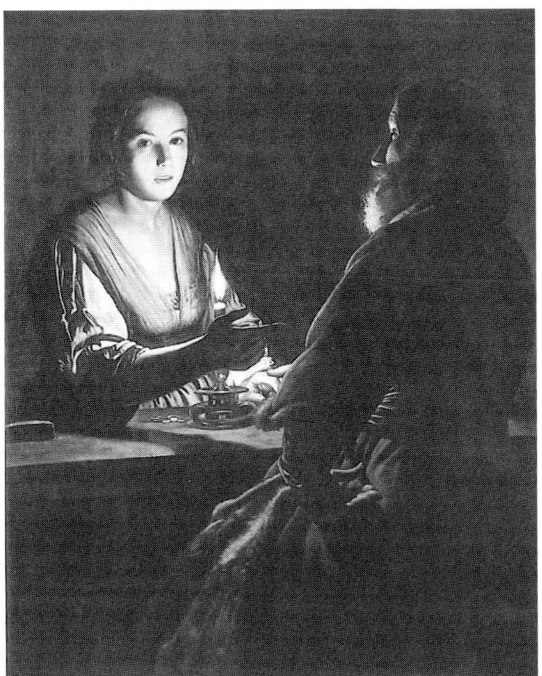

Fig. 19

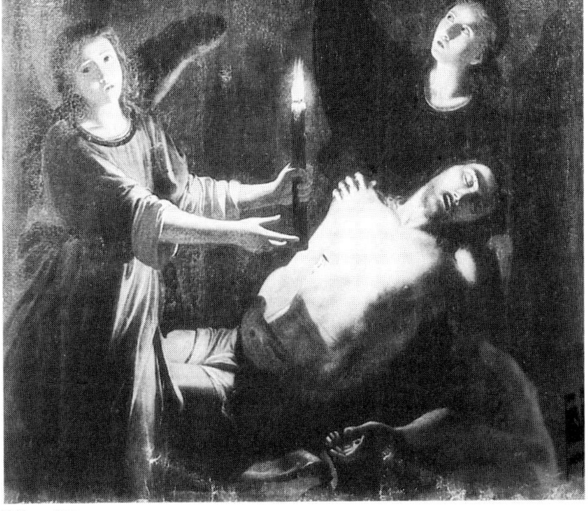

Fig. 20

Fig. 21

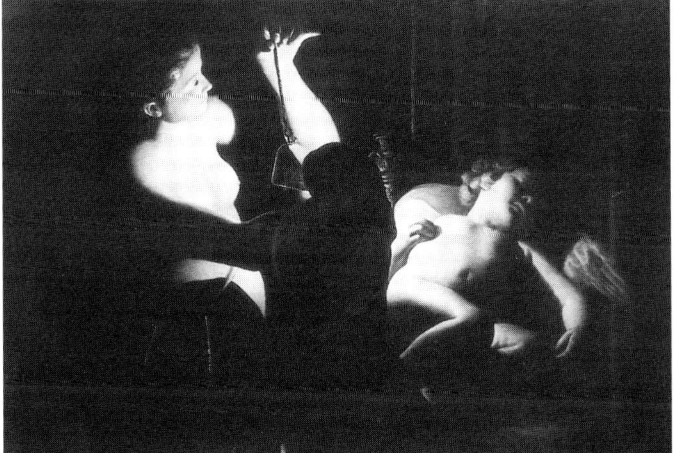

Fig. 22

boys blowing on fire brands while holding swords were painted by both Honthorst and Ter Brugghen around 1623.[77] This aspect of the theme was brought to Italy by Stomer, who painted it several times. By including a sword, Master Jacomo clearly intends to link smoking and fire with the choleric temperament and the hot and dry humor.

Not Master Jacomo

It is also possible to remove a number of pictures from the core Master Jacomo group as well as his circle, including one I placed there erroneously.[78] When the unusual, but much abraded *Hermit with a Bag of Bones* (Fig. 29), present location unknown, was cleaned, it turned out to be a signed and 1629 dated work by Willem van Vliet. This odd picture first appeared in a 1980 London sale,[79] where it was imaginatively titled *The Grave Robber*, and catalogued as Volmarijn. Van Vliet, a Delft painter better known for his portraits, executed a number of innovative Caravaggesque works, many with artificial illumination, for example, his signed and 1624 dated *Pipe Smoker and Bean Eater by Candlelight* (Fig. 30) in Detroit.[80] Like the Candlelight Master, van Vliet's nocturnal works have sometimes masqueraded as Volmarijn. Given the documented contacts between Volmarijn and Delft—he sold pigments to, among others, Leonart Bramer[81]—it seems likely that van Vliet was the source of the Rotterdam painter's small candlelight production rather than Honthorst. The Detroit picture is also of interest for its close-up composition of two heads and, of course, the theme of the bean eater, both of which may be compared with Georges de La Tour *Old Peasant Couple Eating*, in Berlin.[82]

I would also reassign the *Man Masking a Flame with Paper Shade*, in a Milwaukee private collection. This picture, which first appeared in Nicolson's 1979 Bigot lists,[83] appears to be by a Dutch hand, and may be compared with some of the early Caravaggesque works by Jacob Gerritsz. Cuyp, to whom I would tentatively assign it.[84] Physiognomically, the type found in this work is different from Master Jacomo's usual male model. Related to the Milwaukee painting is a work known to me, and apparently to Nicolson, through a photo in the Witt Library's Volmarijn file, *St. Francis in Meditation* (Fig. 31).[85] In 1979, Nicolson thought it was by an artist in contact with Bigot in Rome.[86] Again, Jacob Gerritsz. Cuyp would seem a better choice. I also have serious questions about three pictures Nicolson assigned to his Bigot—my Master Jacomo—group. The most interesting of these, the *St. Paul Visiting St. Peter in Prison*, Marquess of Exeter Collection, Burghley House, Stamford,[87] has some affinity with the pictures I assigned Cuyp, and might turn out to be by him, but at this time I would prefer only to remove the picture from the central Master Jacomo group. I would also set aside two depictions of the *Liberation of St. Peter*, one formerly in the Paris private collection,[88] and the second formerly with Victor Spark, New York (Fig. 32).[89] These works would seem to be by the same hand and may repeat lost Master Jacomo compositions. The execution of the ex-Spark picture, however, which I have studied firsthand, is not of the same quality as other Master Jacomo pictures I have seen. Perhaps they will eventually turn out to be from the studio of Master Jacomo, or even by a follower.

Several pictures from Nicolson's "circle of Bigot in Rome" can also be reassigned to other hands, including the Utrecht painter Peter Wtewael, son of the more famous late mannerist, Joachim. One such picture, the *Card Players* (Fig. 33), Arniston Estate Trustees, Gorebridge, was first assigned to the Candlelight Master by Nicolson in 1960,[90] but disappeared from his 1965 lists. In 1979, however, the picture reappeared, this time assigned to an artist in Rome in contact with Bigot.[91] Earlier, I thought that the somewhat better version of this same composition, in a Cannes private collection, might be by van Vliet.[92] Since both these pictures compare favorably with Peter Wtewael's *Supper at Emmaus* in Oslo,[93] I would now attribute both versions to him. A *St. Jerome Writing*, catalogued by Nicolson as "circle of Bigot" has recently surfaced allowing me to study it firsthand.[94] Now in a New York private collection, there is little question that this striking picture is by Carlo Dolci. There are also several other adjustments I would make to the current Candlelight Master/Bigot lists, but these will have to wait for another article.

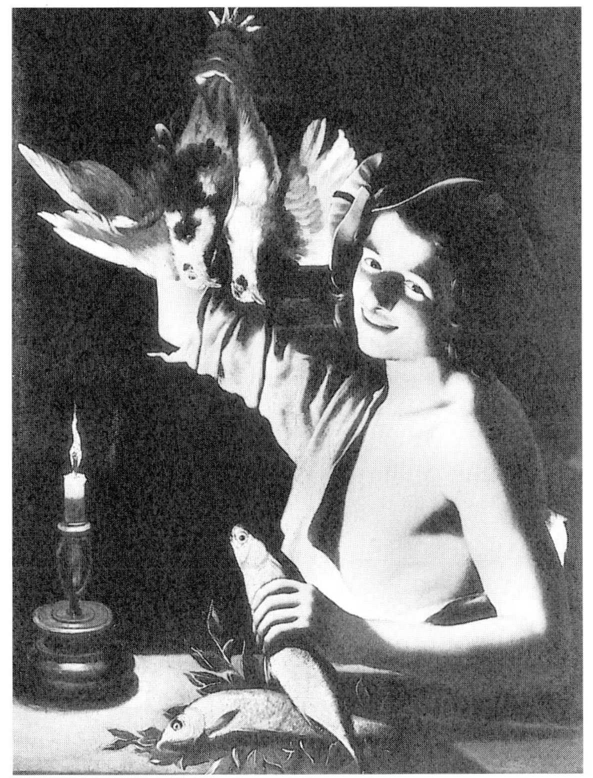

Fig. 23

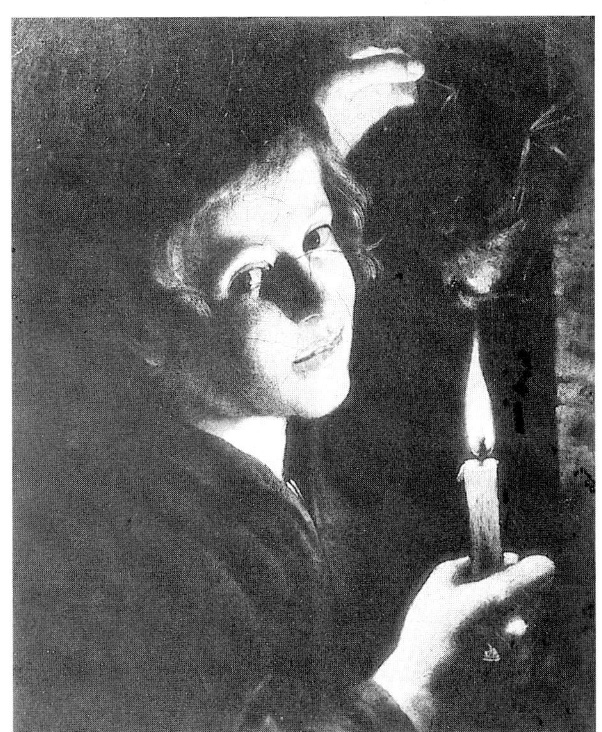

Fig. 24

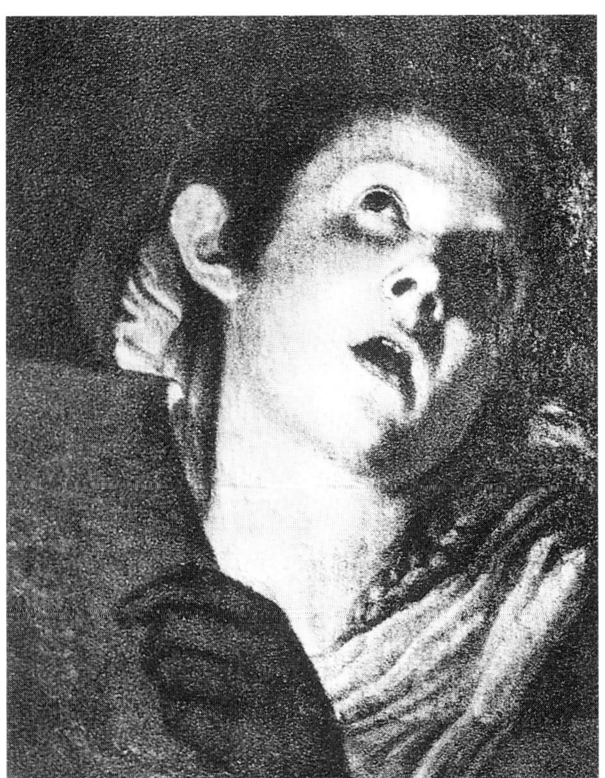

Fig. 25

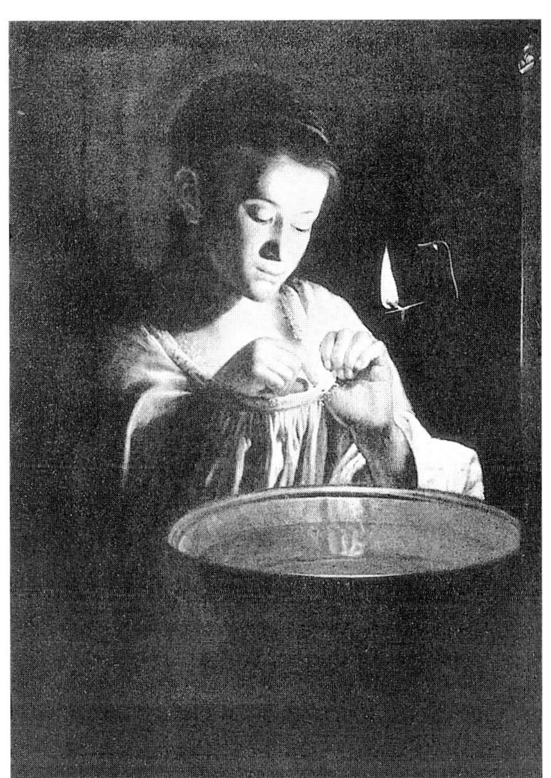

Fig. 26

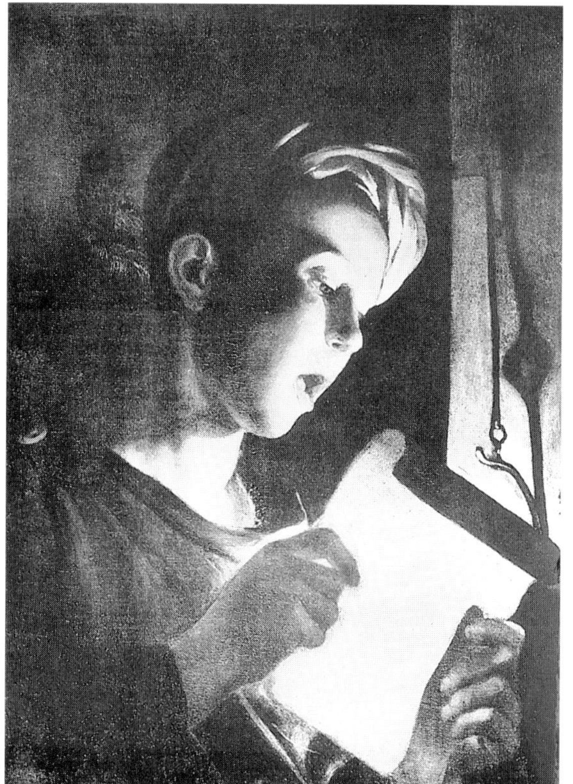

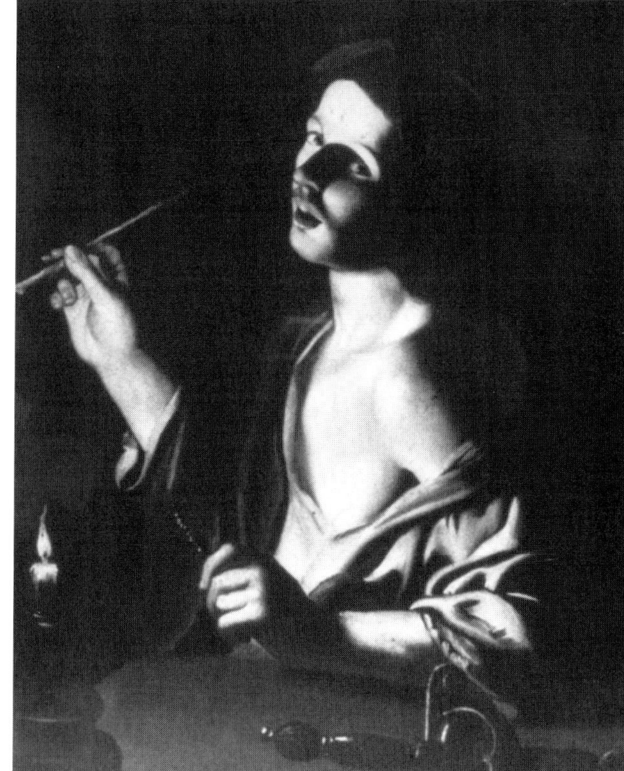

Fig. 27 Master Jacomo, *Singer*. San Francisco, Fine Arts Museums.

Fig. 28 Master Jacomo, *Pipe Smoker*. Milan, Ambrosiana.

Fig. 29 Willem van Vliet, *Hermit with a Bag of Bones*, signed and dated 1629. Present location unknown.

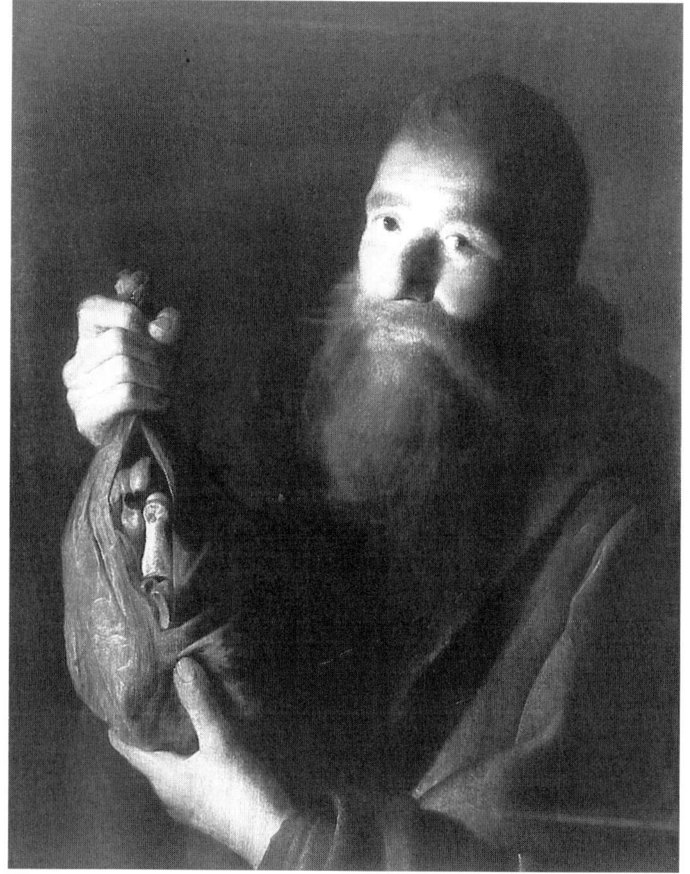

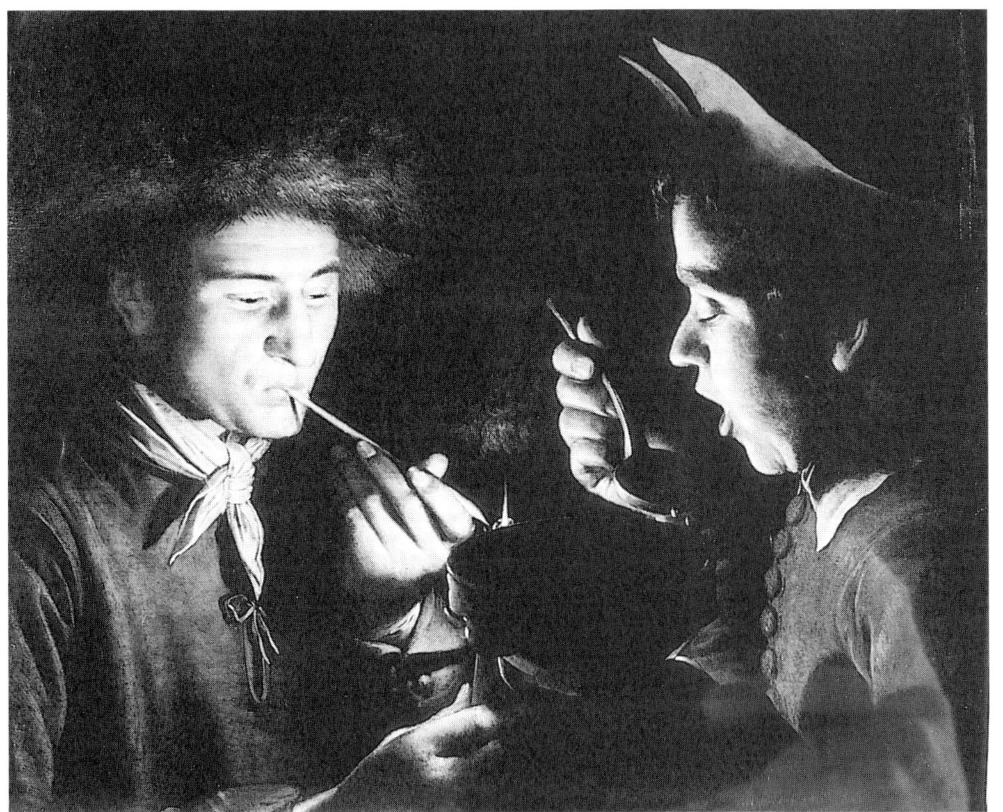

Fig. 30

Fig. 30 Willem van Vliet, *Pipe Smoker and Bean Eater by Candlelight*, signed and dated 1624. Detroit, Detroit Institute of Arts.

Fig. 31 Jacob Gerritsz. Cuyp (?), *St. Francis in Meditation*. Present location unknown.

Fig. 32 Follower of Master Jacomo, *The Liberation of St. Peter*. Present location unknown.

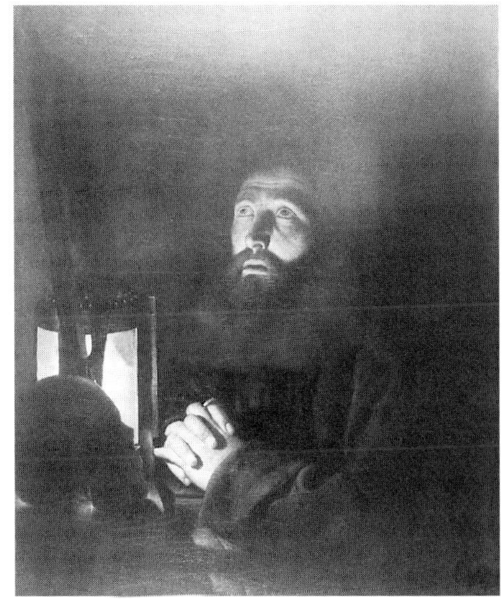

Fig. 31

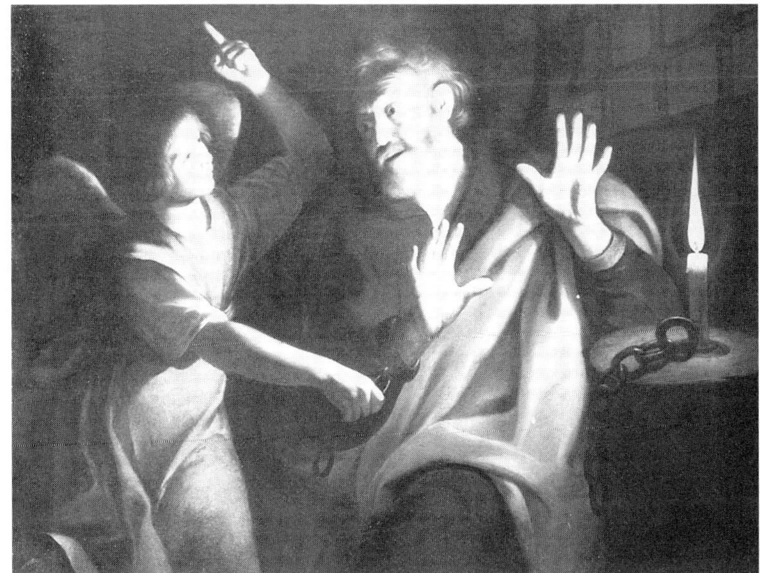

Fig. 32

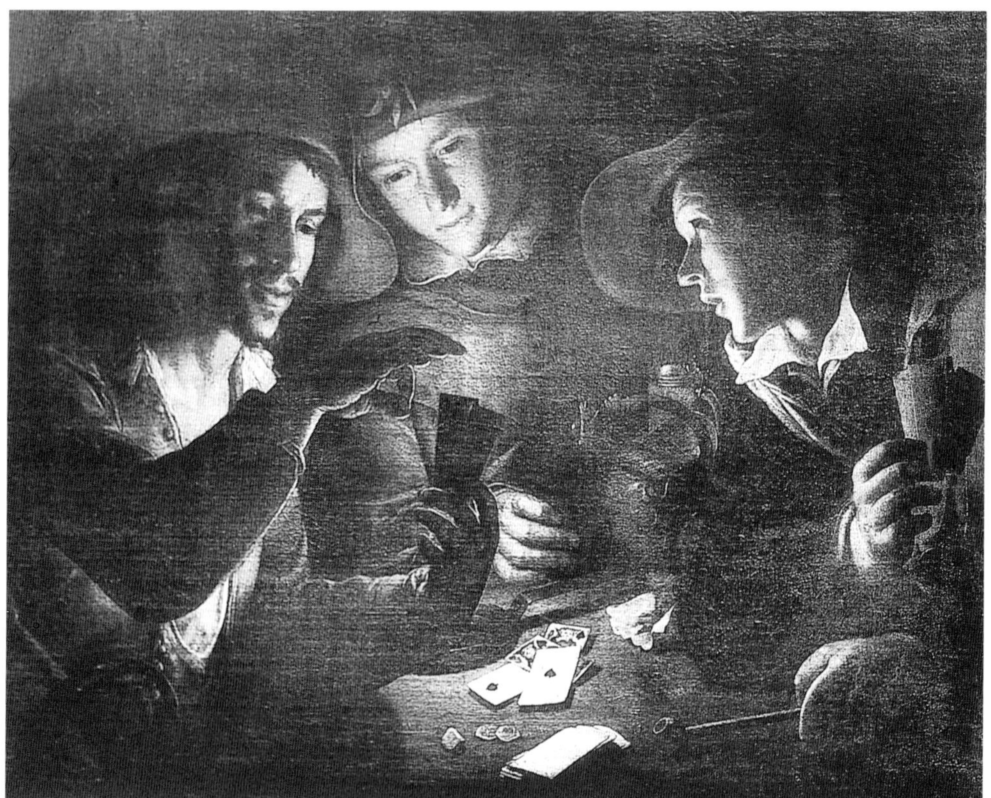

Fig. 33 Peter Wtewael, *Card Players*. Formerly Gorebridge, Arniston Estate Trustees.

Fig. 33

Endnotes

* Some of the research used in this paper was supported by a PSC-CUNY research grant.

1 J. R. Judson, *Gerrit van Honthorst*, The Hague, 1958, cat. nos. 45, 46, and 50, the three paintings in the Passion Chapel, S. M. in Aquiro, Rome.

2 S. M. M. Furness, *Georges de La Tour of Lorraine*, London, 1949, pp. 6–7, 115–16, plate 16; *Doctor Examining a Sample of Urine*, Ashmolean Museum, Oxford.

3 S. J. Gudlaugsson, "Crijn Hendricksz. Volmarijn, een Rotterdamse Caravaggist," *Oud-Holland*, 67, 1952, pp. 241–47, and J. R. Judson, "Possible Additions to Crijn Hendricksz. Volmarijn," *Oud-Holland*, 70, 1955, pp. 181–88.

4 E. S. King, "A newly discovered Stomer," *Burlington Magazine*, 95, 1953, pp. 169–70; the picture is *Judith and Holofernes*, Walters Art Gallery, Baltimore.

5 Benedict Nicolson, "The 'Candlelight Master'—A Follower of Honthorst in Rome," *Nederlands Kunsthistorisch Jaarboek*, 1960, pp. 121 ff.

6 Benedict Nicolson, "The Rehabilitation of Trophime Bigot," *Art and Literature*, 4, Spring, 1965, pp. 66–105. This is an English version of what is essentially the same article published in French in 1964, Benedict Nicolson, "Un caravagiste aixois, le maitre à la chandelle," *Art de France*, 4, 1964, pp. 116–39. All references will be to the improved 1965 English version.

7 Leonard J. Slatkes, "Rembrandt Research Project, vol. I," *The Art Bulletin*, 71, 1989, pp. 139–44.

8 *Michelangelo Merisi da Caravaggio. Come Nascono i Capolavori*, Florence and Rome, 1991.

9 F. Titi, *Ammaestramento nelle Chiese di Roma*, Rome, 1686, pp. 325–26.

10 G. J. Hoogewerff, "Die Werken van Gerard Honthorst te Rome," *Onze Kunst*, 1917, pp. 47–48.

11 Hermann Voss, *Die Malerei des Barock in Rom*, Berlin, 1924–25, p. 469.

12 Judson, 1958, cat. nos. 45, 46, and 50, the three paintings in the Passion Chapel, S. M. in Aquiro, Rome.

13 Nicolson, 1960, pp. 130–32, 150–51, and Nicolson, 1965, cat. nos. 10, 11, and 12. For Nicolson, the *Flagellation* and the *Lamentation* both reveal the participation of an unknown assistant. He considers only the *Christ Crowned with Thorns* to be entirely by the hand of the Candlelight Master.

14 Longhi's opinion is quoted by F. Zeri, *La Galleria Spada*, Florence, 1954, under cat. no. 289.

15 Nicolson, 1965, cat. 6.

16 For the subject of this puzzling picture and a discussion of the various attributions, see Ivan Gaskell, "Vermeer, Judgement, and Truth," *Burlington Magazine*, 126, 1984, pp. 557-61.

17 Judson, 1955, pp. 181–88; see also Gudlaugsson, 1952, pp. 241–47.

18 *Rotterdamse Meesters uit de Gouden Eeuw*, Historisch Museum Rotterdam, 1994, cat. 68; ill. in color, p. 316.

19 Nicolson, 1965, cat. 24.

20 See A. Lefebure, *Chantilly, musée Condé*, Ouest France, 1986, p. 18, no. 124, ill. in color.

21 Nicolson, 1965, pp. 66–105.

22 Jean Boyer, "Un caravagesque français oublié: Trophime Bigot," *Bulletin de la Société de l'Histoire de l'Art Français 1963*, 1964, pp. 35–36. The painting, now lost, was in the Boyer d'Aguilles collection, Aix-en-Provence.

23 François-Georges Pariset, *Georges de La Tour*, Paris, 1948, pp. 404–5, n. 26.

24 Nicolson, 1965, cat. 19.

25 Nicolson, 1965, cat. 33. Benedict Nicolson, *The International Caravaggesque Movement*, Oxford, 1979.

26 A. Blunt, review of Furness, *Georges de La Tour*, *Burlington Magazine*, 91, 1949, p. 297.

27 A. Blunt, review of Pariset, *Georges de La Tour*, *Burlington Magazine*, 92, 1950, p. 145. Pariset, 1948, plate 31, Fig. 1, it should be noted, also published the *St. Jerome*, and like Blunt also thought the St. Leu-St. Gilles picture was by a French artist; however, he believed it repeated a lost Georges de La Tour.

28 Nicolson, 1979.

29 For the Seghers attribution see Nicolson, 1989, p. 174, and Fig. 1428. This picture was apparently unknown to Dorothea Bieneck, *Gerard Seghers*, Lingen, 1992. It is worth noting that the *St. Jerome at his Work Table*, canvas, 82 x 106 cm., sold Paris, Drouot, 4 Dec. 1987, lot 120, ill. in color, as attributed to Trophime Bigot, from the collection of the 5th Earl of Craven, would seem to be close to the Utrecht painter, Jan van Bijlert.

30 *La Peinture en Provence au XVIIe siècle*, Musée des Beaux-Arts, Palais Longchamp, Marseilles, 1978, cat. 3, as "Bigot the Elder."

31 *Ibid.*, pp. 3–9.

32 *Ibid.*, pp. 4–5.

33 *Ibid.*, pp. 6–9.

34 Thuillier was followed by Christopher Wright, *The French Painters of the Seventeenth Century*, Boston, 1985, p. 139, who also lists a Bigot I and Bigot II (the Younger?).

35 Jean Boyer, "The one and only Trophime Bigot," *Burlington Magazine*, 130, 1988, pp. 355–57.

36 Jacques Thuillier, *Georges de La Tour*, Paris, 1993, pp. 174, 178, 196.

37 Marseille, 1978, p. 3.

38 *Ibid.*, p. 3.

39 As early as 1962, I suggested that more than one hand was at work; see Nicolson, 1965, p. 72, n. 16.

40 Benedict Nicolson, *Caravaggism in Europe*, revised and enlarged by Luisa Vertova, 3 vols., Turin, 1989, vol. 1, p. 60.

41 I cannot accept G. Papi's attribution to Circignani, "Sull'attività di Antonio Circignani pittore caravaggesco," *Paragone*, no. 483, 1990, pp. 95–114. This attribution is also rejected by Arnauld Brejon de

Lavergnée, "Le Caravagisme en Europe: A propos de la réédition des Nicolson," *Gazette des Beaux-Arts*, 122, 1993, p. 207, under Fig. 829.

42 Nicolson, 1965, cat. 8, plate 4.

43 *Ibid.*, cat. 9, plate 5. See also *All Museums - Prato. English Guide*, 1985, pp. 37–38, Fig. 2, ill. in color. See also the catalogue *Pitture francese nelle collezioni pubbliche fiorentine*, Florence, Palazzo Pitti, 1977, by Pierre Rosenberg *et al.*, p. 155, cat. 101, ill.

44 Boyer, 1963, pp. 34–51.

45 J. Boyer, "Nouveaux documents inédits sur le peintre Trophime Bigot," *Bulletin de la Société de l'art français*, 1964, pp. 152–158.

46 Joachim von Sandrart, *Academie der Bau-, Bild- und Mahlerey-Künste . . .*, ed. Peltzer, 1925, p. 259.

47 Luigi Salerno, "The Picture Gallery of Vincenzo Giustiniani," *Burlington Magazine*, 102, 1960, p. 98, nos. 107 and 108. The pictures are described as *soprapporte*.

48 Interestingly, another Giustiniani artist, Francesco Parone, from Milan, also worked in S. Maria in Aquiro, although his works have now disappeared. See Salerno, 1960, p. 98, no. 119. Although there is no apparent connection between Parone and the Passion Chapel, the fact that he died in October of 1634 suggests that the Giustiniani may have been involved with obtaining both commissions: that is to say, for Master Jacomo and Parone.

49 J. Bousquet, "Les Relations de Poussin avec le Milieu Romain," *Nicolas Poussin*, Paris, 1960, I, p. 6.

50 Vitaliano Tiberia, "Un'aggiunta per Teofilo Trufamond," *Bolletino d'Arte*, 64, 1991, pp. 71–74.

51 Boyer, 1963, p. 49, and Fig. 3; the picture is in the Parish Church, Saint-Antonin (Bouches-du- Rhône).

52 *Ibid.*, p. 49, Fig. 4, Hôtel de Ville, Éguilles (Bouches-du- Rhône); significantly, the town hall is the former château of the Boyer d'Éguilles family.

53 See Ph. de Pointel, *Recherches sur la vie et les ouvrages de quelques Peintres provinciaux . . .*, Paris, 1, 1847, p. 140, and *Recueil d'Estampes d'après les Tableaux . . . dans le cabinet de M. Boyer d'Aguilles . . .*, Paris, 1744, no. XXIII, and Nicolson, 1965, cat. 4.

54 A version in a private collection, Aix-en-Provence, is illustrated by J. P. Cuzin, "Trophime Bigot in Rome. A suggestion," *Burlington Magazine*, 121, May 1979, pp. 301–5, Fig. 36, as by "Trophime Bigot (?)," and cited in Marseille, 1978, pp. 164–65, ill., Fig. 2, with incorrect dimensions. The painting was sold at Sotheby Parke Bernet, Monaco, 25 June 1984, lot 3364; the correct size is 72 x 91 cm. on an unlined canvas. I might also add that I am not completely convinced by Cuzin's attribution of the unusual *St. Peter and the Servant*, Musée Granet, Aix-en-Provence, to Bigot. It is difficult to relate this odd composition to any certain Bigot picture.

55 Judson, 1958, cat. 27, convent of San Silvestro, Montecompatri, and cat. 27a, Hermitage, St. Petersburg.

56 *Ibid.*, p. 155. The picture does not seem to be by the same hand as the several versions of the composition of the same theme I believe to be by Bigot. See the discussion below.

57 Nicolson, 1989, p. 123, Fig. 1234.

58 Cuzin, 1979, Fig. 39, as by an anonymous painter in Rome, c. 1630; Rome, Circolo degli Scacchi, photo GNF, E 55145.

59 Thuillier, 1993, p. 188.

60 See, for example, Thuillier, 1993, pp. 174, 178, 196.

61 Cuzin, 1979, pp. 301–5, Fig. 37.

62 Judson, 1958, cat. 44, ill. frontispiece. The picture is in the National Gallery, London.

63 Nicolson, 1989, p. 101, Fig. 1598.

64 Bieneck, 1992, cat. A12. However, see also cat. nos. A10, A11, A14, A15, A16, and A17. There was also an even closer three-figured, half-length unpublished Seghers composition of this subject on the London art market.

65 The canvas was on the London art market in 1989 when I saw it and identified it as by the "real" Trophime Bigot, not the Candlelight Master. The work, in poor condition, ended up in a London sale, as Bigot, and has since disappeared.

66 Boyer, 1963, p. 49.

67 Nicolson, 1989, p. 60, Fig. 851.

68 William R. Crelly, *The Paintings of Simon Vouet*, New Haven and London, 1962, cat. 60, p. 176, and Fig. 26.

69 Jacques Bousquet, *Recherches sur le sejour des peintres français a Rome au XVIIème siecle*, Montpellier, 1980, p. 208.

70 See Bousquet, 1980, pp. 73, 76, 202.

71 Nicolson, 1965, cat. 36. Nicolson, 1989, Fig. 868.

72 Nicolson, 1965, cat. 38. Nicolson, 1989, Fig. 867.

73 Nicolson, 1965, cat. 35, plate 10. Although the activity is usually described as catching fleas, this and other related pictures depict delousing. Fleas do not live on the human body, lice do. It is true, as John Moffitt, "*La femme à la puce*: The Textual Background of Seventeenth Century Painted 'Flea-Hunts,'" *Gazette des Beaux-arts*, 110, 1987, pp. 99–103, has shown, that there is a literary tradition of the erotic flea hunt in French and English seventeenth-century poetry. This erotic theme had a certain popularity in Utrecht; see, for example, Honthorst's picture in Basel, Offentliche Kunstsammlung Basel, Kunstmuseum, *Die Nacht*, exh. cat., Haus der Kunst, Munich, 1998–99, cat. 275, ill. in color. The serious nature of the activity in the Doria picture, however, is quite different from Honthorst's treatment and closer to that of Georges de La Tour. See Leonard J. Slatkes, "Georges de La Tour and the Netherlandish Followers of Caravaggio," exh. cat. *Georges de La Tour and his World*, National Gallery of Art, Washington, D.C., 1996–97, pp. 208–9.

74 See, for example, the exhibition catalogue *French Paintings 1500–1825*, Fine Arts Museums of San Francisco, by Pierre Rosenberg and M. C. Stewart, 1987, pp. 41–43.

75 I first published this work in my review of Nicolson, 1979; "Benedict Nicolson, The International Caravaggesque Movement," *Simiolus: Netherlands Quarterly for the History of Art*, XII, 1981–82, pp. 177–78, Fig. 4. This review is apparently unknown to Italian and French scholars. Indeed, the Milan *Pipe Smoker* has not been included or rejected by Vertova, who expanded Nicolson's 1979 lists in 1989, or mentioned by Brejon de Lavergnée in his 1993 review of Nicolson/Vertova. Significantly, there are two other Master Jacomo *Pipe Smokers* known, in Montefortino, Nicolson, 1965, cat. 41, plate 9, and a private collection, France, Marseille, 1978, cat. 9. A copy of the Ambrosiana picture, canvas, 86 x 70 cm., was with Finarte, Milan, and appeared in their catalogue *Asta di dipinti*, p. 27, cat. no. 108, as school of

Honthorst. A cutting from this catalogue is in the Louvre documentation files as Adam de Coster.

76 See the discussion by Leonard J. Slatkes, in *Nieuw Licht op de Gouden Eeuw: Hendrick ter Brugghen en tijdgenoten*, Centraal Museum, Utrecht, Herzog Anton Ulrich-Museum, Braunschweig, 1986–87, under cat. no. 13, the Eger *Pipe Smoker*.

77 See Judson, 1958, cat. 161, Fig. 16, in a private collection, Brussels, and Utrecht, Braunschweig (1986–87), cat. 13, in Eger. The latter is dated 1623.

78 Slatkes, 1981–82, pp. 177–78.

79 Phillips, London, 24 June 1980, lot 181.

80 Slatkes, 1981–82, p. 178.

81 John Michael Montias, *Artists and Artisans in Delft*, Princeton, 1982, p. 207.

82 On the de La Tour, see Slatkes in Washington, 1996–97, p. 205, and cat. 4.

83 Nicolson, 1979, p. 22, plate 63.

84 Compare, for example, with the painting of a *Man with a Pitcher and Glass*, Nationalmuseum, Stockholm; see Alan Chong, "Nieuwe aanwinst: de apostel Paulus uit 1627 door Jacob Gerritsz. Cuyp (1594–1652), *Dordrechts Museum Bulletin*, 13, 1988, pp. 19–23, Fig. 6.

85 Nicolson, 1989, p. 63, plate 671; formerly in the Guest collection, Birmingham.

86 Nicolson, 1979, p. 23.

87 Nicolson, 1960, pp. 135–36, Candlelight Master; Nicolson, 1965, cat. 23, plate 1, Bigot; Nicolson, 1989, plate 855, Bigot.

88 Nicolson, 1989, plate 844.

89 *Ibid.*, plate 847.

90 Nicolson, 1960, plate 14.

91 Nicolson, 1979, p. 23.

92 Slatkes, 1981–82, p. 178.

93 Anne W. Lowenthal, *Joachim Wtewael and Dutch Mannerism*, Doornspijk, 1986, p. 175, cat. D-1, and plate 161. Lowenthal dates the Oslo picture to about 1624. Significantly, a painting depicting cardplayers by Peter Wtewael appears in several inventories of the Wtewael family; see Lowenthal pp. 191–92.

94 Nicolson, 1989, plate 875.

Color Plates

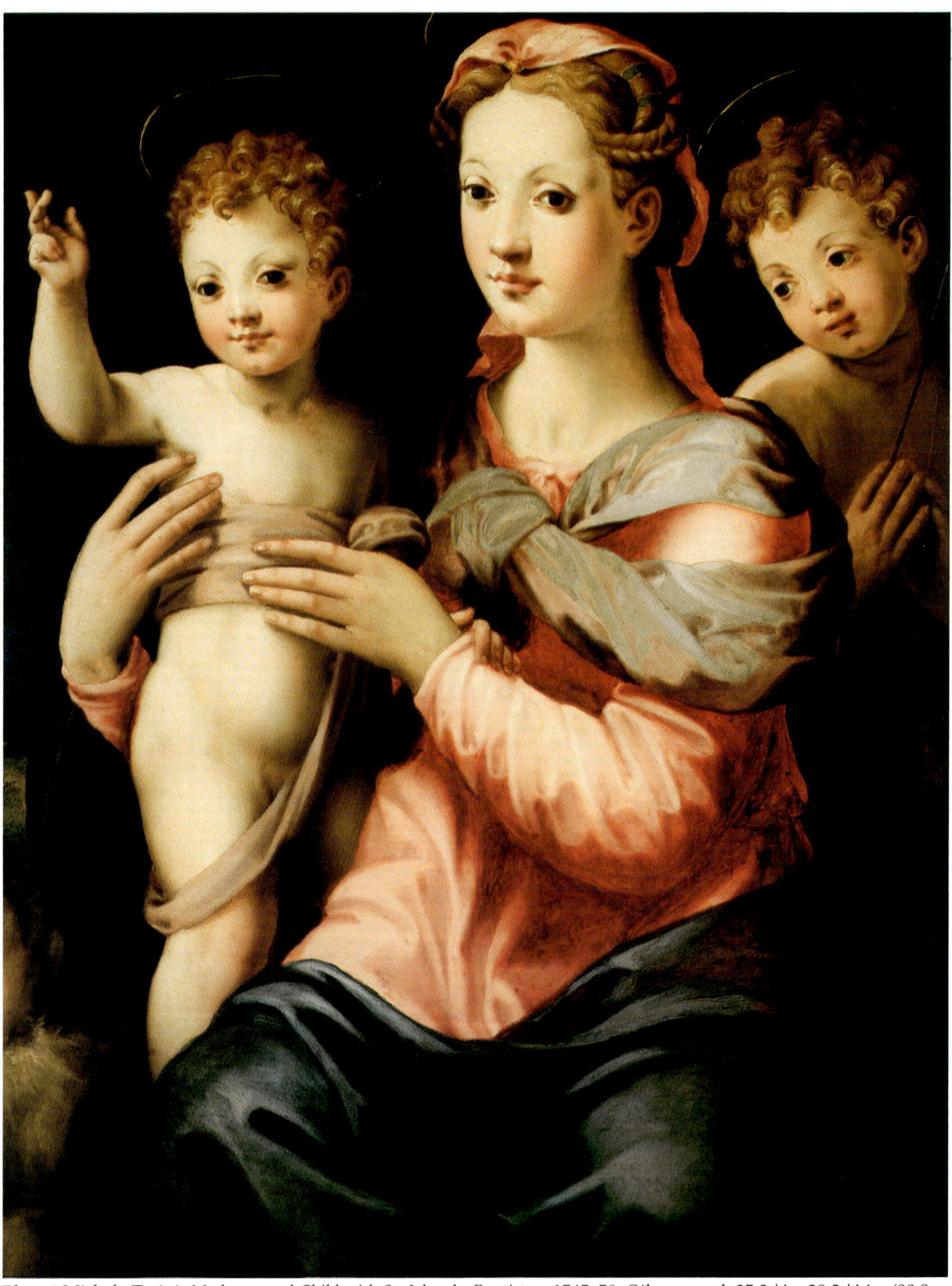

Plate 1 Michele Tosini, *Madonna and Child with St. John the Baptist*, c. 1545–50. Oil on panel, 35 3/4 x 28 3/4 in. (90.8 x 73 cm.). Palmer Museum of Art, The Pennsylvania State University, Purchased by the Friends of the Palmer Museum of Art with supplementary funds provided by the Office of the President, 90.4.

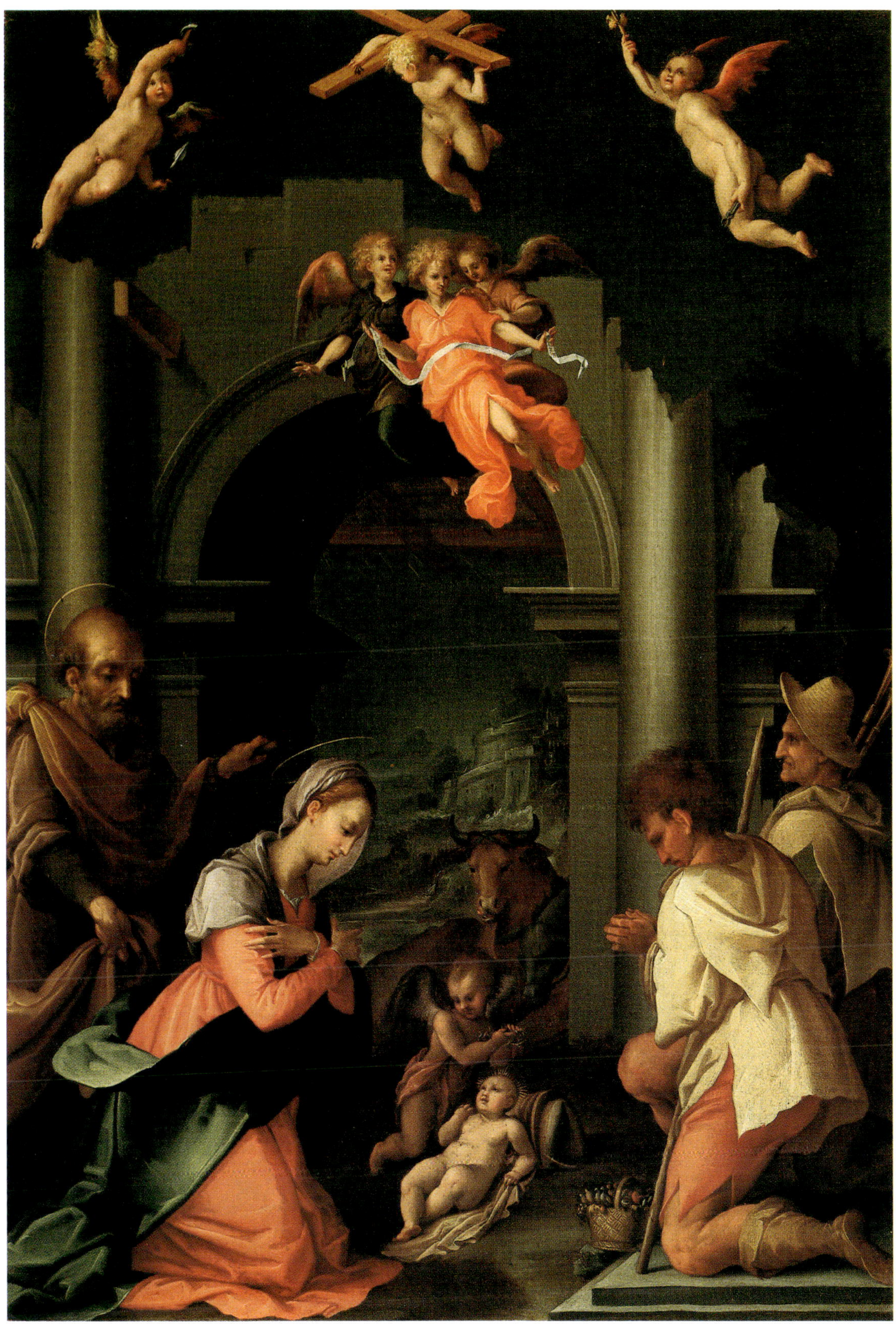

Plate 2 Maso da San Friano, *Adoration of the Shepherds,* c. 1570. Oil on canvas, 28 15/16 x 20 5/16 in. (73.6 x 51.6 cm.). Palmer Museum of Art, The Pennsylvania State University, Gift of the Friends of the Palmer Museum of Art, 87.2.

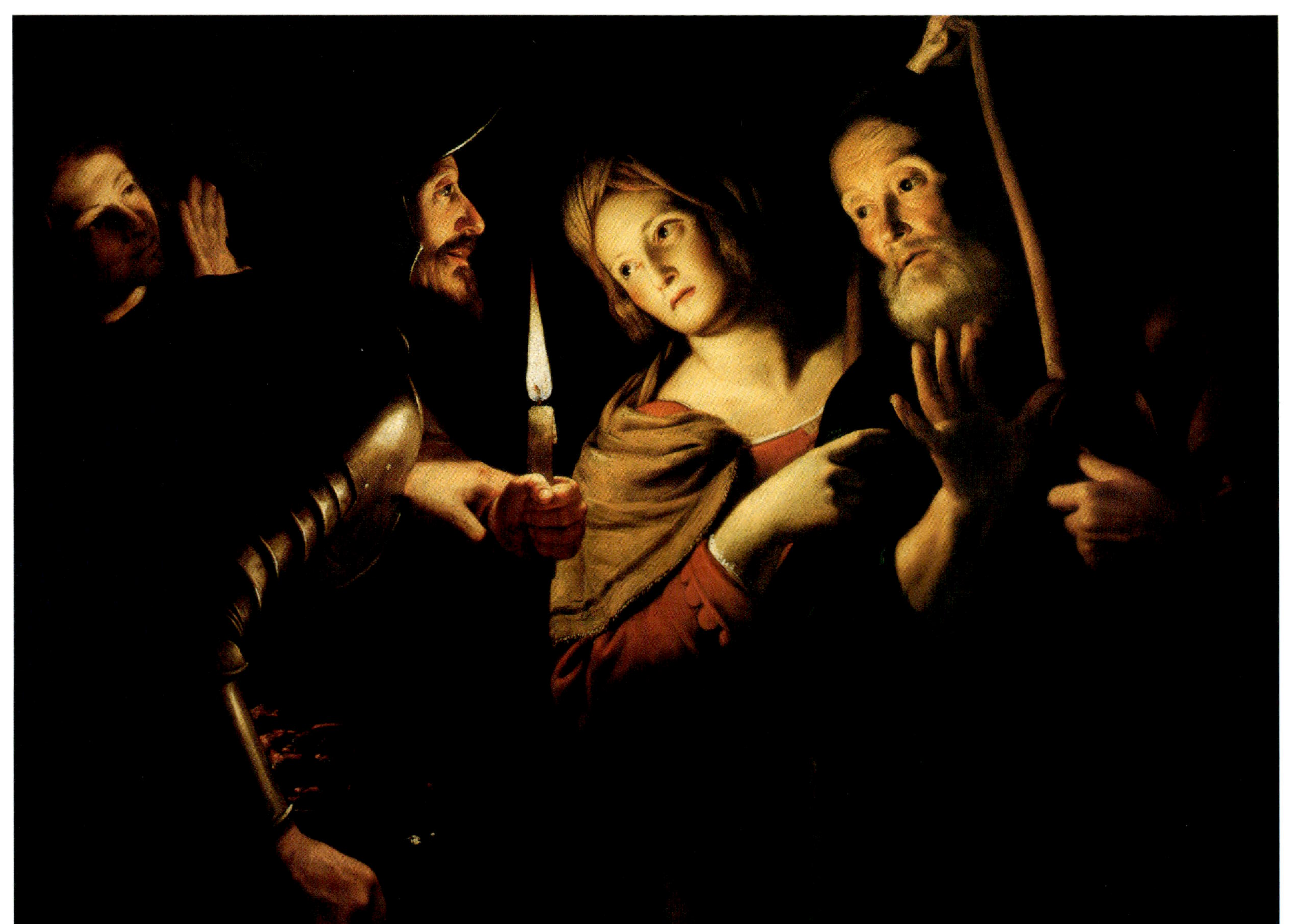

Plate 3 Master Jacomo, *Denial of St. Peter,* c. 1630s. Oil on canvas, 37 1/2 x 50 in. (95.5 x 127 cm.). Palmer Museum of Art, The Pennsylvania State University, 78.3.

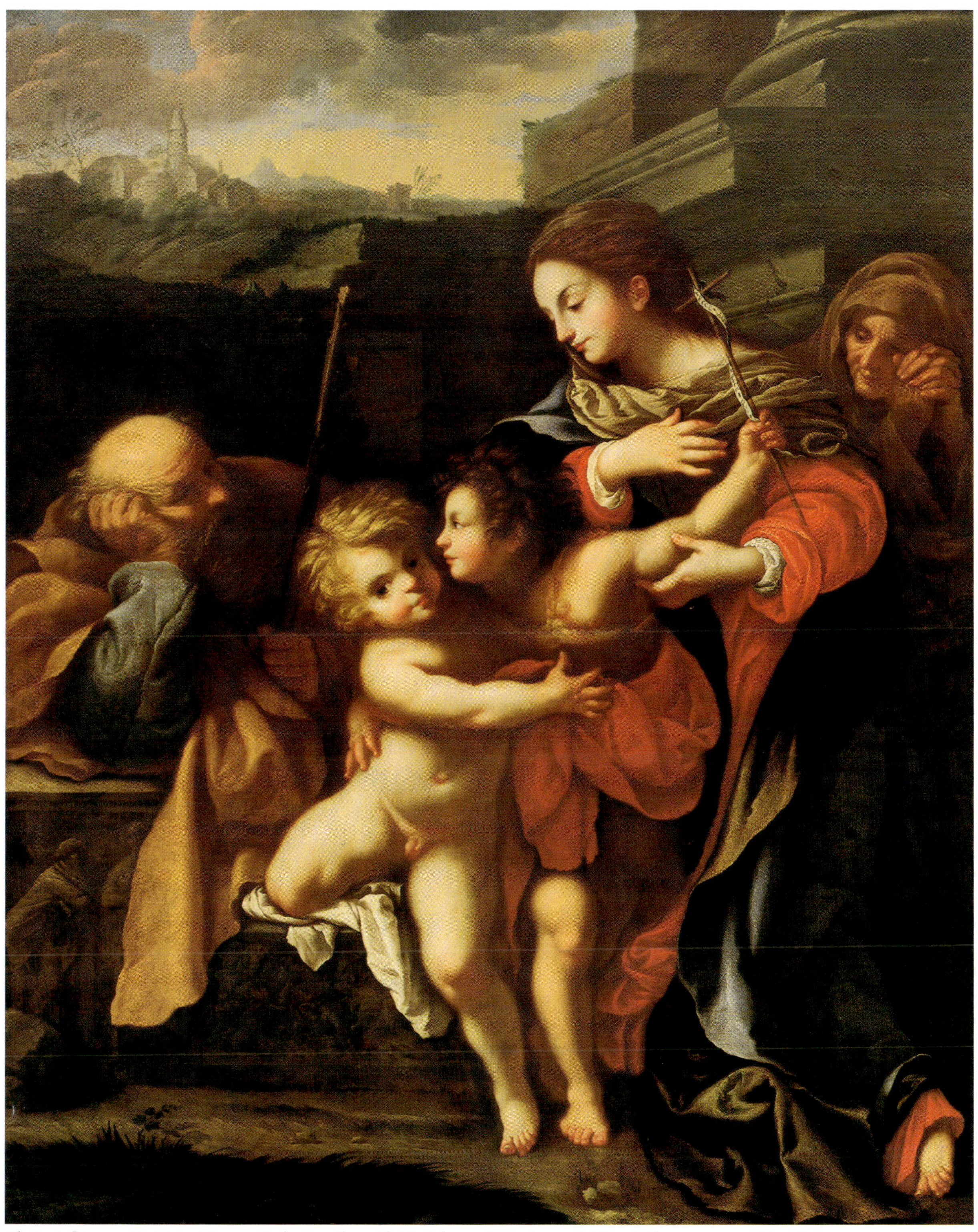

Plate 4 Giovan Battista Vanni, *Holy Family with St. John and St. Anne*, 1640s. Oil on canvas, 70 x 58 in. (177.8 x 147.3 cm.). Palmer Museum of Art, The Pennsylvania State University, 73.118.

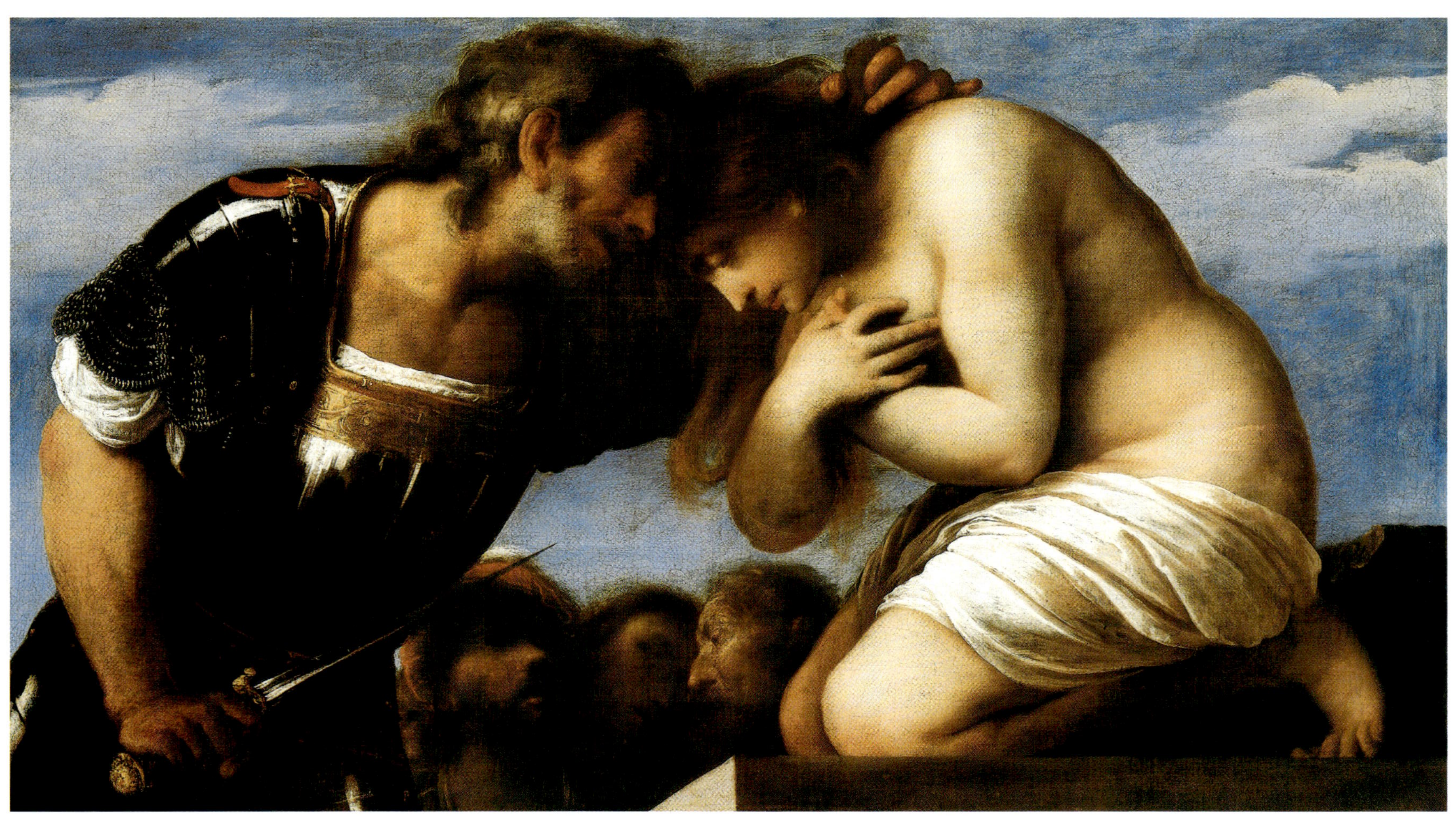

Plate 5 Pietro della Vecchia, *Sacrifice of Jephthah's Daughter*, c. 1650–60. Oil on canvas, 30 1/2 x 54 1/4 in. (77.5 x 137.8 cm.). Palmer Museum of Art, The Pennsylvania State University, Gift of Morton and Mary Jane Harris to honor the members of the staff on the occasion of the opening of the Palmer Museum of Art, August 27, 1993, 93.14.

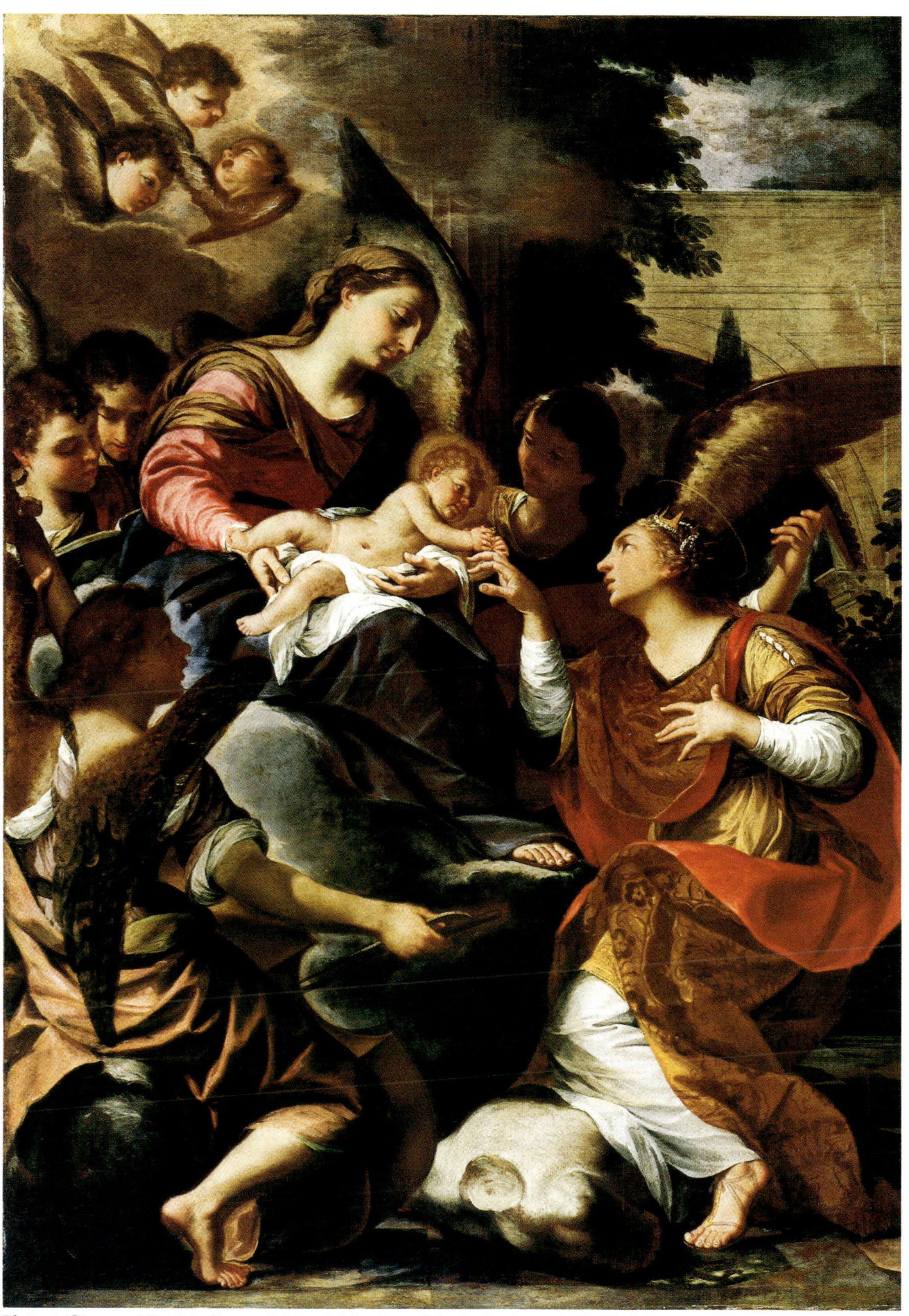

Plate 6 Giovanni Battista Boncori, *Mystic Marriage of St. Catherine*, c. 1673–75. Oil on canvas, 66 x 47 1/2 in. (167.6 x 120.6 cm.). Palmer Museum of Art, The Pennsylvania State University, 76.49.

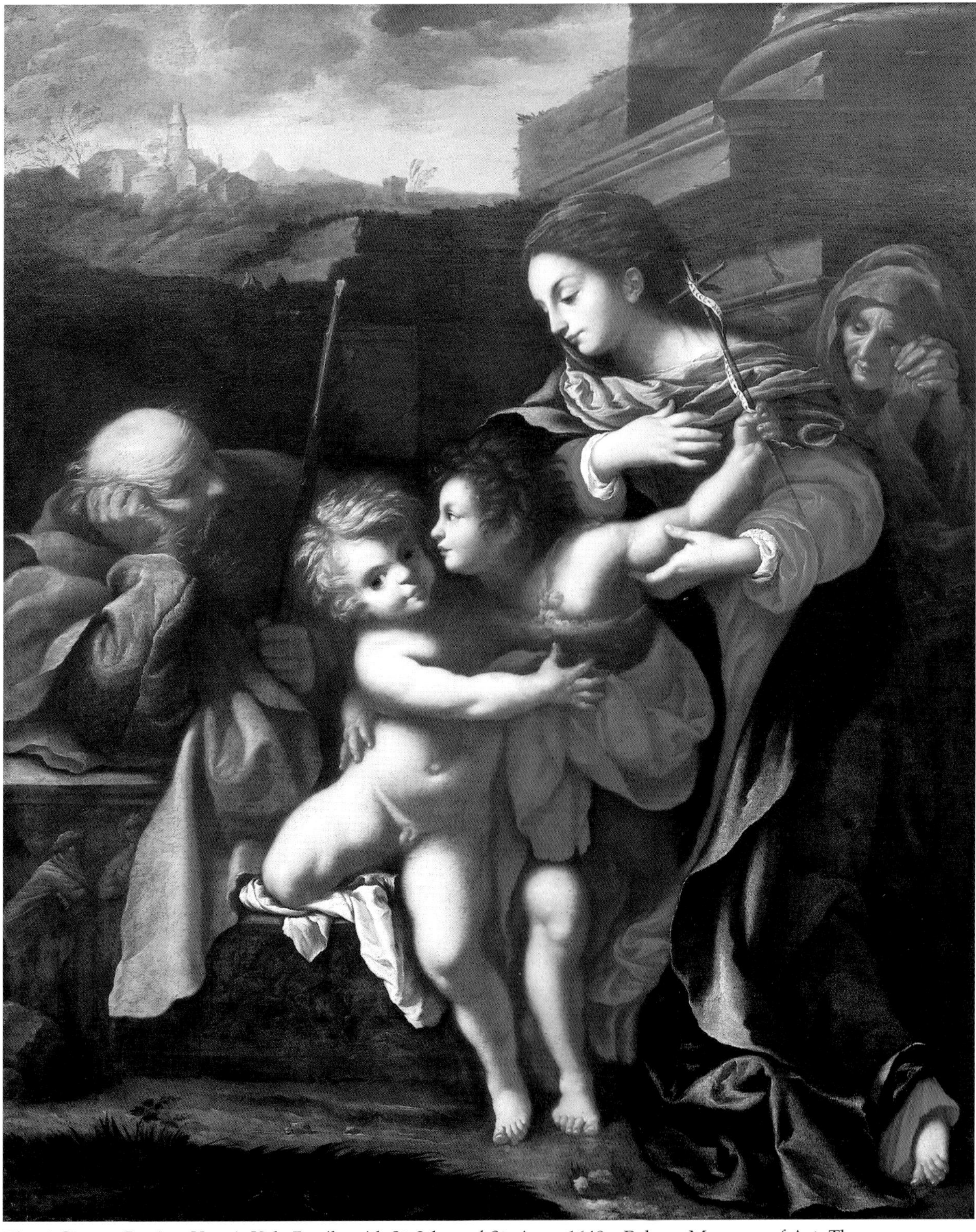

Fig. 1 Giovan Battista Vanni, *Holy Family with St. John and St. Anne*, 1640s. Palmer Museum of Art, The Pennsylvania State University. (See color plate 4.)

The Florentine Baroque: Giovan Battista Vanni

Francesca Baldassari

When I was invited to participate in the symposium, *Continuity, Innovation, and Connoisseurship*, I welcomed the opportunity to examine the Palmer Museum's *Holy Family with St. John and St. Anne* by Giovan Battista Vanni, an artist I had been studying for some years (Fig. 1).[1] Although I cited the painting previously, noting, for the first time, its location at the Palmer Museum, until now I had yet to give it the attention it deserves.[2] Vanni's *Holy Family* is not unknown to scholars. It appeared in an exhibition at the Metropolitan Museum in 1969,[3] the first in America dedicated to Florentine Baroque art. In her catalogue, Joan Nissman stated that Vanni's authorship of the *Holy Family* had been recognized independently by Mina Gregori and Federico Zeri.[4]

In 1969, Vanni was still a rarely studied artist, with the notable exception of the preliminary research of Mina Gregori, who had begun to assemble a corpus of his work. My interest in Vanni began in 1984, when a group of frescoes was uncovered in the small cloister of the monastery of San Benedetto in Pistoia, a Tuscan city once ruled by the Medici Grand Dukes (Fig. 2). I recognized the frescoes as seventeenth-century Florentine, but the artist was not immediately evident. Then, in the archive of the monastery, I discovered documents indicating that they were painted by Vanni with the assistance of his pupil, Cosimo Segoni.[5] This information was corroborated in the biography of Vanni written by Filippo Baldinucci, the prominent seventeenth-century biographer of so many Florentine artists.[6] Baldinucci recorded that the Pistoia frescoes were the last works of Vanni who died in 1660 soon after their completion. I showed the frescoes to Professor Gregori, my advisor at the University of Florence, who confirmed the identification and encouraged me to make the artist the subject of my dissertation. Professor Gregori also offered me an opportunity to work on Vanni for a major exhibition of Florentine Baroque art she was organizing, which would take place at the Palazzo Strozzi in 1986.[7] Vanni, she promised, would be a rewarding subject, and indeed she was right. Today the painter has emerged as one of the significant protagonists of early Florentine Baroque painting.

To understand the place of the Palmer Museum's *Holy Family* in Vanni's oeuvre, it is useful to outline his stylistic development, noting particularly the influence of Correggio and Vanni's interest in landscape and classical antiquity. Giovan Battista Vanni was born in Florence in 1600 during a period of active artistic patronage in the Medici Granducal court and among a group of sophisticated nobles.[8] His father, Orazio, a well-known Florentine goldsmith who had a shop on the Ponte Vecchio, worked for the Grand Dukes and the nobility. It is likely that Orazio introduced his young son to Cardinal Carlo de' Medici, a powerful and discriminating patron for whom Vanni later painted a *Venus and Adonis* (Fig. 11). Baldinucci informs us that Vanni was trained in the workshop of Jacopo Chimenti, called Empoli, and that the master sometimes used his pupil as a model. In Empoli's signed altarpiece of 1617, *St. Ivo Protecting Widows and Orphans*, Baldinucci notes that the young Vanni was the model for the youthful widow on the right who implores the saint to care for her sons (Fig. 3).[9] Baldinucci's observation is confirmed by Empoli's drawing of the attractive youth, preserved at the Uffizi (Fig. 4).[10] In 1618, Vanni enrolled in the Florentine *Accademia del Disegno* and transferred to the studio of Cristofano Allori, where he remained until Allori's death three years later.

St. Benedict Removing the Devil from the Stone is an early work on canvas by Vanni known in two versions: one in the collection of the Cassa di Risparmio in Carrara (Fig. 5)[11] and the other in a Swiss private collection (Fig. 6).[12] Both were commissioned by Vanni's father who, at his death, bequeathed them to his other sons, Nicolò and Jacopo.[13] Documents provide a dating for the Carrara version, executed between 1620 and April 1621, as part of a series of twelve paintings

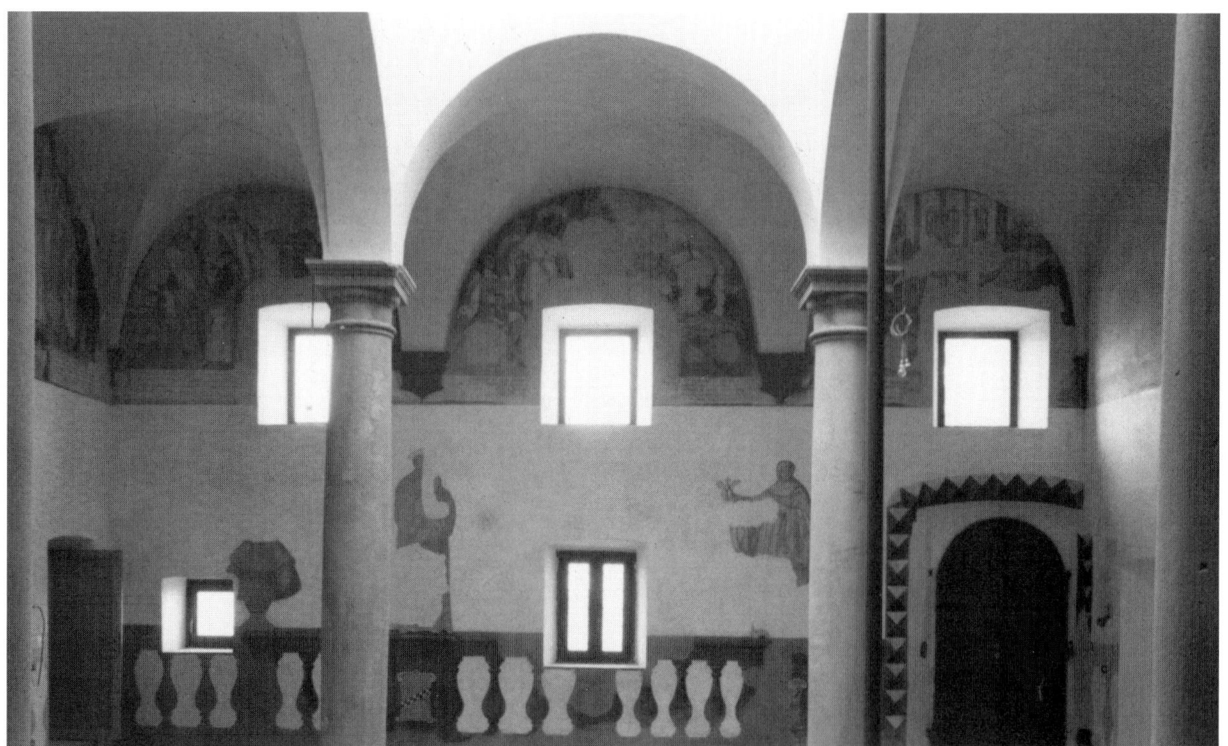

Fig. 2

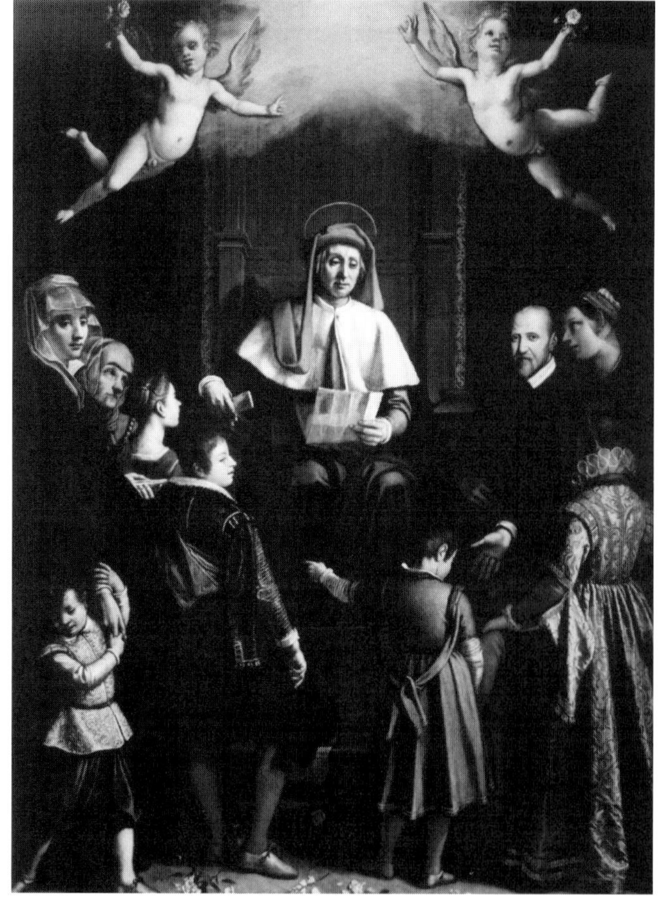

Fig. 3

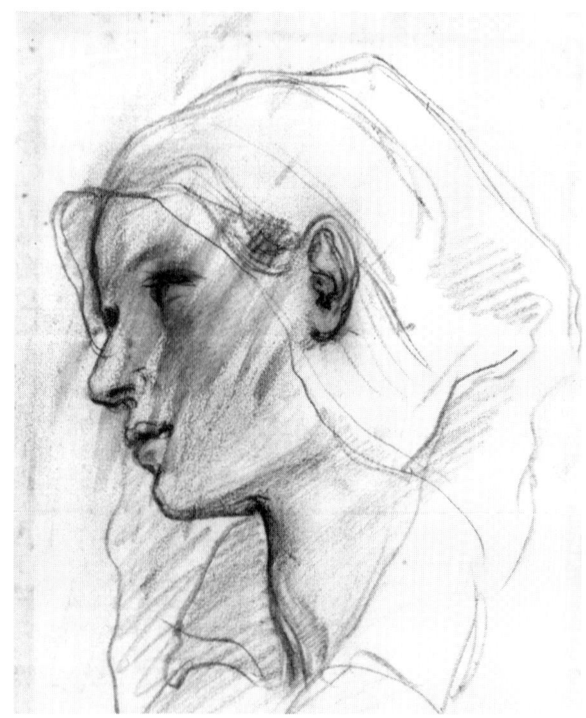

Fig. 4

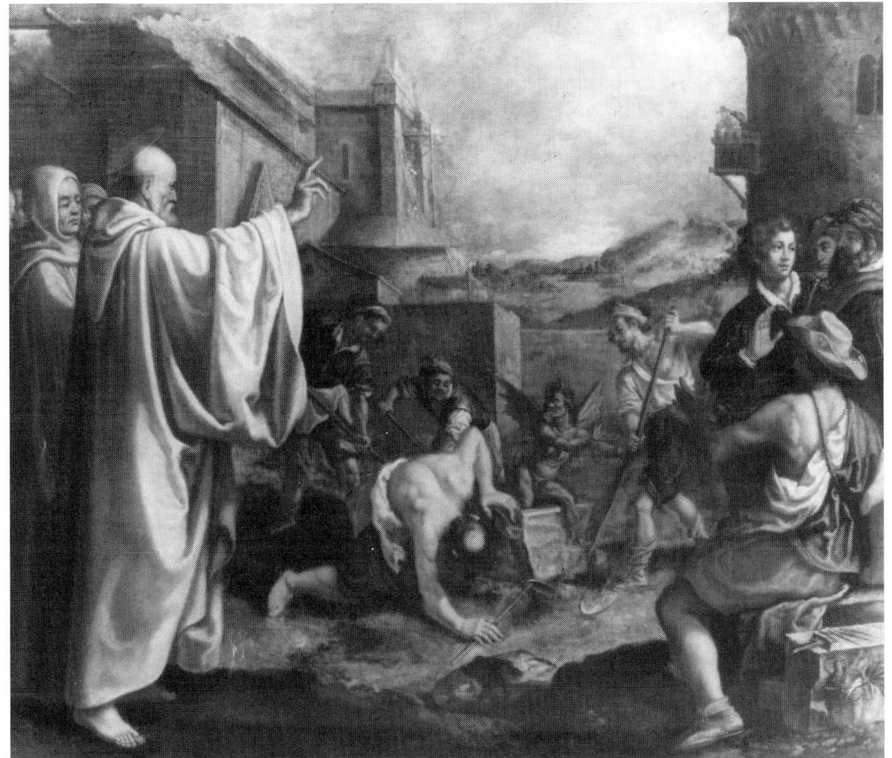

Fig. 5

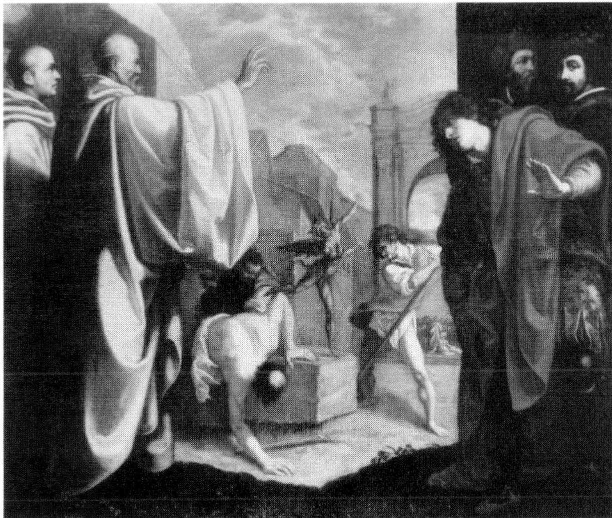

Fig. 6

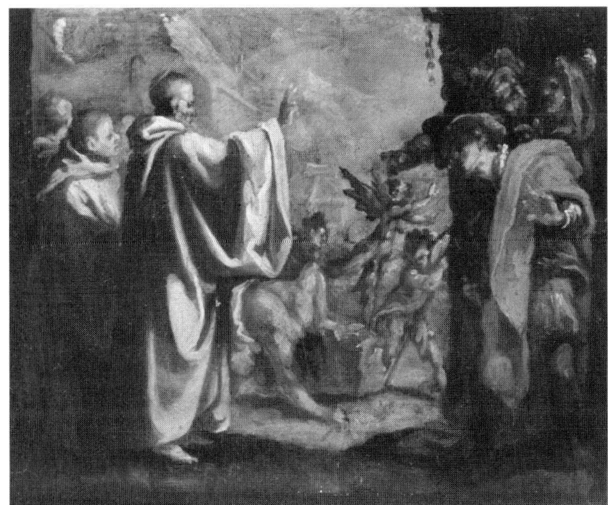

Fig. 7

Fig. 2 Giovan Battista Vanni, assisted by Cosimo Segoni, fresco fragments, 1660. Pistoia, cloister of San Benedetto monastery. Photo: author.

Fig. 3 Jacopo Chimenti, called Empoli, *St. Ivo Protecting Widows and Orphans*, 1617. Florence, Pitti Palace. Photo: The Uffizi, Gabinetto Fotografico, Soprintendenza per i Beni Artistici e Storici di Firenze.

Fig. 4 Jacopo Chimenti, called Empoli, preliminary drawing for *St. Ivo Protecting Widows and Orphans* (portrait of Giovan Battista Vanni?), c. 1617. Photo: The Uffizi, Gabinetto Fotografico, Soprintendenza per i Beni Artistici e Storici di Firenze.

Fig. 5 Giovan Battista Vanni, *St. Benedict Removing the Devil from the Stone*, 1620–1621. Carrara, Cassa di Risparmio. Photo: author.

Fig. 6 Giovan Battista Vanni, *St. Benedict Removing the Devil from the Stone*, 1620–21. Switzerland, private collection. Photo: author.

Fig. 7 Giovan Battista Vanni, Preparatory sketch on panel for *St. Benedict Removing the Devil from the Stone*, 1620–21. See note 13. Florence, private collection. Photo: author.

representing the life of St. Benedict. They were commissioned by the company of San Benedetto Bianco, of which Vanni's father was a member, and were completed by several different artists. Three others of the twelve to survive, by Jacopo Vignali, Fabrizio Boschi, and Carlo Braccelli, were exhibited in 1986 at the Palazzo Strozzi.[14]

The two canvases of St. Benedict, clearly of similar date, testify to the youthful Vanni's skill and reveal his attraction to the innovative style of Ludovico Cigoli, a pivotal figure in the development of the Florentine Baroque. Light is handled freely on the faces, hair, beards, and colorful costumes. The elongated figures recall Bilivert and Cristofano Allori seen through the prism of Cigoli. At the beginning of the 1620s, Vanni participated in two of the important fresco commissions for the Medici Court. In the residential palace, the Casino Mediceo, he executed the *Construction of the Pitti Palace* (Fig. 8). Vanni also did a lunette in the villa of Poggio Imperiale, *Esther before Ahasuerus* (Fig. 9). Both lunettes reflect the influences of Cristofano Allori and Matteo Rosselli.

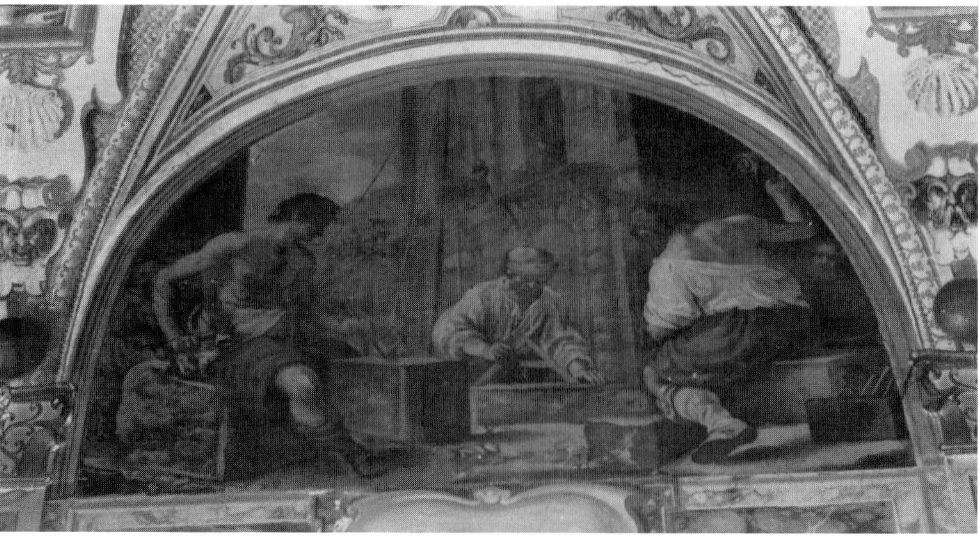

Fig. 8

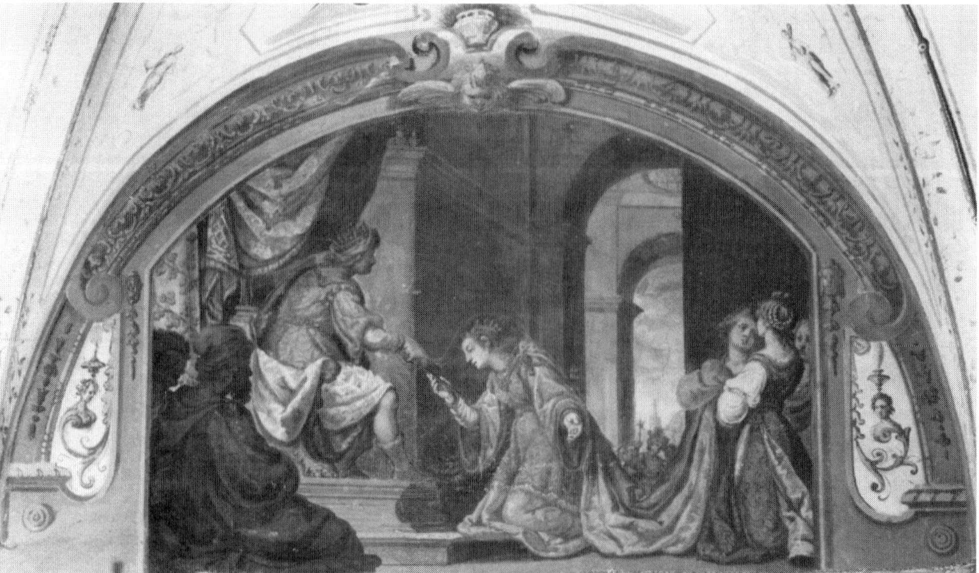

Fig. 9

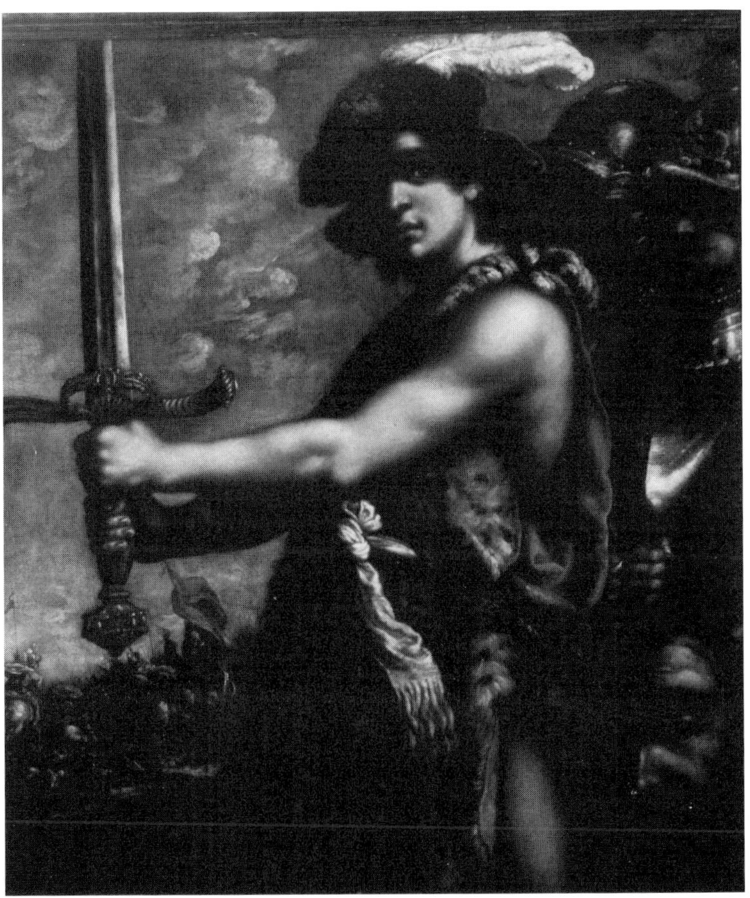

Fig. 10

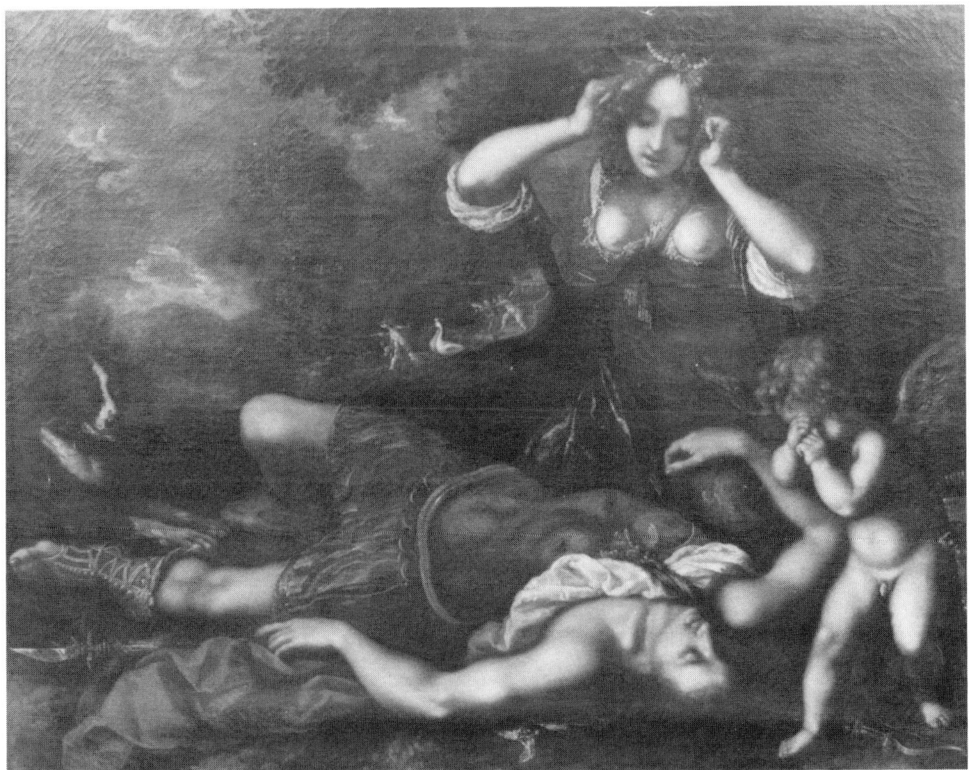

Fig. 11

Fig. 8 Giovan Battista Vanni, *Construction of the Pitti Palace*, early 1620s. Florence, Casino Mediceo. Photo: The Uffizi, Gabinetto Fotografico, Soprintendenza per i Beni Artistici e Storici di Firenze.

Fig. 9 Giovan Battista Vanni, *Esther before Ahasuerus*, early 1620s. Florence, Villa of Poggio Imperiale. Photo: The Uffizi, Gabinetto Fotografico, Soprintendenza per i Beni Artistici e Storici di Firenze.

Fig. 10 Giovan Battista Vanni, *David*, signed and dated 1623. Prato, Palazzo degli Alberti, Galleria. Photo: Prato, Cariprato.

Fig. 11 Giovan Battista Vanni, *Venus and Adonis*, 1624. Florence, Museum of the Opificio di Pietre Dure. Photo: The Uffizi, Gabinetto Fotografico, Soprintendenza per i Beni Artistici e Storici di Firenze.

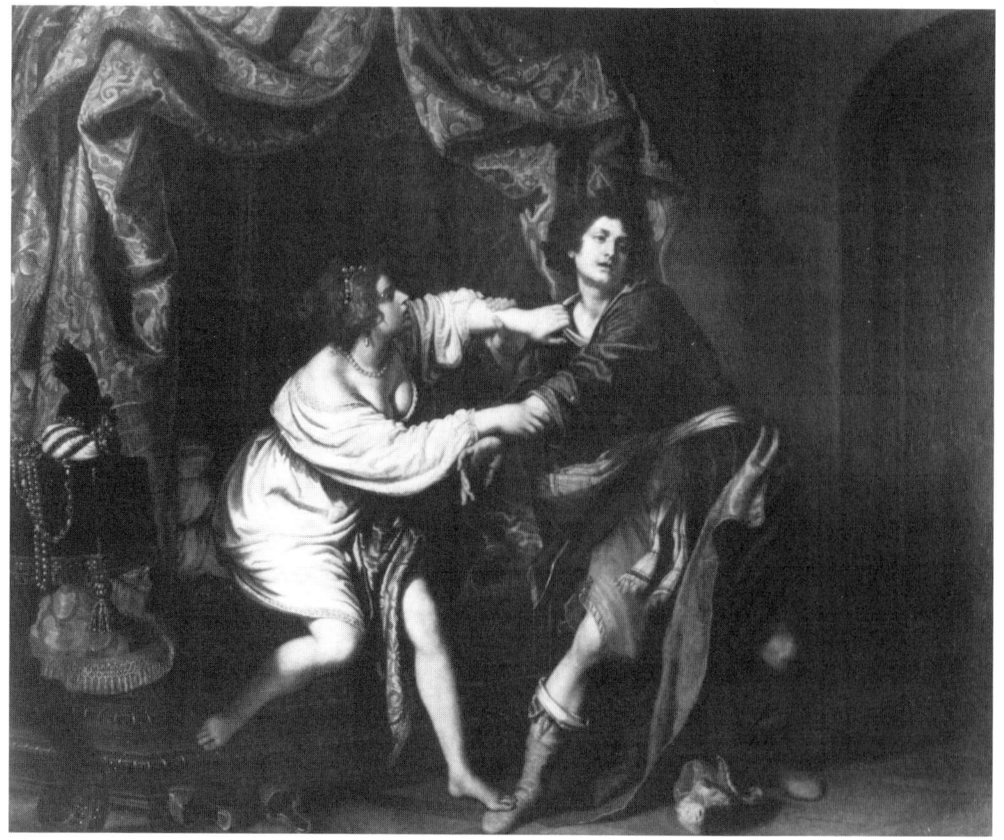

Fig. 14

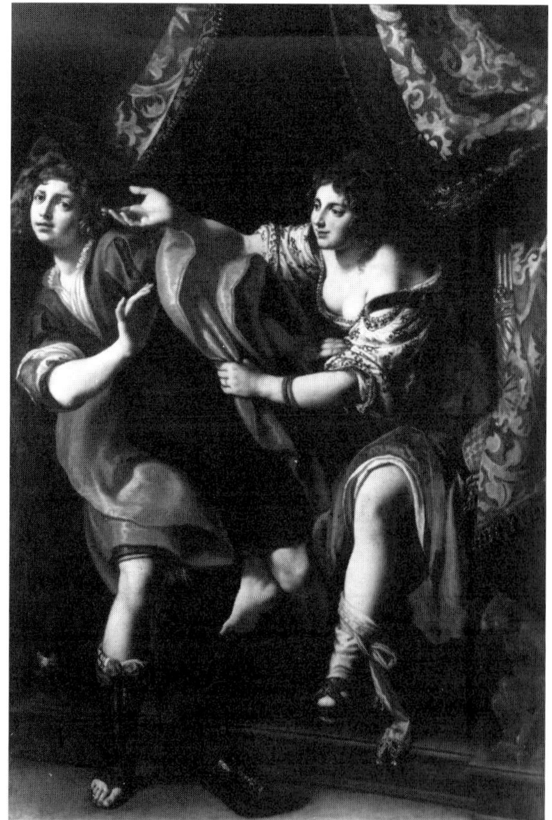

Fig. 13

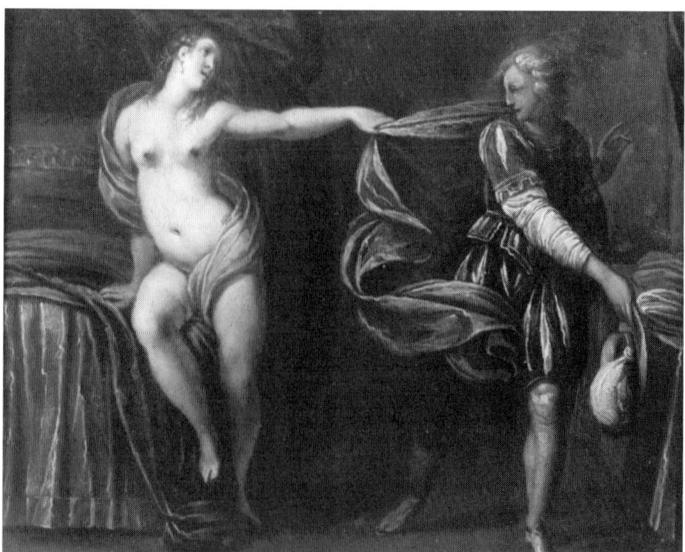

Fig. 12

From 1623, we have a signed and dated *David* (Fig. 10), and in 1624, Vanni was paid by Cardinal Carlo de' Medici for the aforementioned *Venus and Adonis* (Fig. 11).[15] The figure of *Venus* is an early example of *pittura da camera*, a pictorial manner in Florentine baroque art that emphasizes sensuality, which was introduced by Bilivert, Vignali, and Furini.

To this core of documented works I have been able to add others that expand the understanding of Vanni's range. A recently discovered small painting on copper, *Joseph and Potiphar's Wife* (Fig. 12),[16] was probably completed before Vanni's first trip to Rome in 1624 and is still fully Florentine in style and spirit. The subject was popular among the local painters, the most celebrated example being a large canvas of 1610 by Cigoli for the bishop of Arezzo (Fig. 13). In 1619, Bilivert interpreted the subject for Cardinal Carlo de' Medici (Fig. 14), and Vanni adopted his horizontal format as well as his richness of décor, costume, and attention to detail in this little copper. In the Florentine context, the work may be compared with two other diminutive works on copper: Bilivert's modello for *The Temptation of Ubaldo* (Paris, Louvre) and Giovanni da San Giovanni's *Christ Served by Angels* (Florence, Pitti Palace), both datable stylistically to circa 1624. In Vanni's painting, one can detect the influence of Francesco Furini and the *pittura da camera* in the soft treatment of the woman's flesh. Vanni's handling of hair, its waves and ringlets captured in gleaming light, reappears later in the figures of four works conceived with landscape as a prominent element: *Hagar and the Angel in the Wilderness* (Fig. 15), *Tobias and the Angel* (Fig. 16), *The Flight into Egypt* (Fig. 17), and its pendant, *The Finding of Moses.*[17]

These landscape-rich compositions of Vanni should be dated to the 1630s, perhaps just before or contemporaneous with his masterpiece, *St. Sebastian Cured by Pious Women*, executed in Rome (Fig. 18). Vanni is first documented in Rome in 1624 and again during a second visit between 1630 and 1632, after a trip to Parma in 1629 to study Correggio.[18] With the study of

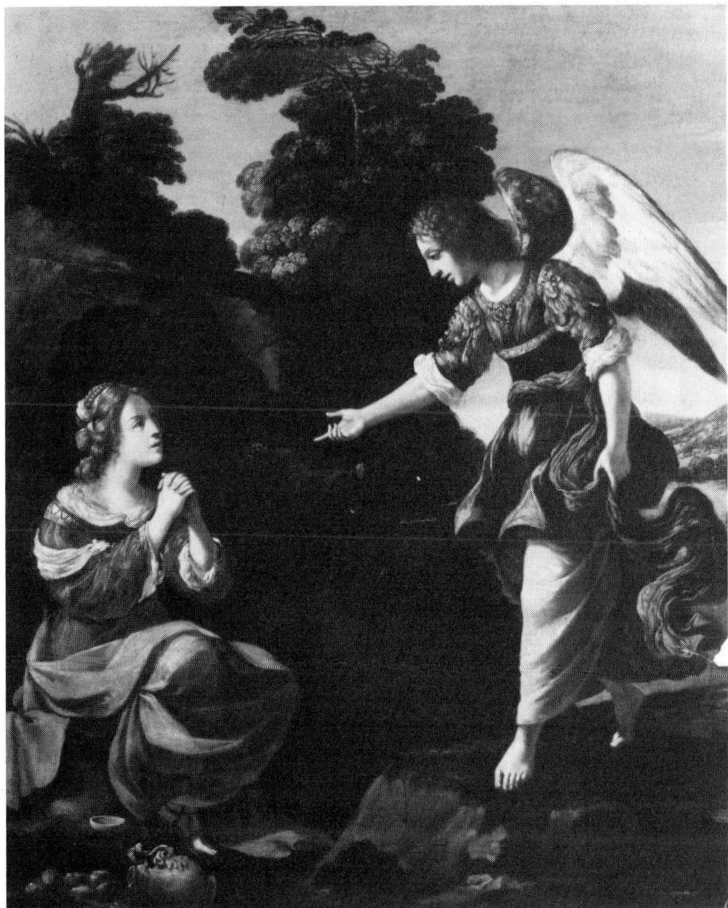

Fig. 15

Fig. 12 Giovan Battista Vanni, *Joseph and Potiphar's Wife*, c. 1624. Private collection. Photo: author.

Fig. 13 Lodovico Cigoli, *Joseph and Potiphar's Wife*, 1610. Rome, Borghese Gallery. Photo: The Uffizi, Gabinetto Fotografico, Soprintendenza per i Beni Artistici e Storici di Firenze.

Fig. 14 Giovanni Bilivert, *Joseph and Potiphar's Wife*, 1619. Florence, Pitti Palace. Photo: The Uffizi, Gabinetto Fotografico, Soprintendenza per i Beni Artistici e Storici di Firenze.

Fig. 15 Giovan Battista Vanni, *Hagar and the Angel in the Wilderness*, 1630s. Formerly in Notre Dame University, Snite Museum.

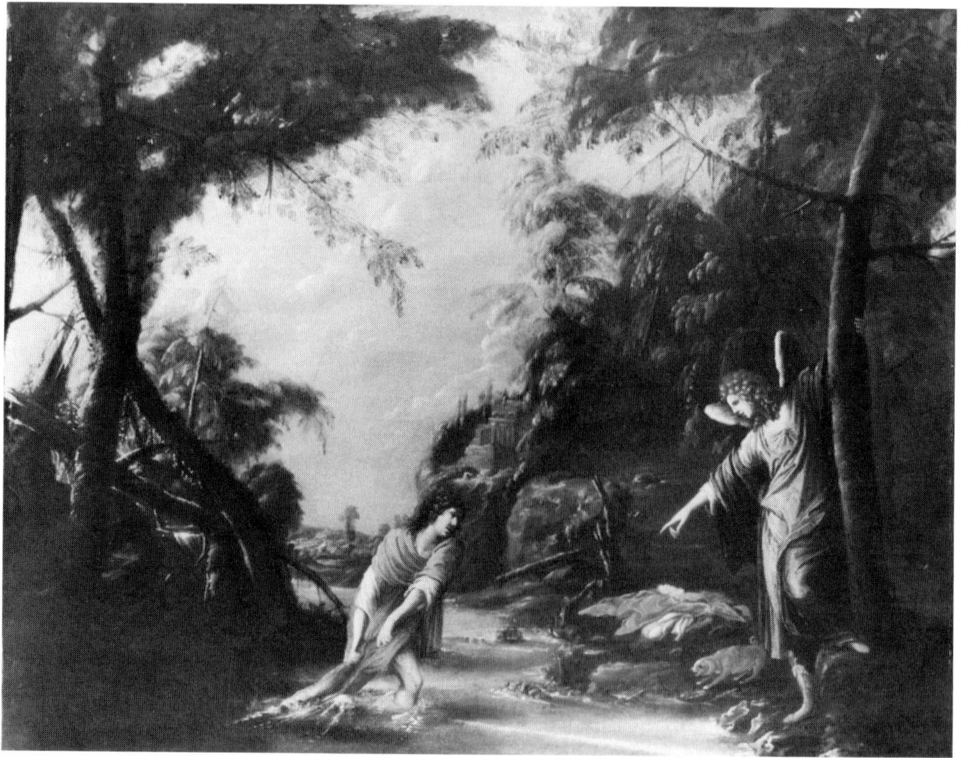

Fig. 16

Correggio and two trips to Rome, his style developed in a new and different manner, revealed dramatically in the *St. Sebastian*. Vanni was deeply impressed by the proto-Baroque art of Correggio, with its subtle use of light, softness of flesh and figure, sweetness of facial expression, and fluidity of paint handling. For Vanni, Correggio served as an enduring source of inspiration.

Documents reveal that Vanni received the commission for the *St. Sebastian* from the prominent Montauto family in 1626 for an altar in San Giovanni dei Fiorentini, the most important Florentine church in Rome.[19] He contracted to complete the work in one year, but in my judgment the commission was not finished until early in the 1630s. The Correggesque faces are not conceivable before Vanni's trip to Parma in 1629. According to Baldinucci, Vanni was probably familiar with the *Mystic Marriage of St. Catherine* by Correggio in the Louvre (Fig. 19).[20] We know that he painted a copy, now lost, of Correggio's *Madonna with St. Jerome* (Fig. 20), and his print after Correggio's *Martyrdom of Saints Placidus, Flavia, Eutichius, and Victorinus* survives (Figs. 21a and 21b). In 1643, Vanni also made engravings after Correggio's famous *Assumption of the Virgin* in the dome of the Cathedral in Parma.[21]

Vanni's *St. Sebastian Cured by Pious Women* (Fig. 18), as well as a *St. Agnes* in Florence (Pratesi collection) dating from the same period (Fig. 22), reveal the artist's keen interest in Roman classical antiquity. Noteworthy are the frieze on the block supporting St. Sebastian, derived from Trajan's Column, and the classically-inspired pose of the saint. The French painter, François Perrier, working in Rome at the same time, shared similar interests, as the drapery suggests in Perrier's *Bacchus and Ariadne* (Fig. 23). His influence can be detected in Vanni's landscapes mentioned above (Figs. 15–17).

The genre of landscape painting was not new in Florentine art. Giulio Parigi and his followers, Remigio Cantagallina and Ercole Bazzicaluva, had been keenly interested in landscape and made many sketches in pen and ink, inspired by Northern prints that were popular in Florence. Baldinucci informs us that numerous Florentine artists, such as Valerio Marucelli, Guasparre Galgagni, Benedetto Boschi, and others still little known, were influenced by Adriano

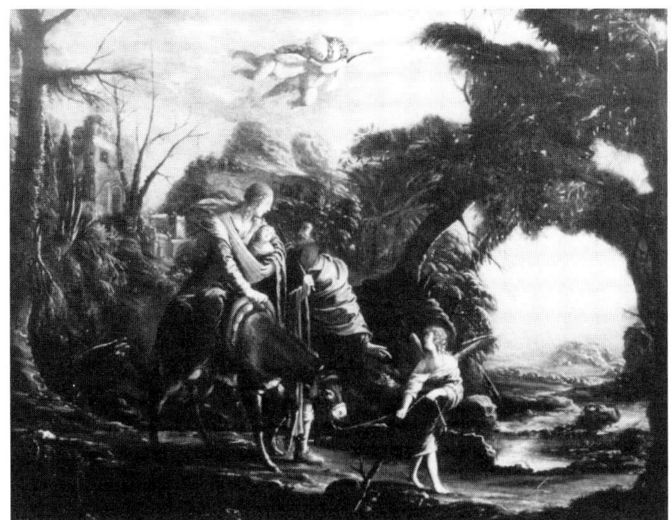

Fig. 17

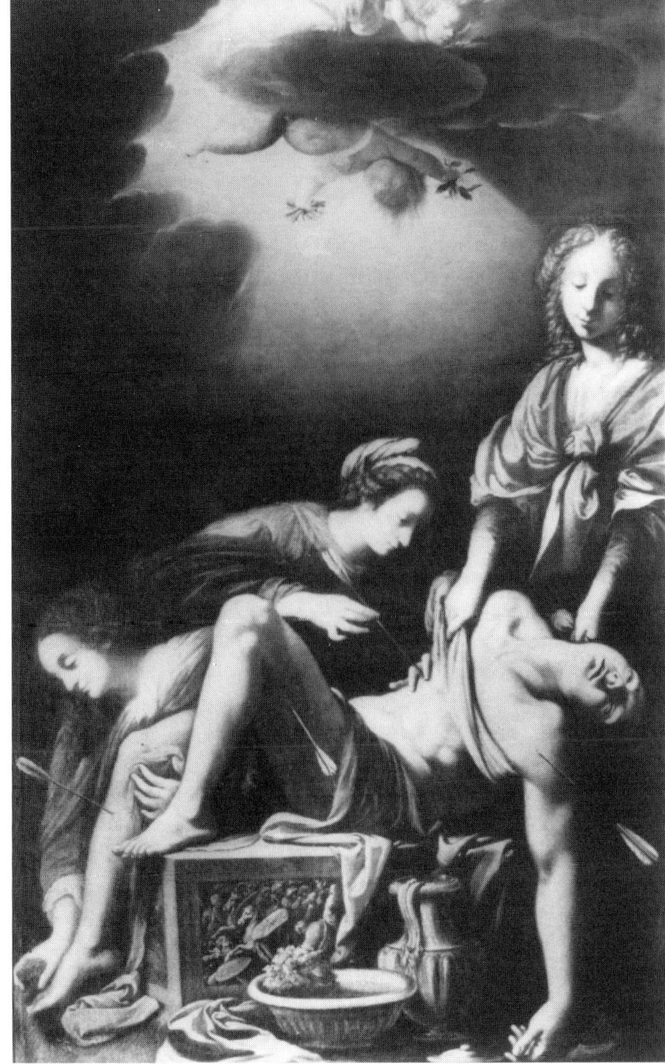

Fig. 18

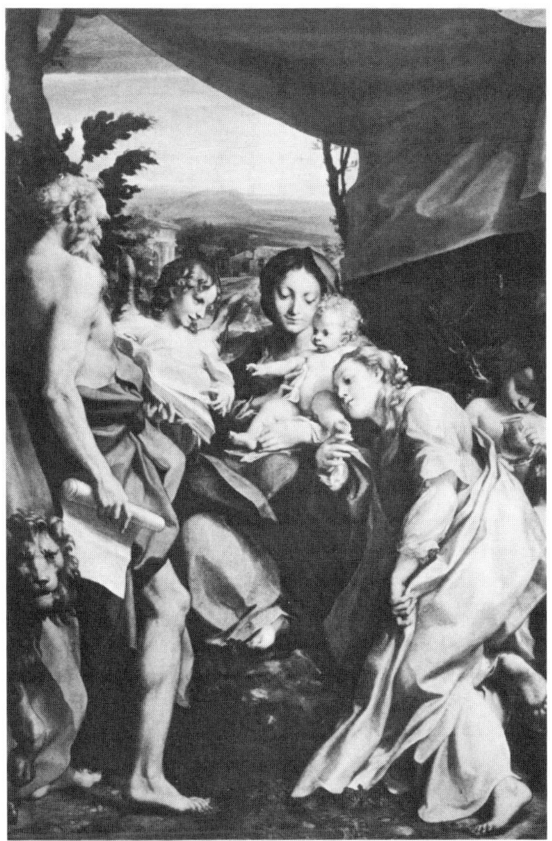

Fig. 20

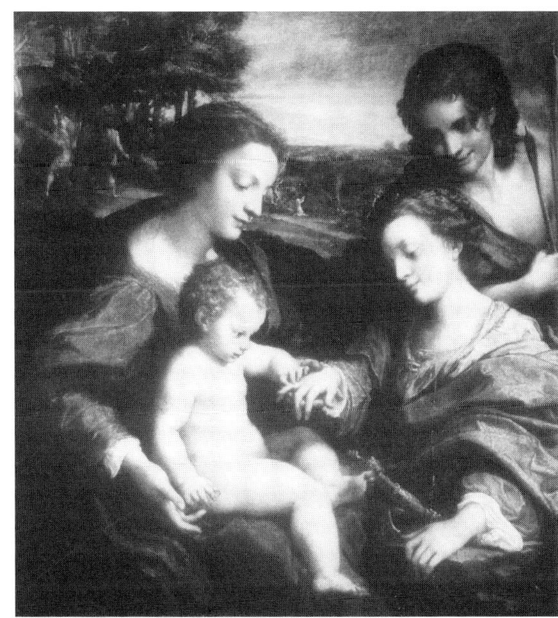

Fig. 19

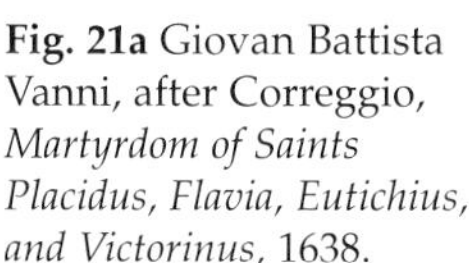

Fig. 21a Giovan Battista Vanni, after Correggio, *Martyrdom of Saints Placidus, Flavia, Eutichius, and Victorinus,* 1638.

Fig. 21b Correggio, *Martyrdom of Saints Placidus, Flavia, Eutichius, and Victorinus,* c. 1524–26. Parma, National Gallery.

Fig. 22 Giovan Battista Vanni, *St. Agnes,* c. 1630. Florence, Pratesi collection. Photo: author.

Fig. 23 François Perrier, *Bacchus and Ariadne.* Austin, Jack S. Benton Museum of Art, University of Texas, Suida-Manning collection, 1999.

Fig. 24 Giovan Battista Vanni, *Abduction of Helen,* c. 1640. Location unknown. Photo: Bologne, Archivo Villani, n. 27278.

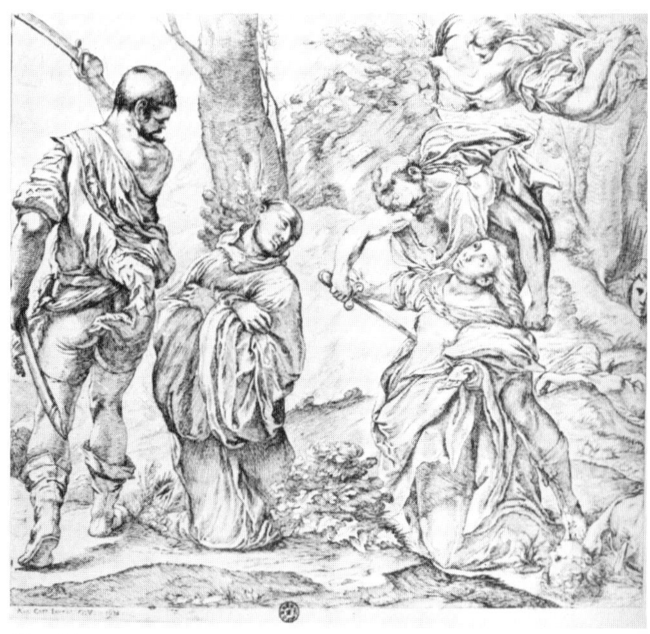

Fig. 21a

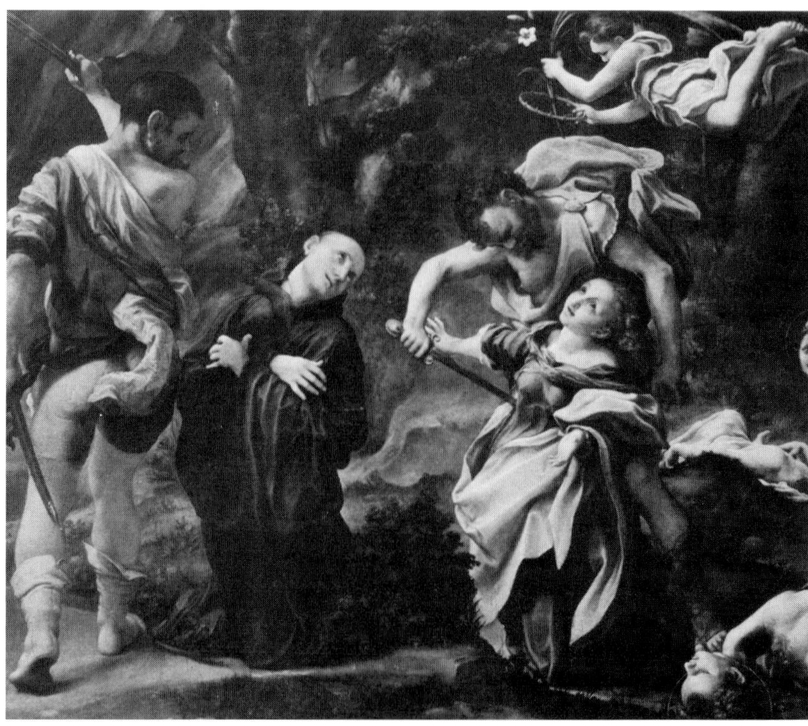

Fig. 21b

Fiammingo (a long-neglected artist awaiting rediscovery), and they all practiced the drawing and painting of landscape.[22] Cristofano Allori produced a number of landscape drawings, some of them copied by his pupil, Vanni, in a sketchbook datable to 1620, early in the latter's career.[23]

The novelty of Vanni's landscapes in Florence was their introduction of French stylistic elements. Perrier's influence has already been mentioned. Vanni's *Hagar and the Angel,* probably one of the earliest, and his *Tobias and the Angel* demonstrate an affinity with Claude Vignon, a French artist working in Rome during Vanni's first visit in the early 1620s. It is not surprising to learn that in 1624, Vanni shared a house on Via Ferratina with Nicolas Poussin and Simon Vouet.[24] His *Flight into Egypt* and *Tobias* anticipate the romantic landscapes of Salvator Rosa,

102

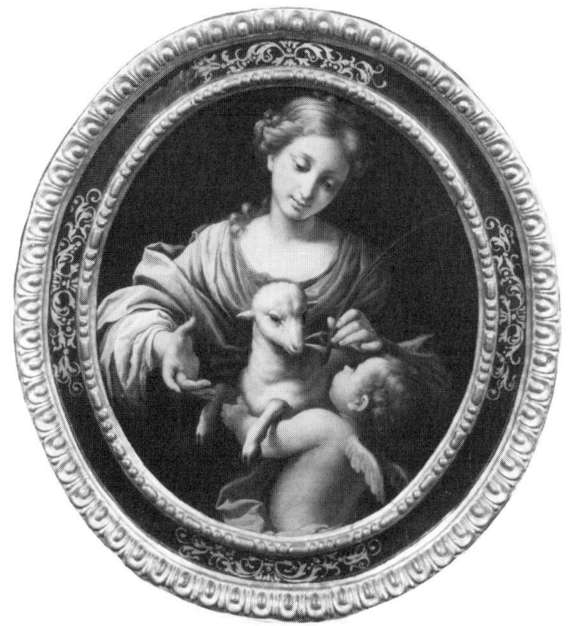

Fig. 22

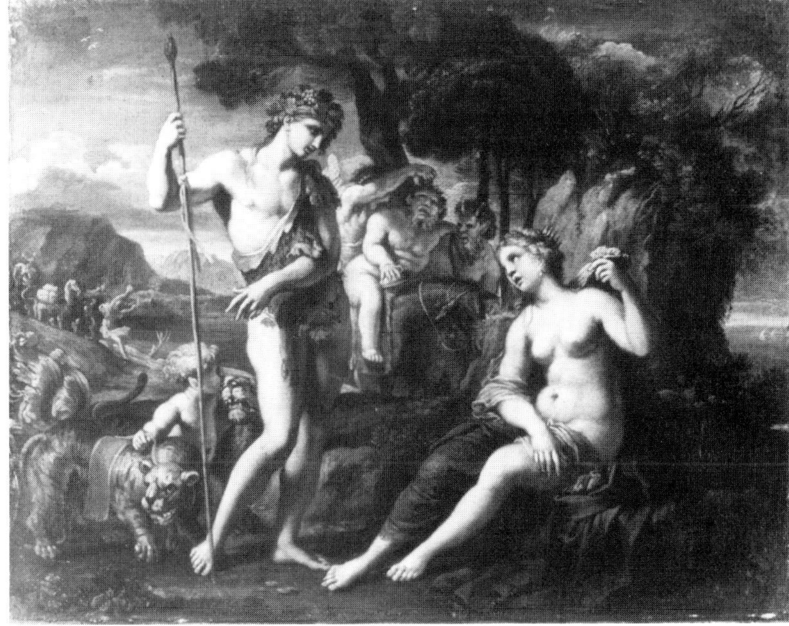

Fig. 23

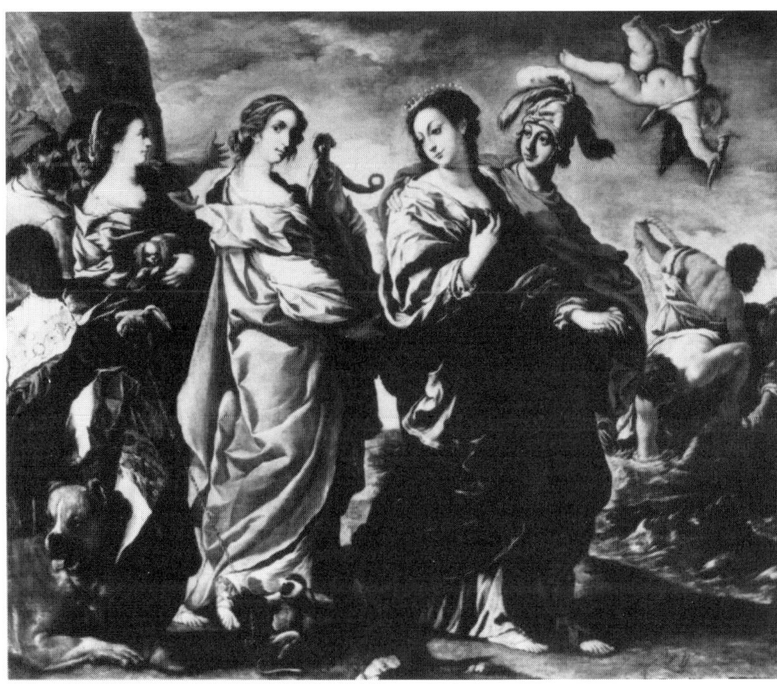

Fig. 24

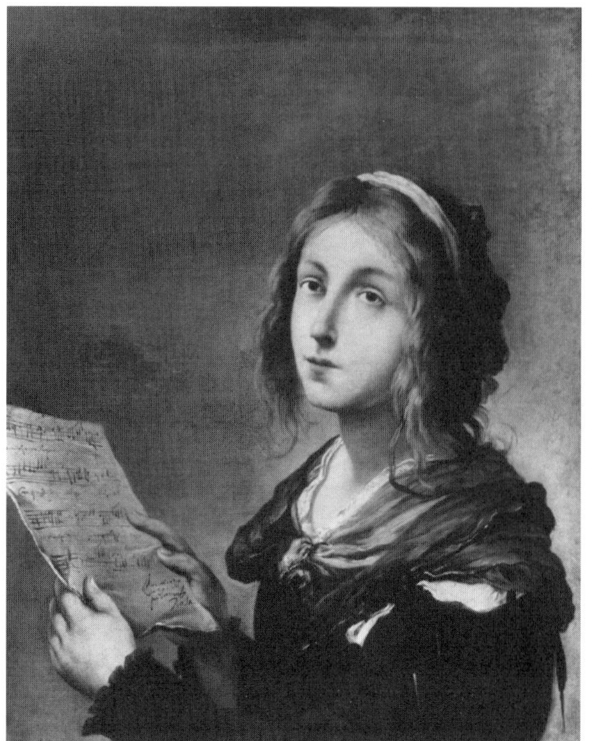
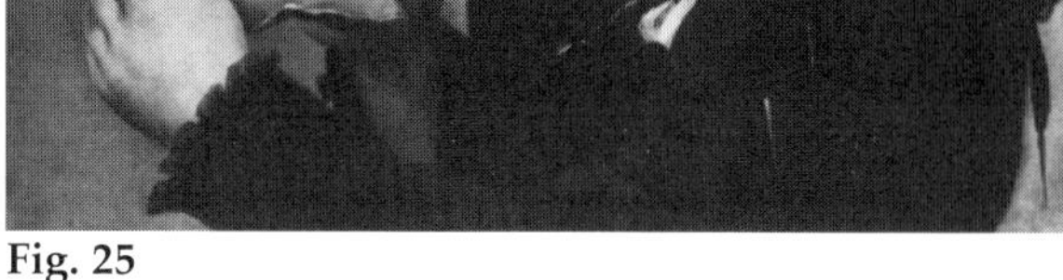

Fig. 25

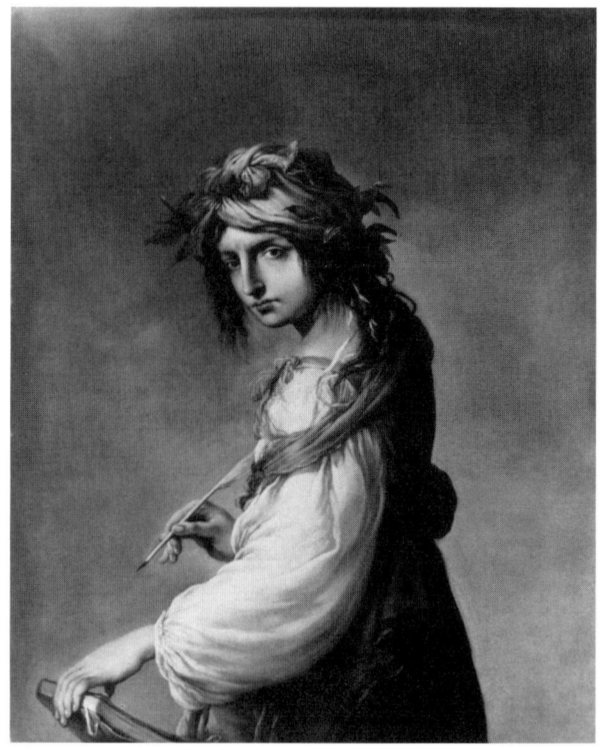

Fig. 26

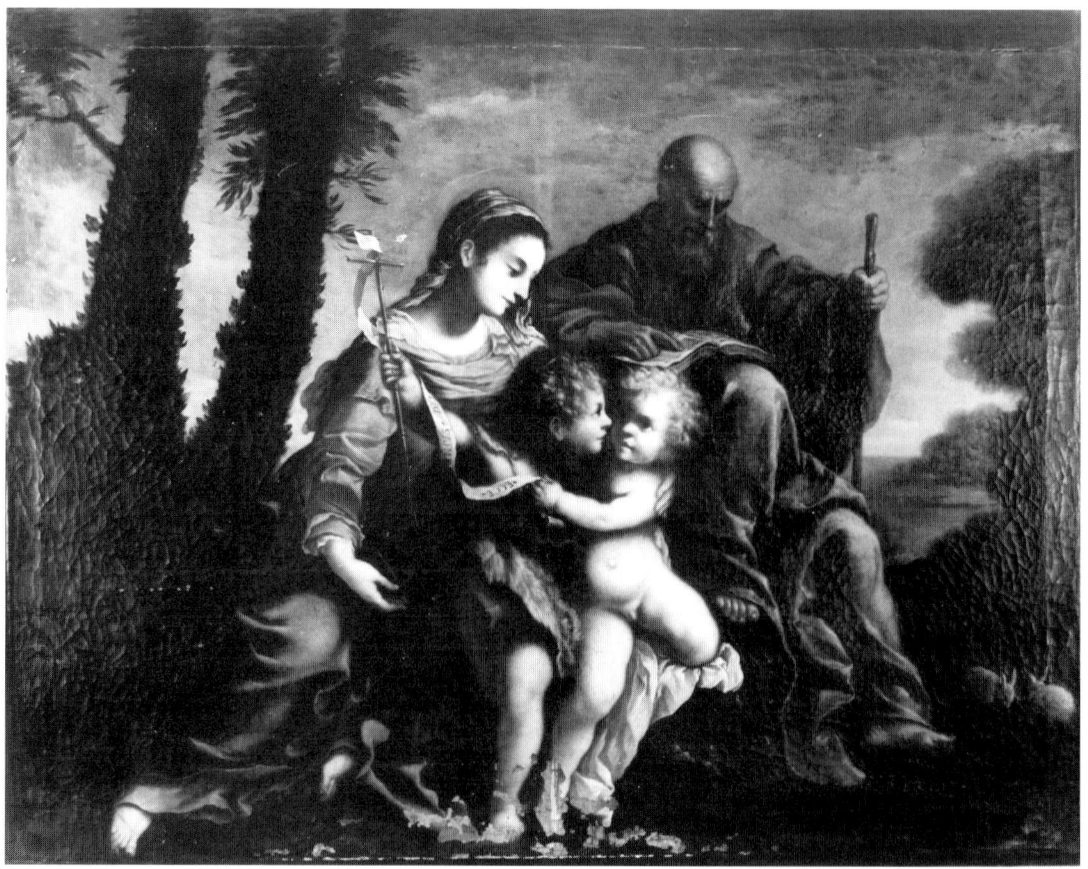

Fig. 27

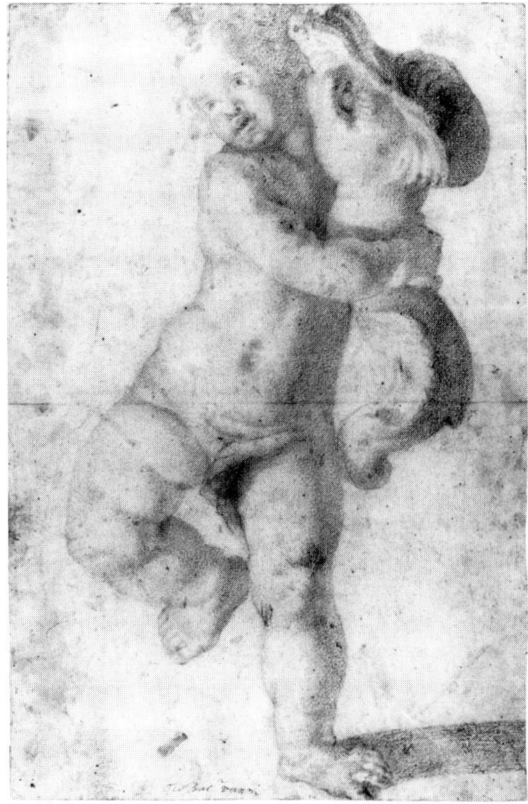

Fig. 28

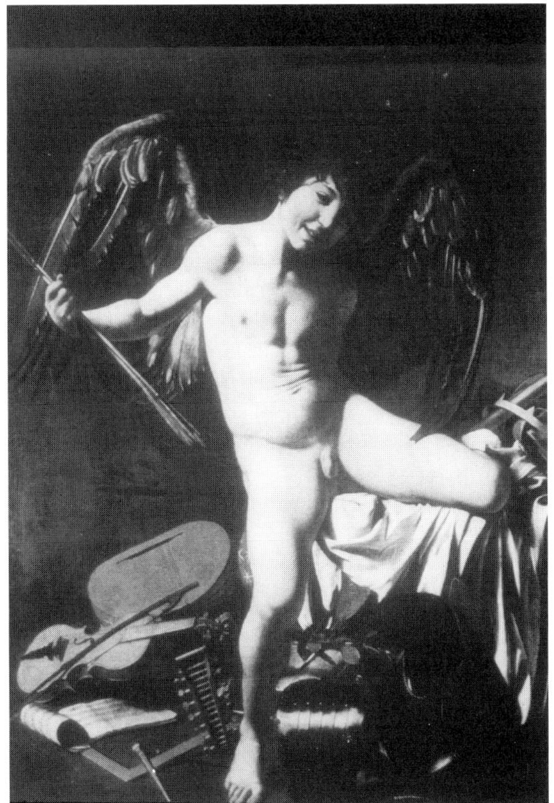

Fig. 29

such as the *Broken Bridge* (Florence, Pitti Palace). The Neapolitan Rosa worked in Florence between 1640 and 1649, and an interchange between the two artists is likely. Rosa's reciprocal influence with Vanni may be reflected in the latter's *Abduction of Helen* (Fig. 24). The gaze of the ancillary figure looking out at the viewer suggests a type favored by Rosa in his *Lucrezia as Music* (Fig. 25) and *Lucrezia as Poetry* (Fig. 26).

With this background, we can understand Vanni as the artist of the Palmer Museum's *Holy Family*. The painting is similar to another *Holy Family* by Vanni in the Cassa di Risparmio, Pistoia, previously in the collection of the Rucellai family of Florence (Fig. 27). In both compositions, the infant Christ embraces St. John. A Vanni drawing, perhaps for the pose of the Christ Child, appeared on the London art market in 1980 (Fig. 28).[25] It is a spirited variation of the embrace in the Palmer and Pistoia paintings. The dolphin may be a Christological reference, as the fish was sometimes used as a symbol for Christ in early Christian art and its significance persisted. The pose of the Christ Child, one leg raised at a sharp angle, is clearly an homage to Caravaggio's *Love Victorious* (Fig. 29), a reference singular in Vanni's oeuvre.

The Palmer *Holy Family* is an example of Vanni's strong interest in the 1640s in the early masters of the Renaissance. The interaction between figures and placement in a well-articulated land-scape reflects the continuing importance of Raphael, especially his Florentine-period Madonnas, such as the *Holy Family* for the Canigiani family (Fig. 30). Vanni's placement of the Madonna's leg and toe echoes Raphael.

Vanni's continued admiration for Correggio is evident in the faces of the infants Christ and St. John, which call to mind the putti of Correggio that fill the dome of the church in the Monastery

Fig. 30 Raphael, *Holy Family with St. John and St. Anne* ('Canigiani' Holy Family), c. 1507. Munich, Alte Pinakothek. Photo: author.

Fig. 31 Giovan Battista Vanni, *Holy Family with Infant St. John and St. Elizabeth*, 1640s, detail of landscape. Palmer Museum of Art, The Pennsylvania State University.

Fig. 32 Giovan Battista Vanni, *St. Francis of Paola Resuscitating a Young Woman*, 1650s. Florence, church of San Giuseppe. Photo: The Uffizi, Gabinetto Fotografico, Soprintendenza per i Beni Artistici e Storici di Firenze.

Fig. 33 Giovan Battista Vanni, *Esther and Ahasuerus*, 1650. Prato, private collection. Photo: author

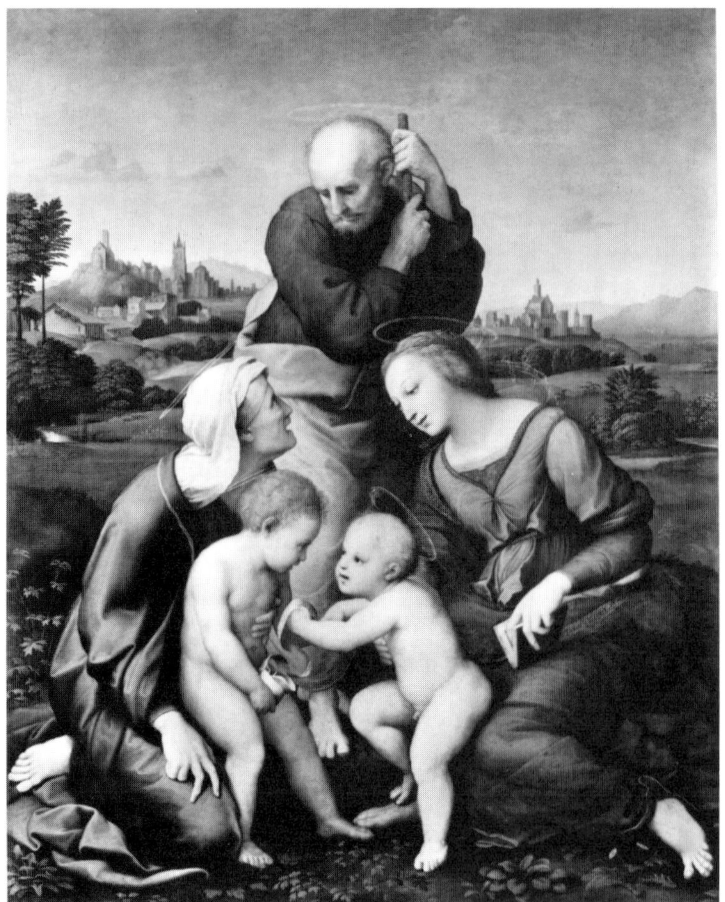

Fig. 30

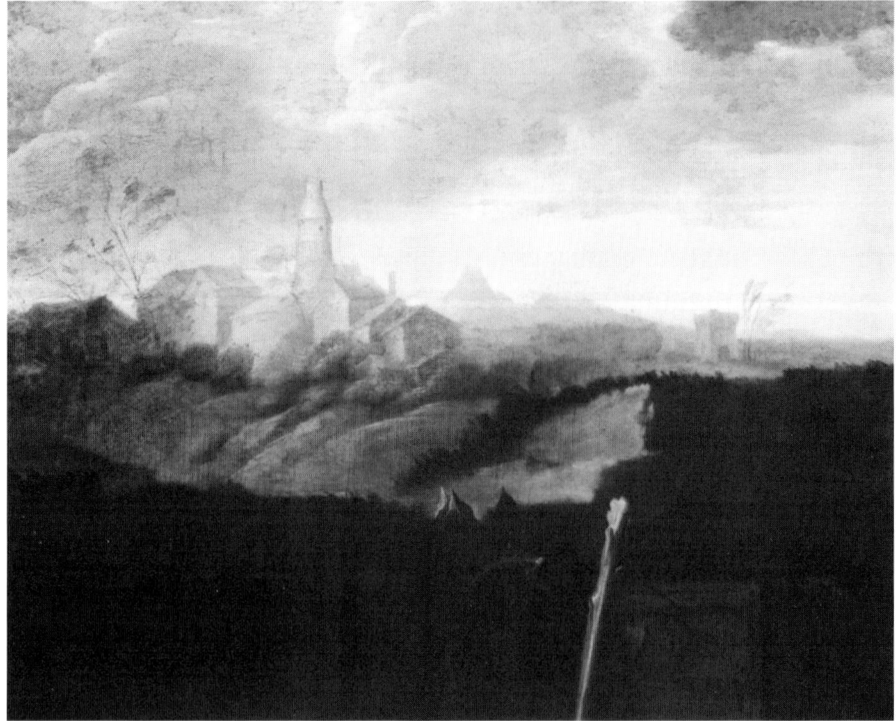

Fig. 31

of St. Paul in Parma. In 1643, Vanni executed drawings for a series of prints after these frescoes,[26] which help us to date the Palmer *Holy Family with St. John and St. Anne* to the 1640s.

In composing the landscape for the *Holy Family* (Fig. 31), Vanni may have worked from a northern print. He repeats the church and the bell tower later in his *St. Francis of Paola Resuscitating a Young Woman* (Fig. 32), one of a series painted by Vanni and others during the late 1650s for the church of San Giuseppe in Florence.[27]

The Palmer *Holy Family* demonstrates the artist's ongoing interest in Roman antiquity; the frieze on the block supporting the Christ child is decorated with antique motifs similar to those in the *St. Sebastian* (Fig. 18). One further observation—the individualized faces of St. Anne and St. Joseph suggest that Vanni may have used live models, a practice common among Florentine painters of the seventeenth century.

The high level of Vanni's art was not sustained in his final years, when he tried unsuccessfully, for example in his *Esther and Ahasuerus* of 1650 (Fig. 33),[28] to emulate the expansive vocabulary of Volterrano.

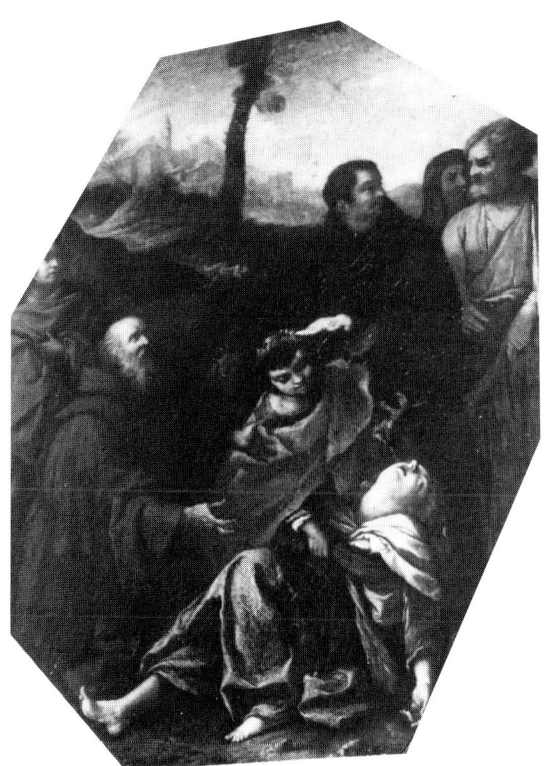

Fig. 32

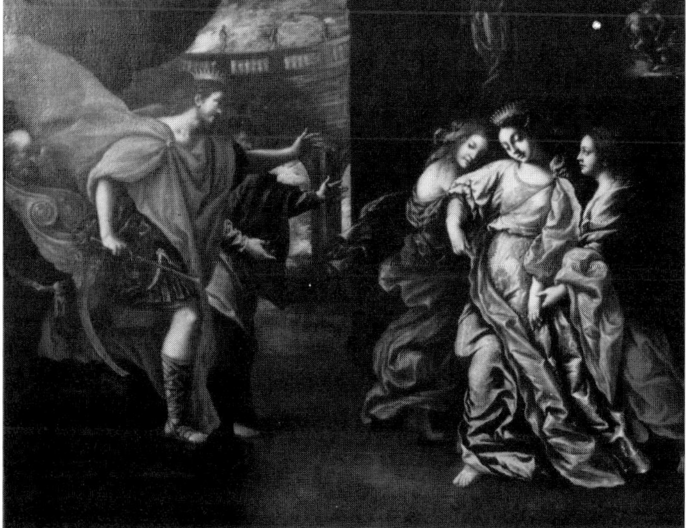

Fig. 33

Endnotes

1 F. Baldassari, "Giovan Battista Vanni e gli affreschi del chiostro di San Benedetto a Pistoia", *Quaderni pistoiesi di storia dell'arte* 5, 1985, pp. 21–37 (Vanni's late frescoes in Pistoia). F. Baldassari, in *Il Seicento fiorentino, Arte a Firenze da Ferdinando I a Cosimo III*, exh. cat. (Palazzo Strozzi exhibition), Firenze, 1986, 3 vols.; vol. I, pp. 290–94 (paintings), vol. II, pp. 291–95 (drawings), vol. III, pp. 178–80 (biography). F. Baldassari, "L'attività pittorica di Giovan Battista Vanni, 1600–1660," Dissertation, University of Florence, 1987–1988, 3 vols. F. Baldassari, "Precisazioni sull'attività giovanile di Giovan Battista Vanni," *Paradigma* 9, 1990, pp. 129–39 (early works). F. Baldassari, "Un inedito di Giovan Battista Vanni," *Paragone* 529/531/533, 1994, pp. 231–34, plates 121–24 (Vanni's *St. Benedict Removing the Devil from the Stone*, Swiss private collection).

2 *Holy Family with St. John and St. Anne*, oil on canvas, 70 x 58 inches (177.8 x 147.3 cm.), Palmer Museum of Art , 73.118. The painting was purchased by the museum in 1973 from Mr. and Mrs. J. O'Connor Lynch, New York.

3 J. Nissman, *Florentine Baroque Art from American Collections*, exh. cat., The Metropolitan Museum of Art, New York, 1969, pp. 40–41, no. 17.

4 *Ibid.*, p. 41.

5 F. Baldassari, 1985, *op. cit.*, pp. 27–37.

6 F. Baldinucci, *Notizie de' professori del disegno da Cimabue in qua*, Firenze 1681–1728, reprinted 1845–47, ed. F. Ranelli, vol. IV, 1846, pp. 534–548; Vanni's authorship of frescoes, p. 547.

7 *Il Seicento fiorentino… op. cit.,* note 1.

8 F. Baldinucci, *op. cit.*

9 Florence, Pitti Palace. See M. A. Bianchini, in *Il Seicento fiorentino… op. cit.*, vol. I, pp. 130–32, no. 1.31.

10 Uffizi inventory no. 9382 F. See E. Testaferrata, in *Il Seicento fiorentino… op. cit.*, vol. II, p. 138, no. 2.85.

11 See F. Baldassari, in *Il Seicento fiorentino… op. cit.*, vol. I, pp. 290–91, no. 1.145.

12 See F. Baldassari, "Un inedito di Giovan Battista Vanni," *Paragone* 529/531/533, 1994, pp. 231–34, plates 121–24.

13 Archivio di Stato di Firenze A.S.F. Notorile Moderno n.13392, Ottavio Amoni 1620-1642, Testamento n.44, c.41 v. See F. Baldassari, *Paragone*, 1994, *op. cit.*, p. 232. A preparatory oil sketch on panel has come to light in a Florentine private collection (Fig. 7).

14 For the series, see G. Pagliarulo, in *Il Seicento fiorentino… op. cit.*, vol. I, p. 246, no. 1.116.

15 *David*, Galleria of the Palazzo degli Alberti, Prato. *Venus and Adonis*, Museum of the Opificio di Pietre Dure, Florence; A.S.F. Possessioni 4169, Cardinale Carlo de' Medici. Libro maestro dal 1617 al 1627 segnato BC c.171 d. e A.S.F., Possessioni 4320, Cardinale Carlo. Entrata e uscita BC dal 1617 al 1624, c.54 r. See F. Baldassari, *Il Seicento fiorentino, op. cit.*, vol. III, p. 178.

16 *Joseph and Potiphar's Wife*, 16 x 21 cm., private collection (previously unpublished). Another small cabinet picture of a *St. John* painted on quartz backed with slate has been identified in the collection of Mark Fehrs Haukohl, Houston, Texas. Both works will be examined in my forthcoming monograph.

17 M. Gregori, in *Il Seicento fiorentino, op. cit.*, vol. I, p. 297.

18 F. Baldassari, *Il Seicento fiorentino, op. cit.*, vol. III, p. 178.

19 F. Baldassari, *Il Seicento fiorentino, op. cit.*, vol. I, pp. 292–94.

20 F. Baldinucci, *op. cit.*

21 A. Caputi and M.T. Penta, *Incisioni italiane del '600 nella raccolta d'Arte Palliara dell' Instituto Suor Orsola Benincasa di Napoli*, Milan, 1987, pp. 201–2, notes 196–202.

22 F. Baldinucci, *op. cit.*, vol. III, p. 723.

23 F. Baldassari, *Il Seicento fiorentino, op. cit.*, vol. II, pp. 291–92.

24 J. Bousquet, "Documents sur le séjour de Simon Vouet à Rome" in *Mélanges d'Archéologie et d'Histoire*, LXIV, 1952, p. 293.

25 Sotheby's, London, 30 October 1980, no. 51, red chalk on white paper, 354 x 235 mm.

26 A. Caputi and M. T. Penta, *op. cit.*, note 21.

27 Vanni, with the help of his workshop, painted six of the nine octagonal pictures depicting the life of St. Francis of Paola, still *in situ* in the church of San Giuseppe in Florence (*The Miracle of Resuscitating a Young Man, Resuscitating a Child, Healing the Crippled, Saving the Shipwrecked, Healing a Blind Man,* and *Saving a Fawn.* (The others were painted by Pignoni and his workshop.) For the series, see R. Contini, "Apocrifi bilivertiani e altri," *Paradigma,* 7, 1986, pp. 63–64, note 34; F. Baldassari, *L'attività pittorica… Il Seicento fiorentino, op. cit.,* II, pp. 259–67; and R. Contini, "Francesco Bianchi Buonavita, primo giovane del Bilivert," *Annali della Fondazione di Studi di Storia dell 'Arte Roberto Longhi,* vol. II, pp. 82–85, Figs. 50a–51b.

28 Prato, private collection, 201 x 262 cm. From documents (Florence, Archivio di Stato, Accademia del Disegno 72, Atti e Sentenze 1620–90, ff. 231–44), we know that a painting of *Esther before Ahasuerus*, probably this, was painted by Vanni in 1650 for the Florentine, Pietro Sacchetti. Since the patron did not pay the agreed fee, Vanni sought the intervention of the Accademia del Disegno. *Esther before Ahasuerus* was then evaluated by the Florentine painters Giovanni Martinelli, Lorenzo Lippi, Mario Balassi, Baccio del Bianco, and Agostino Melissi, who did not come to an agreement. Thus, the painting probably went back to the artist. We do not know when the Serristori family bought it. It appeared, unillustrated, in the sale catalogue of the family as Sienese school XVII century: *Palazzo Serristori, Vendita comprendente importanti dipinti antichi, dipinti del XIX secolo, mobili e oggetti di arredamento, argenti ceramiche europee e orientali, importanti oggetti d'arte, arme antiche*, Sotheby's, Florence, 9–16 May 1977, no. 81.

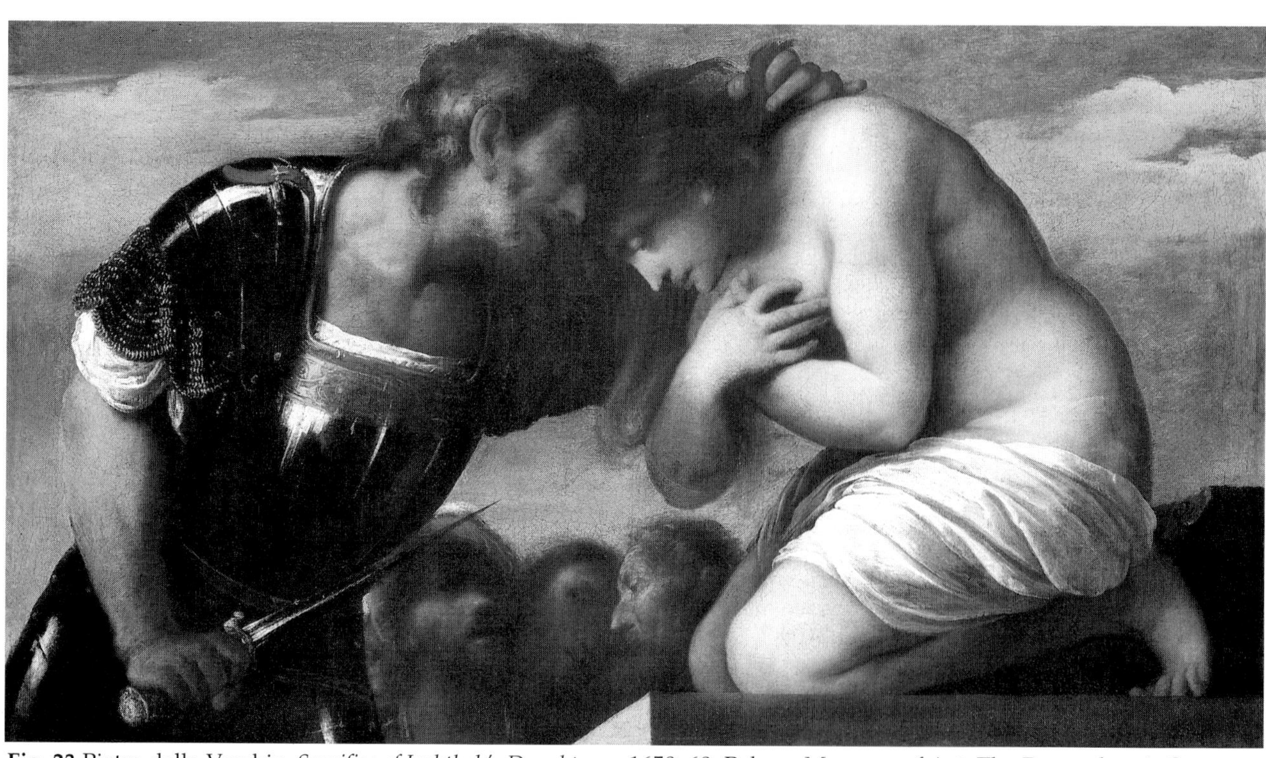

Fig. 23 Pietro della Vecchia, *Sacrifice of Jephthah's Daughter*, c. 1650–60. Palmer Museum of Art, The Pennsylvania State University. (See color plate 5.)

Marvellous Imitations and Outrageous Parodies: Pietro della Vecchia Revisited

Bernard Aikema

If there is one Italian painter from the seventeenth century whose work reflects the dialectics of artistic continuity and change on the one hand, and extraordinary awareness of the demands set by the critical eye of the connoisseur on the other, it is the Venetian, Pietro della Vecchia.

Pietro della Vecchia, who lived and worked in the city of the lagoons between 1603 and 1678, is an anomaly in the history of art. Or so it must seem to those critics who understand the development of art as a linear process, in which one style follows another in a more or less regular way, the Baroque neatly succeeding the late Renaissance, the Rococo, in its turn, following the Baroque, and so forth. In the last few decades, art historians have become increasingly aware that such a schematic and ultimately idealistic view does not do justice to the complexity of artistic forms of the past. More and more, scholars have turned their attention to painterly (and sculptural) oeuvres that do not conform to the established canons of "renaissance" or "baroque." Only by pursuing these studies, that is, by patiently reconstructing the oeuvres of artists in terms of their original cultural milieu, their role in the artistic traditions to which they belong, and the effect they were intended to have on the public for which they were destined, may we expect to come to a historical understanding not only of these fascinating eccentrics, but also the full range of artistic expression in any given era. I sought to do just that in my 1990 monograph on Pietro della Vecchia.[1] I turned my attention to this artist again to add fresh material and insights that were central to the general themes of our 1995 meeting at the Palmer Museum of Art.[2]

I would like to present my observations in the context of the symposium headings, "continuity," "innovation," and "connoisseurship." Instead of using these words, however, I shall translate them into terms that were adopted in the seventeenth century to express similar concepts. "Continuity" I would translate with the two terms *imitatio* and *aemulatio*; "innovation" with the word *meraviglia*; and "connoisseurship," or rather the term "connoisseurs," with that of *dilettanti*, whose *intelligenza* was rigorously tested by Vecchia. In using these Latin and Italian terms, I hope to create a critical framework that enables us to study Vecchia's works in the way I have indicated, in their original cultural milieu, with respect to the artistic traditions of the time relative to their original public.

Our first heading concerns *imitatio* and *aemulatio*. These two words stem from rhetorical instruction and were widely used in the Latin schools during the Renaissance. A good number of artists got their primary education at these schools. In the painters' workshops, training followed a similar pattern. From the beginning, the young pupils were instructed to copy, or *imitate*, the works of the master and of other illustrious examples from the past. The masters, in turn, tried to *emulate* the canonical models, or even to surpass them with virtuosic variations—up to a point where it became difficult to recognize the original prototype. This ability to "hide" the model was considered an important yardstick in judging the quality of a painting. In the words of the Dutch scholar, Eddy de Jongh: "a successful *aemulatio* ... is one in which the work of art in question disguises its borrowings while simultaneously making apparent the similarities with the work that the artist was attempting to better—a matter of subtlety."[3] A matter of subtlety indeed, but a crucial matter, and no one knew how to play the trick better than Pietro Vecchia, as contemporary critics acknowledged. Marco Boschini, author of the treatise, *La carta del navegar pitoresco* (1660), and a guidebook to Venice (published 1664 and 1674), said of Vecchia's work: "although made as imitations of Giorgione, these imitations are not copies, but the products of his intellect."[4] With Giorgione as the role model, small wonder then

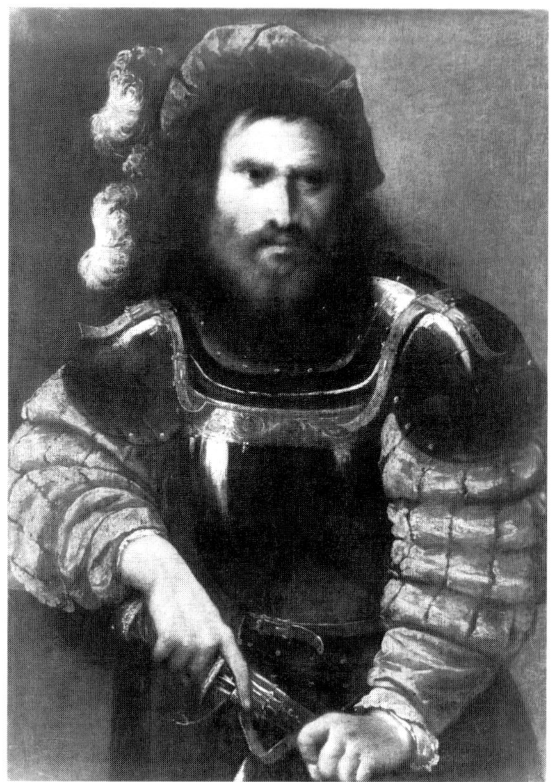

Fig. 1

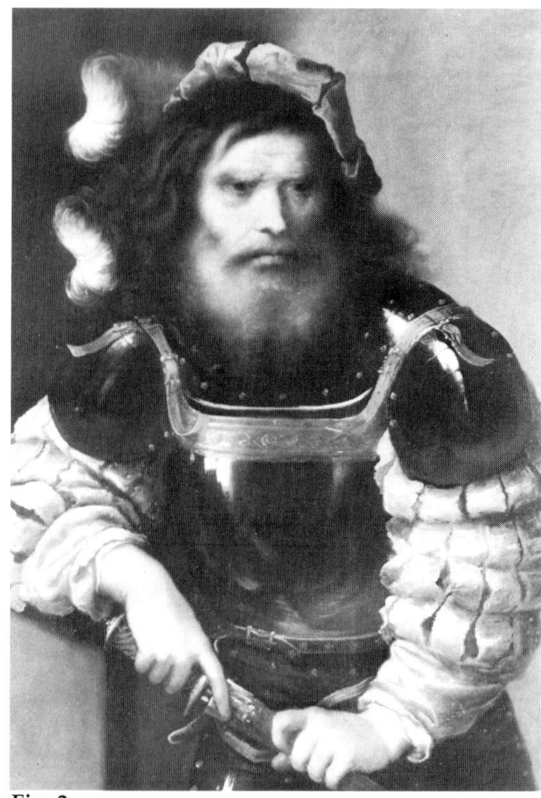

Fig. 2

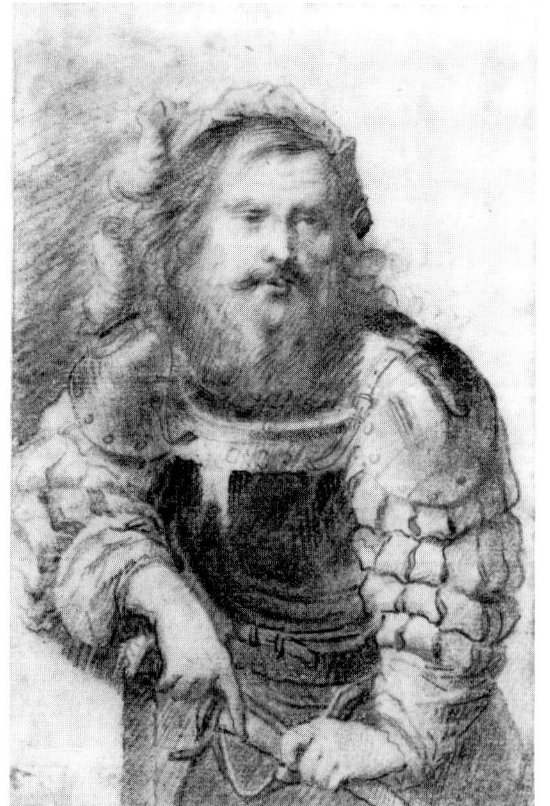

Fig. 3

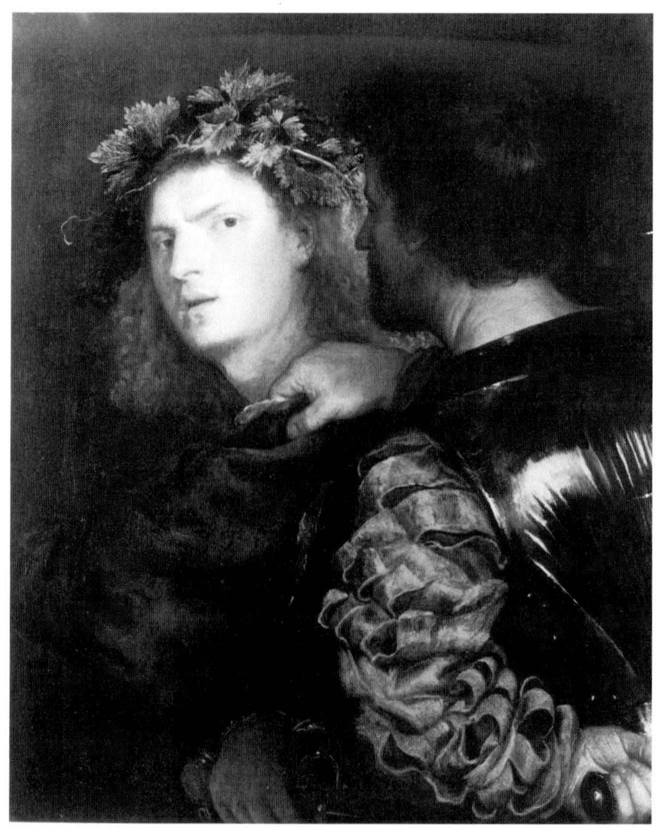

Fig. 4

that Boschini called Vecchia elsewhere the *"simia de Zorzon,"* or "Giorgione's ape."[5] Let us take a look at just a few of these *imitazioni*, in order to understand what it was in Giorgione that attracted Vecchia and his contemporaries.

One of Vecchia's most celebrated compositions is a half-length figure of a redoubtable warrior drawing his sword. A number of slightly different versions are known, including a particularly fine example, first published by Ivanoff in 1944 (Fig. 1).[6] A painting in Salzburg (Fig. 2)[7] and a chalk drawing in an Italian private collection (Fig. 3)[8] are two of the many contemporary adaptations and copies, autograph and by others, which testify to the composition's popularity. The shining armour, the plumed hat, and somewhat exaggerated look of menace of this *"bravo"* create an effect that Ellis Waterhouse, discussing a similar picture, once described rather ungenerously as Vecchia's "Hollywood Giorgionesque" vein.[9] In reality, Pietro Vecchia adapted a prototype believed to be by Giorgione, the famous *Il Bravo* now in the Kunsthistorisches Museum, Vienna (Fig. 4),[10] to Seicento taste by accentuating those very aspects of the sixteenth-century picture that his contemporaries considered quintessential Giorgione. Boschini explained why he so admired Giorgione's *Bravo*: "This is truly such a ferocious action / That whoever sees it wishes to / Raise his hand and say 'stop,' / So real and more than real does it seem."[11] Elsewhere, too, Boschini praises Giorgione for his "rendering of reality" (*maniera del dasseno*), and calls him an artist "with a style that is more lively than living nature itself."[12] For the Seicento public, Giorgione was the artist *par excellence* of naturalism and of the rendering of action, the "snapshot." His art deserved high praise for he was able to take the viewer by surprise with *un ingano de l'ochio* (a deception of the eye).[13] Surprise through deception is an important aspect of Seicento aesthetics that we shall return to later. For the moment we can conclude that Pietro della Vecchia perfectly captured the *maniera del dasseno* in his *aemulatio*, combining in a single figure the shining armour and wide sleeves of the *Bravo* unsheathing his sword and the slightly turned head of the young man being assaulted.

For a seventeenth-century art lover, the name of Giorgione did not stand only for a perfect *maniera del dasseno*. In the *Breve instruzione*, the introduction Boschini wrote to his 1674 guidebook, *Le ricche minere della pittura veneziana*, the critic stated: "For the glory of Giorgione and of Pietro Vecchia, a Venetian painter now living, and for the intelligence of art lovers (*intelligenza de'Dilettanti*), I must say that this Vecchia should be watched, for one will encounter brushstrokes of his that are so transformed into the Giorgionesque form that one will be in doubt whether these are by Giorgione or imitations thereof."[14] The intelligence of the *dilettanti*, in other words, is not only tested by their capability to distinguish particular compositions and motifs, relating them to the artist's prototypes, but also by their perception of the most essential, the most individual aspect of the artwork, the "signature" of the brushwork. According to some seventeenth-century critics, the style of an artist manifested itself most clearly when the brushwork was most visible. In the *Breve instruzione*, in a passage praising the *"colorito veneziano,"* Boschini even went so far as to state flatly that *"la macchia ... è Maniera"* (the visible brushwork... is style).[15] Perhaps he had Vasari's remark in mind, that the marvelously loose brushwork of the late Titian seemed an easy manner, but in reality was most difficult to imitate.[16] Pietro Vecchia met Vasari's implicit challenge. In countless works the Seicento artist imitated the "Giorgionesque" brushwork, most consistently in the many character heads (*teste di carattere*) he produced throughout his long career (Figs. 5, 6).[17] It is perfectly understandable that works of this kind were most popular. With such paintings, the growing number of *dilettanti* could show off wonderfully their skills of connoisseurship—their *intelligenza*. In the eyes of contemporary viewers, these were indeed Vecchia's most "Giorgionesque" works. The connoisseurs, however, did not always succeed in recognizing the artist's *inganno* (deceit). Boschini tells us the story of how he and Vecchia were once shown a self-portrait by Giorgione, which Vecchia laughingly confessed to having painted himself thirty-two years earlier.[18] It should be said, though, that such anecdotes abound in seventeenth-century art literature, and it may be an invented story designed to emphasize the artist's virtuosity.

Fig. 1 Pietro della Vecchia, *Warrior*. Formerly Milan, Coll. P. Tibertelli De Pisis. Photo: Alinari.

Fig. 2 Pietro della Vecchia, *Warrior*. Salzburg, Residenzgalerie. Photo: Residenzgalerie, Salzburg, inv. 313.

Fig. 3 Copy after Pietro della Vecchia, *Warrior*. Italy, private collection. Photo © Speltdoorn, Brussels.

Fig. 4 Attributed to Giorgione, *Il Bravo*. Vienna, Kunsthistorisches Museum. Photo: Kunsthistorisches Museum.

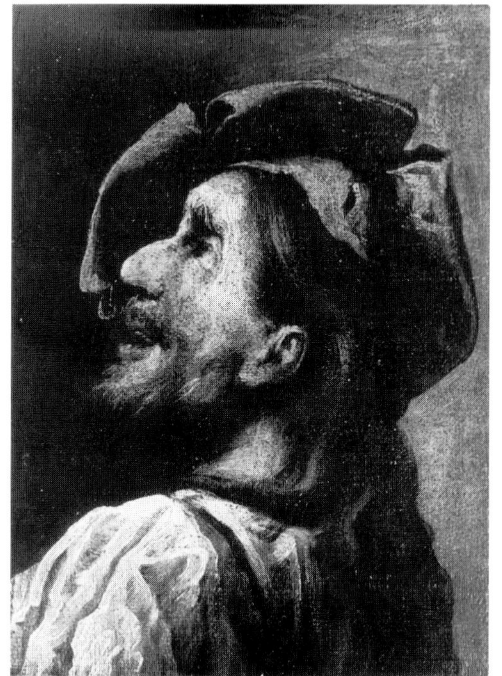

Fig. 5

Fig. 6

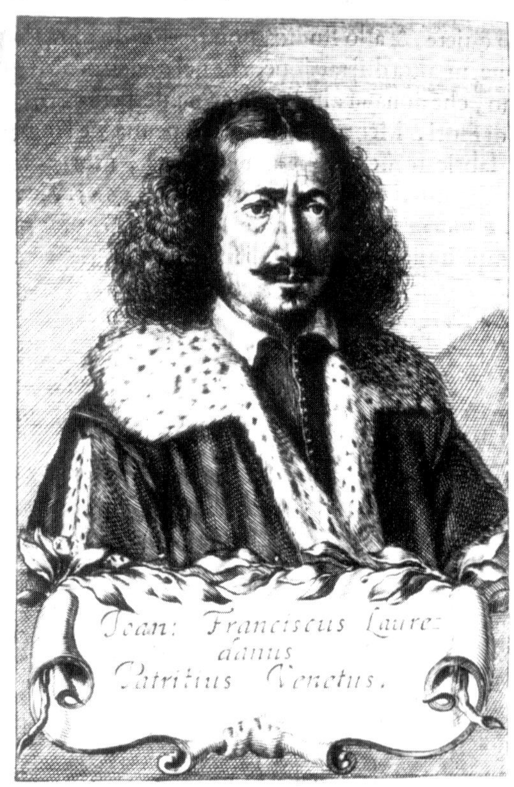

LAVREA. DANTE ipso Phœbo, redimicula geſtat:
Et potiseſt alijs LAVREA Serta DARE.

Fig. 7

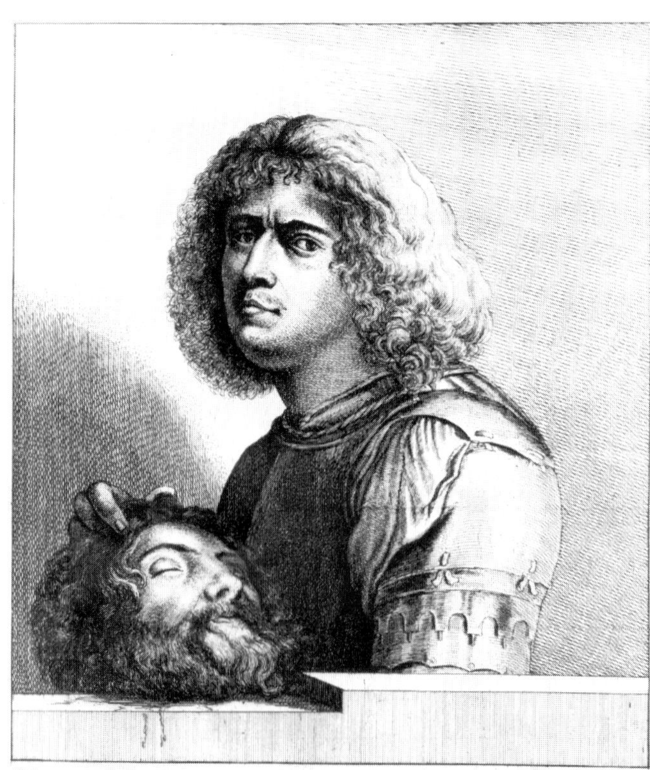

VERO RITRATTO DE GIORGONE DE CASTEL FRANCO
da luy fatto come lo celebra il libro del VASARI.

Fig. 8

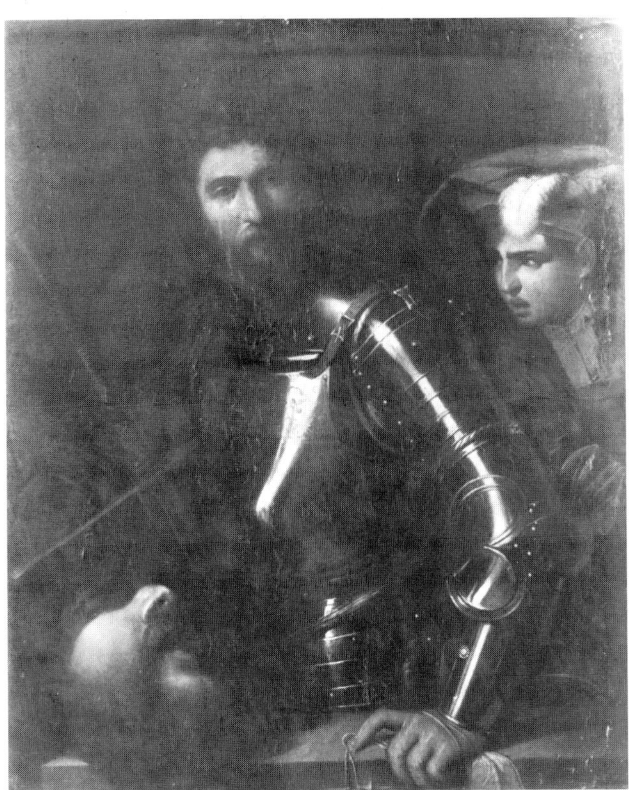

Fig. 9

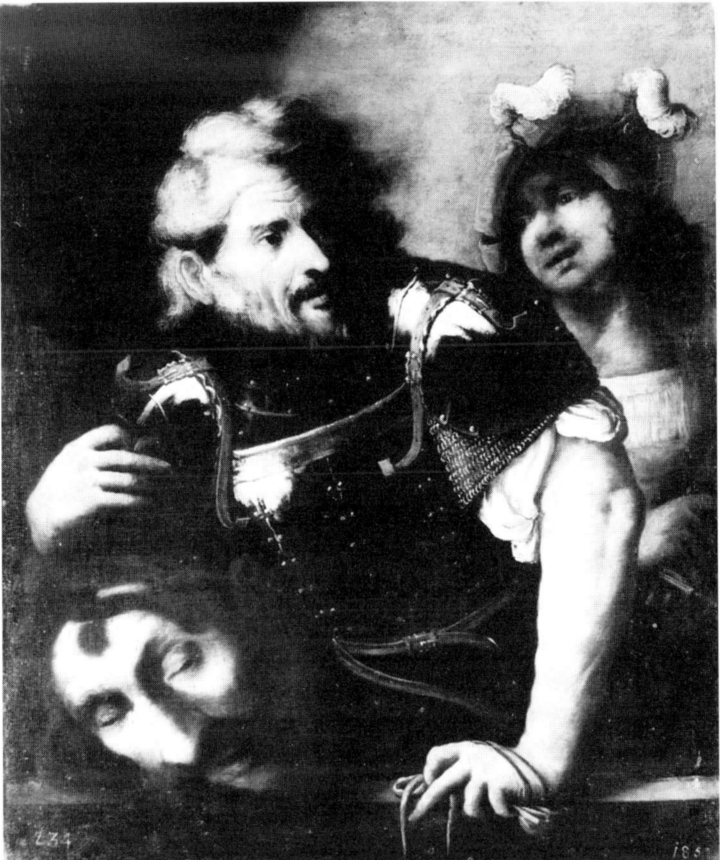

Fig. 10

Fig. 5 Pietro della Vecchia, *Picturesque Head*. Venice, private collection. Photo: author.

Fig. 6 Pietro della Vecchia, *Picturesque Head*. Paris, Louvre. Photo: Documentation photographique de la Réunion des musées nationaux.

Fig. 7 Giovanni Picini after (?) Nicolas Régnier, *Giovan Francesco Loredano.* Published in *La Gloria de gli Incogniti*, Venetia, 1647, p. 244. Photo: author.

Fig. 8 Wenzel Hollar after Giorgione, *David and the Head of Goliath*, 1650. Photo: author.

Fig. 9 "Amico friulano del Dossi," *Saul, David and the Head of Goliath.* Stuttgart, Staatsgalerie. Photo: Gemäldegalerie Stuttgart.

Fig. 10 Pietro della Vecchia, *Saul, David and the Head of Goliath*. Dresden; Staatliche Kunstsammlungen. Photo: Staatliche Kunstsammlungen (Pfauder).

L'ingano de l'ochio could take various forms. When viewing a work of art, the Seicento spectator wanted to be surprised, to experience the marvels of a creation as wonderful, as unusual, as paradoxical, as unexpected as possible. Satire and grotesque humour, daring eroticism and abstruse philosophy, pseudo-science and witchcraft could provide appropiate themes to achieve the desired effect of *meraviglia*, the term used in Seicento poetry and literary criticism to describe such effects. It stems from the poet Giovan Battista Marino,[19] who greatly influenced the *Accademia degli Incogniti*, a literary circle in Venice headed by the patrician, Giovan Francesco Loredano (Fig. 7).[20] Pietro Vecchia had close ties with the *Incogniti*. This is borne out by the unusual themes he preferred, which were perfect pictorial renderings of *meraviglia*. The following examples will illustrate the point.

Vecchia's use of the motif of David with the head of Goliath is an excellent illustration of how the artist parodied pictorial traditions and is quite in line with the literary practice of the *Incogniti*, who were capable, for instance, of writing grotesque love poems on themes such as a *Bellissima Gobba* (a beautiful crippled woman), or a *Bellissima Matta* (a beautiful crazy woman).[21] Vecchia's points of departure are a painting by Giorgione, shown here in the 1650 print after it by Wenceslaus Hollar (Fig. 8),[22] and a composition (known in several versions) which may originate in a work by the anonymous sixteenth-century Northern Italian artist known as *amico friulano del Dossi* (Fig. 9).[23] The *amico friulano* composition evidently reflects Giorgione's invention, but the principal figure is Saul, while David is relegated to a secondary position in the right margin. This composition seems to correspond with the description of a picture that the Venetian seventeenth-century critic Carlo Ridolfi attributed to Giorgione: "two half-length figures in one painting, with Saul grasping by the hair the head of Goliath brought by the young David, and in the latter one admires the courage and in the former the royal majesty."[24] There is a picture by Pietro Vecchia, also known in several versions, which fits this description at least as well, if not better (Fig. 10).[25] For while Saul's right hand in the Stuttgart picture disappears in a deeply shaded section, the same hand in the painting by Vecchia unmistakably holds Goliath's head by the hair, as described by Ridolfi. It would seem that the usually well-informed Ridolfi was deceived by yet another clever *aemulatio* by Pietro Vecchia.

Another picture by Vecchia is more remarkable, or perhaps we should say, more outrageous. This relatively early work, the present location of which is unknown to me, shows not two but six figures behind a parapet, one of whom is an elderly woman (Fig. 11).[26] The iconography seems very unusual at first. I think we should rule out the possibility that the woman represents Herodias and the severed head John the Baptist. The menacing *bravo* holding the head of Goliath should be identified as King Saul, whereas the youth on the extreme left, who curiously enough looks more like a seminarian than a valiant young shepherd, must represent David. The startling element is the gruesome head of Goliath, which bears an awful grin. Why did Vecchia choose to include this horrible detail in the picture? Certainly in order to shock, to provoke the onlooker: a *meraviglia* indeed, although of somewhat doubtful taste in our eyes. But the provocation might be more than a simple pun and have a deeper meaning. According to Vasari, Giorgione's self-portrait is included in his *David and Goliath*. John Shearman has argued, convincingly in my opinion, that the bearded head of Goliath is Giorgione's self-portrait and not the head of David, as had always been assumed.[27] In my 1990 book, I raised the question of whether there may be an analogy to Vecchia's painting. Could the repulsive head also be a self-portrait? I rejected the possibility mainly on the basis of the fact that the short beard of the severed head in the picture does not seem to fit the fashion of the 1630s as we know it.[28]

At the time this appeared logical, but I feel now that I may have viewed the matter a bit too easily. I have come to this conclusion after reconsidering another curious picture by the master, formerly in the Papafava collection in Padua (Fig. 12).[29] It also shows a group of half-length figures behind a parapet. The principal character, a man with unkempt hair, a beard, and a rather long, aquiline nose, holds with his right hand a severed head on a platter while simultaneously poking his left middle finger into the dead man's mouth. His neighbor on the right fixes us with his gaze while at the same time drawing our attention to his companion's strange action. It is not easy to determine the subject of this peculiar image. The platter would seem to indicate that it is a representation of John the Baptist—but who are the accompanying figures?

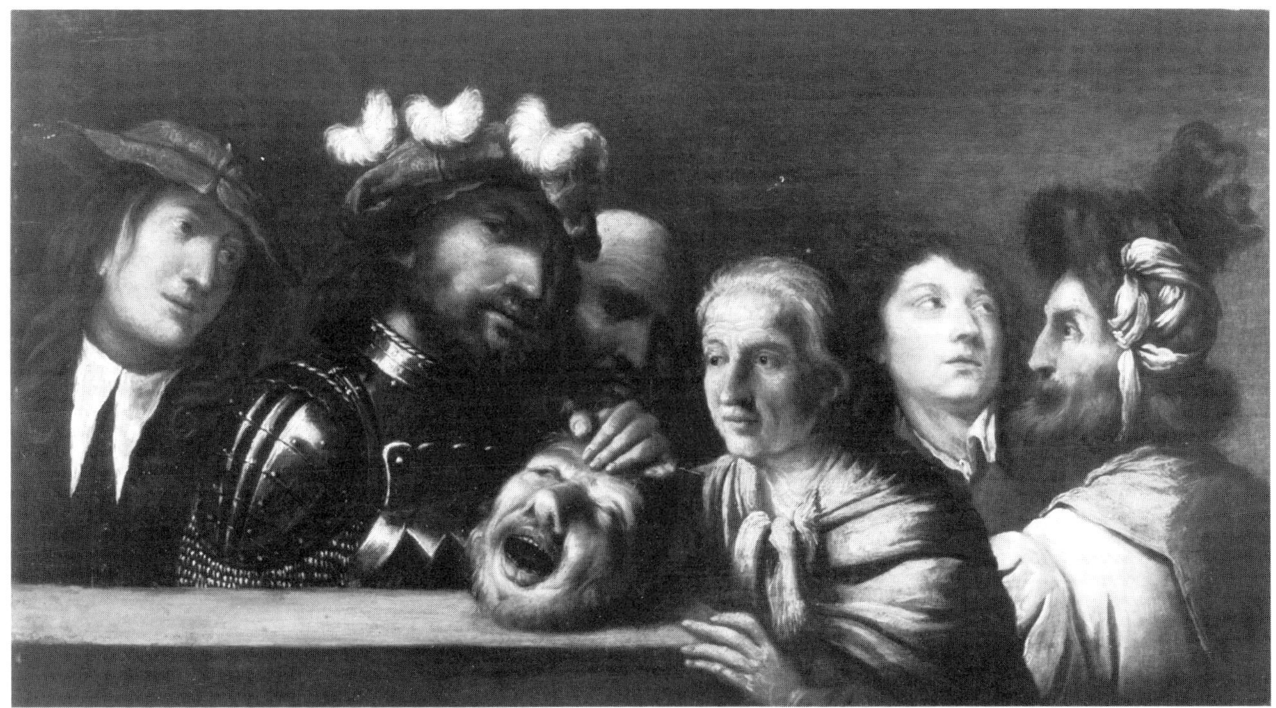

Fig. 11

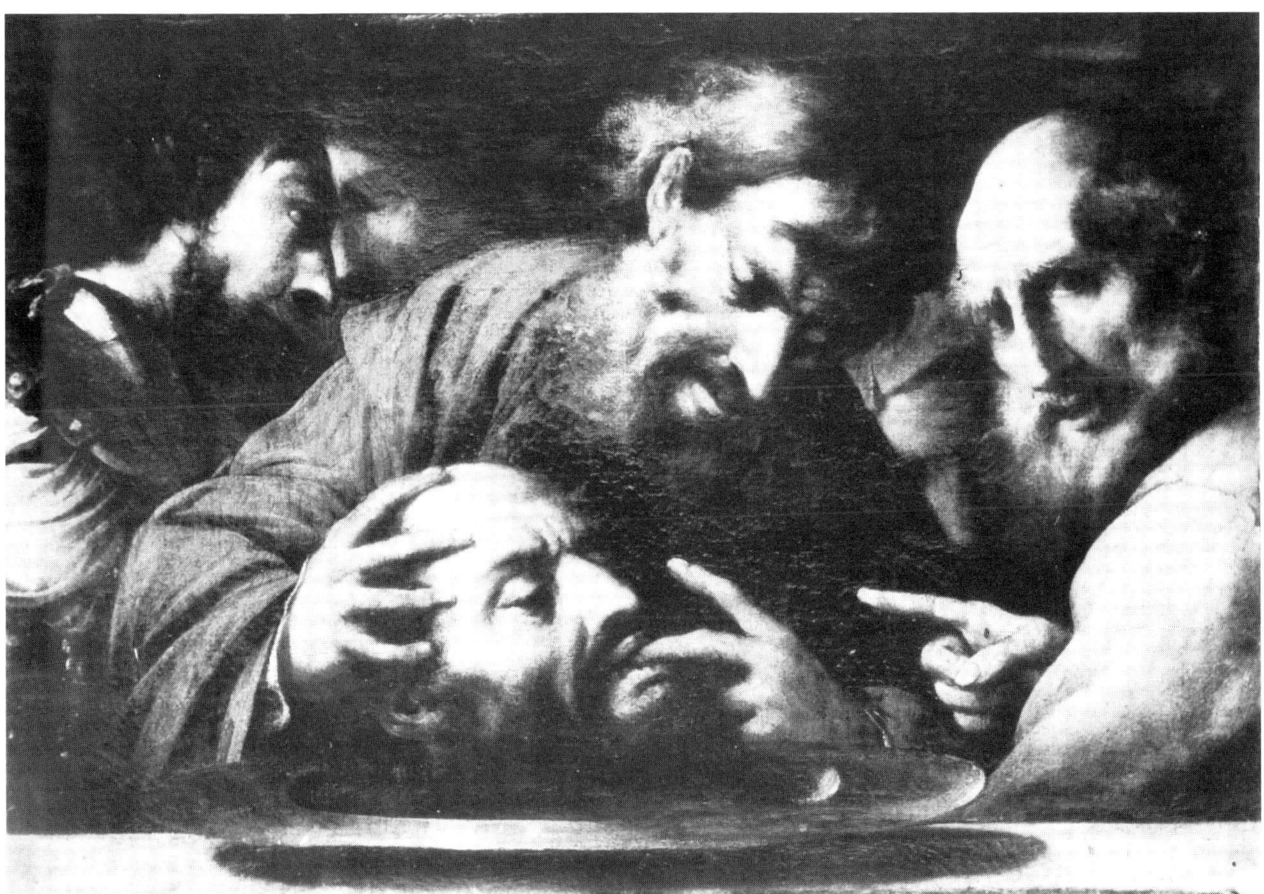

Fig. 12

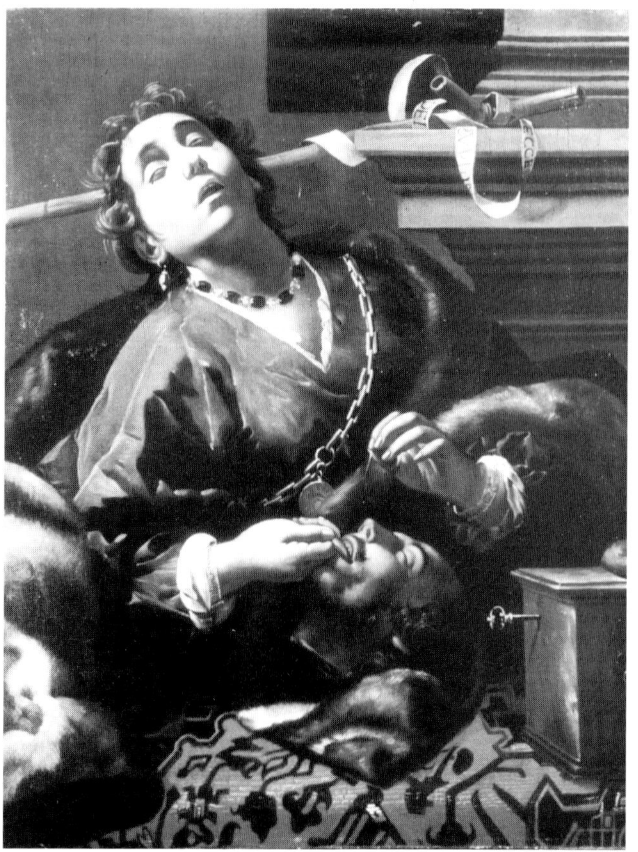

Fig. 13

There is a Seicento iconographical type in which Herodias is shown with the head of Saint John, whose tongue she has pierced out of vengeance.[30] Several paintings by Francesco Cairo are magnificent examples of this imagery (Fig. 13).[31] Although Vecchia's picture seems to allude to this episode, its theme is certainly different. Actually, the picture has no "real" subject at all. Instead, it represents an amalgam of two themes: that of Saul and the head of Goliath and that of Herodias piercing the tongue of Saint John. A quite sophisticated *astratto del suo intelletto* (product of his intelligence), Vecchia's picture challenges the visual memory of the *dilettanti* but leaves them in the end with an open question: what is the subject? To my knowledge, the picture is unique in the seventeenth century: a history piece without a theme. Of course, this is already a perfect *meraviglia* by itself. But I venture to suggest that Vecchia went even further in his erudite play on established pictorial traditions. The head of Saint John is evidently modelled after that of Goliath in the picture by Giorgione. Supposing the artist knew that the latter was a self-portrait by Giorgione, Vecchia's representation might contain another, rather startling surprise. For who could the strange man be, poking his finger into Giorgione's mouth? As a hypothesis I would suggest that perhaps this person is Pietro Vecchia himself, visualizing his irreverent "play" on the generally respected Cinquecento tradition in a most unusual and direct manner. There is no way to prove this idea. All we know of Vecchia's appearance is that he was short and thin ("*piccolo, e smunto*").[32]

The only external argument we can propose to lend weight to the hypothesis is another picture by Vecchia (Fig. 14).[33] This painting shows exactly the same composition as the ex-Papafava picture, with one cardinal difference: instead of a severed head, the central character is holding a celestial globe. It has been convincingly suggested that this picture is a representation of the Greek philosophers, Democritus and Heraclitus, a theme popular in Seicento Italy and the Netherlands, especially among the followers of Caravaggio.[34] From his own paintings and printed sources, we have evidence that Vecchia had a keen interest in scientific and pseudo-scientific pursuits, such as chiromancy, cabalism, astronomy, and astrology (Figs. 15, 16).[35] Could

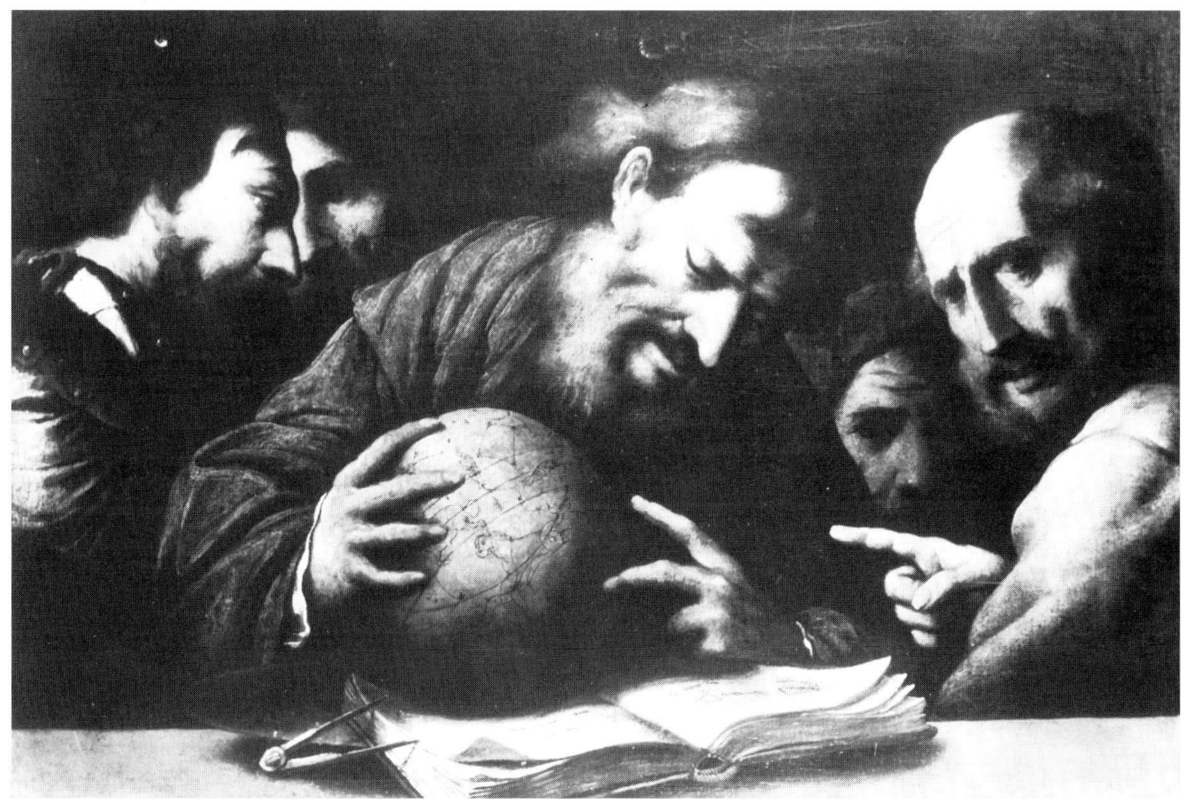

Fig. 14

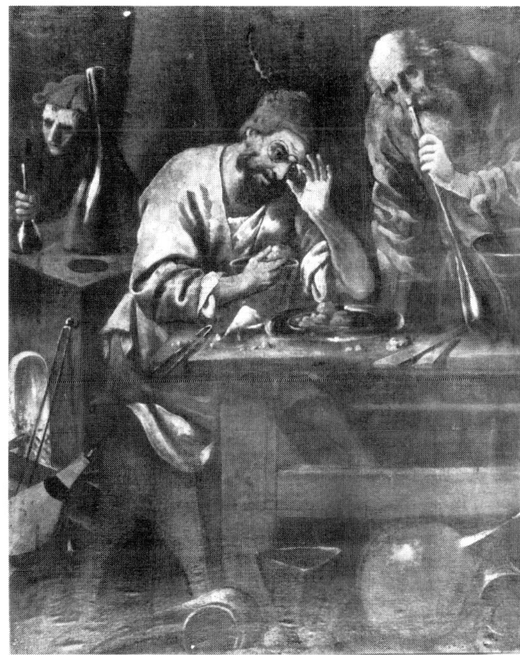

Fig. 15

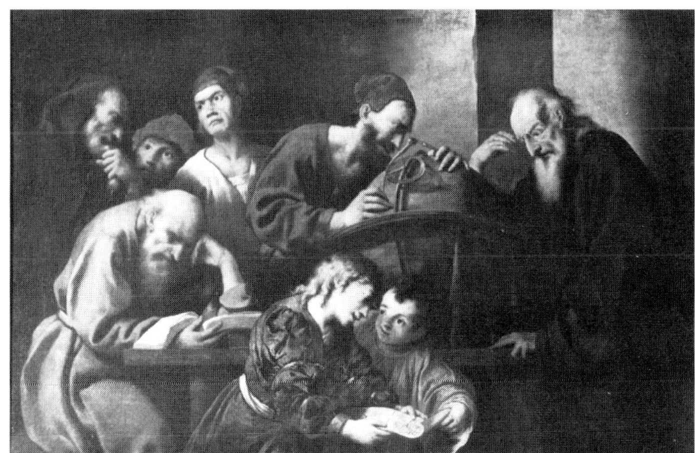

Fig. 16

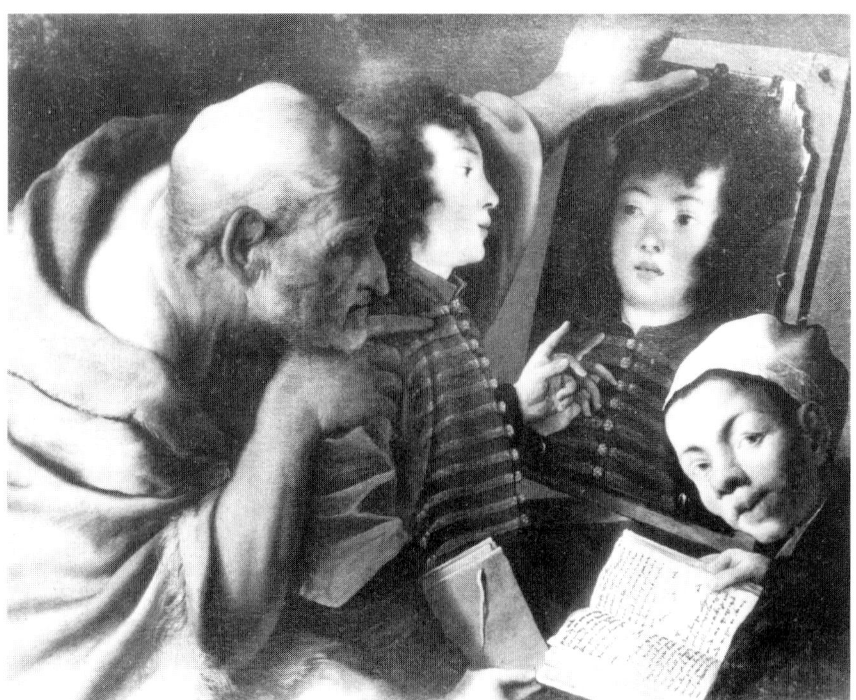

Fig. 17

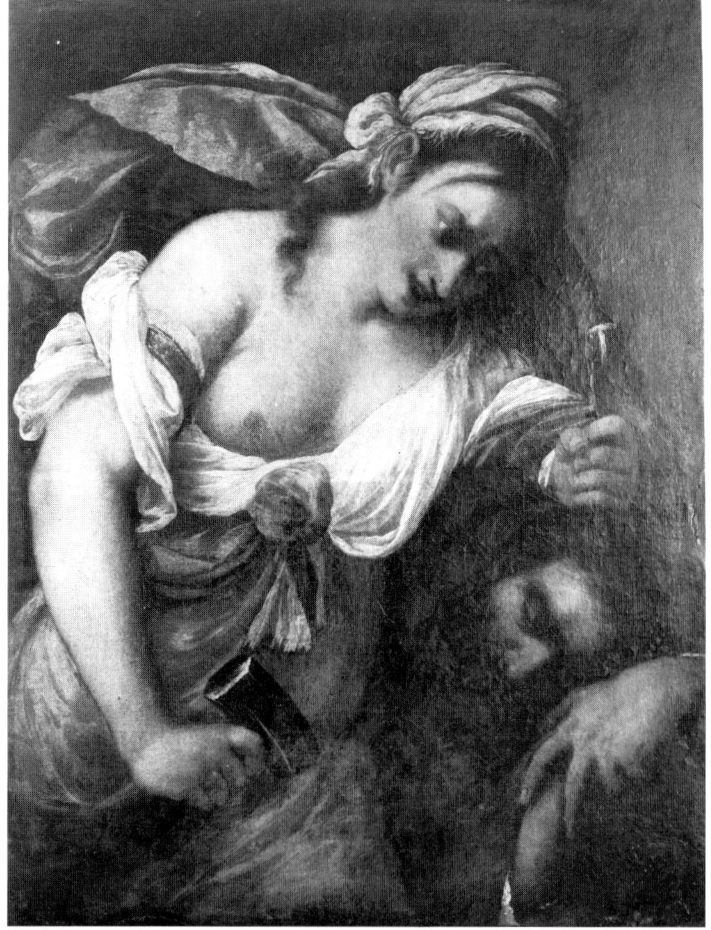

Fig. 18

Vecchia, returning to the similar compositions—with severed head and a globe—have portrayed himself in both related works with the intention of illustrating two quintessential aspects of his art: pictorial tradition and (pseudo) science?[36] It is true that the proposed self-portraits look more like one of Vecchia's many *teste di carattere* than a specific individual, but that, too, might be an *inganno* of the artist vis-à-vis his public. I should make it clear that I would not have dared to put forward such an audacious, if not extravagant, hypothesis for any other artist than Pietro della Vecchia, master of the *inganno* and the *meraviglia*.

Just how challenging Vecchia's pictures could be at times is excellently illustrated in his works with erotic or eroticizing themes. In my book, I argued that a painting in a private collection depicting Socrates and two students is clearly homosexual in tone (Fig. 17).[37] Without repeating my arguments extensively, I limit myself to pointing out the almost exaggerated contrast between the ugly pupil looking in our direction and the beautiful boy, held closely by the old philosopher, whose face is reflected together with that of his teacher in the mirror, which is not only a means of "knowing thyself" but also a traditional erotic symbol. Moreover, Vecchia's interpretation of the theme of Socrates and his pupils is directly paralleled in one of the most notorious literary works to appear in Venice during this period, the novella, *Alcibiade fanciullo a scuola*. Published around 1650 through the sponsorship of Giovan Francesco Loredano, it was probably written by Antonio Rocco, a member of Loredano's circle. The novella is in essence a plea for homosexual love in the form of a dialogue between Socrates and his beloved pupil, Alcibiades.[38] Vecchia's painting shows such clear affinities with *Alcibiade fanciullo a scuola* that we may safely assume it was directly inspired by the novella. In Vecchia's oeuvre, indeed in the whole of Seicento art, this picture is an exception, albeit a significant one. As a rule, the artist's more or less erotic pictures are firmly heterosexual, for example a *Jael and Sisera* from Vecchia's later period (Fig. 18),[39] and a slightly earlier *Roman Charity* (Fig. 19).[40]

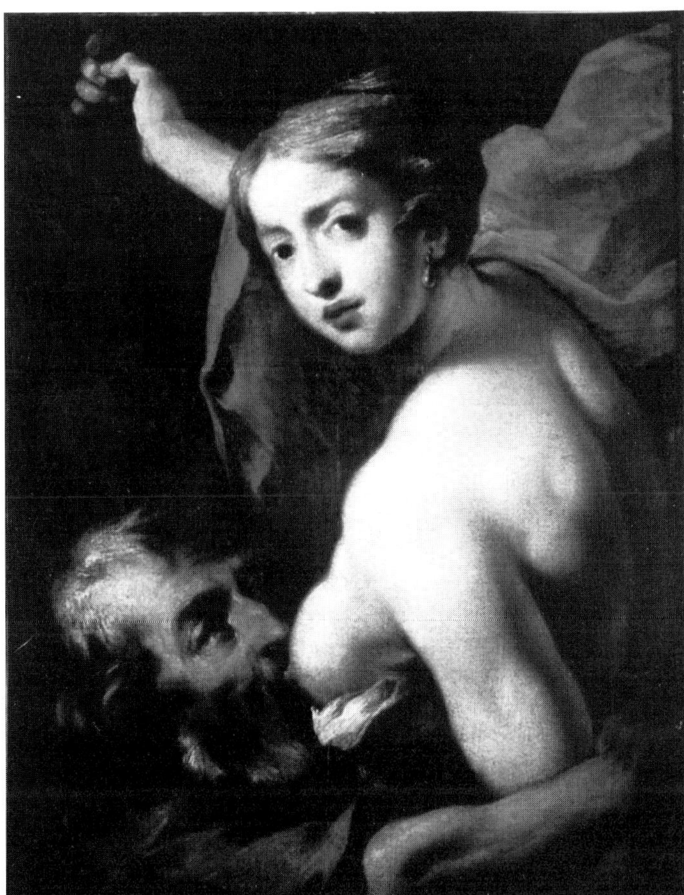

Fig. 19

Fig. 17 Pietro della Vecchia, *Socrates and His Pupils*. Present location unknown.
Photo: author.

Fig. 18 Pietro della Vecchia, *Jael and Sisera*. Formerly France, private collection. Photo: Louvre, les Archives Photographiques d'art et d'histoire.

Fig. 19 Pietro della Vecchia, *Roman Charity*. Orléans, Musée des Beaux-Arts. Photo: author.

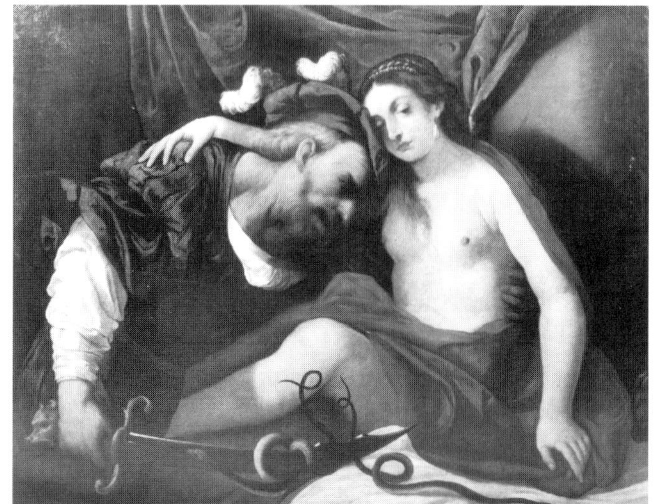

Fig. 20

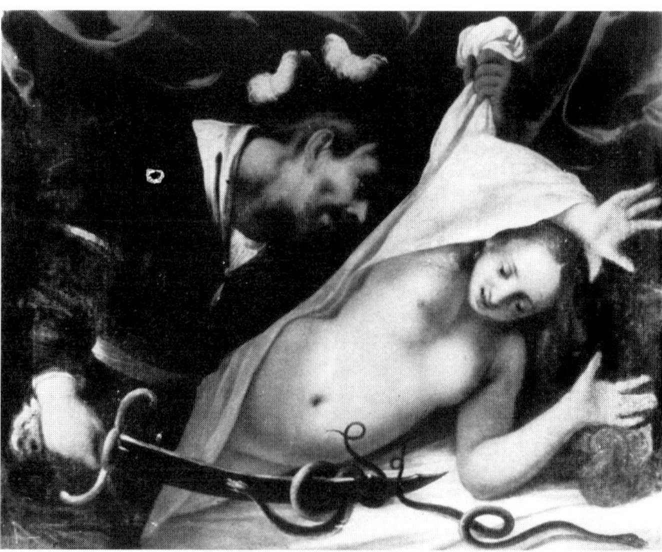

Fig. 21

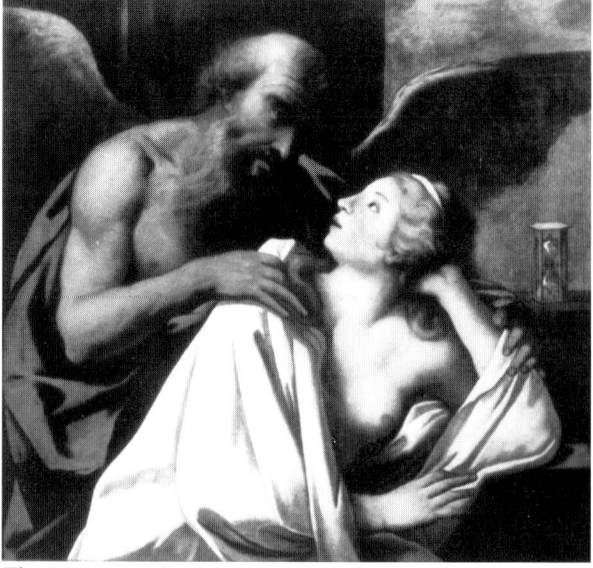

Fig. 22

A more interesting subject is that of the seer, Tiresias, who, at one point in his life, was changed from a man into a woman and who lived as such for seven years before turning back into a man again.[41] In Vecchia's two renderings of the theme, the metamorphosis takes the form of a violent action (Figs. 20, 21).[42] If we had not recognized the theme from the two serpents that, according to Ovid's tale, were struck by Tiresias, we would probably have interpreted the subject as a scene of rape.

This undertone of male violence is typical for Pietro Vecchia's erotic scenes, and it might be considered typical for the attitude of the *Accademia degli Incogniti* in general. Giovan Francesco Loredano's literary society was firmly conservative, and although its members could admire a female composer and musician like Barbara Strozzi, a vehemently "feminist-*avant-la-lettre*" writer like Arcangela Tarabottini, or female painters like Chiara Varotari and Artemisia Gentileschi, their admiration never touched the ethical heart of the matter but only the form, the *meraviglia*, of the paradox of women excelling in artistic and intellectual activities that were usually reserved for men. Many of the *Incogniti's* poems betray a violent, oppressive attitude toward women. Two works by della Vecchia also display this attitude. *Time Discovering Truth*, in an Italian private collection, is clearly not a "neutral" rendering (Fig. 22).[43] The touch of Time's claw-like fingers is aggressive and threatening, and the young woman seems fearful.

The Palmer Museum's *Sacrifice* is another example of this attitude (Fig. 23, p. 106).[44] Again, the painting's subject presents us with some uncertainties. There are three frequently depicted narratives in seventeenth- and eighteenth-century Venetian art in which a young girl is sacrificed: those of Iphigenia, Polyxena, and Jephthah's daughter. It is improbable that the Palmer picture represents the first, for Iphigenia is always shown with a deer, the sacred animal of Diana, to whom she was to be sacrificed. Due to the lack of attributes, however, it is almost impossible to decide whether we are dealing with Jephthah's daughter or with Polyxena. In my book, I opted for the latter. However, in view of our earlier discussion of the ex-Papafava picture with its half-length figures and severed head (Fig. 12), I am now inclined to view the problem in a somewhat different way. Perhaps here, too, Vecchia relied on the dilettante's *intelligenza* to recognize the representation as a conflation of the traditional scenes of sacrifice. The picture's *meraviglia* consists of what Boschini calls "*due opposti d'affetti,*"[45] in other words, the artist's ability to convincingly render the contrast between the executioner's brute violence and the girl's almost palpable helplessness and fear.

Most of the themes and issues we have discussed up to this point find expression in a painting from a private collection in Vicenza (Fig. 24). Quite large (182 x 161 cm.), this previously unpublished work is a high point in Pietro Vecchia's mature style. The dramatic use of chiaroscuro, the weird, exaggerated movements of the figures, and the almost stifling lack of space invite comparison with two canvases from what must have been the most important commission of Vecchia's later years: a series of paintings for the second courtyard of the Jesuit monastery in Venice (1664–1674).[46] No doubt the Vicenza picture was done at about the same time. The painting's subject is not difficult to determine. The five full-length figures evidently represent the Ages of Man. This theme had enjoyed a certain popularity with Venetian painters of the early sixteenth century, for example Titian's early picture in the National Gallery of Scotland, Edinburgh, which shows three groups of figures in a landscape representing Childhood, Adolescence, and Old Age (Fig. 25). Titian's painting constitutes the prototype for a series of renderings of the theme done in the later sixteenth century, and it is the model Vecchia consciously chose to emulate, as closer inspection reveals.

First we notice that Titian, following a venerable tradition, has depicted three ages, whereas Vecchia, in accordance with a different convention just as old, has chosen to divide the *aetas hominis* into four parts. In the picture we recognize from the left, Old Age, Adolescence, Childhood, and Adulthood.[47] This is not Vecchia's only representation of the Ages of Man. Three other versions of the theme by Vecchia are known, all showing four instead of three ages.[48] Evidently, Vecchia's was a conscious choice, as if to establish a sort of dialogue with the Cinquecento master. This impression seems to be confirmed when we consider two of the other

Fig. 24 Pietro della Vecchia, *Four Ages of Man*. Vicenza, private collection. Photo: Alfonsi, Antique Paintings, Vicenza.

Fig. 25 Titian, *Three Ages of Man*. Edinburgh, National Gallery of Scotland. Photo: National Gallery of Scotland, Edinburgh.

Fig. 26 Pietro della Vecchia, *Childhood*. Ponce, Museum of Art. Photo: Museo de Arte de Ponce, The Luis A. Ferré Foundation, Inc., Ponce, Puerto Rico.

Fig. 27 Pietro della Vecchia, *Adulthood*. Ponce, Museum of Art. Photo: Museo de Arte de Ponce, The Luis A. Ferré Foundation, Inc., Ponce, Puerto Rico.

Fig. 28 Pietro della Vecchia, *Maturity*. Ponce, Museum of Art. Photo: Museo de Arte de Ponce, The Luis A. Ferré Foundation, Inc., Ponce, Puerto Rico.

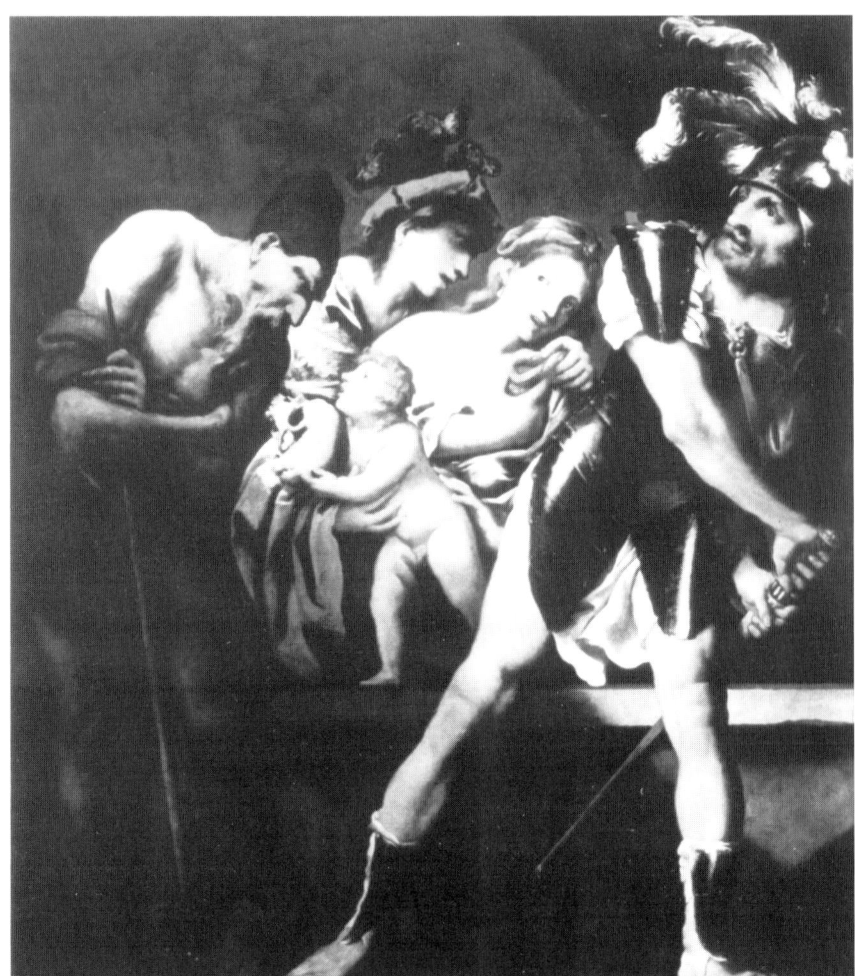

Fig. 24

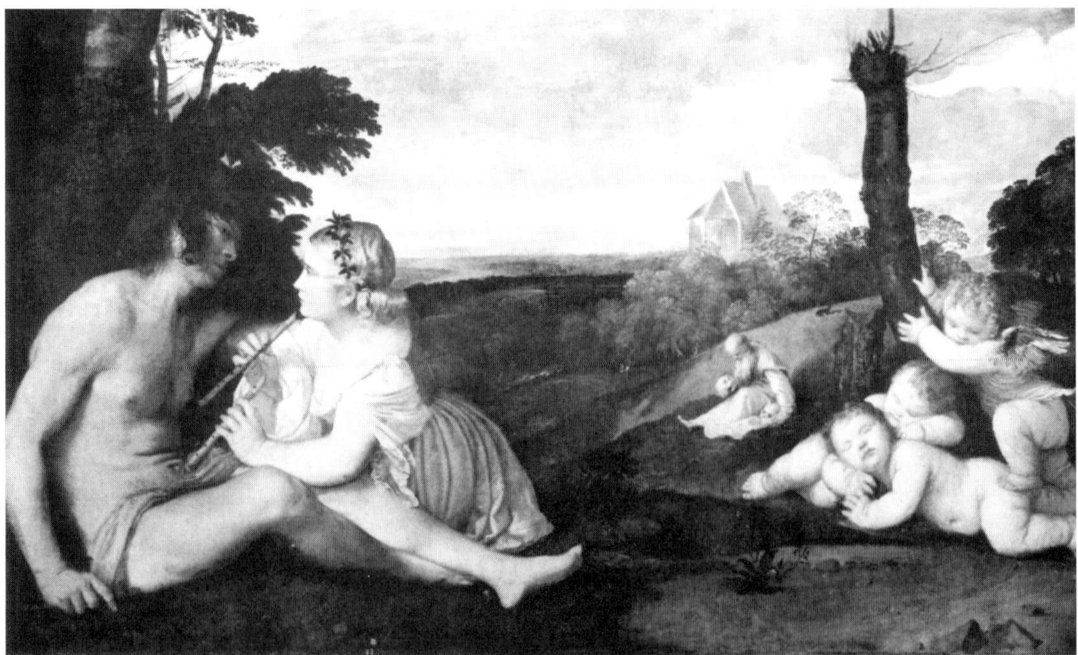

Fig. 25

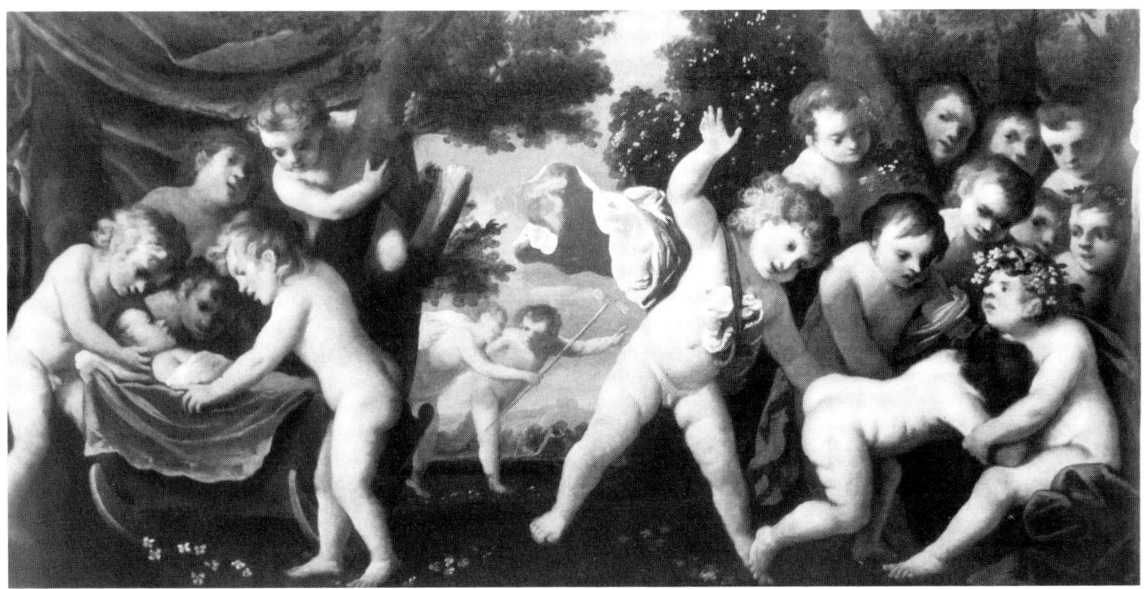

Fig. 26

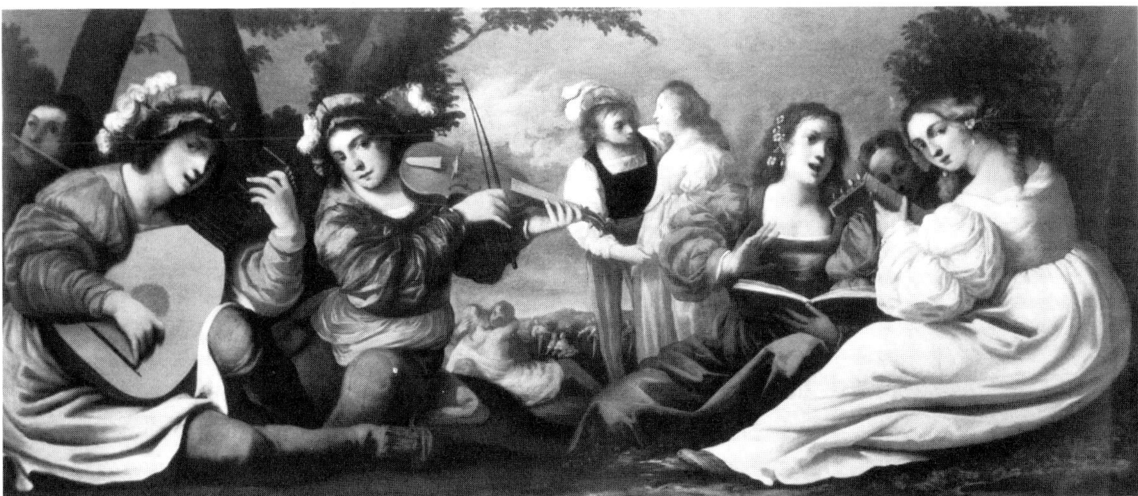

Fig. 27

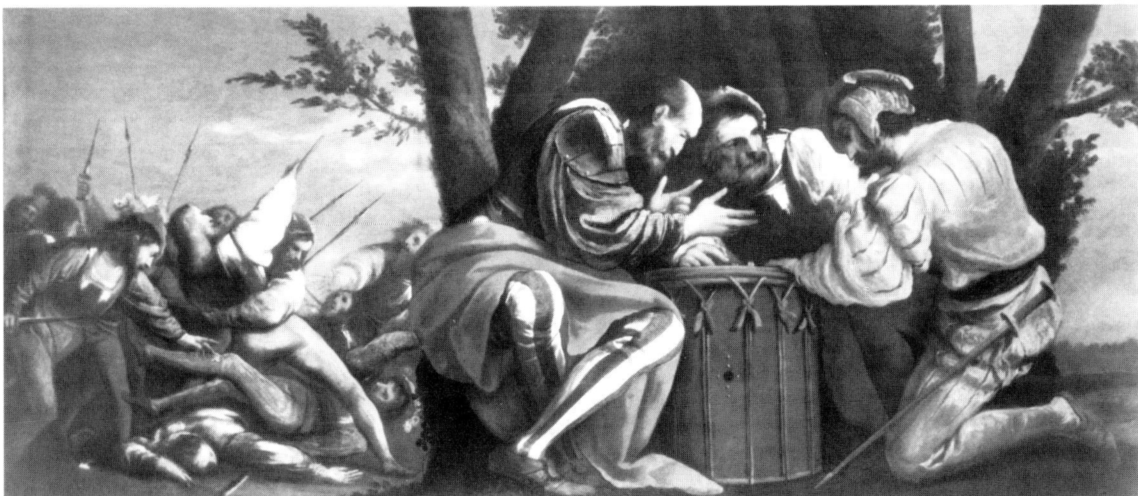

Fig. 28

versions. In a cycle of four pictures in the Museum of Ponce, Puerto Rico, Childhood is shown as a group of nude children (Fig. 26), Adolescence as youths amusing themselves with music and love (Fig. 27), Adulthood in the form of a male-dominated world of gambling and battling (Fig. 28), and Old Age as a group of old men in discussion in the foreground while in the background an old woman is receiving alms (Fig. 29).[49] Another painting by Vecchia in a Roman private collection also deals with this theme, although probably not an autograph work, but rather produced as a workshop piece (Fig. 30).[50] Obvious differences notwithstanding, its basic conception is similar to that of the four pictures in Ponce: going counterclockwise, two young children (dressed) are playing merrily; a young couple is making love; a fearsome warrior places his foot on a skull, symbol of the transitory nature of all earthly things; and, at the right, an old man sits pondering his past. Again we notice that, according to Vecchia and his *entourage*, the world is male-dominated. Gentleness is merely transitory. Life is really about melancholy, war, and violent death.

In Titian's painting, human life is presented rather differently. Certainly, Titian knows perfectly well that life is transitory—note that the old man in the background is contemplating *two* skulls instead of one, a clear reference to the lovers on the left—but his world is decidedly less male-dominated and grim than Vecchia's. Recent studies have argued, moreover, that in Titian's conception, man would seem potentially capable of elevating himself to the sublime virtue of Platonic *eros*, which overcomes the limits of earthly love.[51] Vecchia's images, by contrast, show no trace of such gentleness, let alone sublime ideals. This is clear from the painting in Vicenza. Consider the girl holding the baby. She is being embraced by the young man at her side, but instead of a tender sign of love, the embrace seems an almost violent act. The comparison with the harmonious couple in Titian's picture is telling. In Vecchia's world, there is no room for harmony or delicacy. Typically, the dominating figure in the picture is the menacing warrior to the right.

These observations bring us back once more to Pietro Vecchia's position as an artist in a period considered by those who lived in it as a *"secolo di ferro,"* an iron age, as compared to the *"secolo d'oro,"* the golden age of the preceding Cinquecento. "But what can we do? Those painters are dead, those who stole glory from eternity with the art of their brushes," lamented Giovan Francesco Loredano and Pietro Michiel in the introduction to their *Il Cimiterio: Epitafi giocosi*, a collection of strangely irreverent, rhymed epitaphs from 1645.[52] Vecchia's *aemulationes* are an answer to this complaint. In 1648, Carlo Ridolfi described in great detail a painting of the Ages of Man that he attributed without hesitation to Giorgione himself: "In the middle there is a stalwart fully armoured man, a hot-blooded youth ready to avenge even the slightest offence and to shed blood for the sake of glory, and whose fury is not even stopped by another man, who shows him an image of death.... Nearby one saw a youngster discussing with philosophers, dealing with tradesmen and with an old woman, to show the various occupations of youth, and finally one saw a nude man, bent by old age, with wavy, snow-white hair, who was meditating upon a skull...."[53] The description is that of a picture close to Vecchia's two paintings in Rome and Vicenza.

Unfortunately nothing is known about the original location of the Vicenza picture, which is unusually large for a work by Vecchia with this kind of subject matter. There is, however, an unpublished drawing in Chicago that may throw some light on its artistic genesis (Fig. 31).[54] The sheet has the same composition as the painting. As the drawing style is typical for Vecchia, it would seem that we have a preparatory drawing for the picture. A closer look at the sketch reveals, however, an architectural backdrop rendered *sottinsù*. This suggests that the Chicago drawing was done for a ceiling. Either the Vicenza painting is a variant of this ceiling or the ceiling was developed from the easel painting. Whichever alternative is correct, the sheet in Chicago is directly related to the picture. This is an interesting discovery, for until now only two drawings by Vecchia were known that bear direct relation to a painting: one in a private collection in Ulm, Germany, done in preparation for the early *Crowning of Thorns* (Venice, collection Donà delle Rose),[55] and a drawing of the *Conversion of Francesco Borgia* (Paris, private collection), which is preparatory to the painting of the same subject, executed between 1664 and 1674, in the Musée Municipal, Brest, France.[56] The Chicago drawing is only the third, certain,

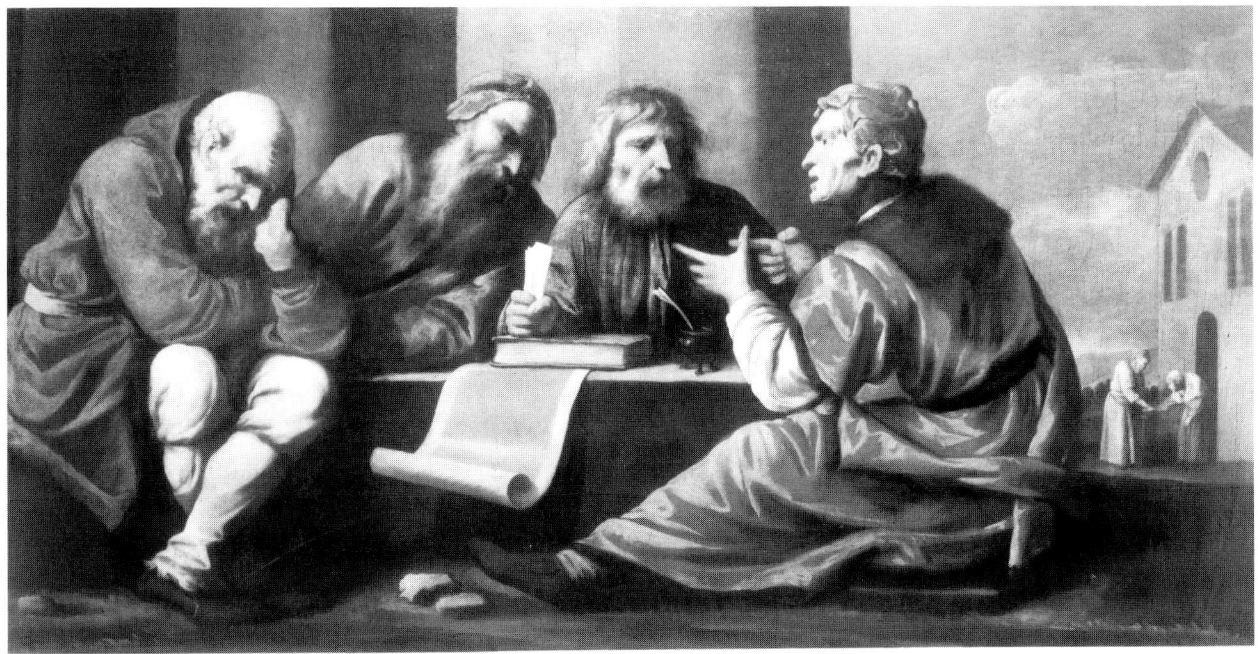

Fig. 29

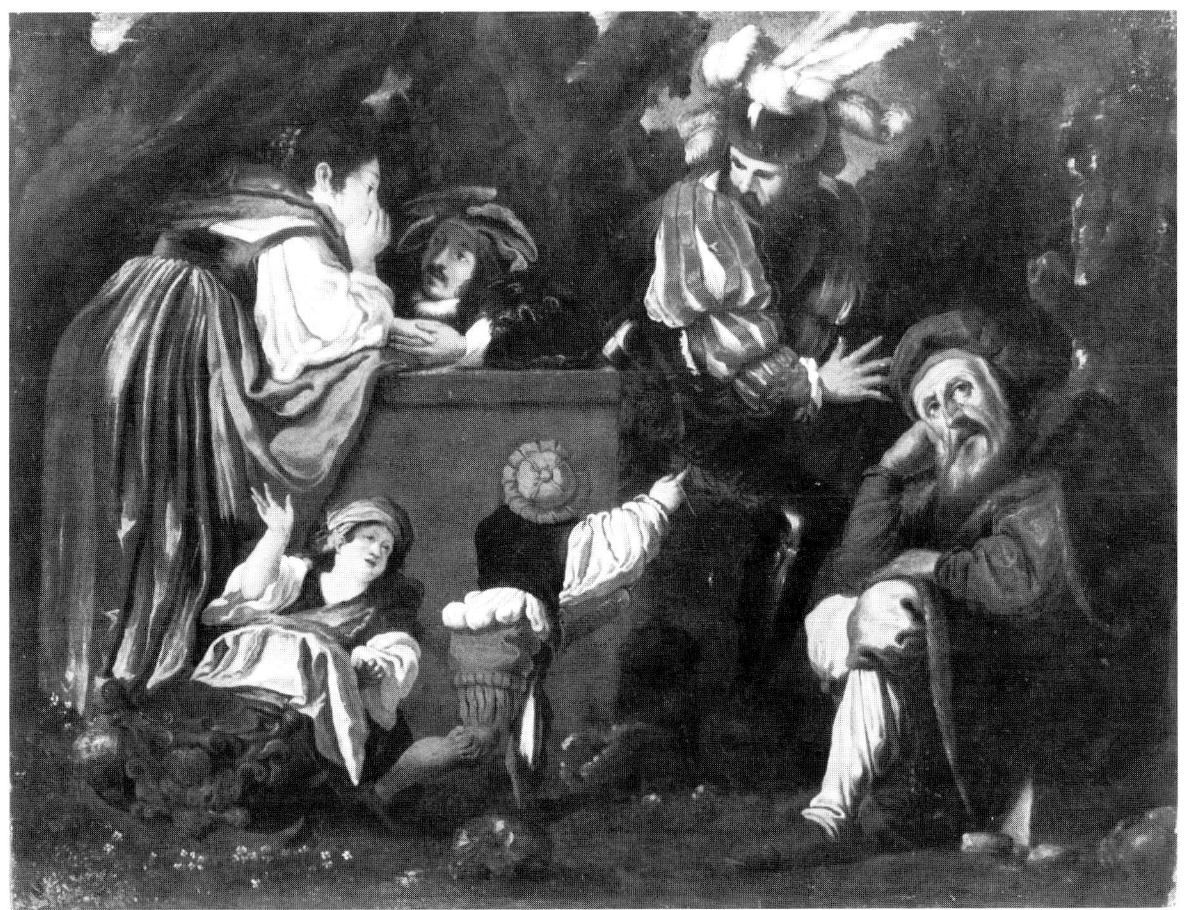

Fig. 30

relatable drawing by Pietro Vecchia that has come down to us. Around these three sheets, however, we can group a small number of drawings with similar characteristics that can be attributed with confidence to the artist. Among them is the *Three Grotesque Heads* from a private collection in Venice,[57] and an unpublished drawing in The Art Institute of Chicago, *Joseph the Carpenter with the Christ Child* (Fig. 32).[58]

In conclusion, let us take a look at the Chicago drawing of the Ages of Man. Over the central group hovers a winged figure of Time or Death, which is lacking in the Vicenza picture. Even more than in the painting, the drawing stresses the artist's message that life on earth is pervaded by the awareness of omnipresent death. "Man is like a soldier (*soldà*)," wrote the seventeenth-century poet and librettist, Giovan Francesco Busenello, "the world is his quarter," and though "he often has his day" (*vien spesso a zornada*), "good fortune will never hold for long and he will inevitably end belly up" (*con la panza in alto*).[59] This gloomy view of an unhappy century has been interpreted by Pietro Vecchia in a body of deeply impressive works of art.

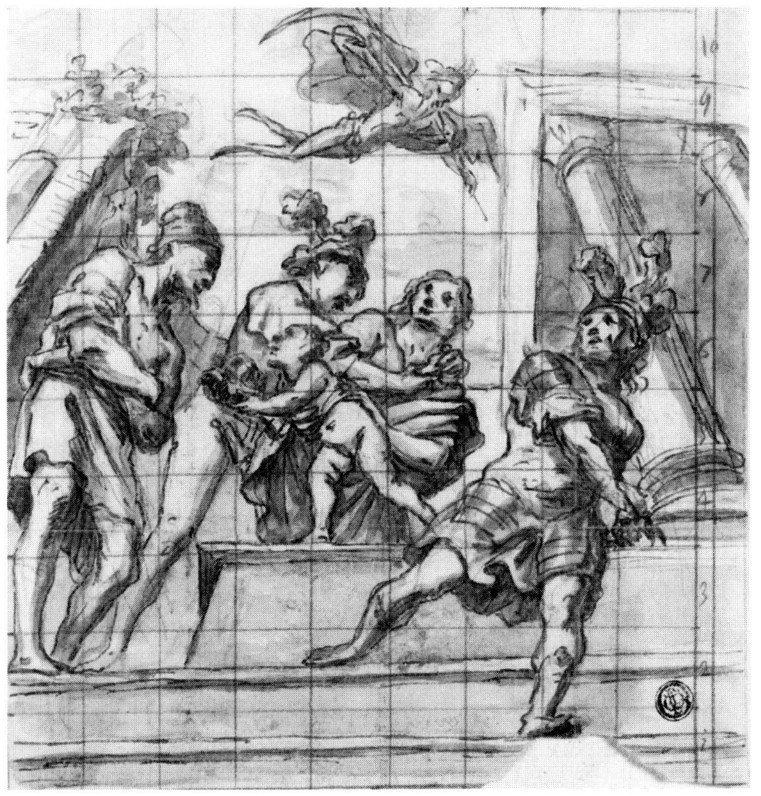

Fig. 31

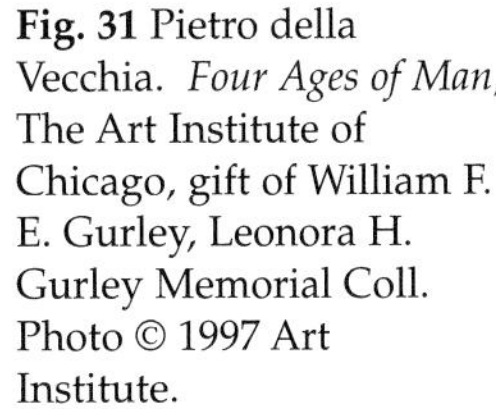

Fig. 31 Pietro della Vecchia. *Four Ages of Man*, The Art Institute of Chicago, gift of William F. E. Gurley, Leonora H. Gurley Memorial Coll. Photo © 1997 Art Institute.

Fig. 32 Pietro della Vecchia, *Joseph the Carpenter with the Christ Child*. The Art Institute of Chicago, gift of William F. E. Gurley, Leonora H. Gurley Memorial Coll. Photo © 1997 Art Institute.

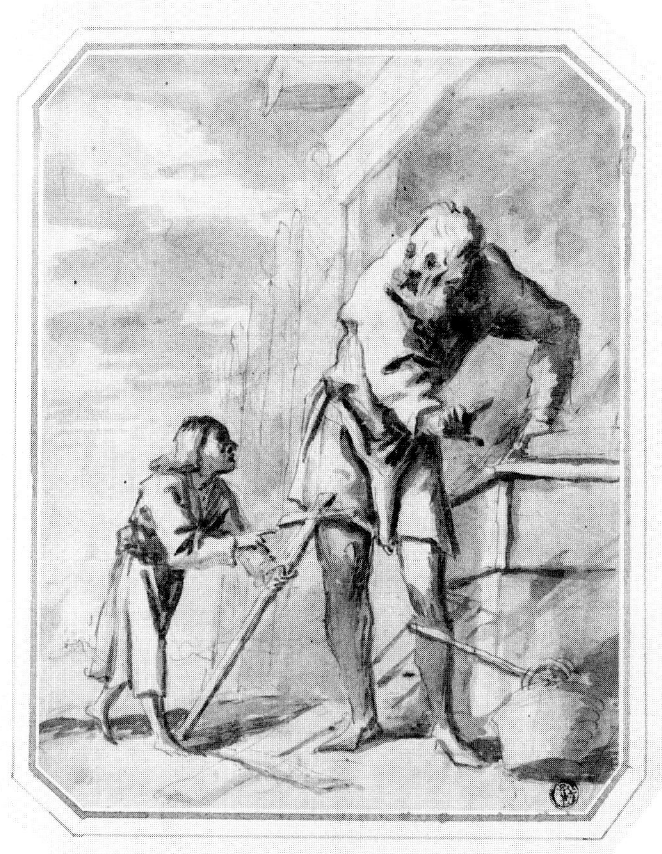

Fig. 32

Endnotes

I wish to thank Mary Jane Harris for her kind invitation to participate in the symposium.

1 B. Aikema, *Pietro della Vecchia and the Heritage of the Renaissance in Venice*, Florence, 1990 (hereafter cited as Aikema, *della Vecchia*).

2 Recently, new documentary evidence concerning Pietro Vecchia's biography was made available by A. Lemoine, "Nicolas Régnier et son entourage: nouvelles propositions biographiques," in *Revue de l'Art* 117, 1997, pp. 57–59. Lemoine discovered that Pietro Vecchia married Clorinda, the daughter of fellow-painter Nicolas Régnier, only in 1649 and not in the 1620s, as I had hypothesized. Although it is still possible that the young Pietro Vecchia first met the Régnier family in Rome during the early 1620s, it cannot be maintained any longer, as I had proposed, that Vecchia played a key role in convincing his (future) father-in-law to take residence in Venice. Among the witnesses to the marriage was the well-known merchant and business associate of Vecchia and Régnier, Paolo del Sera. As the godfather of their first daughter, Caterina Bastiana, who was baptized on 14 June 1655, Pietro and Clorinda chose the great architect, Baldassare Longhena. Further evidence of Vecchia's strong links with the Régnier clan derives from the fact that in 1668 and 1669 he acted as the Venetian procurator of the Parma-based half-brother of Nicolas Régnier, the painter Michele Desubleo.

3 E. de Jongh, "The Spur of Wit: Rembrandt's Response to an Italian Challenge," in *Delta* 12 (no. 2), 1969, p. 183.

4 "E queste imitazioni non sono coppie, ma astratti del suo intelletto, bensì per imitare i tratti Giorgioneschi" (M. Boschini, *Le ricche minere della pittura veneziana*, Venice, 1674, Breve instruzione, section b 3). On Boschini's life, works, and cultural ambience see, most recently, M. F. Merling, *Marco Boschini's "La Carta del Navegar Pitoresco:" Art Theory and Virtuoso Culture in Seventeenth-Century Venice*, 2 vols., Ph.D. diss., Brown University, 1992, with full bibliography.

5 M. Boschini, *La carta del navegar pitoresco*, ed. A. Pallucchini, Venice and Rome, 1966, p. 536 (orig. pub., Venice, 1660, p. 500).

6 N. Ivanoff, "Il grottesco nella pittura veneziana del Seicento: Pietro il Vecchia," in *Emporium* 99, 1944, p. 88 (ill.); Aikema, *della Vecchia*, p. 149, cat. 210.

7 Aikema, *della Vecchia*, p. 149, cat. 210A.

8 Black and red chalk, 136 x 90 mm. Previously unpublished.

9 E. Waterhouse, *Italian Baroque Painting*, London, 1969, p. 117. It should be remarked at this point that during the seventeenth century, the term "bravo" was never employed to describe Vecchia's pictures of extravagantly dressed warriors. In modern art-historical literature, these figures by Vecchia are usually called "bravi," probably under the influence of the description of such figures in Alessandro Manzoni's *Promessi sposi* (which in turn must be based upon paintings like those here under discussion). For more on this, see Aikema, *della Vecchia*, p. 23, note 35.

10 T. Pignatti, *Giorgione*, London, 1971, p. 141, cat. no. A 61; J. Anderson, *Giorgione. Peintre de la "brièveté poétique*,*"* Paris, 1996, pp. 342, 344.

11 "In verità che l'è una azion sì fiera, / Che a chi la vede ghe vien volontà / De petar man e de dir: ferma là, / Tanto la par dasseno e più che vera." Boschini, 1966, *op. cit.*, p. 56 (orig. ed. 1660, p. 38).

12 "Zorzon con muodi più vivi del vivo / Mostrerà la maniera del dasseno." Boschini, 1966, *op. cit.*, p. 62 (orig. ed. 1660, p. 43).

13 The quotation is again from Boschini, 1966, *op. cit.*, p. 86 (orig. ed. 1660, p. 65). The full verse runs as follows: "Perchè in fin la Pitura non è altro / Che un ingano de l'ochio certamente / E quel, che in l'inganar xe più valente, / Xe certo anche stimà per el più scaltro."

14 "A gloria di Giorgione e di Pietro Vecchia, Pittor vivente Veneziano, e a intelligenza de' Dilettanti, devo dire che abbino l'occhio a questo Vecchia, perchè incontreranno tratti di questo pennello trasformati nelle Giorgionesche forme in modo, che resterano ambigui se siano parti di Giorgione, o imitazioni di quello." Boschini, 1674, *op. cit.*, Breve instruzione, section b 4.

15 Boschini, 1674, Breve instruzione, section "Colorito." Quoted by P. Sohm, *Pittoresco. Marco Boschini, his critics, and their critiques of painterly brushwork in seventeenth- and eighteenth-century Italy*, Cambridge, 1991, p. 153.

16 G. Vasari, *Le vite de' più eccellenti pittori scultori ed architettori*, ed. G. Milanesi, Florence, 1906, vol. VII, p. 452: "E questo modo [i. e. Titian's late style] è stato cagione che molti, volendo in ciò immitare e mostrare di fare il pratico, hanno fatte di goffe pitture: e ciò adiviene perchè, se bene a molti pare che elle siano fatte senza fatica, non è così il vero, e s'ingannano; perchè si conosce che sono rifatte, e che si è ritornato loro addosso con i colori tante volte, che la fatica la si vede."

17 The examples I illustrate are from a Venetian private collection (Fig. 5, previously unpublished) and the Louvre (Fig. 6, inv. no. MNR 541), catalogued as anonymous Venetian seventeenth century.

18 L. and U. Procacci, "Carteggio di Marco Boschini con il Cardinale Leopoldo de'Medici," in *Saggi e Memorie di Storia dell'Arte* 4, 1965, p. 107.

19 J. V. Mirollo, *The Poet of the Marvellous: Giambattista Marino*, New York and London, 1963, pp. 115–20. See also J. Kenseth, ed., *The Age of the Marvelous*, exh. cat., Hood Museum of Art, Dartmouth College, Hanover, New Hampshire, 1991, for additional bibliography.

20 Illustration from *La Gloria de gli Incogniti*, Venetia, 1647, p. 244. This volume contains a series of biographies of the foremost members of Loredano's circle. On stylistic grounds, the *inventor* of the print can be identified with either Tiberio Tinelli or, more probably, with Pietro Vecchia's father-in-law, Nicolas Régnier (see also Aikema, *della Vecchia*, p. 83). For Vecchia's ties with Loredano's circle, see Aikema, *della Vecchia*, pp. 70–73 and 109–10.

21 The titles—obvious parodies of the Petrarchesque tradition of love poetry—are those of poems by G. M. Milcetti, *Le bellissime diffettuose, i capricci poetici, con altri componimenti*, Venice, 1667. See the analysis by P. Getrevi, *Dal picaro al gentiluomo. Scrittura e immaginario nel Seicento narrativo*, Milan, 1986, pp. 146–149; and also the remarks by L. Giachino, "La senualità in Barocco. L'esperienza lirica di Pietro Michiel tra erotismo e concettismo," in *Quaderni Veneti* 33, 2001, p. 81.

22 Pignatti, 1971, *op. cit.*, Fig. 216.

23 According to Roberto Longhi, see F. Gibbons, *Dosso and Battista Dossi, Court Painters at Ferrara*, Princeton, 1968, p. 259. Another version of this composition, in Rome, Galleria Borghese, was recently discussed by Anderson, 1996, *op. cit.*, p. 340, ill., who labels the work as a replica after Dosso Dossi. According to A. Ballarin, "Une nouvelle perspective sur Giorgione," in *Le siècle de Titien: L'âge d'or de la peinture à Venise*, Paris, 1993, p. 290, Fig. 12, the composition records a lost prototype by Giorgione. Neither this proposal nor Ballarin's reconstruction of Giorgione's later *oeuvre* in general seems completely convincing to me. See also A. Ballarin, "Una nuova prospettiva su Giorgione: la ritrattistica degli anni 1500–1503," in *Giorgione: Atti del Convegno Internazionale di Studi 1978*, Venice, 1979, pp. 227–51 (earlier version of the text in the 1993 French catalogue just cited).

24 "Due mezze figure in una stessa tela di Saule, che stringe ne'capelli il capo di Golia recatogli dal giovinetto Davide, ed in questi ammirasi l'ardire, in quello la regia maestà." The picture belonged to "Li Signori Leoni da San Lorenzo." C. Ridolfi, *Le maraviglie dell'arte ovvero le vite degli illustri pittori veneti e dello stato*, Venice, 1648, vol. I, p. 102.

25 Aikema, *della Vecchia*, p. 121, cat. no. 35.

26 Aikema, *della Vecchia*, p. 132, cat. no. 108.

27 J. Shearman, "Cristofano Allori's 'Judith'," in *Burlington Magazine* 121, 1979, p. 9.

28 Aikema, *della Vecchia*, p. 45.

29 Aikema, *della Vecchia*, p. 132, cat. no. 107. (First illustrated in this paper.)

30 A. Pigler, *Barockthemen*, Budapest, 1974, vol. I, pp. 482–83. A similar subject is that of Fulvia, who pierces the tongue of Cicero's severed head (Pigler, vol. II, p. 392).

31 Two are discussed in the exhibition catalogue *Francesco Cairo 1607–1665*, Varese, 1983, pp. 116–17, cat. no. 18 (Museo Civico, Vicenza) and pp. 117–18, cat. no. 19 (Museum of Fine Arts, Boston). The picture illustrated here as Fig. 13 is an early work by Cairo that has not been published before.

32 T. Temanza, *Zibaldon*, ed. N. Ivanoff, Venice and Rome, 1963, p. 75.

33 Formerly on the Milanese art market. Aikema, *della Vecchia*, p. 140, cat. no. 161.

34 The suggestion was made verbally by Leonard Slatkes. On the theme, see A. Blankert, "Heraclitus en Democritus; in het bijzonder in de Nederlandse kunst van de zeventiende eeuw," in *Nederlands Kunsthistorisch Jaarboek* 18, 1967, pp. 31–124; O. Ferrari, "L'iconografia dei filosofi antichi nella pittura del sec. XVII in Italia," in *Storia dell'Arte* 57, 1986, pp. 103–81, especially pp. 156–57 and 162–63.

35 Aikema, *della Vecchia*, respectively p. 141, cat. no. 162 and p. 140, cat. no. 158. For the picture at Padua, see also E. Saccomani, in D. Banzato, A. Mariuz, G. Pavanello, eds., *Da Padovanino a Tiepolo: Dipinti dei Musei Civici di Padova del Seicento e Settecento*, Milano, 1997, pp. 139–140, cat. no. 50.

36 The pictures measure, respectively, 68 x 102 cm. and 73 x 115 cm. In theory, they could have been a pair of (most extravagant) pendants.

37 Aikema, *della Vecchia*, pp. 61–62, 136, cat. no. 132.

38 L. Coci, "*L'Alcibiade fanciullo a scola.* Nota bibliografica," in *Studi Seicenteschi* 26, 1985, pp. 301–22.

39 Aikema, *della Vecchia*, p. 121, cat. no. 32. (First illustrated in this paper.)

40 Exh. cat. *L'allégorie dans la peinture: La représentation de la charité au XVIIe siècle*, Caen (Musée des Beaux-Arts), 1986, cat. no. 22; A. Brejon de Lavergnée-N. Volle, *Musées de France: Répertoire des peintures italiennes du XVIIe siècle*, Paris, 1988, p. 451; exh. cat. *Italies: Peintures des musées de la région Centre*, Tours, Orléans, and Chartres 1996–97, pp. 218–19, cat. 60 (given as Venetian, second half of the seventeenth century).

41 The story seems to have been rarely depicted in Seicento Italy. It does not appear in the repertory compiled by Pigler, 1974, *op. cit.*

42 One is in the Musée des Beaux-Arts, Nantes. See B. Sarrazin, *Catalogue raisonné des peintures italiennes du musée des Beaux-Arts de Nantes: XIIIe-XVIIIe siècle*, Nantes, 1994, pp. 189–90, cat. no. 138. The other was auctioned in Milan (Finarte, 4 Novembre 1986, no. 107). It is mentioned by Sarrazin, 1994, *op. cit., loc. cit.*

43 Previously unpublished.

44 Aikema, *della Vecchia*, p. 135, cat. no. 128B.

45 "Due oppositi d'affetti, che formano un concerto pittoresco, che più non può far l'Arte." Boschini, 1674, *op. cit.*, Breve instruzione, section b 3, on the aforementioned *Bravo* now in Vienna, attributed by some to Giorgione.

46 Aikema, *della Vecchia*, pp. 30–31, and 128, cat. no. 77, Fig. 68; p. 133, cat. no. 110, Fig. 69.

47 For the concept of the Ages of Man in general, see E. Sears, *The Ages of Man. Medieval Interpretations of*

the Life Cycle, Princeton, 1986. For Titian and his adaptation of the system of the Three Ages, see E. Panofsky, *Problems in Titian, Mostly Iconographic*, New York, 1969, pp. 94–96.

48 Aikema, *della Vecchia*, p. 137, respectively, cat. nos. 136–39, 140–43, 144.

49 Aikema, *della Vecchia*, p. 137, cat. nos. 136–39.

50 Aikema, *della Vecchia*, p. 137, cat. no. 144, Fig. 99.

51 A. Gentili, *Da Tiziano a Tiziano: Mito e allegoria nella cultura veneziana del Cinquecento*, Milan, 1980, pp. 55–57.

52 "Ma, che si può fare? Son morti quei pittori, che con gli scherzi de' pennelli rubbavano l'eternità alla gloria." *Il Cimiterio: Epitafi giocosi*, Venice, 1680, p. 7.

53 The full quotation is: "Nel mezzo eravi un huomo di robusto aspetto tutto armato, inferendo il bollore del sangue dell'età giovanile, pronto nel vendicare ogni picciola offesa e preparato negli aringhi di Marte à versar il sangue per lo desio della gloria, il quale punto non ralenta il furore, benche altro gli rechi annanzi il simolacro di morte, ò volesse ingegnosamente dimostrare il Pittore (secondo il detto del pacientissimo) la vita dell'huomo altro non essere, che una spezie di militia sopra la terra & i giorni suoi simili à quelli de'mercenari. Poco lungo vedevasi un giovinetto in dispute co'Filosofanti, e tra negotiatori, e con una vecchiarella, per dinnotare le applicationi varie della gioventù, e finalmente vedevasi un vecchio ignudo curvo per lo peso degli anni, ondeggiante il crine di bianca neve, che meditava il teschio d'un morto, considerando come tante bellezze, virtù e gratie del Cielo all'huomo compartite divenghino in fine esca de vermi entro ad un'oscura tomba, qual Pittura dicesi essere in Genova appresso de'Signori Cassinelli." Ridolfi, *op. cit.*, 1648, vol. I, p. 101.

54 Pen and wash over red chalk, squared, 212 x 204 mm., The Art Institute of Chicago, Acc. No. 1922.813.

55 Aikema, *della Vecchia*, p. 157, cat. of drawings no. 1.

56 P. Rosenberg, "Un dessin de Pietro della Vecchia", in *Arte Veneta* 30, 1976, pp. 182–83; Aikema, *della Vecchia*, p. 157, cat. of drawings no. 3. Two other drawings, showing respectively *Soldiers Throwing Dice* (Oxford, Christ Church Picture Gallery; Aikema, *della Vecchia*, p. 157, cat. of drawings no. 2) and *Three Warriors in a Landscape* (Milan, Raccolte Civiche del Castello Sforzesco, coll. Giovanni Morelli; Aikema, *della Vecchia*, p. 35, and G. Bora, *I disegni della collezione Morelli*, Bergamo, 1988, pp. 210–11, cat. no. 77) are also unmistakably related to pictures by Vecchia, although they are not exactly preparatory studies.

57 Aikema, *della Vecchia*, pp. 157–158, cat. of drawings no. 4, ill. See also M. Muraro, *Mostra di disegni veneziani del Sei e Settecento*, Florence, 1953, p. 32, cat. no. 54.

58 Pen and wash over black chalk, 254 x 201 mm., Acc. No. 1922.812. It might be useful to repeat my point of view, expressed before in Aikema, *della Vecchia*, pp. 34 and 158, cat. of drawings no. 7, that the drawing most frequently associated with Pietro della Vecchia, the *Allegory of Poverty*, executed in pen and wash, from the Janos Scholz collection, now in the Pierpont Morgan Library, New York, is not an autograph work but a copy, done by an anonymous seventeenth-century draughtsman after a lost painting by Vecchia.

59 Quoted by G. Benzoni, *I "Frutti dell'Armi:" Volti e risvolti della guerra nel '600 in Italia*, Rome, 1980, p. 45. A similar image of the life of man can be found in a poem by Marino (in *La lira*, Venetia, 1630, p. 90), which was quoted, significantly, by Ridolfi, 1648, *op. cit.*, vol. I, p. 100, in his *vita* of Giorgione.

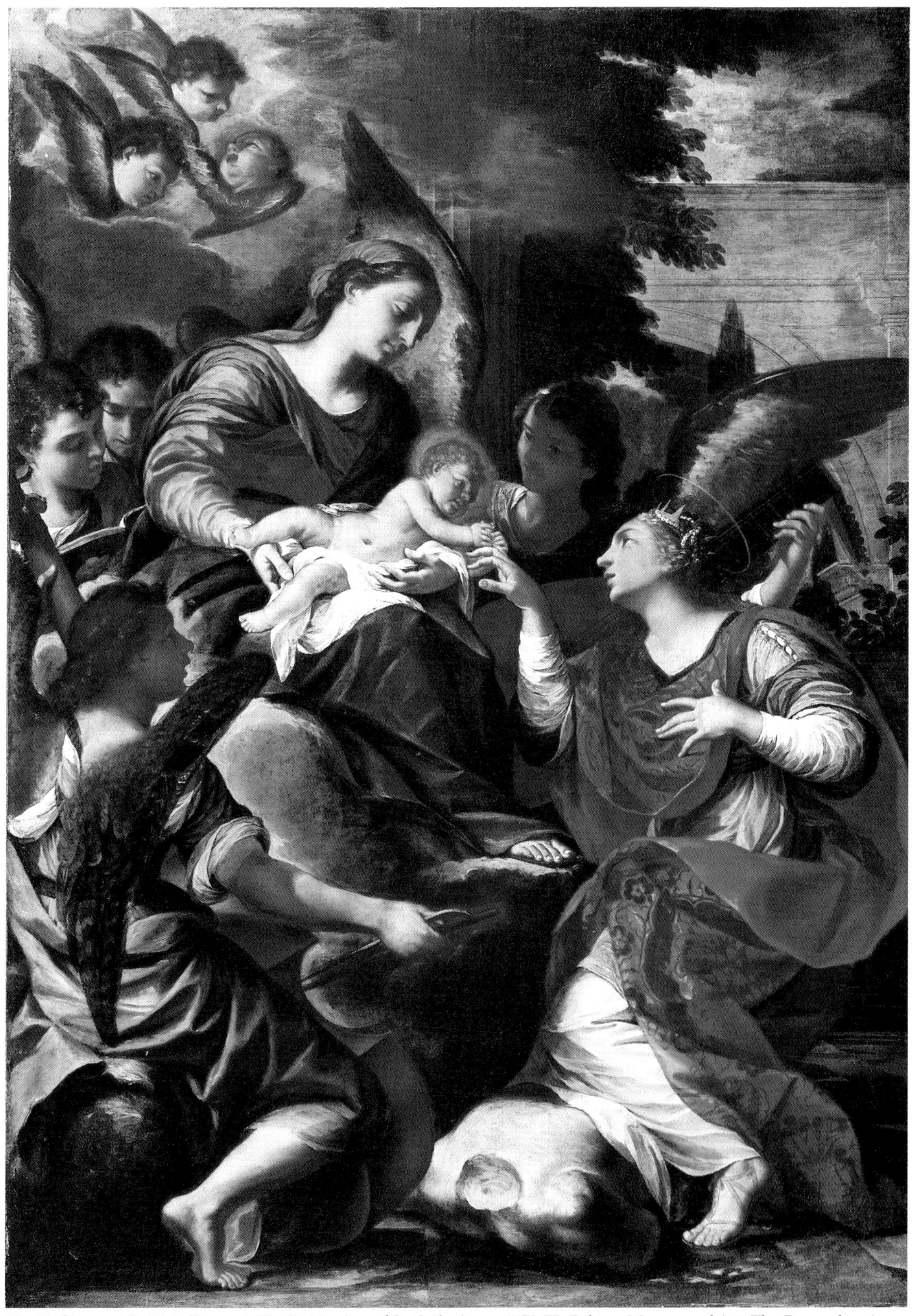

Fig. 1 Giovanni Battista Boncori, *Mystic Marriage of St. Catherine*, c. 1673-75. Palmer Museum of Art, The Pennsylvania State University. (See color plate 6.)

The Mystic Marriage of St. Catherine:
An Unknown Work of Giovanni Battista Boncori,
c. 1673–1675, in the Palmer Museum of Art

Erich Schleier

In 1976, the Palmer Museum of Art at Penn State acquired an impressive baroque painting representing the *Mystic Marriage of St. Catherine* (Fig. 1). The Virgin, seated on clouds as if on a throne, appears to the kneeling St. Catherine. She is surrounded by four large adolescent angels; one of them is playing the *viola da gamba* in the left foreground. Two others are singing while holding a book, and one is playing the lute. The figures of the Madonna and Child are emphasized by a column, which is partly hidden behind clouds. Behind the column are the foliage of trees and an architectural arch. Above is a passage of the clouded night sky lit by the hidden moon. The size, the vertical format of the picture, its subject, and its diagonal composition with the Virgin enthroned on clouds appearing to a kneeling female saint point to its probable original function as a small altarpiece in a side chapel of a church.[1] The museum acquired it from a New York art dealer, Clyde Newhouse, as a work of Pier Francesco Mola, an artist who worked in Rome from the early 1630s, notably in the forties, fifties, and sixties and who died there in 1666. Not much is known about its previous history.[2] Strangely, with its attribution to Mola, the picture has not received critical attention and has remained virtually unpublished. It became increasingly clear, however, to Kahren Arbitman, director of the museum from 1990 to 1996, and to Mary Jane Harris, benefactor, advisory board member, and guest curator, that the attribution to Mola could not be correct. A color transparency was sent to me for my opinion.

Although the picture shows some similarities with Mola's style in a general sense, I felt that it was probably the work of an artist influenced by Mola, who belonged to the following generation working in Rome in the later seventeenth century after Mola's death. The composition, with its strong play of diagonals, is more dynamic than any of Mola's pictures, which are mostly characterized by a static structure and a prevailing calm lyrical mood, as exemplified in his *Adoration of the Shepherds* in the Kunsthistorisches Museum, Vienna (Fig. 2), and his *Rest on the Flight* and *Encounter of Jacob and Rachel* in the Hermitage, St. Petersburg.[3] Above all, the forms and proportions of the figures are much heavier, more massive and ponderous than Mola's figures ever are, and the facial types are different.

After having first been led astray by the type and proportion of the Virgin's face, which prompted me to believe for a while that the Palmer Museum picture could be the work of Giuseppe Ghezzi[4], not far from his altarpiece on the high altar of S. Maria del Suffragio (Fig. 3),[5] the *Madonna of the Rosary with St. Joseph and St. Dominic* in the oratory of the same church,[6] or the altarpiece in S. Giuseppe dei Falegnami,[7] I had to change my mind when I remembered the color reproduction of an altarpiece by Mola's pupil Giovanni Battista Boncori, in an article by Rosella Carloni published in 1989.[8] Although her article was not the first publication on this little known painter,[9] it made accessible for the first time Boncori's production of altarpieces, compositions with large size figures rather than his previously better known landscapes with small figures. Only one ceiling fresco survives by the artist in a Roman church, whereas two altarpieces published by Carloni are in Boncori's birthplace, Campli, a small town in Abruzzo, ten kilometers north of Teramo, and in nearby Ascoli Piceno in the Marches. The stylistic similarity of the painting in the Palmer Museum to these two altarpieces traditionally attributed to Boncori is so striking as to leave absolutely no doubt that it must be by the same artist.

The *Presentation of the Virgin in the Temple* (Fig. 4) served until recently as the painting of the main altar in the small church of S. Maria della Misericordia in Campli.[10] In 1989, when Carloni published her article, the altarpiece was still on the back wall above the high altar. Soon after-

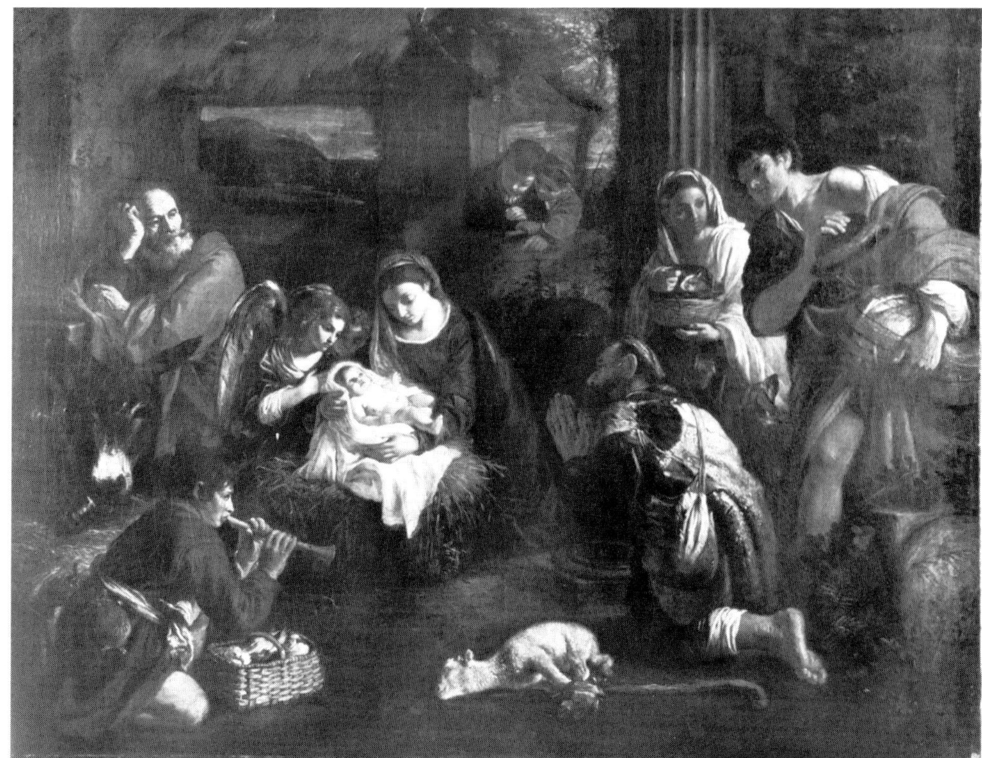

Fig. 2

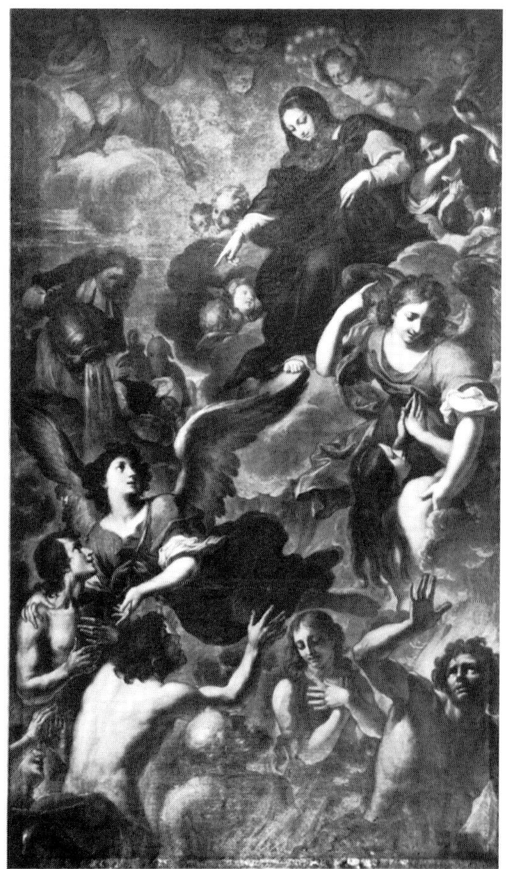

Fig. 3

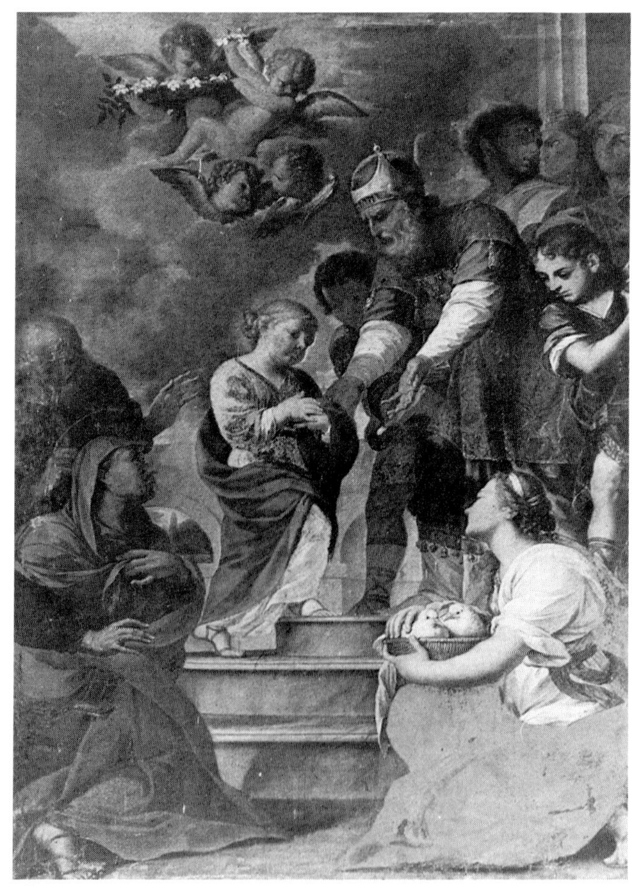

Fig. 4

wards, the church was permanently closed and the altarpiece transferred to the sacristy of the cathedral, where it hangs today. Even more striking than the altarpiece's stylistic affinity with the figures in the Campli *Presentation of the Virgin* is how it compares compositionally with Boncori's other altarpiece nearby, the *Madonna Enthroned with SS. Hyacinth and Vincent Ferrer* (Fig. 5) in the Dominican church of S. Pietro Martire in Ascoli Piceno.[11] Even if the attributions of the two altarpieces go back only to the late eighteenth and early nineteenth century respectively, one need not question their validity.[12] The poses of the Madonna and the Child in the Ascoli painting are extremely similar, almost identical to the analogous group in the Palmer Museum painting, as is the group of three cherubim in the upper left. Their poses and spatial relationship to each other are virtually identical, as are the facial types, with their somewhat squeezed, awkward features. The putti also appear in a very similar fashion in the Campli picture. Here the characteristic facial type of the young acolyte holding the candelabra is extremely similar to the singing angel on the left of the Palmer picture, a facial type somewhat reminiscent of Mola, yet highly individual, betraying perhaps Venetian memories of Boncori's earlier trip to Venice in the late 1660s, where he saw the works of Veronese.

The altarpieces in Campli and Ascoli Piceno differ stylistically from each other because they belong to two different moments of the artist's career, as Carloni has established.[13] In the Campli picture, the figures have somewhat robust, even rustic features and compact, sturdy bodies. The adolescent Mary is awkwardly plump in a way that reminds us of certain figures of Mola—for instance, Rebecca in the painting of *Rebecca and Eliezer at the Well* in the Colonna Gallery, Rome (Fig. 6)[14]—and of Antonio Gherardi, another of Mola's pupils. Carloni rightly stresses "un suo particolare gusto realistico nella raffigurazione quasi popolaresca della Vergine."[15] The composition is static: the kneeling figures of Anne and the woman holding the doves, symbols of the Virgin's purity, frame the composition. Other features in the Palmer Museum painting can be compared with the Campli alterpiece, but there is an increased dynamism in the Palmer example that distinguishes it from the static solidity and gravity of the Campli picture. The ponderous, heavy forms, however, are quite similar; the large angel on the left with its head in profile can be compared, within certain limits, to the rustic St. Anne.

The proportions and forms are quite different in the Ascoli painting. They are more slender and elegant. The swift diagonal movements and rhythms generated by the figures of the kneeling and adoring saints, the infant St. John, and the Madonna, are totally absent in the Campli example. Whereas Boncori is strongly indebted to his teacher, Mola, in the Campli piece, the Ascoli painting shows a classicizing elegance that puts Boncori in the vicinity of artists like Luigi Garzi, with whom Boncori worked almost side-by-side when both painters executed ceiling frescoes in S. Carlo al Corso in Rome, Boncori in 1679 (Fig. 7) and Garzi in 1681 (Fig. 8). Boncori's fresco has virtually nothing to do with the Mola-esque style of the Campli painting, and only the facial types of the putti allow us to recognize in both the

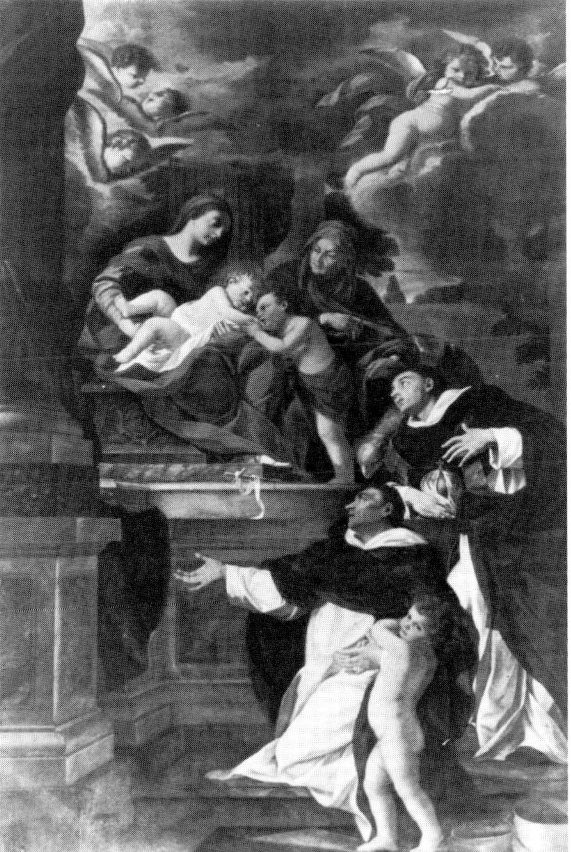

Fig. 5

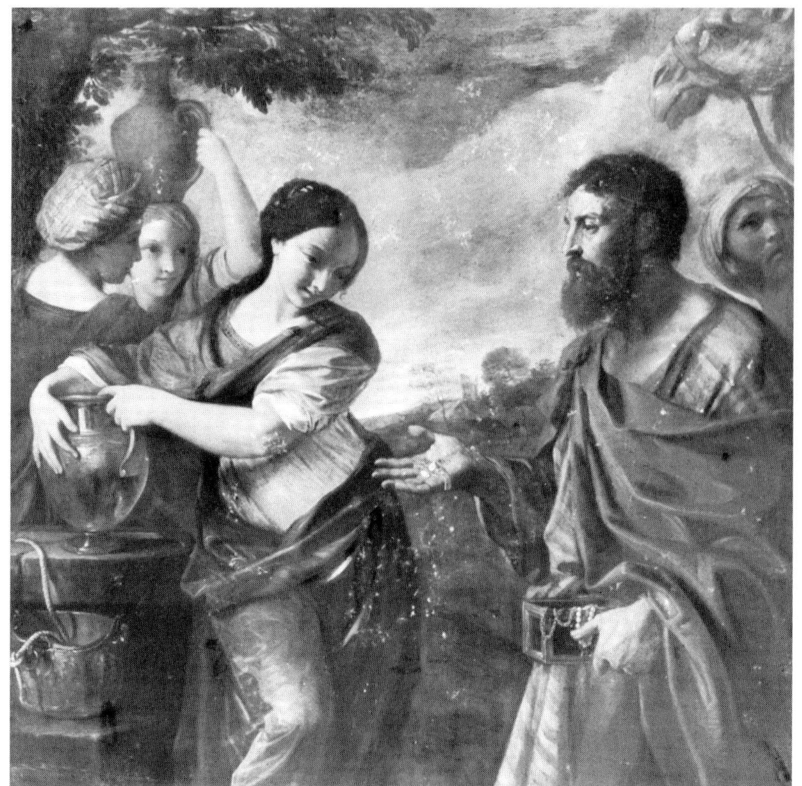

Fig. 6

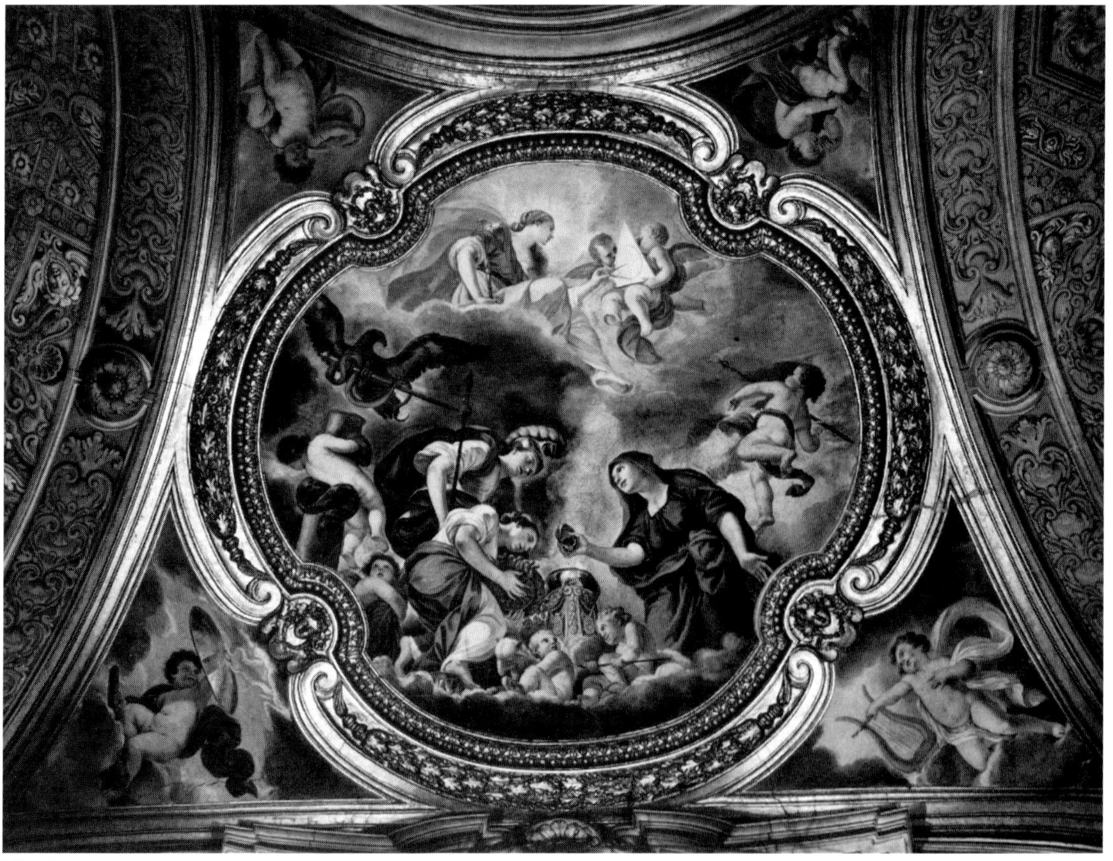

Fig. 7

hand of the same master. It is therefore very plausible that Carloni dates the Campli picture around 1670, soon after his trip to the north, which apparently took place between 1665 and 1669 when Boncori is not listed in the Roman Stati d'Anime. She dates the Ascoli painting to the early 1680s after the fresco in S. Carlo al Corso. It seems likely to me that the Palmer Museum picture has to be placed between 1670 and 1679, and probably closer to the Campli picture than to the end of that decade. The ponderousness of forms, the painterly, almost Guercinesque, chiaroscuro, and the warm, twilight, neo-venetian, Mola-like colors (in contrast to the cooler tones in the Ascoli painting) speak in favor of a rather early date, perhaps 1673–75. Thus, it pre-dates the Ascoli work by at least five, if not ten years. At Ascoli, the figures and figure groups are more loosely distributed in the pictorial space and are seen from a greater distance. In the Palmer composition, they are close to the picture plane and more closely fitted into the rectan-gular field. It would seem that the pose of the Christ Child seated on his Mother's lap and lean-ing toward St. Catherine was first invented for the *Mystic Marriage of St. Catherine* at the Palmer, and the position of his right arm and hand was later adapted to the motive of extending his hand toward the infant St. John who kisses him in the Ascoli picture.

The clouds on which the Virgin is sitting in the Palmer painting are substituted by an architec-tural throne in the Ascoli painting, and elements of St. Catherine are echoed in the figures of two Dominican saints. Her head in profile, looking upwards, survives in the facial pose of the kneeling St. Vincent Ferrer, and the devotional gesture of her left hand with outspread fingers survives in the analogous gesture of the hand of the standing St. Hyacinth.

The Virgin's face in the Ascoli picture is quite close to that in our painting. It also compares with the face of the Virgin in Boncori's Mola-like landscape *Rest on the Flight*, in the Arcevia collec-tion in Rome, formerly in the Marefoschi collection in Macerata. The *Rest* was first published by Salerno, then reproduced by Busiri Vici and again by Carloni (Fig. 9).[16] Another landscape, without flying cherubim and putti, appeared at auction in London in 1985 and 1986.[17] Here the drapery folds of the Virgin and Joseph are quite similar to those of the large angel, the Virgin, and the St. Catherine in our picture. Thus, we can fit these rather early landscapes into the group formed by the three altarpieces.

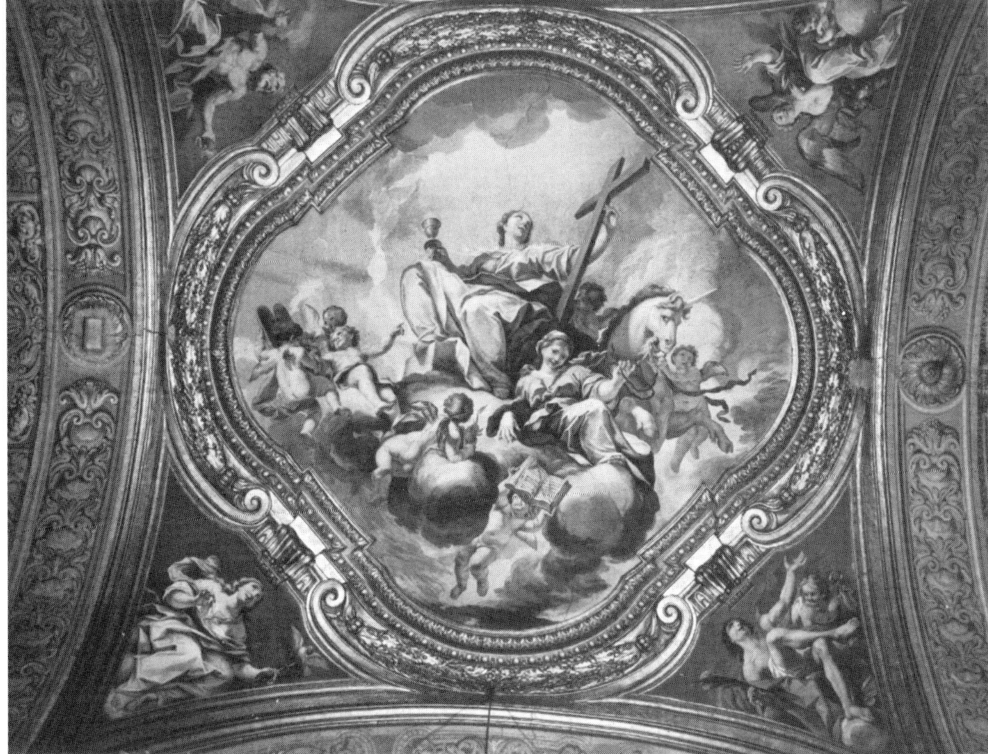

Fig. 8

What do we know about Giovanni Battista Boncori? There is a great discrepancy between the wealth of information offered by his two principal eighteenth-century biographers, Lione Pascoli[18] and Nicola Pio,[19] and the scarcity of surviving pictorial material. Only the three altarpieces, the church ceiling fresco, two easel paintings for collectors, and two academic drawings survive, much less than the surviving material of other and better known pupils and followers of Mola, such as Antonio Gherardi, Girolamo Troppa, and Giovanni Bonati.[20]

Lione Pascoli, who published Boncori's *Vita* in 1736, says he was born in Campli and he gives 1643 as the year of his birth. Nicola Pio, who dated his *Vite* 1724, said Boncori was born in Rome in 1640 and died there in 1701. The latter date is given in the inscription of Grecolini's portrait drawing in Stockholm, which was done for Pio's collection of biographies. There he is called *Pictor Ascolanus*, painter from Ascoli.[21] We now know that Boncori actually died in Rome on May 22, 1699, in the parish of SS. Vincenzo e Anastasio.[22] The death note says that he was 66 years old and that he had been born in Campli, diocese of Ascoli Piceno. According to this citation, he was born in 1633. As Carloni established, Boncori probably came to Rome at the age of 26 in 1659, where his presence is first documented in 1662, the same year in which his teacher, Pier Francesco Mola, was elected *Principe* of the Academy of St. Luke. He always lived in the Rione Trevi, in the parish of SS. Vincenzo e Anastasio. His earliest residence (in 1662–63) was the second courtyard of the Quirinal palace. Carloni leaves open whether this is actually the papal palace or Palazzo Mancini, later Rospigliosi, on the Quirinal.[23] In 1670–71, he lived as a guest of Cardinal Francesco Maria Mancini, the brother of Lorenzo Mancini, Cardinal Mazarin's brother-in-law, in the Palazzo Mancini on the Quirinal. Cardinal Mazarin had bought Palazzo Mancini in 1641 from the Marchesi Bentivoglio, and the Mancinis sold it in 1708 to the Rospigliosi, hence its later name, Rospigliosi Pallavicini.[24] From 1673 to his death in 1699, Boncori lived in the "Orto dei Signori Fiorentilli al presente de' Signori Mazzarini" or "Giardino dei Mazzarini" or "Orto dei Mancini".[25]

Both biographers state that he was a pupil of Pier Francesco Mola but, only Pio, not Pascoli, notes that he had first been a pupil of Pietro da Cortona, before making a trip to northern Italy and entering the studio of Mola. The Accademia di San Luca has two classicizing competition

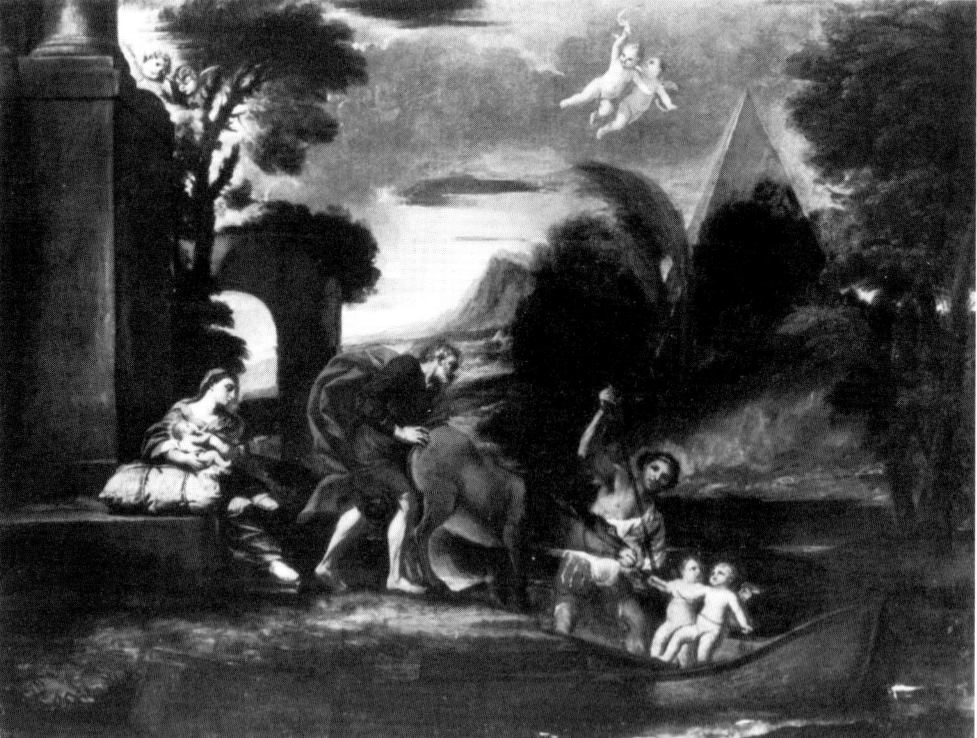

Fig. 9 Giovanni Battista Boncori, *Rest on the Flight*. Rome, private collection. Photo: author.

Fig. 9

drawings that bear Boncori's name. One, the *Shepherds Finding Romulus and Remus* of 1663, combines elements of both Cortona and Mola. The second, the *Sacrifice of Numa Pompilius*, for which the 31-year-old Boncori won third prize in 1664, is very Cortonesque in figure style and composition. By 1670, however, all elements of Cortonism had vanished in the altarpiece at Campli, where instead the influence of Mola is dominant.

According to Pascoli, Boncori began in the studio of Mola "Nella celebre scuola del .... celebrato Mola bevve il primo latte della professione"[26] and only then went on the trip to northern Italy. If we bear in mind that the academy drawing documented 1664 shows little Mola influence and that Mola died in 1666, it would seem that Boncori's decisive shift from Cortona to Mola must have taken place in 1665. Pascoli reports that Boncori's trip led him to Parma and for some longer time to Venice, then to Ferrara, Cento, and Bologna, where he saw the works of Guercino, which had been strongly recommended to him by Mola (himself greatly indebted to Guercino). In Venice Boncori studied, of course, the great masters of the sixteenth century: Titian, Veronese, and Tintoretto, in other words, Venetian color.

In Ferrara, he could have seen the works of Dosso Dossi, Scarsellino, Bononi, and those works of Guercino that were visible in churches of the city. We may mention parenthetically that Giovanni Bonati, another Mola pupil who was actually from Ferrara, had access to Guercino's studio in Bologna from 1658 to 1661 before he reached Rome in 1662 and became Mola's pupil from 1662 to 1665. An additional connection with Ferrara lies in the fact that another Mola follower, Girolamo Troppa, sent three paintings to the church of San Giuseppe in Ferrara in the 1660s.

Antonio Gherardi from Rieti, like Boncori, combined influences of Mola and Cortona. Five years younger than Boncori, he arrived one or two years earlier in Rome, around 1657–58, and became Mola's pupil about the same time. It is likely that the two painters met in Mola's studio. There are similarities in the figural repertoire between Boncori's Campli altarpiece of circa 1670 and Gherardi's famous ceiling paintings in S. Maria in Trivio in Rome, executed 1668–70.

Pascoli mentions a number of large format pictures (*fuori di misura*) that Boncori did in Rome before his trip to the North; none, however, has survived or been identified. An annotation in an Academy document of 1664 quoted by Carloni mentions Boncori as a pupil of the landscape painter Giovanni Francesco Grimaldi,[27] and it is worth noting that he owned several landscapes by Grimaldi. Next to his teacher, Mola, Grimaldi is the artist most frequently mentioned in the inventory after Boncori's death.

As we have said, Boncori lived in 1670–71 in the palace of Cardinal Francesco Maria Mancini on the Quirinal. The Cardinal had inherited the palace from Cardinal Mazarin, who had died in 1661. He had the *juspatronato* of two chapels in S. Maria in Aracoeli, the Cappella Bufalini, which he also inherited from Cardinal Mazarin, whose mother was Ortensia Bufalini, and the Mancini chapel, the chapel of his father's family. Around 1670, Cardinal Mancini conceived the idea to redecorate this latter chapel, dedicated to St. James. By the time of his death in 1672, the chapel was probably finished. The Cardinal commissioned his protégé, Boncori, to paint the altarpiece that represented St. James with St. Stephen and St. Hippolyte. According to Titi's *Ammaestramento* of 1686, the architectural design was done by Carlo Rainaldi, who worked extensively for the Mancini family, but according to Casimiro's book on S. Maria in Aracoeli (1736), the entire decoration, including the *stucchi*, was done by Boncori.

The *stucchi* are still extant, but the paintings in the lunettes, in the pendentives, and in the now empty oval field of the small dome are lost. The altarpiece disappeared at the latest by 1823, when the chapel passed to the Marini family, who dedicated it to St. Michael and placed a new painting on the altar. Apparently around 1670–71, Boncori painted a portrait of Cardinal Mancini, which remained unfinished in his own collection probably due to the sudden death of the sitter. Carloni quite plausibly argues that because of close family ties between the Mazzarini-Mancini family and the Colonna (Maria Mancini had married Lorenzo Onofrio

Colonna, Gran Connestabile of the Kingdom of Naples), it was Cardinal Mancini as protector and patron of Boncori who introduced him to the Colonna. The 1783 catalogue of the Colonna collection mentions a ceiling painting in the *palazzetto alla pilotta*, depicting *Alexander the Great at the Siege of Tyrus*, and an easel painting of *Venus and Mars* by "Buoncori Scolare del Mola sullo stile veneziano."

The two sons of Lorenzo Onofrio Colonna and Maria Mancini, Carlo Colonna, later a Cardinal, and Filippo II, Gran Connestabile, both owned pictures by Boncori and lent some to exhibitions in the cloister of San Salvatore in Lauro in the 1680s and 1690s.[28] Boncori himself lent his own pictures several times to these exhibitions. Carloni pointed out that another painting, listed in a Rospigliosi inventory, depicting Santa Rosa da Lima, who had been canonized in 1671 with Santa Rosa da Viterbo, was probably painted in connection with the canonization, and that Boncori secured the Dominican commission either through the Colonna or the Costaguti, Boncori's early patrons, who had strong ties with the Dominicans and who had a family chapel in SS. Domenico e Sisto with an altarpiece by Mola. We may recall that the altarpiece in Ascoli Piceno is in a Dominican church. Unfortunately, the Rospigliosi picture is also lost.

In 1678, Boncori was nominated to the Academy of St. Luke. He soon held various posts and functions, and in 1683, he began teaching at the Academy. In 1679, he contributed to the decoration of the aisle vaults and the ambulatory of SS. Ambrogio e Carlo al Corso, together with Ludovico Gimignani, Luigi Garzi, Giov. Batt. Benaschi, Girolamo Troppa, and other smaller masters, some of them connected with Boncori, such as Carlo Ascenzi. All worked under the direction of Giacinto Brandi, who had decorated the dome, transept, and the vault of the nave. As Carloni rightly pointed out, in the early 1680s Boncori painted his altarpiece for S. Pietro Martire in Ascoli Piceno, and probably in 1681, he painted the high altarpiece (now lost) of the *Visitation* for S. Maria degli Orfanelli, known as S. Maria in Aquiro, in Rome, which Titi mistook for a work of Maratta. It disappeared probably in a fire in 1845. Another altarpiece in Rome mentioned by Pascoli, featuring the Madonna with SS. John, Joseph, and Elizabeth, was in S. Niccolò ai Cesarini. As hinted by Pascoli, it was apparently executed from Boncori's design by a pupil, who, according to Titi, was Lorenzo Nelli. There was also in the same church an altarpiece by Carlo Ascenzi, whom we have already encountered in S. Carlo al Corso. Ascenzi and Nelli were the two painters who did the inventory and evaluation of works of art (published by Carloni) belonging to Boncori at his death. The two altarpieces were probably done in connection with the Padri Somaschi's redecoration of the church soon after 1695, near the end of Boncori's life. That he did not execute the painting himself concurs with Pascoli's statement that during the last four or five years of his life he had virtually given up painting. His altarpiece must have been removed at a very early date, as Carloni has established, and the church itself was demolished in the 1920s.

Pascoli tells us that Boncori had made enough money painting works for private collectors to live comfortably. He probably continued teaching. On January 11, 1699, he was elected *Principe* of the Academy of St. Luke, but held the office only for four months. Weakened by illness, he died in May of 1699, and Carlo Maratta succeeded him as *Principe*.

Luigi Lanzi in his "Storia Pittorica dell'Italia," published at the end of the eighteenth century, stated that Pier Francesco Mola "Vi formò tre allievi che aspirando alla gloria del colorito lo cercarono a que' fonti, a'quali lo aveva attinto il maestro; e viaggiarono per tutta Italia. Eccogli: Antonio Gherardi da Rieti, che morto il Mola frequentò la scuola del Cortona . . . : Gio.Batista Boncuore abruzzese, pittore sempre di grand' effetto, ma talora un po` pesante; Giovanni Bonatti ferrarese."[29] To these we can add Francesco Giovane and Giovanni Battista Pace from Rome and Carlo Ascenzi from Genazzano as pupils, and Girolamo Troppa from Rocchette in Sabina as a follower of Mola. As mentioned, Bonati and Troppa both have a conspicuous oeuvre of extant works. Bonati's recently established catalogue of surviving paintings comes to twelve. Francesco Giovane, a much older pupil of Mola, marks the other extreme: only one painting, the altarpiece of the *Baptism of Christ* on the second side altar to the right in S. Maria del Carmine in

Ascoli Piceno.[30] In addition, there are nine etchings, some of his own invention, others after Maratta and Mola. Further attributions and additions to his painted oeuvre that have been made on stylistic grounds are inconclusive.[31]

In the case of Giovanni Battista Pace, who probably worked in Mola's studio in the 1660s, only three extant paintings are documented as his, but his *oeuvre* has recently been enlarged to fourteen works through attributions on stylistic grounds.[32] The undocumented, yet convincing and accepted, extant works by far exceed the documented extant works. The case of Boncori is just the opposite. The number of his documented but lost works far exceeds those few that have survived or have thus far been identified (namely only six if we limit ourselves to the paintings). It is difficult to say whether this is due just to bad luck, as in the cases of the three lost altarpieces formerly in Roman churches. Certainly the circumstance of the two surviving altarpieces in Ascoli and Campli, which remained unpublished until 1989, did not allow us to form an idea of his artistic personality. Until then he was mistakenly considered only as a painter of Mola-esque landscapes with small figures.

As I indicate above, the contrast between the altarpieces in Campli and Ascoli is considerable and the stylistic development shown in the Ascoli example is remarkable. The early picture is domestic. The characterization of St. Anne in the left foreground is rustic, the rendering of her face bordering on caricature. Lanzi's comment "talora un pò pesante" applies well to such a figure. The compact, inelegant features of the young Mary as a peasant girl with puffy cheeks are vaguely reminiscent of certain figures by Antonio Gherardi, but the Veronese quality of Gherardi's figures is totally absent here. The rustic and domestic elements go directly back to Mola, as does the static character of the composition.

In the Ascoli Piceno picture, with its slender and elegant proportions and soft, polished modeling, there is nothing rustic or heavy in the figures and their rhetorical gestures, but instead a classicizing character that points in the direction of Carlo Maratta. By this time, Boncori had easily mastered the grand format of four meters, almost twice the size of the Campli picture. He overcame the compactness and crowding of the earlier picture but at the cost of a certain blandness. The Palmer Museum picture, which can be situated between them, is probably closer to the earlier picture, but it combines the virtues of both. With the Campli work it shares the full-bodied forms, heavy proportions, and the predilection for strong local colors that have become deeper. The glowing red and gold of St. Catherine's cloak recall the strong reds in many of Mola's pictures, such as the Vienna *Adoration of the Shepherds* (Fig. 2), a work which furnished the prototype for the countenance of Boncori's Virgin.[33] One could also mention Mola's altarpiece in SS. Ambrogio e Carlo al Corso for the colors, the combination of architectural and landscape elements, and the crepuscular *chiaroscuro* atmosphere. The ponderousness and dramatic *chiaroscuro* of the Palmer Museum picture place Boncori at this moment in a certain parallel to Giuseppe Ghezzi (my initial idea for its attribution), whereas the lighter, more pleasing and elegant tones in the later fresco in SS. Ambrogio e Carlo al Corso (Fig. 7) and the Ascoli painting place him among artists like Luigi Garzi. In all three altarpieces, however, the facial types of the cherubim are identical. They become a kind of signature, convincing evidence that the three pictures are by his hand. Because of Carloni's publication of the two altarpieces and the identification of the altarpiece in the Palmer Museum of Art, it is highly probable that other works by Giovanni Battista Boncori will emerge.

Postscript, 2002

In the closing line of my 1995 paper, I speculated on the likelihood that other works by Giovanni Battista Boncori would emerge. Just lately I have come across an altarpiece in a small Roman church, San Giovanni della Pigna, which on stylistic grounds I believe can be attributed to him. In the second side-altar to the left, there is a *Christ Appearing to St. Theresa of Avila* (Fig. 10). The style strongly suggests the mode of Mola and even the young Guercino, but is clearly a work of the second half of the seventeenth century, comparing well with the Palmer *Mystic Marriage of St. Catherine* and the altarpieces in Campli and Ascoli Piceno in its weightiness, earthy colors, bulky forms, and characteristic, virtually "signature" facial types of the cherubim. The only Roman guidebook to list the *St. Theresa* is Filippo Titi's "Descrizione delle Pitture, Sculture e Architetture esposte al Pubblico in Roma," Rome 1763,[34] where it is given as the work of Antonio Gherardi.[35] Though not that artist, it lingers in the circle of Mola. With further study, if my attribution holds, it would be Boncori's only altarpiece remaining in a Roman church.

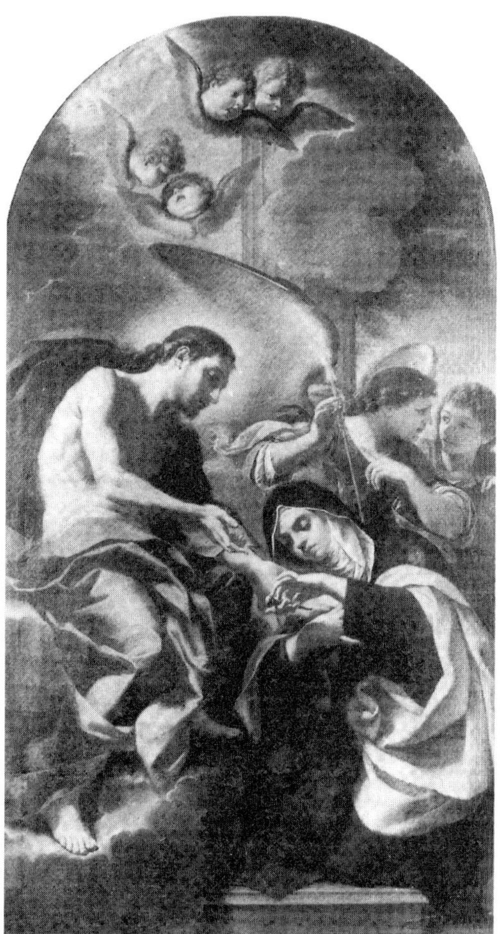

Fig. 10 Giovanni Battista Boncori, *Christ Appearing to St. Theresa of Avila,* c. 1670–75. Rome: San Giovanni della Pigna.

Endnotes

I am grateful to Mary Jane Harris not only for having invited me to the symposium at Penn State on April 1, 1995, where this paper was presented, but also for having helped to prepare my English text for publication.

1 Oil on canvas, 66 x 47 1/2 in. (167.6 x 120.6 cm.), inv. no. 76.49.

2 As a letter from Clyde Newhouse of May 3, 1976, explains to Olga K. Preisner, then registrar of The Pennsylvania State University Museum of Art, the painting can be traced back to the early 1950s, when it was in the collection of a certain Kurt Schmitt in Zürich, who sold it around 1953 to an American collector, who in turn sold it to Newhouse Galleries (and a partner) around 1974. The painting was cleaned and restored for Newhouse Galleries by Marco Grassi in 1974–75. From July 8, 1974, we have a statement from the late Giuliano Briganti, declaring the painting "a typical work by Pier Francesco Mola." Mary Jane Harris kindly obtained this information from Joan Pope of Newhouse Galleries.

3 See the catalogue of the exhibition *Pier Francesco Mola*, Lugano, 1989, nos. I.23 and I.26.

4 With this attribution the picture is mentioned in a booklet, "Palmer Museum of Art," University Park, Pennsylvania, 1993, p. 26.

5 See Valentino Martinelli, "Introduzione a Giuseppe Ghezzi pittore 'erudito e bravo maestro' padre di Pier Leone 'Di lui più celebre,'" in: *Giuseppe e Pier Leone Ghezzi*, Rome 1990, p. 10, Fig. 2. I am grateful to Dieter Graf, former director of the Fototeca of the Bibliotheca Hertziana, for providing a photo of the painting and for giving his permission to reproduce it.

6 Fiorella Pansecchi, "Giuseppe Ghezzi. Tre Quadri fuori sede," in *Scritti in onore di Federico Zeri*, Milan 1984, II, pp. 724–29.

7 Martinelli, *loc. cit.*, p. 13, Fig. 6.

8 Rosella Carloni, "Una traccia per Giovanni Battista Boncori e la sua scuola," in *Bollettino d' Arte* 55 LXXVI, 1989, pp. 57–74; in the literature Boncori's name appears variously as Boncore, Boncori, Bonocore, Boncuore, and Buoncuore. Carloni found the artist's signature spelled "Boncori" in a document of a payment receipt. We follow her spelling as the most authentic one.

9 It was preceded by an article by the late Andrea Busiri Vici, "La Fuga in Egitto di Giovanni Battista Buoncuore," in *Scritti di storia dell'arte in onore di Federico Zeri*, Milan, 1984, II, pp. 730–735.

10 R. Carloni, 1989, p. 61, Fig. 5, and color plate I.

11 *Ibid.*, pp. 61–62, Fig. 6.

12 The attribution of the altarpiece in Campli can be traced back to a Visitation report of 1833. The attribution of the altarpiece in Ascoli Piceno goes back to Orsini's *Guida* of 1790. See R. Carloni, 1989, p. 68, note 49.

13 R. Carloni, 1989, pp. 61–62.

14 See Eduard A. Safarik, *Catalogo sommario della Galleria Colonna, Dipinti*, Busto Arsizio, 1981, p. 93, no. 124.

15 R. Carloni, 1989, p. 61.

16 L. Salerno, *Pittori di paesaggio del Seicento a Roma*, III, Rome, 1980, p. 932, Fig. 11a; A. Busiri Vici, *loc. cit.*, 1984, pp. 730–35; R. Carloni, 1989, p. 62, Fig. 7.

17 Christie's, London, October 25, 1985, lot 235; Christie's, London, May 23, 1986, lot 81.

18 Lione Pascoli, *Vite de'pittori, scultori, ed architetti moderni* (Rome, vol. II, 1736), edizione critica dedicata a Valentino Martinelli, Perugia 1992, pp. 716–24 ("Giambatista Buoncore," edited by Chiara Santucci).

19 Nicola Pio, *Le Vite di Pittori Scultori et Architetti* (1724), ed. with intro. by Catherine and Robert Enggass, Città del Vaticano, 1977, pp. 85–86.

20 See L. Ficacci, "Giovannin del Pio: notizie su Giovanni Bonati pittore del Cardinale Carlo Francesco Pio di Savoia," in *Quadri Rinomatissimi, il collezionismo dei Pio di Savoia*, Modena, 1994, pp. 199–226.

21 A. Busiri Vici, 1984, p. 734, Fig. 726; R. Carloni, 1989, p. 66, note 1.

22. R. Carloni, 1989, p. 66, note 8.

23 R. Carloni, 1989, p. 66, note 10.

24 *Ibid.*

25 *Ibid.*, and pp. 59 and 63: "in via quae à Quirinale, et praecise à caupona nuncupata de' Cavallegieri retro Palatium Ex.mi Ducis de Nivers descendit ad viam vulgo de' serpenti." It may have been one of those houses that can be discerned on Falda's map of 1676, where the Orto Mancini is clearly visible, as it is on Nolli's map of 1748. The houses in that area were destroyed at the latest soon after 1870, when the new Via Nazionale cut through it and the Banca d'Italia was erected.

26 L. Pascoli, 1992, p. 716.

27 R. Carloni, 1989, p. 59.

28 See Giulia de Marchi, "Mostre di Quadri a S. Salvatore in Lauro, Stime di Collezioni Romane," *Note e Appunti di Giuseppe Ghezzi*, Rome, 1987, passim; E. A. Safarik, *The Colonna Collection of Paintings Inventories 1611–1795, Italian Inventories* 2, Munich, 1996, passim; R. Carloni, 1989, pp. 59–60.

29 Luigi Lanzi, *Storia Pittorica della Italia dal Risorgimento delle Belle Arti fin presso al fine del XVIII secolo*, 4th ed., Pisa, 1815, 2, p. 173.

30 No specific work by Giovane is given in Nicola Pio's short paragraph on the artist, see ed. Enggass, 1977, p. 37. The earliest mention and rather extensive description is in Baldassarre Orsini, *Descrizione delle Pitture, Sculture Architetture ed altre cose rare della insigne Città di Ascoli nella Marca*, Perugia, 1790, pp. 87–88 (not mentioned by Bellini 1983, 1987); Paolo Bellini, "Francesco Giovane: catalogo descrittivo," *in Rassegna di Studi e di Notizie, Raccolta delle Stampe* A. Bertarelli, XI, Milan, 1983, p. 54; id., The *Illustrated Bartsch* 47 (Commentary, Part 1), *Italian Masters of the Seventeenth Century*, New York, 1987, p. 55; Antonio Rodilossi, Ascoli Piceno città d'arte, 1987, p. 216.

31 See E. Schleier, "Pier Francesco Mola e la pittura a Roma," in the catalogue of the exhibition *Pier Francesco Mola*, Lugano, 1989, p. 82.

32 *Ibid.*, pp. 83–85 and 319–22, cat. IV, 13 and 14; E. Schleier., "Per Giovanni Battista Pace e Pier Francesco Mola," *in Antichità Viva* XXXI, 5-6 1992, pp. 13–18. To these fourteen paintings we may tentatively add another one, *Moses Striking the Rock* (oil on canvas, 87.6 x 117.3 cm.), belonging to the Agnes Etherington Art Centre, Queen's University, Kingston, Ontario, acc. no. 28-203 (1985). See D. MacTavish, *Telling Images, Selections from the Bader Gift of European Paintings to Queen's University*, Queen's University, Kingston, Ontario, 1988, p. 66, no. 16, with an unconvincing attribution to Sébastien Bourdon. I am very grateful to David de Witt, Bader Curator of European Art, Agnes Etherington Art Centre, for bringing the picture to my attention.

33 See the catalogue of the Mola exhibition, Lugano, 1989, p. 69, no. I.18. One could also quote the St. Petersburg *Rest on the Flight*, cat. I. 23.

34 In the modern critical edition of Titi's guidebooks by B. Contardi and S. Romano, it is listed and illustrated as "manner of Antonio Gherardi." See *Filippo Titi, Studio di Pittura, Scoltura, et Architettura, nelle chiese di Roma (1674–1763)*, edizione comparata, Florence, 1987, I, p. 87; II, Fig. 638. The location cited is San Giovanni della Pigna, third altar to the left. W. Buchowiecki (Handbuch der Kirchen Roms, vol. 2, Vienna, 1970, p.116) mentions the altarpiece as an anonymous work of the seventeenth century. C. Pietrangeli (*Guide Rionali di Roma*, Rione IX, Pigna, II, Rome, 1977, p. 90) cites the picture as by an "anonimo del sec. XVIII."

35 See T. Pickrel, *Antonio Gherardi, Painter and Architect of the Late Baroque in Rome*, Ph.D. diss., University of Kansas, 1981, Ann Arbor UMI Prints, 1981. On p. 281, the *St. Theresa* is listed among Gherardi' s lost works, with a note that it does not appear in any other Roman guidebook other than Titi and was not mentioned by Gherardi' s biographer, Lione Pascoli. Pickrel apparently did not check the picture in the little church.

Closing Remarks

Kahren J. Arbitman, *director, Palmer Museum of Art*, April 2, 1995

I stand before you this morning full of wonder. I will now admit that as the initial plans for this event unfolded, I was the naysayer who said that this weekend wasn't possible. I was certain we could not attract over one hundred people to central Pennsylvania for anything not attached to a sporting event. A touch football game in the sculpture garden or a bowling tournament in the lobby maybe, but a symposium on Old Master art? Never.

In taking this initial stance, I clearly underestimated two things: one, the ingenuity and tenacity of those dedicated to the study of Old Master art, and two, the indomitable spirit of Mary Jane Harris.

How many of you, when learning that the symposium was to be held at University Park, Pennsylvania, looked at a map to find out just where this is? Anyone who undertook this search knows that University Park is not on the map. You'll find the town of State College, but not University Park, which is the mailing address of Penn State. It's enough to make one abandon the idea of venturing into this part of the world. But you didn't give up. You persevered.

Having made the decision to come, you then found out that securing lodging was going to be difficult because we had the audacity to schedule the symposium the same weekend as fraternity and sorority pledge formals—and a majority of hotel rooms were reserved six months ago for after-formal parties and whatever else students do in hotel rooms. Despite this, you still persevered.

I must ask your forgiveness for underestimating you, and I must thank all of you, particularly those who came great distances, for making the extraordinary effort to get here to be part of the symposium.

I have to extend a special thank you to the speakers for the time, effort, and talent it took to prepare your presentations. I know that the time commitment for something like this is always greater than anticipated when you agreed to come. But the success of any scholarly symposium is measured by the quality of the presentations, and I must say that this has been the most successful symposium that I have ever attended. Since this reflects directly onto the reputation of the museum, I want to make sure you all know how grateful the Palmer Museum of Art is to you.

I would also like to thank our sponsors. Because we were determined to make the symposium free to the public, we needed financial support to cover the costs. We were delighted and gratified at the response from both foundations and individuals. The Samuel H. Kress Foundation and the Robert Lehman Foundation were extremely generous, as were the Piero Corsini Gallery and Hester Diamond. Benedetta Corsini and Hester Diamond are here. Would you please stand so that everyone can see you?

The great part about being a museum director is that I get all of the credit for the wonderful things that happen around here, despite the fact that I have little to do with them. That being the case, I would be remiss if I didn't take this occasion to thank Patrick McGrady, our curator of education and in-house techno wiz, whose responsibility it was to get you all here and keep you all happy. That's a fairly daunting task, but he did it with great style. Pat, thank you very much; you make me look terrific.

And finally, I am left with the impossible task of trying to find the words to thank Mary Jane Harris. Unfortunately, I am not sure that the right words exist. Mary Jane is the soul behind this weekend's events. She was the inspiration for the symposium. She knew what its focus should be, and who should address the issues. She also had the idea for the exhibition to accompany the symposium. Usually the exhibition comes first, but our exhibition evolved because Mary Jane wanted symposium visitors to enjoy an exhibition created specifically with them in mind.

Now having ideas is one thing—I cannot tell you how many people wander into my office with "great ideas" they think I should carry out. But Mary Jane had more than ideas; she had the knowledge, contacts, enthusiasm, and drive to see her ideas through to reality. Should we try to create a list of what Mary Jane did for both the symposium and the exhibition, it would be book length—and that's if we single space.

A few examples will give you an idea of what I'm talking about. In the middle of the March 1994 blizzard, Mary Jane took the train from New York to Philadelphia so that she could look at a drawing at the Philadelphia Museum of Art. She stayed until the entire museum shut down early because the staff was panicked by the ice storm. Mary Jane then blithely took the train back to New York.

Then there was the time she took the 6 a.m. flight from New York to Pittsburgh, drove into the city to meet with private collectors, drove out to the University of Pittsburgh for more meetings with possible lenders, visited the Carnegie Museum to search its collection, drove two hours to Latrobe to see another painting, toured the campus at St. Vincent, drove back out to the airport in time to run to catch the last plane that evening back to New York. I could go on and on, but I think you get the picture.

So Mary Jane, the word thank you simply doesn't capture how grateful we are for everything you have done. Unfortunately, the English language doesn't offer any better alternatives. Because of you, art historians, critics, collectors, and enthusiasts from around the country, and even around the world, have now heard of the Palmer Museum of Art. You have done what Rand McNally could not. You have put us on the map.

Biographical Notes on the Symposium Speakers

Bernard J. H. Aikema is professor of art history at Katholieke Universiteit Nijmegen, The Netherlands, and Sotheby's professor of art history at Katholieke Universiteit, Leuven (Louvain, Belgium). Internationally prominent as a scholar, lecturer, and writer on the cultural history and art of Venice, he is the author of the monograph on Pietro Vecchia, a book on the iconography of Jacopo Bassano, and a catalogue, *Tiepolo and His Circle, Drawings in American Collections*, for which he selected the drawings exhibited at Harvard University and The Pierpont Morgan Library, New York, in 1996–97. With Beverly Louise Brown, he co-organized a landmark exhibition, *Renaissance Venice and Northern Painting in the Age of Bellini, Dürer, and Titian*, at the Palazzo Grassi, Venice, September 5, 1999–January 9, 2000.

Francesca Baldassari, an independent scholar in Florence, is a noted specialist on Florentine art of the seventeenth and eighteenth centuries. She has published monographs on Carlo Dolci (1995) and Cristoforo Munari (1998). She organized an exhibition of still-life paintings by Munari and his circle in Reggio Emilia in 1999 for which she also wrote the catalogue. Her monograph on Giovanni Domenico Ferretti was published in 2002 by the Cassa di Risparmio di Pistoia and Pescia S.p.A. Her dissertation subject was Giovan Battista Vanni.

Philippe Costamagna, an independent scholar in Paris, is the author of a monograph and catalogue raisonné on Jacopo Pontormo, *Pontormo, L'Opera Completa* (1994), and of many scholarly essays and entries for exhibition catalogues. In 1998–99, he was a Fellow at Harvard's Villa I Tatti, Florence, and is currently writing a two-volume work on sixteenth-century Florentine portraiture. He completed his graduate studies at the École du Louvre and the Sorbonne and received his doctorate in 1994.

Mina Gregori lives in Florence, Italy, and has achieved international recognition as an educator, scholar, writer, lecturer, and organizer of a vast range of revelatory exhibitions. A student and later the assistant of Roberto Longhi, she succeeded him in 1976 as chair of art history at the University of Florence, where she held the position *Professore ordinario di storia dell'arte mediovale e moderna* until 1997. Her exhibitions and publications range from monographic—Altobello Meloni, Camillo Boccaccino, Morazzone, Moroni, Ceruti, the Campi, Sofonisba Anguissola, Titian, Raphael, Manfredi, and Caravaggio—to encyclopedic, such as her exhibition of Florentine seventeenth-century paintings, drawings, and decorative arts at the Palazzo Strozzi in 1986. Professor Gregori is the president of the Roberto Longhi Foundation and directs the scholarly art history periodical, *Paragone*. She was appointed Samuel H. Kress Professor at the Center for Advanced Studies in Visual Arts, National Gallery of Art, Washington, for the academic year 1999–2000, and is preparing a monograph on Giovanni da Milano. Professor Gregori has recently been inducted as Chevalier into France's Legion of Honor.

Heidi J. Hornik holds the position of associate professor of art history and director of the Martin Museum of Art at Baylor University, Waco, Texas. She earned her doctorate in art history at Penn State. A catalogue raisonné on her dissertation artist, Michele Tosini, is being prepared for publication. In May 2000, Heidi took a sabbatical to work on a cross-discipline volume, *Illuminating Luke: Themes from the Annunciation to the Ascension in Italian Renaissance and Baroque Art*, co-authored with her husband, Mikeal Parsons.

Erich Schleier was the curator of Italian, Spanish, and seventeenth-century French paintings in the Gemäldegalerie, Staatliche Museen, Berlin, from 1971 until his retirement in 1999. He has published fundamental studies on Giovanni Lanfranco and the Italian and French artists who worked in Rome in the seventeenth and eighteenth centuries. He has contributed essays and entries for catalogues of significant exhibitions: *Canaletto, Painting in Naples 1606–1705, The Age of Caravaggio, The Age of Correggio and the Carracci, Pier Francesco Mola*, and *Pietro da Cortona*. Dr. Schleier organized the recent catalogue and exhibition of Giovanni Lanfranco, the artist on whom he is the foremost scholar, under the title *Giovanni Lanfranco, un pittore barocco tra Parma, Roma e Napoli*, Milan, 2001. In 2000, he received an honorary degree from the Seconda Università di Napoli.

Leonard J. Slatkes is professor of art history at Queens College of the City University of New York, where he joined the faculty in 1966. He is highly regarded for his scholarship and extensive publications on seventeenth-century Dutch painting and the northern followers of Caravaggio. Recipient of many grants and awards, he has written monographs on Rembrandt, Vermeer, van Baburen, which he recently revised, and Ter Brugghen, soon to appear. Professor Slatkes received his Ph.D. in 1962 at the University of Utrecht.

Continuity, Innovation, and Connoisseurship

Old Master Paintings, Drawings, and Prints
from Pennsylvania Collections

EXHIBITION CHECKLIST

Palmer Museum of Art
February 28 through April 30, 1995

EXHIBITION CHECKLIST: PAINTINGS

Girolamo Romanino
(Brescia, 1484/87–Venice, 1560)
Portrait of a Gentleman, 1520
Oil on canvas, 30 x 25 5/8 inches
Allentown Art Museum,
Samuel H. Kress Collection, 1960.23

Circle of Andrea del Sarto
(Florence, 1486–1530)
and Pontormo
(1494–Florence, 1557)
Cupid and Apollo
Oil on canvas, 24 x 18 5/8 inches
Samuel H. Kress Collection,
Center Gallery, Bucknell University,
Lewisburg, Pennsylvania

Trophime Bigot
(Arles, c. 1579–1650)
The Dead Christ and an Angel
Oil on canvas, 44 x 38 inches
La Salle University Art Museum,
Philadelphia

Giovanni Martinelli
(Florence, 1600/04–1659)
The Holy Family
Oil on canvas, 44 1/2 x 38 inches
La Salle University Art Museum,
Philadelphia

Attributed to Mariotto Albertinelli
(Florence, 1474–1515)
The Adoration of the Christ Child
Oil on panel, 6 5/8 x 23 3/8 inches
The John G. Johnson Collection,
Philadelphia Museum of Art

Fra Bartolommeo
(Florence, 1472–1517)
Adam and Eve with Two Children
Oil on panel, 12 3/8 x 9 3/4 inches
The John G. Johnson Collection,
Philadelphia Museum of Art

Circle of Matthias Stom (Stomer)
(Amersfoort, c. 1600–after 1650)
Christ and Nicodemus
Oil on canvas, 40 5/8 x 56 inches
Saint Vincent Archabbey Art Collections,
Latrobe, Pennsylvania

Jacopo Chimenti, called Jacopo da Empoli
(Empoli, 1537–1640)
Study for *The Martyrdom of St. Barbara,* 1603
Pen, ink, and wash over black chalk,
13 5/8 x 9 inches
The Carnegie Museum of Art, Pittsburgh;
Gift of Herbert DuPuy, 1923

Attributed to Claude Vignon
(Tours, 1593–Paris 1670)
St. Paul Writing
Pen and ink, 15 13/16 x 10 1/8 inches
The Carnegie Museum of Art, Pittsburgh;
Gift of Dr. and Mrs. Daniel Fishkoff, 1976

Cristofano Allori
(Florence, 1577–1621)
Half-Length Study of a Boy and *Study of Clasped Hands*
Red chalk, 8 x 8 inches
Philadelphia Museum of Art: The Muriel and
Philip Berman Gift. Acquired from the John
S. Phillips Bequest of 1876 to the
Pennsylvania Academy of the Fine Arts.

Carlo Maratti
(Camerano, 1625–Rome, 1713)
Head of a Child
Red chalk on blue paper, 14 x 9 7/8 inches
Philadelphia Museum of Art

Antonio Molinari
(Venice, 1655–1704)
Crucifixion of St. Peter (?) *Martyrdom of St. Lawrence* (?)
Pen, brown ink, and brown wash over
graphite, 12 x 9 5/8 inches
Philadelphia Museum of Art: John S. Phillips
Collection. Acquired with the Edgar V. Seeler
Funds (by exchange) and with funds con-
tributed by Muriel and Philip Berman.

Francesco de'Rossi, called Francesco Salviati
(Florence, 1510–Rome, 1563)
Kneeling Figure, c. 1551
Black chalk on white laid paper,
14 7/8 x 10 15/16 inches
Philadelphia Museum of Art: The Muriel and
Philip Berman Gift. Acquired from the
John S. Phillips Bequest of 1876 to the
Pennsylvania Academy of the Fine Arts.

Pier Francesco Mola
(Coldrerio, 1612–Rome, 1666)
Studies of Fighting Men, c. 1669
Pen, ink, and wash, 6 13/16 x 11 1/2 inches
Private collection, Pittsburgh

Pier Francesco Mola
(Coldrerio, 1612–Rome, 1666)
Hagar and Ishmael, c. 1650
Pen and ink, 4 7/8 x 7 9/16 inches
Private collection, Pittsburgh

Jan van der Straet (Johann Stradanus)
(Bruges, 1523–Florence, 1605)
Adriaen Collaert, engraver
(1560–1618)
Philipp Galle, printer
(1537–1612)
Christ before King Herod, c. 1590
Engraving, 10 3/8 x 7 5/8 inches
The Trout Gallery, Dickinson College,
Gift of Dr. David Robertson, 83.9.1

Adam Elsheimer
(Frankfurt, 1578–Rome, 1610)
Hendrik Goudt, engraver
(Utrecht, 1585–1630)
*Jupiter and Mercury in the House of Philemon
and Baucis,* 1612
Engraving, 6 1/2 x 8 3/4 inches
Philadelphia Museum of Art

Adam Elsheimer
(Frankfurt, 1578–Rome, 1610)
Hendrik Goudt, engraver
(Utrecht, 1585–1630)
The Mocking of Ceres, 1610
Engraving, 8 1/2 x 9 3/8 inches
Philadelphia Museum of Art: The Muriel and
Philip Berman Gift. Acquired from the John
S. Phillips Bequest of 1876 to the
Pennsylvania Academy of the Fine Arts.

Salvator Rosa
(Arnella, 1615–Rome, 1673)
Diogenes and His Bowl, c. 1662
Etching, 17 7/8 x 10 3/4 inches
Philadelphia Museum of Art:
The Charles M. Lea Collection

Salvator Rosa
(Arnella, 1615–Rome, 1673)
The Infant Oedipus Hung from a Tree, c. 1663
Etching, 28 7/8 x 18 7/8 inches
Philadelphia Museum of Art:
The Charles M. Lea Collection

Esaias van de Velde
(Amsterdam, c. 1591–The Hague, 1630)
Wooded Landscape with Travelers, called *The
Square Landscape,* 1614–1624
Etching and engraving, 6 7/8 x 7 1/8 inches
Philadelphia Museum of Art: The Muriel and
Philip Berman Gift. Acquired from the John
S. Phillips Bequest of 1865 to the
Pennsylvania Academy of the Fine Arts, with
funds contributed by Muriel and Philip
Berman and the gifts (by exchange) of Lisa
Norris Elkins, Bryant W. Langston, the
Samuel S. White 3rd and Vera White
Collection, with additional funds (by
exchange) given by John H. McFadden, Jr.,
Thomas Skelton Harrison, and the Philip H.
and A. S. W. Rosenbach Foundation.

Continuity, Innovation, and Connoisseurship
Old Master Paintings, Drawings and Prints from Pennsylvania Collections

From the Suida-Manning Collection, Forest Hills Gardens, New York
(Now in the Jack S. Blanton Museum of Art, College of Fine Arts, The University of Texas at Austin)

Francois Perrier
(French, 1590–1650)
Bacchus and Ariadne
Oil on canvas, 13 1/2 x 17 1/2 inches

Giovanni Battista Gaulli, called Il Bacciccio
(Italian, 1639–1709)
Rinaldo and Armida
Oil on canvas, 15 1/8 x 19 1/4 inches

Claude Vignon
(Tours, 1593–Paris, 1670)
St. Cecilia with Valerian and Tibertius
Oil on copper, 9 1/4 x 11 7/8 inches

Pier Francesco Mola
(Coldrerio, 1612–Rome, 1666)
Domenico Segni Tied to a Tree with Four Kidnappers, 1650
Pen and brown ink, brown wash over black pencil on paper, 8 3/8 x 14 1/2 inches

Giovanni Francesco Barbieri, called Il Guercino
(Cento, 1591–Bologna, 1666)
The Infant Christ Holding a Bird, and St. Joseph, c. 1621–23
Pen, brown ink, and brown wash on laid paper, 7 3/4 x 9 15/16 inches

From the Collection of Morton and Mary Jane Harris, New York

Giovanni Balducci
(Florence, 1560–Naples, after 1631)
Christ in Glory with Apostles and Saints, c. 1586
Bozzetto for altar in the Oratorio dei Pretoni, Florence
Oil on panel, 23 3/4 x 17 inches
Given to the Palmer Museum of Art in 1996

Girolamo Forabosco
(Venice, 1604/05–1679)
David with the Head of Goliath, c. 1650-1660
Oil on canvas, 46 x 35 inches
Given to the Palmer Museum of Art in 1996

Giovanni Francesco Barbieri, called Il Guercino
(Cento, 1591–Bologna, 1666)
Study for the *Assumption of the Virgin* (recto and verso), c. 1650
Red chalk on laid paper,
12 13/16 x 8 15/16 inches

Cristofano Allori
(Florence, 1577–1621)
Half Figure of a Youth Pointing, c. 1621
Study for *The Inspiration of Michelangelo*, Casa Buonarroti, Florence
Black chalk on paper, 8 3/8 x 6 5/8 inches

Baldassare Franceschini, called Il Volterrano
(Italian, 1611–1689)
Studies for the *Madonna and Child with Infant St. John* (recto and verso)
Black chalk, pen, and brown ink on paper,
9 3/4 x 14 inches